The Use of Psalms in the Narrative Structure of Mark

The Use of Psalms in the Narrative Structure of Mark

JUNGWOO LEE

Foreword by Andrew D. Streett

WIPF & STOCK · Eugene, Oregon

THE USE OF PSALMS IN THE NARRATIVE STRUCTURE OF MARK

Copyright © 2025 Jungwoo Lee. All rights reserved. Except for brief quotations in critical publications or reviews, no part of this book may be reproduced in any manner without prior written permission from the publisher. Write: Permissions, Wipf and Stock Publishers, 199 W. 8th Ave., Suite 3, Eugene, OR 97401.

Wipf & Stock
An Imprint of Wipf and Stock Publishers
199 W. 8th Ave., Suite 3
Eugene, OR 97401

www.wipfandstock.com

PAPERBACK ISBN: 979-8-3852-4851-3
HARDCOVER ISBN: 979-8-3852-4852-0
EBOOK ISBN: 979-8-3852-4853-7

VERSION NUMBER 09/29/25

Scripture quotations marked (NIV) are taken from the Holy Bible, New International Version®, NIV®. Copyright © 1973, 1978, 1984, 2011 by Biblica, Inc.™ Used by permission of Zondervan. All rights reserved worldwide. www.zondervan.comThe "NIV" and "New International Version" are trademarks registered in the United States Patent and Trademark Office by Biblica, Inc.™

Scripture quotations marked (ESV) are taken from the Holy Bible, English Standard Version® (ESV®) © 2001 by Crossway, a publishing ministry of Good News Publishers. All rights reserved.

Dedicated to
my wife,
Minjeong Kum

Contents

Foreword by Andrew D. Streett | ix

Acknowledgments | xi

List of Abbreviations | xiii

1   Introduction | 1
2   The Structure and the Purpose of Mark | 25
3   Psalm 2 in Mark | 63
4   Psalm 118 in Mark | 91
5   Psalm 110 in Mark | 123
6   Psalm 22 in Mark | 158
7   Conclusion | 192

Bibliography | 201

Index of Authors | 225

Index of Scripture and Other Ancient References | 233

Foreword

I met Jungwoo Lee in August 2019 when I was fairly new to Southwestern Seminary and was just beginning to dip my toes into doctoral supervision. One could not ask for a better first doctoral student. Jungwoo, already a seasoned missionary, had recently completed comprehensive exams. He expressed interest in the use of the OT in the NT and quickly devoured the major classic and contemporary works in the field, ultimately choosing to pursue research in the use of the Psalms in Mark since I could offer the best supervision in that area due to my own research. From that first meeting it took him only eighteen months to submit the defense draft! Such focus and quality of work are becoming all too rare among PhD students, especially those who remain active in family life and ministry as Jungwoo did.

The resulting dissertation showed balance in methodology, precision in scope and goals, depth in primary and secondary research, and clarity in writing and argumentation. Most importantly, it made a meaningful contribution to the fields of Markan narrative analysis and the use of the Psalms in Mark.

This work explores how the Gospel of Mark employs Pss 2, 22, 110, and 118 to develop its structural and theological agenda. Arguing from a narrative-critical perspective, Lee demonstrates that these psalms appear at key junctures in Mark to present Jesus as the Messiah, the Son of God, who inaugurates the kingdom of God and fulfills the Scriptures.

Lee first exposes the reader to the context of each psalm in the literary and canonical contexts of the OT and subsequent use in Second Temple literature. Then he shows how Mark read each psalm in its broader context and used it to make a unique contribution to the workings of the narrative. Psalm 2, used at the baptism and transfiguration, forms a theological framework for the Gospel, portraying Jesus as the messianic king who conquers his enemies. Psalm 118, cited during Jesus' entry into Jerusalem and in the parable of the wicked tenants, gives a scriptural blueprint for Jesus' passion and resurrection and forms the climax of his Davidic messianic identity as the one who founds a new temple and leads a new exodus. Psalm 110 is used in the Davidsohnfrage episode and the trial scene, revealing Jesus' identity as priest-king and anticipating his heavenly enthronement and second coming. Psalm 22 is quoted and alluded to throughout 15:20-16:7, showing Jesus to be the Righteous Sufferer who is ultimately vindicated by God. At once literary and theological, his treatment of this scriptural texture of Mark will prove to be useful for anyone working in this field.

I am very glad that Jungwoo Lee's revised work will be available more broadly through this publication, so that scholars and all who seek to understand the Gospel of Mark and the work of Christ may be helped by it.

Easter 2025
Andrew D. Streett
Associate Professor of Biblical Studies
Southwestern Baptist Theological Seminary

Acknowledgments

This book is a revised version of my PhD dissertation at Southwestern Baptist Theological Seminary, Fort Worth. Having worked in the Third World, it has been my sincere desire to help local churches to be equipped with the strong foundation of God's word. This book is a stepping stone to accomplish my dream. Since I studied theology years ago, the study on the use of the OT in the NT has been my keen interest. Thankfully God has provided me the most appropriate dissertation supervisor for me, who has introduced me to scores of standard books on the use of the OT in the NT, which has both enlarged my understanding of the field and helped me narrow down my research interests. During my initial research, I observed that most works on the use of the OT in the Gospels have not paid enough attention to its relationship with the narrative structure of the Gospels. This book is an attempt to explore what roles the use of specific psalms plays in Mark's narrative structure. The book of Psalms is one of my favorite books of the bible. Studying the Gospel of Mark surprised me, as I discovered the depth and the richness of Mark that I had not known before. I hope that my book will somehow help readers appreciate the Gospel more, as I did.

My book is the fruit of many people's efforts. My dissertation supervisor, Dr. Andrew Streett, was a perfect Doktorvater for me. His keen insight and prompt responses were immense help for me to make progress in writing. He has encouraged me to publish the book and graciously wrote forward of the book. I cannot imagine how I could finish it without his competent guidance and gracious care. Some churches and individuals supported me financially and with prayers, so that I could finish the writing project and serve the nations. I really appreciate their faithful support. Of these churches and individuals, I would like to express my special thanks to Dallas Youngnak church, which has supported me faithfully since 2008. Of course, my family has been my biggest source of support. Thank you, Hope, Faith, and Love Lee, who have patiently waited for your daddy to finish the book-writing. Most of all, my wife, Minjeong, has been supporting me wholeheartedly, so that we may go and serve God where he calls us. I dedicate this work to her.

Finally, I thank God for his sufficient grace for me to be a part of the servants who train and equip future Arab church leaders in the Middle East after finishing my PhD program. It is my prayer that God would continue to give me grace to equip God's churches in Arab world with his word faithfully and diligently until he calls me home. εἴ τις θέλει ὀπίσω μου ἀκολουθεῖν, ἀπαρνησάσθω ἑαυτὸν καὶ ἀράτω τὸν σταυρὸν αὐτοῦ καὶ ἀκολουθείτω μοι (Mark 8:34).

List of Abbreviations

Journals

AR	*Approaching Religion*
ATR	*Anglican Theological Review*
BBR	*Bulletin of Biblical Research*
Bib	*Biblica*
BibInt	*Biblical Interpretation*
BR	*Biblical Research*
BSac	*Bibliotheca Sacra*
BT	*Baptistic Theologies*
BTB	*Biblical Theology Bulletin*
BZ	*Biblische Zeitschrift*
CBR	*Currents in Biblical Research*
CBQ	*Catholic Biblical Quarterly*
CTR	*Criswell Theological Review*
CTM	*Concordia Theological Monthly*
Dir.	*Direction*
DSD	*Dead Sea Discoveries*
EC	*Early Christianity*
ECL	*Early Christianity and Its Literature*
EvQ	*Evangelical Quarterly*
HTR	*Harvard Theological Review*

IBS	*Irish Biblical Studies*
IrTheologQ	*Irish Theological Quarterly*
JBL	*Journal of Biblical Literature*
JES	*Journal of Ecumenical Studies*
JETS	*Journal of the Evangelical Theological Society*
JJMJS	*Journal of the Jesus Movement in Its Jewish Setting*
JJS	*Journal of Jewish Studies*
JQR	*The Jewish Quarterly Review*
JR	*Journal of Religion*
JSHJ	*Journal for the Study of the Historical Jesus*
JSJ	*Journal for the Study of Judaism in the Persian, Hellenistic and Roman Period*
JSP	*Journal for the Study of the Pseudepigrapha*
JSNT	*Journal for the Study of the New Testament*
JSOT	*Journal for the Study of the Old Testament*
JSS	*Journal of Semitic Studies*
JTI	*Journal of Theological Interpretation*
KJOTS	*Korean Journal of Old Testament Studies*
KRT	*Korea Reformed Theology*
NovT	*Novum Testamentum*
NTS	*New Testament Studies*
OTE	*Old Testament Essays*
OtSt	*Oudtestamentische Studien*
PRSt	*Perspectives in Religious Studies*
Proc.	*Proceedings*
RB	*Revue biblique*
RF&P	*Reformed Faith & Practice*
Restor. Q.	*Restoration Quarterly*
RevExp	*Review and Expositor*

RdQ	Revue de Qumran
RevScRel	Revue des sciences religieuses
Salm	Salmanticensis
SBJT	Southern Baptist Journal of Theology
SC	Sacra Scripta
SEÅ	Svensk Exegetisk Årsbok
SJOT	Scandinavian Journal of the Old Testament
Theol. Beitr.	Theologische Beiträge
TLZ	Theologische Literaturzeitung
TRE	Theologische Realenzyklopädie
TToday	Theology Today
VT	Vetus Testamentum
ZAW	Zeitschrift für die alttestamentliche Wissenschaft
ZNW	Zeitschrift für die neutestamentliche Wissenschaft und die Kunde der älteren Kirche
ZThK	Zeitschrift für Theologie und Kirche

Commentaries

AB	Anchor Bible Commentary
BNTC	Black's New Testament Commentaries
BCOTWP	Baker Commentary on the Old Testament Wisdom and Psalms
BECNT	Baker Exegetical Commentary on the New Testament
EGGNT	Exegetical Guide to the Greek New Testament
EBC	Expositor's Bible Commentary
JPSTC	JPS Torah Commentary
NAC	New American Commentary
NCBC	New Cambridge Bible Commentary

NICNT	New International Commentary on the New Testament
NICOT	New International Commentary on the Old Testament
NIGCT	New International Greek Testament Commentary
NIVAC	New International Version Application Commentary
OTL	Old Testament Library
PC	Proclamation Commentaries
PNTC	Pillar New Testament Commentary
SPS	Sacra Pagina Series
TOTC	Tyndale Old Testament Commentaries
WBC	Word Biblical Commentary
ZECNT	Zondervan Exegetical Commentary on the New Testament

Others

AB	The Aramic Bible
ABRL	The Anchor Bible Reference Library
AGJU	Arbeiten zur Geschichte des antiken Judentums und des Urchristentums
AUSDDS	Andrews University Seminary Doctoral Dissertation Series
ANRW	Aufstieg und Niedergang der römischen Welt: Geschichte und Kultur Roms im Spiegel der neueren Forschung Part 2
BDAG	Danker, Frederick W., Walter Bauer, William F. Arndt, and F. Wilbur Gingrich. *Greek-English Lexicon of the New Testament and Other Early Christian Literature.* 3rd ed. Chicago: University of Chicago Press, 2000.
BBB	Bonner Biblische Beiträge

BETL	Bibliotheca Ephemeridem Theologicarum Lovaniensium
BThST	Biblisch-Theologische Studien
BU	Biblishe Untersuchungen
BZAW	Beihefte zur Zeitschrift für die alttestamentliche Wissenschaft
BZNW	Beihefte zur Zeitschrift für die Neutestamentliche Wissenschaft und die Kunde der Älteren Kirche
CO	Corpus Reformatorum, Ioannis Calvini Opera Quae Supersunt Omnia
DJD	Discoveries in the Judean Desert
DJD	Early Judaism and Its Literature
FAT	Forschungen zum Alten Testament
FOTL	Forms of the Old Testament Literature
HBM	Hebrew Bible Monographs
HThKNT	Herders Theologischer Kommentar zum Neuen Testament
JSJSup	Supplements to the Journal for the Study of Judaism
JSNTSup	Journal for the Study of the New Testament Supplement Series
JSOTSup	Journal for the Study of the Old Testament Supplement Series
LHBOTS	The Library of Hebrew Bible/Old Testament Studies
LNTS	Library of New Testament Studies
NTMon	New Testament Monographs
NovTSup	Novum Testamentum Supplement
NTTSD	New Testament Tools, Studies, and Documents
LXX	Septuagint

MT	Masoretic Text
NSBT	New Studies in Biblical Theology
NT	New Testament
OT	Old Testament
RNT	Regensburger Neues Testament
SBB	Stuttgarter Biblische Beitrage
SB	Studies in Biblical Theology
SBLDS	Society of Biblical Literature Dissertation Series
SBLMS	Society of Biblical Literature Monograph Series
Soc. Biblic. Lit. Semin.	Society of Biblical Literature Seminar Papers
SCS	Septuagint and Cognate Studies
SNTSMS	Society for New Testament Studies Monograph Series
SSN	Studia Semitica Neerlandica
STDJ	Studies on the Texts of the Desert of Judah
TSAG	Texte und Studien zum antiken Judentum
VTSup	Supplements to Vetus Testamentum
WdF	Wege der Forschung
WUNT	Wissenschaftliche Untersuchungen zum Neuen Testament

1

Introduction

The Gospel of Mark is replete with scriptural quotations, allusions, and echoes. Of these references, ones from Isaiah occur most often, followed by ones from Psalms. The fact that Psalms is the most frequently cited book of the OT in Mark after Isaiah is not surprising when one considers that (1) a messianic overtone is found in many psalms, and (2) the book of Psalms is one of the most commonly quoted Scriptures of Israel among the Jews at Qumran, some of whom were contemporary with Mark, the author of the Gospel.

Because of the numerous occurrences of Psalms, literature abounds about Mark's use of Psalms; however, these books and articles tend to focus on specific categories of Psalms or on individual psalms. Though some scholars have addressed the overall scriptural function of the Psalter in the Gospel of Mark, no one has produced a book-level publication. This book is an endeavor to fill that lacuna. To identify the organic function of Psalms in Mark, one must consider not only the immediate context of Mark but also the whole narrative of Mark. Thus, I will pay attention to the scriptural function of Psalms in the entire narrative of the Gospel of Mark.

THESIS

In his presentation of the good news, Mark consistently focuses on Jesus' identity, his mission to usher in God's kingdom, and discipleship. These overarching themes are undergirded by Scripture. Indeed, Mark's Gospel is filled with scriptural quotations, allusions, and echoes to demonstrate how the Scriptures are fulfilled. Of these, this book focuses on the use of the four most explicitly cited psalms in Mark (i.e., Pss 2, 118, 110, 22). I will argue that Mark uses Pss 2, 118, 110, and 22 at the key junctures of the narrative of the Gospel of Mark to present Jesus as the Messiah, the Son of God, who inaugurates the kingdom of God. To validate the above thesis, I will explore the narrative structure and the purpose of Mark in chapter 2. Then, chapters 3–6 will examine the use of each of the four psalms in the Gospel of Mark in light of the narrative structure and the purpose of Mark.

In chapter 2, the structure of the Markan narrative is discerned through narrative criticism (i.e., Mark 1:1—8:21, Jesus' ministry in Jerusalem–[Mark 8:22-26, transition]–Mark 8:27—10:45, on the way–[Mark 10:46-52, transition]–Mark 11:1—16:8, Jesus' ministry in Jerusalem). Based on the structure of Mark, I will propose that the purpose of the Gospel of Mark is to (1) present Jesus as the Messiah, the Son of God, who brings about the kingdom of God, to (2) exhort its readers to follow the king, and to (3) affirm that the Scriptures are fulfilled in all these matters. The structure and the purpose of Mark will serve as the foundation for the examination on Mark's use of four psalms in chapters 3–6. Therefore, each of chapters 3–6 will seek to elicit the significance of these psalms not only in their immediate contexts but also in the context of the whole Markan narrative.

Chapter 3 will show that Mark's allusions and echo to Ps 2:7 in Mark 1:11, 9:7, and 15:39 serve as the key framework of the entire narrative of Mark. The close location between the Son of God language above and the kingdom of God language in Mark 1:15, 9:1, and 15:43 will reveal that Jesus' identity as the Messiah, the Son of God and the kingdom of God function as the overarching themes of Mark. Moreover, the allusion to Ps 2:7 in Mark 9:7 (God's witness to the disciples about Jesus' sonship) connects Jesus' messianic sonship to discipleship. The chapter will also show that Mark has the whole context of Ps 2 (God's rule via his messiah and the subjugation of his enemies) in mind.

Chapter 4 will demonstrate that Mark presents Jesus as the eschatological Davidic Messiah who ushers in God's kingdom through his salvation (i.e., the new exodus) and brings a new temple order. In doing so, Mark appropriates Ps 118:25-26 in Mark 11:9-10 (Jesus' entry to Jerusalem, the final destination of his ministry) as the culmination of the Davidic messiah motif in the Markan narrative. Also, Mark quotes

Ps 118:22–23 in Mark 12:10–11 as the conclusion of the parable of the wicked tenants that projects Jesus' death and resurrection as the consummation of the salvation history and serves as the blueprint for the rest of the Markan narrative. Also, the quotation of Ps 118:22–23 clearly portrays Jesus' death and resurrection as the foundation of the new temple order and the cause of the wonder (i.e., the new exodus).

Chapter 5 will discuss one quotation and one allusion to Ps 110:1 in Mark 12:35–37 and 14:62. The chapter will show that the first citation serves as the counterattack on the temple establishment that Jesus is more than the Son of David. It builds up the literary tension about Jesus' identity that is finally resolved in Mark 14:62. The second citation is placed at the crux of the Markan narrative (Mark 14:61–62), where Jesus' full identity as the Messiah, the Son of God, and the Son of Man is revealed. In tandem with other scriptural allusions (Ps 80:18 and Dan 7:13), the allusion to Ps 110:1 functions to (1) recapitulate Jesus' full identity; (2) present Jesus as the king who will bring a new temple order; (3) forecast Jesus' resurrection, the heavenly enthronement, and the Parousia; (4) consummate God's kingdom via his Messiah and the subjugation of his enemies envisaged by the allusions to Ps 2; and finally, (5) serve as the partial fulfillment of the passion prediction (i.e., arrest) and lead to the rest of the anticipated passion (i.e., death and resurrection) in the Markan narrative.

Chapter 6 will explore the significance of a group of citations to Ps 22 in the Markan narrative. The section will show that Mark employs Ps 22 at the climax of the Markan narrative (i.e., the crucifixion; Mark 15:20–39) to highlight that Jesus' passion fulfills the Scriptures. Mark uses Ps 22 typologically; thus, he presents Jesus as the Messiah and the Righteous Sufferer in the pattern of David in his struggle to bring God's kingdom. The unique features of Ps 22 (i.e., the vivid description of suffering and humiliation, exuberant praise and proclamation of God's rule) seem to explain why Mark uses Ps 22 more than any other Davidic lament psalms and locates all of them at the climax of the Markan narrative. Furthermore, the chapter will demonstrate that, though Mark uses only lament section of Ps 22, his placement of the citations of Ps 22 in the Markan narrative indicates that he has also vindication section of the psalm in mind (Ps 22:21–31; Mark 15:38—16:7).

HISTORY OF SCHOLARSHIP

Since a plethora of literature on the subject of Mark's use of Psalms exists, even a book-length literature review would not be adequate to give an exhaustive survey on the scholarship. So, we will selectively review some key literature relevant to our interest.[1] Though not focusing on the use of Psalms, Joel Marcus's *The Way of the Lord: Christological Exegesis of the Old Testament in the Gospel of Mark* is a classic work on Mark's use of Scripture. As the subtitle indicates, his focus is Markan Christology. Methodologically, he claims to employ redaction and narrative criticism as well as contemporary Jewish interpretation and the historical/cultural situation of the Markan community. Though his book has many exegetical gems, one thing looks particularly problematic. He asserts that his interpretation of scriptural uses aligns with the whole narrative of Mark. But instead of doing exegesis by observing the overall literary narrative of Mark first and then by identifying the use of Scripture in the narrative, he allows external criteria (i.e., Old Testament) to control the exegesis of the narrative.[2]

Adela Yarbro Collins's "The Appropriation of the Psalms of Individual Lament by Mark"[3] broaches the question of how differently the first-century Christians appropriated the Old Testament from other Jewish practices of OT appropriation. She focuses on a diachronic history of the appropriation of the psalms of individual lament and concludes that these psalms have been reread and reappropriated by different communities for their own situations.[4] One can find the conspicuous example of rereading and reappropriation in the scroll of the Qumran community that appropriated the suffering of the Davidic lamenter in the psalms in such a way that the suffering of the Teacher of Righteousness was predestined because they considered the Teacher an "eschatological catalyst."[5]

---

1. The literature review mainly focuses on important books, articles, and essays that are specifically devoted to the use of Psalms in Mark. Joel Marcus's *Way of the Lord* is an exception due to its significance to the use of the OT in Mark. We must admit that our selection of importance is subjective but inevitable due to the scope of the book.

2. Like Rikki Watts, for Marcus, the Isaianic new exodus motif is the hermeneutical key. Rikki E. Watts's book *Isaiah's New Exodus and Mark* elaborates in detail how Isaianic new exodus motif found in Mark 1:2–3 with Malachi's judgment of Lord motif is programmatic for the interpretation of the whole Gospel. We will briefly examine the validity of his claim in chapter 2.

3. Collins, "Appropriation," 223–41.

4. Collins, "Appropriation," 225.

5. Collins, "Appropriation," 227.

Following the exegetical method of his contemporaries, she argues, Mark reappropriated the psalms of individual lament to present Jesus' suffering as "the predestined suffering of the messiah."[6] Probably because the allusion to lament psalms in the passion narrative is well recognized, she reinforces her argument with two allusions to lament psalms "outside of the passion narrative in Mark" (Ps 22:7 in Mark 9:11–13 and Ps 69:9 in Mark 3:20–21).[7] She concludes that Christian appropriation of Psalms was not "an act of disappropriation or a violent theft of part of the Jewish heritage."[8] Her argument strengthens the claim that Mark's use of Old Testament, at least the use of the lament psalms, aligns with Jewish tradition of scriptural use. However, her article neither takes into account the narrative of Mark nor treats the use of Psalms in Mark comprehensively.

In his article, "Das Markusevangelium, Psalm 110,1 und 118,22f . . . Folgetext und Prätext," Breytenbach examines "the referential intertextuality," that is, the relationship between *follow-up text* (i.e., the Gospel of Mark) and *pre-text* (i.e., Psalms).[9] He focuses on the two cited psalms in Mark: Ps 110:1 (Ps 109:1 LXX) in Mark 12:35–37 and 14:62 and Ps 118:22 (Ps 117:22f. LXX) in Mark 8:31 and 12:10f. He argues that the author of the Gospel intended the intertextual references in the text to be recognized by the readers.[10]

Methodologically, Breytenbach analyzes follow-up text first and then pre-text, since he believes the priority should be given to the narrative of Mark. As for the analysis of the pre-text, his interest is in the effects of the transformation of pre-text.[11] Having analyzed the relationship between follow-up texts (Mark) and the pre-texts (Psalms) mentioned above, he concludes that the quotations (i.e., Pss 110:1 and 118:22) are related to certain themes in early Christianity. These themes are the eschatological reign of Christ at the right hand of the Almighty and the rejection and restoration of Jesus which are firmly linked to the narrative.[12]

Breytenbach's work is noteworthy in that he gives the priority to the function of the cited text in the narratival interpretation of the follow-up text. However, his focus on the effects of the transformation of pre-text

6. Collins, "Appropriation," 231–32.
7. Collins, "Appropriation," 232–36.
8. Collins, "Appropriation," 240.
9. Breytenbach, "Markusevangelium," 199.
10. Breytenbach, "Markusevangelium," 201.
11. Breytenbach, "Markusevangelium," 210.
12. Breytenbach, "Markusevangelium," 221.

does not seem to pay sufficient attention on the context of the pre-text, perhaps because of his methodological commitment to the notion of intertextuality that underlines the interaction between text and reader rather than author.

Robert D. Rowe's book *God's Kingdom and God's Son: The Background to Mark's Christology from the Concepts of Kingship in the Psalms*, as the subtitle indicates, consistently investigates the kingship motif as the background for Jesus' messianic kingship in Mark.[13] For that task, he examines the ideas of kingship in Psalms, the latter part of Isaiah, early Judaism, and the Gospel of Mark. He argues that Psalms, Isaiah, and some early Jewish literature consistently evince a "two-tier kingship," that is, God's kingship represented by Davidic messianic kingship.[14] Having traced the two-tier kingship motif in the OT and some early Jewish literature, Rowe finally seeks to find this two-tier kingship concept in the use of the OT in the Gospel of Mark. He sees the kingdom of God motif in the use of Isaiah in Mark. Especially, he focuses on the four royal psalms (i.e., Pss 2, 118, 110, and 22) and concludes that these psalms corroborate the idea that Jesus is the messianic king who discloses the kingdom of God on earth, climaxing in his death and resurrection.[15]

Rowe's thorough research on the background of the kingship idea in Old Testament and early Judaism is admirable. Also, this book agrees with Rowe that the focus of the Gospel of Mark is the kingdom of God. However, despite his meticulous analysis and the similar view with this book, his methodology and argument have a fatal weakness: as it will be argued further in this book, instead of making a claim based on one's presupposition that the Gospel is about the kingdom of God, one should thoroughly analyze the entire narrative of Mark to see if one can reach the theological conclusion that the Gospel is about the kingdom of God.[16] Unfortunately, Rowe does not relate the four psalms with the structure of the entire narrative of Mark. Instead, his book only focuses on how kingship motif is manifested in the use of these Psalms in Mark. In conclusion, Rowe approaches the kingship motif in the Gospel of Mark shaped

---

13. Rowe, *God's Kingdom*.
14. Rowe, *God's Kingdom*, 310.
15. Rowe, *God's Kingdom*, 307.
16. It is possible that Rowe's presupposition that Mark is "a theological (as well as a historical) document" possibly drives him to focus on the theology (i.e., kingship motif as a part of Christology) instead of approaching these four psalms in light of the entire narrative of Mark. Rowe, *God's Kingdom*, 9.

by the OT rather than by the use of the OT in light of the narrative of Mark.

Rikki Watts's two articles, "The Psalms in Mark's Gospel" and "The Lord's House and David's Lord: The Psalms and Mark's Perspective on Jesus and the Temple," contain in essence the same content in spite of differences in some details.[17] In these two articles, Watts treats the use of four psalms that are either cited or clearly alluded to in Mark (Pss 2, 118, 110, and 22). He carefully expounds the original context of these psalms, their use by contemporary Jewish literatures, and their function in the narrative of Mark. He proposes that these four psalms play a significant role in the narrative of Mark. In a nutshell, he argues,

> Mark's careful arrangement of his psalm citations presents Jesus as both Israel's Davidic Messiah (Pss. 2, 118) and the temple's Lord (Ps. 110) who, coming to purge Jerusalem but rejected by the temple authorities, announces the present structure's destruction and, through his death and vindication (Ps. 22), its replacement with a new people-temple centered on himself.[18]

In other words, Watts proposes that the four psalms serve to present Jesus as the Davidic Messiah and the Lord of the temple, who will replace it through his death and vindication. His proposal has some merit. Also, though he wrote a relatively short article, he loads it with a considerable amount of information and insights. The book will interact with Watts's article in due course.

Here it will suffice to mention just one thing: Watts considers that Mark merges "Jesus as David's messianic son" with Isaiah's new exodus motif, which is "the overarching paradigm" for the Gospel of Mark.[19] His interpretation of each psalm consistently reveals how they pertain to the Isaianic new exodus paradigm of Mark. Considering that he already argued strongly for the paradigm in his book, *Isaianic New Exodus in Mark*, his insistence on the close-knit relationship between Psalms and the new exodus motif in Mark is not surprising.[20] Although hardly any Markan scholars doubt that the Isaianic new exodus motif is one of the dominant themes in the Gospel of Mark, whether the motif is programmatic for the

17. Watts, "Psalms," 25–45; Watts, "Lord's House," 307–22.

18. Watts, "Lord's House," 307.

19. Watts, "Psalms," 25, 44. Watts also wrote about the use of Old Testament in Mark, where he consistently presented Isaianic new exodus motif as the overarching paradigm. Watts, "Mark," 111–250.

20. Watts, *Isaiah's New Exodus*.

whole Gospel or not is a disputed point.[21] In addition, how much the use of Psalms is related to the motif may not be as definite as Watts claims. Yet, despite its brevity, Watts's article is one of the few writings that deal with the use of Psalms in Mark's Gospel as a whole.

Stephen P. Ahearne-Kroll's *The Psalms of Lament in Mark's Passion* examines the LXX version of the four lament psalms evoked in the Markan passion narrative.[22] Ahearne-Kroll challenges the interpretation that Jesus accepts his suffering as God's prescribed will in Scriptures. Rather, Ahearne-Kroll's reading of the lament psalms projects Jesus as a Davidic lamenter who "goes to his death challenging God to answer his cries from the cross."[23] Ahearne-Kroll elicits his concept of Jesus as a Davidic lamenter from his understanding that Davidic praise and thanksgiving in the lament psalms are only means to persuade God to grant salvation.[24]

As a result, Ahearne-Kroll is reluctant to consider that God vindicated Jesus through resurrecting him. Even though he denies the absolute significance of the lament psalms for interpreting Jesus' death, his understanding of lament psalms affects heavily the interpretation of passion narrative. In conclusion, despite the contribution he makes by offering a commentary on the Septuagintal lament psalms, his interpretation fails

---

21. Watts argues that three themes of Isaianic new exodus—(1) "Yahweh's deliverance and healing of the exiles"; (2) Yahweh's leading "blind Israel" on a journey; 3) Yahweh's "arrival in Jerusalem"—correspond to three stages of Mark's literary progression: (1) Jesus' might manifested in "words and deeds"; (2) blind disciples led by Jesus on the way; and (3) Jesus' arrival in Jerusalem. Watts, *Isaiah's New Exodus*, 371. However, some scholars question Isaianic new exodus motif as the overarching structure of Mark. For instance, Larson questions it as following: "Watts writes concerning the first major division of the gospel, 'Jesus' healings of the blind, deaf, and lame likewise echo Yahweh's healing of the exiles in the INE' (2000: 372). However, there are no miracles of sight in the first major division of the gospel. Likewise, in what sense can one say that the exiled people are delivered and healed? The end of the first major section of Mark, 8.14–21, hardly suggests deliverance and healing." Larsen, "Structure of Mark's Gospel," 148. See the heated debates among the scholars on the validity of the new exodus motif as the overarching paradigm in Mark in Smith, "Uses of 'New Exodus,'" 224–26.

22 Ahearne-Kroll, *Psalms of Lament*. The evoked psalms (LXX) are (1) Ps 40:10 in Mark 14:18; (2) Pss 41:6, 12, and 42:5 in Mark 14:34; (3) Ps 68:22 in Mark 15:23, 36; and (4) PsS 21:19, 8, and 2 in Mark 15:24, 29, 34 respectively; Ahearne-Kroll, *Psalms of Lament*, 63–77.

23. Ahearne-Kroll, *Psalms of Lament*, 224; According to Ahearne-Kroll, Mark portrays that Jesus is a suffering royal figure like David, who "challenges God's role in his suffering, who searches for understanding of his suffering in light of his past relationship with God, and who finally attempts to shame God to act on his behalf only because he is suffering." Ahearne-Kroll, *Psalms of Lament*, 38. The term "Davidic lamenter" reflects Ahearne-Kroll's understanding of Jesus in the passion narrative.

24. Ahearne-Kroll, *Psalms of Lament*, 108.

to pay close attention to the vindication motif present in the original context of the psalms. In addition, he does not consider the overall literary structure of Mark's Gospel that clearly exhibits the motif of vindication through resurrection of which the passion narrative is a part.

Holly Carey's *Jesus' Cry from the Cross* specifically deals with the use of Ps 22:2 (MT) in Mark 15:34.[25] She propounds that Mark 15:34 reflects the original context of the whole Ps 22, that is, vindication after suffering, because the entire narrative of Mark supports "Jesus' impending vindication via resurrection."[26] She also consistently claims that the first "implied readers" would have read Mark 15:34 in the whole context of Ps 22, that is, with the suffering and vindication of the Righteous Sufferer in mind.[27] She supports her thesis in four different ways: (1) She argues that the Gospel of Mark stresses the importance of resurrection: the three "passion-resurrection predictions" and many other passages connect Jesus' suffering and vindication through resurrection.[28] (2) Having examined the methodology of OT quotations and allusions in Mark's Gospel, Carey concludes that Mark sometimes employed OT quotations and allusions contextually.[29] (3) She also examines the use of Psalms in Mark's contemporary Jewish social and cultural context and found the existence of a righteous sufferer motif.[30] (4) Likewise, she proposes that Mark also appropriated this motif in the use of lament psalms in the Gospel.[31] Thus, the implied readers of Mark were aware of the vindication of the righteous sufferer concept and understood Mark 15:34 with that interpretation strategy. In conclusion, she admirably validates her argument by taking the overall narrative into account instead of only the immediate context in Mark (i.e., the passion narrative) as well as by considering the social context of the first-century implied readers.[32]

---

25. Carey, *Jesus' Cry*.

26. Carey, *Jesus' Cry*, 171.

27. Carey, *Jesus' Cry*, 172. Carey does not explain why she capitalizes "the Righteous Sufferer." In chapter 6, I capitalize the word (i.e., the Righteous Sufferer) for Jesus only and thus distinguish it from other righteous sufferer figures in Old Testament and Second Temple Jewish literature because of Jesus' unique role as the ultimate eschatological Righteous Sufferer. See more detail in chapter 6.

28. Carey, *Jesus' Cry*, 68.

29. Carey, *Jesus' Cry*, 92–93.

30. Carey, *Jesus' Cry*, 124–25.

31. Carey, *Jesus' Cry*, 137–38.

32. Carey, *Jesus' Cry*, 23.

Timothy J. Geddert's article "The Use of Psalms in Mark," covers five quotations and one allusion (Ps 107:28 in Mark 4:39) in Mark.[33] Geddert's article does not interact with the literature of early Judaism like that of Watts. Instead, it mainly focuses on explicating the original context of Psalms and their function in the Gospel of Mark. The article is not heavily academic, but he tries to dig into "the meaning below the surface of the text."[34] He often connects each psalm in the context of the overall narrative. The article, however, is not thorough, and it does not offer comprehensive ideas on the use of Psalms.

In his article, "Mein Gott, mein Gott, warum hast du mich verlassen?," Martin Stowasser states his desire to explore whether the use of the citation of Ps 22:2 in Mark 15:34 implies the whole context of Ps 22 or not.[35] To situate it in the broader context of the Gospel of Mark, he first observes randomly some OT allusions and quotations in passion narrative and non-passion narrative in Mark to find out whether Mark uses them with the immediate OT context in mind or not.[36] He claims that they all turn out to be used atomistically; they enhance the development of the Markan train of thought. Thus, he tentatively concludes that any cited text that points to its OT context would be exceptional.[37]

Stowasser only finds three occasions (Mark 14:27, 34; 15:34) in the passion narrative that take the immediate context of the OT into consideration.[38] Mark 14:27 and 14:34 break the narrative flow probably "to create space for these expanding thoughts for the readers."[39] As for Mark 15:34, where the cry of righteous sufferer in Ps 22:2 (MT) is cited, the citation has the immediate context (Ps 22:3) in mind because Ps 22:3 is the paraphrase of Ps 22:2. Mark seems to intend to emphasize God's abandonment of Jesus by citing Ps 22:2.[40] But other allusions of Ps 22 in the passion narrative do not imply their immediate OT contexts. Stowasser motivates the reader to consider what kind of relationship the use

---

33. Geddert, "Use of the Psalms in Mark," 179–92. His five quotations are from the four psalms (Pss 2; 118; 110; 22). But he does not provide the reason why he omitted the use of Ps 2 in Mark 9:7.

34. Geddert, "Use of the Psalms in Mark," 182.

35. Stowasser, "Mein Gott, mein Gott," 161.

36. Stowasser, "Mein Gott, mein Gott," 162.

37. Stowasser, "Mein Gott, mein Gott," 171.

38. Stowasser, "Mein Gott, mein Gott," 173, 182.

39. Stowasser, "Mein Gott, mein Gott," 177.

40. Stowasser, "Mein Gott, mein Gott," 182, 184.

of Psalms, especially Ps 22, has with its original context. However, his research does not sufficiently interact with the narrative of Mark.

Bernardo Cho's *Royal Messianism and the Jerusalem Priesthood in the Gospel of Mark* does not devote itself solely to the use of Psalms in Mark.[41] Yet the book includes the interpretation of Pss 110, 118, and 22 in Mark to support his argument. Cho's chief interest is the relationship between "the Royal Messiah" and "the Jerusalem priesthood." He claims that the late Second Temple period literature evidences the expectation in Jesus' time that the Jerusalem priesthood would play a significant role in consummating the royal messianism in the eschatological era. Mark's Gospel reflects how the Jerusalem priests fail to actualize this anticipation by rejecting Jesus as the Royal Messiah. In turn, they are rejected by God, but Jesus is "vindicated by God and enthroned above his enemies."[42] Although Cho does not focus solely on the use of Psalms in the Gospel of Mark, his eclectic approach, which especially takes heed to the overall narrative of the Gospel, enhances his readers' understanding of the given biblical passages. And yet, since Cho's interest is the relationship between royal messianism and the Jerusalem priesthood, his book selectively deals with the relevant psalms according to his focus. Thus, Cho does not give a comprehensive picture of the narrative use of the Psalms in Mark.

The brief survey of scholarship on Mark's use of Psalms shows that there is a need for comprehensive research on Mark's use of Psalms not only in its immediate context but also in the whole narrative context of Mark. The only exception would be Watts's articles, which still do not provide the full-scale study on the major citations to Psalm in Mark due to their scopes. While not claiming to be exhaustive since our topic is limited to the four psalms, this book attempts to engage in the thorough study of the most often cited psalms in Mark so that it may contribute to understanding Mark's use of Psalms in light of the Markan narrative.

METHODOLOGY

The Use of the OT in the NT

Since the research on the use of Psalms in the Gospel of Mark falls into the field of use of the OT in the NT, I will clarify some methodological

---

41. Cho, *Royal Messianism*.
42. Cho, *Royal Messianism*, 20–21.

issues related to the use of the OT in the NT. Before clarifying of the methodological issues, I need to justify why I use the phrase "the use of the OT in the NT" instead of "intertextuality." Often biblical scholars use the word "intertextuality" interchangeably with the phrase "the use of the OT in the NT," as they often define intertextuality as the study of the intertextual relationship between the OT and the NT. In spite of its wide use in biblical study, the term "intertextuality" is problematic in at least two dimensions: (1) The different groups of scholars create confusion by using varying definitions of intertextuality.[43] (2) The great dissonance between the origin of the term and its use by biblical scholars creates a potential problem for those who use this term without thoughtful reflection on this dissonance.[44]

Almost all scholars agree that it is Julia Kristeva who popularized the term intertextuality, influenced by Ferdinand de Saussure, the proponent of Structuralism, and Mikhail Bakhtin, who proposed dialogism.[45] Kristeva's intertextuality synthesized the concepts of sign, dialogism, and polyphony from Saussure and Bakhtin with her own political and cultural ideology. Kristeva contends that "any text is constructed as a mosaic of quotations; any text is the absorption and transformation of another."[46] As a result, she resists "every totalitarian, unitary truth claim" via "dialogue of texts" (i.e., intertextuality).[47] Though many biblical scholars define "intertextuality" in a limited sense, without Kristeva's ideological connotation (i.e., Richard B. Hays), as Moyise demonstrated, the term is too inclusive to be used for this study.[48] Therefore, to avoid possible unintended connotations attached to the term "intertextuality," I will use

---

43. Moyise classifies intertextuality into three categories to "indicate the individual scholar's particular interest or focus": (1) Intertextual echo ("[A] particular allusion or echo can sometimes be more important than its 'volume might suggest'"); (2) Dialogical intertextuality: ("The interaction between text and subtext is seen to operate in both directions"); (3) Postmodern intertextuality: ("Meaning can only result if some interactions are privileged and others are silenced"). Moyise, "Intertextuality," 17–18.

44. Yoon, "Ideological Inception," 58–76.

45. According to Yoon, Kristeva synthesized the notion of *sign* as "a symbol that communicates a particular message" from Saussure and that of *dialogism* ("the text creates the dialogue between the text and the reader") and *polyphony* ("a plurality of meanings") from Bakhtin. Yoon, "Ideological Inception," 61–65. As for the dialogue of voices purported by Bakhtin, see Bakhtin, "Discourse in the Novel," 263.

46. Kristeva, "Word, Dialogue, and Novel," 37.

47. Alkier, "Intertextuality and the Semiotics," 6; Kristeva, "Word, Dialogue, and Novel," 37.

48. See footnote 43.

"the use of the OT in the NT" to limit the focus to how NT authors used the OT.[49]

As for the methodology of the OT in the NT, this book will articulate "Context," "Interpretive Technique," "Textual Form."[50] Also, I will specifically explore criteria for OT quotations, allusions, and echoes. Finally, I will briefly justify the reason why the book focuses on Mark's intention, rather than how Mark's first readers would understand the use of Psalms in Mark.

Contextual vs Atomistic

Whether NT writers used OT texts with their wider contexts in mind or they used OT texts atomistically has been an ongoing debate in the field of the use of the OT in the NT since Dodd's concise but significant book *According to the Scriptures*, which initially highlighted this crucial issue.[51] Up until now, scholars have not reached a consensus and their

---

49. It was definitely Richard B. Hays who popularized the term "intertextuality" in the field of biblical study in his epochal book, *Echoes of Scripture in the Letters of Paul*. Yoon, however, argues that while acknowledging Kristeva's influencing on intertextuality, Hays distances himself with Kristeva by not following Kristeva's definition of "intertextuality" in that he excludes Kristeva's ideological motivation. Yoon also points out that even Hollander's book *The Figure of Echo*, from which Hays claims to receive a lot of insights, does not explicate the notion of intertextuality. Thus, Yoon contends, Hays insufficiently justifies his use of the term intertextuality. Yoon, "Ideological Inception," 68–71. The writer is aware of some scholars' arguments that the term "Old Testament" is anachronistic, since the canonization of the OT was still in the process during the writing of the NT. However, NT authors were conscious that they were citing Israel's Scripture, and since we call Israel's Scripture "the Old Testament," I will use the term "the use of the OT in the NT."

50. David M. Allen suggests four "core themes" of the field: "Context," "Interpretive Technique," "Textual Form," and "Macro versus Micro." Allen, "Introduction," 7. Allen explicates that "macro" readings are "attuned to a wider narrative . . . and thus are shaped by, and generative of, a wider, expansive reading of the scriptural material," whereas "'micro' readings are more concerned with fine textual detail . . ." Allen, "Introduction," 11.

51. Asserting that the OT is "the substructure of NT theology," Dodd argues NT authors considered the wider context of the OT when they used the OT in the NT. Dodd, *According to the Scriptures*, 126–27. In contrast to Dodd, Barnabas Lindars, in his book *New Testament Apologetic*, argues that New Testament writers used the OT apologetically (and atomistically) and that the apologetic starting point is the resurrection of Christ. Lindars, *New Testament Apologetic*, 13, 72–73. His argument is, however, open to criticism since it is based on unsubstantiated assumption. For instance, Marshall points out two things: (1) Unlike Lindars's assumption, the NT's use of the OT goes beyond the apologetic use. (2) It seems that resurrection is not the starting point of

opinions fall into the spectrum between respect for OT context and atomistic interpretation. For example, one of the prominent proponents of the view that NT writers were aware of the wider context is Gregory K. Beale. Borrowing the concept from Eric Donald Hirsh, Beale gives an illustration of an apple ('meaning') picked up from a tree and placed in a new setting ('significance'). For Beale, the meaning of OT text remains the same in the NT, even though the significance of the text may change in a new context.[52] However, Steve Moyise, though not totally against respect for OT context, is much more cautious of the idea that NT authors respected OT context. Taking some examples from Paul's use of the OT, he concludes that one's definition of "the respect for OT context" determines if Paul used the quotations in coherence with OT contexts or not.[53] However, his inclination toward reader's response (i.e., Paul's use of the OT as a rhetorical device for his readers) and his criticism of those who consider the wider context (i.e., the contexts of book, OT narrative, and theme) discloses Moyise's thought that Paul, more often than not, did not respect OT contexts.[54]

Arthur Keefer observes that scholars reach different conclusions on "the OT/NT relationship" because their definitions of context are different. And even those who consider the same OT context for NT text

---

all the uses of the OT in the NT. Marshall, "Assessment of Recent Developments," 8–9. In a similar vein, Donald Juel also proposes the atomistic use of the OT in the NT, however, with different motives. In his book *Messianic Exegesis*, Juel postulates that the early Christians' confession on the crucified and risen Messiah led them to "adopt" the non-traditional messianic passages as messianic passages, following the hermeneutical method of their Jewish contemporaries. Juel, *Messianic Exegesis*, 26–29. Juel's argument is still a disputed point. For example, as for view that Second Temple Jews were conscious of OT contexts, see Instone-Brewer, *Techniques and Assumptions*. The contrasting view is proposed by Wold. Wold, "Old Testament Context," 115–25. In summary, Wold's argument indicates that NT writers appropriated OT texts atomistically.

52. Beale, *John's Use*, 51–52. Walter Kaiser also proposes the similar concept. See also Kaiser, "Single Meaning, Unified Referents," 45–89. Kaiser also seems to draw on the concept from Hirsch. See Hirsch., *Aims of Interpretation*, 2–3.

53. He argues that "Paul did not always respect the context of his quotations" if one considers OT contexts as "the language of the original," "the historical situation of the original authors," and "the surrounding verses of the quotations." However, he contends, if one regards "a serious engagement with the actual words of the quotation and relating them to similar texts elsewhere in Scripture" and "discerning the meaning of a quotation by relating it to the main contours of Scripture or a major section of Scripture", Paul "does sometimes (or often) respect the context of his quotations." Moyise, "Does Paul Respect," 112–13.

54. Moyise, "Does Paul Respect," 101–12. As for the idea that Paul quoted the OT for the rhetorical effects on his readers, see especially Stanley, *Arguing with Scripture*.

INTRODUCTION 15

may have contrasting interpretive results based on their hermeneutical presuppositions.[55] His observation helps identify the methodological problem in studying the use of the OT in the NT. He lists eight categories of OT contexts scholars often utilize:

(a) the language of the original (linguistic/grammatical);

(b) the surrounding verses of the quotations;

(c) similar texts elsewhere in the OT;

(d) major section(s) of the OT (esp. a single book);

(e) OT theme(s);

(f) God's redemptive-historical action (salvation history/theology);

(g) the historical situation of the original authors;

(h) the meaning within the mind of the original authors.[56]

Keefer points out that the modern interpreter's hermeneutical presupposition influences the "notion of context" and one's interpretation of the OT.[57] Though Keefer's analysis does not solve the problem of different opinions, it helps us to identify different definitions of OT context and to know the relationship between the choice of definitions and the interpreter's hermeneutical commitment. Instead of restricting itself to a specific definition, this book will selectively utilize these different categories to explore the relationship between OT and NT texts. That is, in each chapter, we will interpret the target psalm (i.e., the immediate context), the canonical context of the target psalm (i.e., the psalm in the Psalter), and the relationship of the psalm with OT texts outside of the Psalter (i.e., the lexical, structural, and thematic parallels between the given psalm and OT texts).

Having identified how the interpreter's hermeneutical presupposition affects one's understanding of the context, instead of imposing one's own hermeneutical presupposition, it would be wise to consider what NT authors' presuppositions would be and to see if their interpretation presupposes OT context or not. Moo and Naselli call it a "hermeneutical axiom" of NT writers.[58] According to Moo and Naselli, the NT's funda-

55. Keefer, "Meaning and Place," 83.
56. Keefer, "Meaning and Place," 84.
57. Keefer, "Meaning and Place," 85.
58. According to Moo and Naselli, hermeneutical axioms are "a community's basic convictions about Scripture, its own identity, and God's movement in history."

mental hermeneutical axiom is "the authors' conviction that the God who had spoken in the OT continued to speak to them and that it was this final divine context for all of Scripture that determines the meaning of any particular text."[59] Thus, the NT can not only apply the meaning of the OT but also *extend* and *deepen* it.[60] Moo and Naselli do not mean the *change* of meaning as the proponents of the atomistic approach argue but the *application* and *extension* of OT meaning. The application and extension of OT meaning cohere with the NT authors' hermeneutical axiom that God who spoke through OT authors now continues to speak in light of Christ's event (i.e., Heb 1:1–2). Moo and Naselli's notion of *application and extension of meaning* explains better than that of *meaning and significance* purported by Beale and Kaiser that the seemingly atomistic OT texts in the NT are actually used contextually. Therefore, on the one hand, this bookwill accommodate Moo and Naselli's approach concerning OT context. On the other hand, this study is still open to the possibility of atomistic use of NT authors because, as Moo and Naselli admit, their conclusion does not necessarily "prove" that NT authors interpreted the OT always correctly (i.e., contextually) but does demonstrate that their OT interpretation is based on their hermeneutical axiom shared with other "early Christians."[61]

Interpretive Technique and Textual Form

An increasing number of scholars recognize the parallels between NT authors' exegetical techniques and that of early Jewish literature, especially

---

Another important concept is "appropriation technique." It is "specific, 'on the surface' method(s) that authors use to appropriate a text for a new situation." Moo and Naselli, "Problem," 716. Moo and Naselli argue that NT authors used similar appropriation technique—which is conscious of OT context—with their contemporary Jews but had different hermeneutical axiom. Moo and Naselli, "Problem," 715–19.

59. Moo and Naselli, "Problem," 737. They propose three approaches particularly significant in rendering "a rationale for the NT's use of the OT": (1) The canonical approach provides the interpretive framework by answering the "why" questions. (2) Typology describes one critical way in which the two testaments within the one canon can be seen to relate to each other—the "how." (3) And *sensus plenior* is the "what": the fuller, or deeper, sense that NT writers find in OT texts as they read canonically. The NT authors discern a "fuller" meaning in OT passages by placing these texts in a wider context than the original authors could have known. Moo and Naselli, "Problem," 736–37.

60. Moo and Naselli, "Problem," 737.

61. Moo and Naselli, "Problem," 745.

Dead Sea manuscripts and rabbinic literature.⁶² As mentioned above, NT authors shared the common appropriation technique with their contemporary Jews. They shared even the common pool of the texts with other Jews but arrived at different conclusions. ⁶³ Indeed, the book of Psalms is one of the most commonly cited biblical books in Second Temple Jewish literature, as well as in the NT, including Mark. Therefore, this book will compare both interpretive techniques and hermeneutical axioms of the relevant psalmic passages in the contemporary Jewish literature with Mark to discover how they may shed light on the use of Psalms in Mark.

In regard to the textual form, Lim informs us of two lessons from "Post-Qumran textual criticism" that relate to the use of the OT in the NT: (1) "the pluriformity of the biblical texts of ancient Judaism between approximately 200 BCE and 100 CE" and (2) the need to differentiate between "language and textual classification in assessing the biblical citations in the New Testament."⁶⁴ These lessons suggest two implications for the study: (1) We should be more open to the possibility that what looks like a "variant created by the (NT) author" (i.e., Mark) is a citation of "a textual variant attested in the biblical scrolls."⁶⁵ (2) We should not necessarily assume that the Septuagint would be the text-type of the citation (i.e., Psalms) just because the citation is written in Greek.

Authorial Intention vs Reader's Response

The tension between authorial intention and reader's response has been an ongoing issue for interpreters.⁶⁶ Which side one takes drastically affects his/her exegesis.⁶⁷ In the spectrum of author–text–reader, the authorial intent approach emphasizes that the author's intention, which is reflected in the text, attempts to shape a reader's response. On the contrary, a reader-response approach is not interested in the author's

---

62. For instance, Brewer, *Techniques and Assumptions*; Lim, *Holy Scripture*; Docherty, "New Testament Scriptural Interpretation," 1–19.
63. Lim, "Qumran Scholarship," 72.
64. Lim, "Qumran Scholarship," 69–71.
65. Lim, "Qumran Scholarship," 69.
66. For instance, see Hirsch, *Validity in Interpretation*; Kevin J. Vanhoozer, *Meaning in This Text*; Beale, "Questions of Authorial Intent," 1–26 for authorial intention. As for reader's response, see Barthes, "Death of the Author," 142–48; Fish, *Is There a Text*; Moyise, *Evoking Scripture*, 125–41.
67. Miller, "Intertextuality in Old Testament," 284–89.

intention. Intertextuality and multiple meanings of the text presuppose a reader's control over the text.

Since the subject has many corollaries, and for the sake of the methodology relevant to our topic, we will limit ourselves to only one question: should we seek to focus on Mark's authorial intention in the use of Psalms in Mark or on how Mark's first readers would resonate with his use of Psalms in the Gospel of Mark? The work of Christopher Stanley, one of the most outspoken scholars about the relationship between OT citations and the first readers of the NT, is a good test case for our subject matter. If Hays deals with modern readers' response in his discussion of the seven criteria for stretching an allusion,[68] Stanley is interested in how Paul used OT citations in order to persuade his readers to recognize his apostolic authority.[69] In other words, according to Stanley, Paul's intention to use OT citations is rhetorical persuasion so his readers may accept his authority. Porter, however, correctly objects to Stanley's assumption of Paul's readers' literary status because we do not know how much the readers of Paul were aware of Paul's citations.[70] Due to Stanley's presupposition of Paul's readers, unfortunately, Stanley only focuses on the explicit citations to the detriment of neglecting less explicit citations.[71] In addition, Abasciano notes that Stanley's methodology is limited because Stanley interprets Paul's letters by way of the first readers' response instead of searching for authorial intention from the text.[72] Porter and Abasciano's critiques on the weaknesses of Stanley's study are convincing. The book will focus on Mark's authorial intention inscribed in the text when he used Psalms in the Gospel. And by advocating the authorial intention, the effort to establish the criteria for quotation, allusion, and echo is theoretically justified.

The Definitions and Criteria for Quotation and Allusion

Hays makes an incisive comment on the relationship among quotation, allusion, and echo. He says, "Quotation, allusion, and echo may be seen as points along a spectrum of intertextual reference, moving from the

---

68. Hays, *Echoes of Scripture in Paul*, 29–32.
69. Stanley, *Arguing with Scripture*, 34–36.
70. Porter, "Further Comments," 105–6.
71. Porter, "Further Comments," 101; Abasciano, "Diamonds in the Rough," 165.
72. Abasciano, "Diamonds in the Rough," 177–80.

explicit to the subliminal."⁷³ While scholars generally concur with Hays's statement, the consensus on the definitions of quotation, allusion, and echo has proven elusive. Since this study investigates the use of the quotations and clear allusions of Psalms in the Gospel of Mark, we will focus on defining quotation and allusion.⁷⁴

One of the most representative definitions of quotation is Stanley's. Instead of "quotation," he uses the term "citation." According to Stanley, citations "are introduced by an explicit citation formula," "are accompanied by a clear interpretive gloss," and "stand in clear syntactical tension with their present linguistic environment."⁷⁵ However, Porter thinks that the scope of Stanley's definition is "too narrow."⁷⁶ The book consents with Porter that the definition of quotation should include both "formulaic quotation" and "direct quotation without an introductory formula."⁷⁷

Concerning allusion, Hays's seven criteria in his book *Echoes of Scripture in the Letters of Paul* has continued to impact the subsequent discussion on the subject matter.⁷⁸ Numerous scholars have adopted his seven criteria to identify allusion and echo. It, however, does not mean that all of them wholeheartedly followed Hays's criteria. They either selectively used Hays's or added more criteria.⁷⁹ Some scholars even question the validity of Hays's criteria; having evaluated some of the literature that applied Hays's criteria, Paul Foster finds the echoes and allusions they present to be quite "speculative." Foster warns about "radical reader-response" without sufficient effort to "ascertain authorial intention."⁸⁰

---

73. Hays, *Echoes of Scripture in Paul*, 23.

74. However, sometimes it is inevitable to mention echo alongside allusion because many scholars tend to lump them together in their discussion.

75. Stanley, *Paul and the Language of Scripture*, 4.

76. Porter, "Further Comments," 101.

77. Porter, "Further Comments," 107–8.

78. Hays suggests "seven tests" to hear "intertextual echoes": (1) availability, (2) volume, (3) recurrence, (4) thematic coherence, (5) historical plausibility, (6) history of interpretation, (7) satisfaction. Hays, *Echoes*, 29–32. Though he uses the term "echo," his seven criteria include "allusion." The difference between allusion and echo is the degree of certainty. Hays, *Echoes of Scripture in Paul*, 29.

79. Allen, "Use of Criteria," 135–36. For instance, Beale modifies Hays's seven criteria: He pairs up thematic coherence and satisfaction into one criterion as availability and historical plausibility. Beale, *Handbook*, 34.

80. Foster, "Echoes Without Resonance," 96.

Similarly, Porter criticizes that some of Hays's seven criteria disclose Hays's openness to reader's response.[81]

Agreeing with Foster and Porter, the study is wary of following Hays's criteria despite the wide use of his criteria by other scholars. Rather the study seeks to adopt a definition and criteria that faithfully ascertain authorial intent. Thompson introduces a good point of departure for the definition of allusion. He claims that "literary critics concur that allusion involves (1) the use of a sign or marker that (2) calls to the reader's mind another known text (3) for a specific purpose."[82] Thus, he states that allusion will "refer to statements which are intended to remind an audience of a tradition they are presumed to know as dominical."[83] Based on his definition of allusion, Thompson proposes eleven criteria for identifying them.[84] However, the fundamental difficulty to adopt Thompson's criteria is that his study is not about the OT and NT relationship but about Paul's allusion and echo of Jesus' teaching. Despite this difficulty, Thompson's observation on literary critics' consensus on allusion provides the basis to define allusion. However, once again, one needs to adopt the definition that befits the use of the OT in the NT.

As for allusion in the use of the OT in the NT, two scholars' definitions deserve to be noted. G. K. Beale briefly defines allusions as "a brief expression consciously intended by an author to be dependent on an OT passage."[85] Beale's definition of allusion rightly emphasizes the authorial intention but is not as specific as it should be. In that sense, Porter's definition of allusion fills the gap in the two previous definitions. He says,

---

81. Porter especially finds *availability* to be "highly problematic" because identifying availability depends on "the shifting levels of knowledge of the audience." Porter, "Further Comments," 103. Also, Porter argues that Hays's last four criteria are dependent on the interpretation of readers. Porter, "Use of the OT," 83. Nevertheless, one should remember that Hays does not negate the intention of the author. The following statement of Hays shows that he embraces both authorial intention and reader's recognition. "The concept of allusion depends both on the notion of authorial intention and on the assumption that the reader will share with the author the requisite "portable library" to recognize the source of the allusion;" Hays, *Echoes of Scripture in Paul*, 29.

82. Thompson, *Clothed with Christ*, 29.

83. Thompson, *Clothed with Christ*, 30.

84. They are: (1) verbal agreement, (2) conceptual agreement, (3) formal agreement, (4) place of the Gospel saying in the tradition, (5) common motivation rationale, (6) dissimilarity to Graeco-Roman and Jewish traditions, (7) presence of dominical indicators, (8) presence of tradition indicators, (9) presence of other dominical echoes or word/concept clusters in the immediate context, (10) likelihood the author knew the saying, and (11) exegetical value. Thompson, *Clothed with Christ*, 31–36.

85. Beale, *Handbook*, 31.

Allusion is concerned to bring an external person, place, literary work, or similar entity into the contemporary text, whereas echo does not have the specificity of allusion and is reserved for language that is thematically related to a more general or abstract notion or concept. The use of both concepts seems to imply an intentional use by the author for a particular textual purpose, such as exemplifying or supporting a particular concept. The appeal is based in common knowledge that is thought to be shared with the readers, although an allusion or an echo can still be present if the recipients fail to know or recognize their presence, since they are determined by the intention of the author.[86]

Porter's definition on allusion specifies and refines the three elements of literary critics' definition of allusion that Thompson introduced. Also, Porter underlines the importance of authorial intention. His definition of allusion seems to be more specific and clearer than most definitions proposed by other scholars. Thus, the study will follow Porter's definitions of allusion.

Next, one needs to establish the solid criteria for allusion. After defining allusion in his book *Sacred Tradition in the New Testament*, Porter demonstrates how he applied his definition to interpreting the OT in the NT in the rest of the book. Yet, Porter does not provide clear criteria for finding allusions. I have already noted that some of the criteria of Hays and post-Hays scholars are open to a reader's interpretation. If we follow Porter's definitions of allusion, the criteria for finding allusion should be author-oriented and, thereby, should be identifiable in the text itself.

Some scholars posit criteria suitable to the above requirements. Jon Paulien's internal evidence for allusion seems to be appropriate for authorial intention approach because his criteria focus on the textual evidence. He proposes three criteria to identify allusion: (1) *verbal parallel* (at least two words are identical between the two texts), (2) *thematic parallel* (the two texts share common a theme or motif), and (3) *structural parallel* (the two texts have similar literary, or theological, or historical structure).[87] Similar to Paulien, Miller suggests lexical similarities, the presence of similarities in content ("theme, motif," or "character"), and "similarity in form or structure."[88] Beale also seems to propose a similar idea with those of Paulien and Miller when he states, "The telltale key to

---

86. Porter, *Sacred Tradition*, 46–47.
87. Paulien, "Elusive Allusions," 41–43.
88. Miller, "Intertextuality," 295–97.

discerning an allusion is that of recognizing an *incomparable or unique parallel in wording, syntax, concept, or cluster of motifs in the same order or structure.*"[89] Considering the similar opinions of these scholars, it seems that these three criteria (verbal, thematic, and structural parallels) are essential to verify allusions, at least for those who are convinced that one should find out the author's intention in the text.

This study is aware that the presence of diverse views on the criteria illustrates the difficulty to pin down the criteria. Even those who share the three basic criteria (lexical, thematic, and structural parallels) may end up identifying different allusions in the same text. Even if the study adopts Porter's definition, still the ambiguity remains because one cannot be completely free from subjectivity. Nevertheless, in order to avoid uncontrollable subjectivity that depends on the readers, I consider the above three elements as the basic criteria for allusion.

Literary Approach

The Gospel of Mark has been often a favorite test case for many scholars to apply their hermeneutical methodologies. Since World War II, form criticism, redaction criticism, narrative criticism, and recently, performance criticism, have been eagerly applied in interpreting the Gospel of Mark. While each approach has its strengths and weaknesses, narrative criticism seems to have gained the favor of the most Markan interpreters up to now.[90] Possibly the greatest merit of narrative criticism is that it provides opportunity to those who desire to interpret the Gospel as a whole since its major focus on the plot, characters, setting, and rhetoric presupposes reading the book as a unified text. Moreover, the genre of the Gospels belongs to narrative, which is the main target of narrative criticism.[91] Finally, the narrative approach's commitment to the text and

---

89. Beale, *Handbook*, 31.

90. Many scholars give an overview of these approaches and their strengths and weaknesses. As for the comparison among form, redaction, and narrative criticism, see Malbon, "Narrative Criticism," 29–32.

91. However, as time has gone on, scholars have begun to show interest on the orality of the Gospels. In the early church, the gospel was read publicly to the local Christian community. Thus, performance criticism investigates what effects the performance— the act of publicly reading the gospel—would have generated on the hearers. See Horsley, *Text and Tradition*. Therefore, the emphasis of narrative criticism is text while that of performance criticism is hearers. However, performance criticism, just as narrative criticism, considers the whole narrative as one unit. Because their commonalities are

the entire narrative is amenable to reading a text according to the authorial intent.[92] In light of these aspects, the narrative approach would be most appropriate to investigate the narrative of the Gospel as a unified text.

This study seeks to examine the use of Psalms in Mark in light of the entire narrative of the Gospel of Mark utilizing the methodology of the use of the OT in the NT and narrative approach. Thomas R. Hatina's critique of scholarship on the use of the OT in the NT provides a solid basis for this endeavor. He argues that most of the study on the function of Scripture in the Gospels tends to assume the historical approach; scholars make efforts to search for the original context of the Scripture and the context of contemporary Judaism to compare with the use of Scripture in Mark. All these efforts have merits on their own, which the book will utilize also. Yet, interpreters can be absorbed in these external factors to the detriment of neglecting the internal factor, that is, the whole narrative of the Gospel of Mark. Even if interpreters consider the literary context of the Gospel of Mark, they tend to treat only the immediate context of NT text.

Therefore, Hatina suggests the study of the scriptural function that integrates the triple dimensions: history, literature, and theology.[93] In regard to the relationship of these three dimensions, Hatina thinks that historical research should be subordinated to the whole narrative of the Gospel of Mark rather than the other way around because the narrative criticism assumes Mark as "a unified literary work."[94] As for theology, it is a "by-product" of literary and historical dimensions.[95]

Like Hatina's critical observation, the literature review relevant to this study reveals that scholars hardly consider the whole narrative when they treat the use of Psalms in the Gospel of Mark. Also, they tend to

---

much greater than their differences, some scholars are even suspicious of the endeavors to study them as separate entities. Nevertheless, the focus of our study is the scriptural function of Psalms with Mark's authorial intention in mind. As a result, narrative criticism would suit the purpose of this study best.

92. "Narratology posits an authorial voice inscribed in the text and supposes that the authorial audience is comprised of actual readers who, during the time of reading, share the presuppositions of the authorial voice. Reading this way, the authorial audience experiences the effect of meaning which is "intended." This intention is a textual effect, not a psychological disposition." Lochrie, "Scripture and Authorial Intent," 315.

93. Hatina, *In Search of a Context*, 48.

94. Hatina, *In Search of a Context*, 50–51.

95. Hatina, *In Search of a Context*, 50. Hatina's point is well taken by some scholars also. See Carey, *Jesus' Cry*, 10–12; Hays, *Echoes of Scripture in the Gospels*, 98.

focus on either the passion narrative or specific psalms. There is no book-length study on the quotations and allusions to Psalms throughout the Gospel of Mark to see how these psalms contribute to the structure and the purpose of the whole narrative of Mark. The goal of the study is to fill the lacuna in the scholarship. Therefore, in agreement with Hatina's argument, this study will present the structure of the entire narrative of the Gospel of Mark as the literary context of the Psalms in the Gospel of Mark.[96] Then using the methodology of the use of the OT in the NT explicated above, we will examine the scriptural function of Psalms in Mark in light of the entire narrative of Mark. However, due to the limitation on the scope of the study, the book cannot treat all the quotations, allusions, and echoes of Psalms in the Gospel of Mark. Thus, the study will focus on relatively explicit and recurring psalmic references that are at the same time significant to the narrative of the Gospel of Mark: Pss 2, 110, 118, and 22.[97]

---

96. This writer is aware that other Synoptic Gospels such as Matthew have some different details about the same incidents. For instance, the voice from heaven at the baptism of Jesus says, "this is my Son" in Matt 3:17, while the same heavenly voice in Mark 1:11 says, "you are my Son." However, this study will deal only with Mark.

97. In subsequent chapters of this book, I will show that the references to these four psalms in Mark are relatively explicit and recurring based on the criteria adopted in this chapter and that they play significant roles at the key junctures of the Markan narrative.

2

THE STRUCTURE AND THE PURPOSE OF MARK

As the book seeks to identify how the use of Psalms contributes to the Markan narrative, this chapter aims to establish the narrative structure and the purpose of Mark. By doing so, the study will be able to lay a foundation for articulating what role each psalm plays not only in the immediate context of Mark but also in light of the entire narrative of Mark. Furthermore, identifying the purpose of Mark will enable us to provide the basis for why Mark uses certain psalms. As mentioned in chapter 1, I will mainly utilize narrative criticism to present the structure of Mark. First, I will present the structure of the Markan narrative employing narrative criticism after a brief overview of the literary factors of narrative criticism. Second, based on the structure of the Markan narrative, I will suggest the purpose of Mark.

LITERARY FACTORS OF NARRATIVE CRITICISM

Since narrative criticism has become the dominant method of Gospel study, more and more scholars pay attention to the literary factors in examining the structure of Mark[1]

---

1. Some scholars question the validity of applying the modern methodology (i.e., literary criticism) suitable for modern readers to an ancient narrative which aims for oral listeners like Mark. See Moore, *Literary Criticism and the Gospels*, 87. However, as Dinkler argues, "many recent narratological developments are closely aligned with the concepts and questions of classical antiquity." Also see Dinkler, "New Testament

Narrative criticism typically treats settings, plot, characters, and rhetoric.[2] *Settings* contain space and time. *Plot* is an event of a story, and "conflict is a key to Markan plot."[3] Many scholars have focused on the conflict between the characters (i.e., Jesus, Jewish authorities, disciples, Satan, etc.).[4] *Characters* are closely related to plot, since conflict occurs between different characters in a story. Scholars tend to stress the specific character's narrative role in the narrative structure of Mark, such as the disciples,[5] Jesus,[6] the minor characters.[7] *Rhetoric*, according to Rhoads and Michie, is "'how' the story is told to create certain effects on the reader."[8]

Of the elements of rhetoric that Rhoads and Michie suggest, the ideological point of view and narrative patterns are especially related to the structure of Mark.[9] Hatina posits "kingdom of God" in Mark 1:14–15 to be

---

Rhetorical Narratology," 214. Apart from narrative criticism, geographical and theological approaches are employed by Markan scholars. As for geographical approach, many scholars continue to recognize the geographical framework in Mark's Gospel. For example, France partitions Mark into three acts according to geography apart from Mark 1:1–13 (i.e., Mark 1:14—8:21 "Act One: Galilee," 8:22—10:52 "Act Two: On the Way to Jerusalem," 11:1—16:8 "Act Three: Jerusalem"). France, *Mark*, 13–14. Some of them outline not only the major sections but also their subsections according to spatial change, i.e., Hendrick, "What Is a Gospel," 257–60. Other scholars organize the structure based on different theological themes in Mark such as Jesus' title in Mark 1:1 (i.e., "the Son of God," "Christ"), the new exodus motif, "the Way" motif, the interaction between Jesus and his disciples (i.e., Christology and discipleship), and Christology and discipleship in light of the nature of Jesus' mission, that is, the advent of the kingdom of God through Jesus' "miracle and cross." See Achtemeier, *Mark*, 34; Stein, *Mark*, 35; Watts, *Isaiah's New Exodus*, 371; Heil, *Mark*, 18; Perrin, *New Testament*, 147; Thompson, "Literary Patterns," 222, 233–38; Henderson, *Christology and Discipleship*, 27.

2. It also follows the diagram of reading process that Chatman popularized: Real Author→ Implied Author→ Narrator→ Narratee→ Implied Reader→ Real Reader. Chatman, *Story and Discourse*, 267. Traditionally, the narrator's and implied author's points of views have been regarded to be the same and to be the most important in Mark's Gospel. However, Malbon, who used to consider these two to be the same, now differentiates them. See "Mark's Jesus: Characterization as Narrative Christology." Malbon, *Mark's Jesus*, 16.

3. Malbon, "Narrative Criticism," 33.
4. i.e., Kingsbury, *Conflict in Mark*; Shively, *Apocalyptic Imagination in Mark*, 9–10.
5. Tannehill, "Disciples in Mark," 386–405.
6. Kingsbury, *Christology of Mark's Gospel*, 173–76; Malbon, *Mark's Jesus*.
7. Williams, *Other Followers of Jesus*.
8. Rhoads and Michie, *Mark as Story*, 35.
9. Rhoads and Michie suggest "narrator," "points of view and standard of judgment," "style," "narrative patterns," and "other literary features" as the elements of rhetoric. Rhoads and Michie, *Mark as Story*, 35–62.

the ideological point of view of Mark's Gospel. He argues that kingdom of God has "programmatic" and "paradigmatic" importance and functions as the "interpretive framework" for the entire narrative of Mark.[10] Mark employs a variety of narrative patterns that affect delineating the narrative structure such as chiasm (i.e., concentric structure),[11] intercalation,[12] summary statements,[13] *inclusio*, and doublets.[14] The following section is allotted to establishing the structure of Mark by following the literary approach such as reading process, settings, plot, characters, and rhetoric (i.e., an ideological point of view, narrative patterns, and other literary features).

NARRATIVE STRUCTURE OF MARK[15]

As we observe in the previous section, many scholars acknowledge the existence and significance of narrative patterns and literary features in Mark such as chiasm, intercalation, summary statement, *inclusio*, doublets, etc., even though they may disagree with the details. The above narrative patterns and literary features belong to rhetoric. In addition to these narrative patterns and literary features, the present section will pay attention to an ideological point of view of narrator, implied author, and character, especially Jesus since the Gospel is about the life of Jesus. Also, I will focus on the shift in settings, plot, and characters in shaping the narrative structure of Mark.

---

10. Hatina, *In Search of a Context*, 90–135; Marshall, *Faith as a Theme*, 36–43.

11. van Iersel, *Mark: Reader-Response Commentary*, 84; Scott, "Chiastic Structure," 18; Dewey, *Markan Public Debate*, 131–67.

12. It is called also "sandwich technique" or "A-B-A pattern." Edwards, "Markan Sandwiches," 193–94. Like a sandwich, the one episode is inserted in between the other episode. The original story and inserted story are to be interpreted mutually. See also Shepherd, *Markan Sandwich Stories*, 388–92.

13. Schmidt, *Rahmen der Geschichte Jesu*, 13.

14. For example, Mark 4–8 contains two feeding episodes (Mark 6:30–44; 8:1–10), two boat episodes (Mark 4:35–41; 6:45–52). Fowler, *Loaves and Fishes*, 113. As for some good examples of commentaries and article that apply narrative criticism to outline the narrative structure of Mark, see Moloney, *Mark*, 16–22; Boring, *Mark*, 4–6; Williams, "Outline," 523–25.

15. Since our study focuses on the narrative structure of Mark, we will assume the reliability of the Greek text of Mark (i.e., Nestle-Aland Novum Testamentum Graece 28th edition). Those who are interested in the matter may refer to Hurtado, "P45 and the Textual History," 132–48; Lafleur, *Famille 13*.

Scholars do not agree on the macro-level divisions of the Markan structure. They tend to divide either into two, three, or seven parts based on the criteria such as summary statements with topographical shift,[16] geographical,[17] and thematic markers.[18] Regardless of different divisions by these scholars, it seems that many of them pay attention to the geographical shifts in Mark.[19] Many other scholars also recognize the importance of the geographical change from Galilee to Jerusalem in the Markan structure.[20] Apart from Jesus' ministries around Galilee and Jerusalem, some scholars rightly notice the transitional nature of 8:22–26 and Mark 10:46–52 that frame Mark 8:27—10:45 (i.e., on the way to Jerusalem).[21] Therefore, it seems that the tripartite schema (i.e., Mark 1:1–8:21, Jesus' ministry in Galilee–[Mark 8:22–26, transition]–Mark 8:27—10:45, on the way–[Mark 10:46–52, transition]–Mark 11:1—16:8, Jesus' ministry in Jerusalem) seems to be the most plausible macro-level divisions of the Markan structure.[22] The present section adopts this tripartite schema. I will explain more in the appropriate part of this section.

Prologue: Mark 1:1–15

Mark 1:1–15 begins with the title (Mark 1:1) that exhibits the content of the Gospel (i.e., Jesus) and the identity of Jesus. Thus, in Mark 1:1, the narrator informs implied readers that the Gospel is about Jesus and that Jesus' identity as the Messiah, the Son of God, plays a key role in the Gospel.[23] Then the narrator introduces the forerunner of Jesus, John the

16. i.e., Perrin, *New Testament*, 147.
17. i.e., France, *Mark*, 13–14; Tolbert, *Sowing*, 113–14; Williams, "Outline," 513.
18. Collins, *Mark*, 88.
19. Perrin, *New Testament*, 147; Collins, *Mark*, 88; Tolbert, *Sowing*, 13–14; Williams, "Outline," 513.
20. Lane, *Mark*, 29–31; Boring, *Mark*, 4–6; Taylor, *Mark*, 107–11.
21. Best, *Following Jesus*, 134–45; van Iersel, *Mark*, 122–41; Williams, "Outline," 518–19; Boring, *Mark*, 231; Moloney, *Mark*, 163.
22. i.e., Boring, *Mark*, 4–5. The majority of Markan scholars consider Mark 16:8, instead of Mark 16:20, as the ending of Mark. See, for example, Wedderburn, *Beyond Resurrection*, 135–44; Williams, "Literary Approaches," 26–35; Stein, "Ending of Mark," 86–88.
23. Two things need to be mentioned about Mark 1:1 that affect the interpretation of the entire narrative of Mark: (1) Scholars interpret Ἰησοῦ in τοῦ εὐαγγελίου Ἰησοῦ to be either subjective genitive ("the gospel announced by Jesus") or objective genitive ("the gospel about Jesus"). We agree with those who view it as objective genitive ("the gospel about Jesus"). While it is true that Jesus proclaimed the gospel in the narrative of

Baptist, with the composite scriptural quotations (Exod 23:20; Mal 3:1; Isa 40:3) in Mark 1:2–3.[24] In the composite scriptural quotations, YHWH sends his messenger to prepare the way of the Lord and the messenger cries out in the wilderness to people to prepare the way of the Lord. The focus of the quotations is the forerunner, John. However, the quotations also indicate the close link between the forerunner and the Lord: Jesus is bringing God's eschatological kingdom, and John is his forerunner to prepare the heart of people to welcome their king, Jesus. In Mark 1:4–8, John's role as Jesus' forerunner is further described. He prepares the hearts of people with the baptism of repentance (Mark 1:4–5). Moreover, he proclaims Jesus as the stronger one who will baptize with the Holy Spirit (Mark 1:7–8).[25]

As the forerunner introduces the coming of Jesus in Mark 1:7–8, Jesus appears to be baptized by John in Mark 1:9. The shift in character in Mark 1:9 indicates Mark 1:9–15 as the subsection of Mark 1:1–15. Jesus is confirmed by God in heaven as the messianic Son of God with the

---

Mark (i.e., Mark 1:15), the inseparable relationship between Jesus and the gospel gives more weight to consider Ἰησοῦ as objective genitive (i.e., Mark 8:35, 37). (2) The textual evidences are evenly divided between the omission and the presence of υἱοῦ θεοῦ. While it is difficult to side with either position, since the existence of υἱοῦ θεοῦ can be defended textually and its existence perfectly fits in the narrative flow of Mark, we will consider υἱοῦ θεοῦ as an authentic text of Mark. Therefore, the Son of God is the apposition of the Messiah (Χριστοῦ υἱοῦ θεοῦ). Readers can refer to Metzger, *Textual Commentary*, 62; Botner, "Role of Transcriptional Probability," 467–80; When we consider the Son of God as the apposition of the Messiah, we may wonder what the Son of God means in Mark. The two suggestions seem to be most likely: (1) The most probable meaning of the Son of God is the Messiah. Thus, the Son of God is not only appositional but also identical to the Messiah in Mark 1:1. Beateman, "Defining the Titles," 559. (2) When we consider the sociopolitical context of Mark, the implied author may have intended to challenge the Roman empire. Evans, "Beginning of Good News," 83–100.

24. Scholars offer different opinions about whether Mark 1:2–3 is connected to the previous verse (Mark 1:1) or the following verse (Mark 1:4–8). Because of the space limit, I will just introduce the representative studies on the issue. Geulich posits the argument for the connection between verse 1 and 2. Geulich, *Mark 1—8:26*, 7–8. His argument is sufficiently refuted by Johnson. See Johnson, "Form and Function," 58–71, Other strong proponents of the connection between Mark 1:1 and 1:2 are Joel Marcus and Watts. Based on the connection between verse 1 and 2, they propose the new exodus motif as the overarching theme of the narrative of Marcus, *Way of the Lord*, 12–47; Watts, *Isainic New Exodus*, 53–90. However, their arguments are also evidently counterargued by Hatina who shows the connection between Mark 1:2–3 and Mark 1:4 and who argues that the new exodus motif is one of the major themes of Mark but not the governing interpretive framework of Mark. Hatina, *In Search of a Context*, 138–83.

25. The description on John the Baptist as a figure like Elijah in Mark 1:6 (cf. 2 Kgs 1:8) both echoes Malachi 4:5, thus Malachi 3:1 in Mark 1:2 and foreshadows the identification of John the Baptist with Elijah in Mark 9:11–13. Stein, *Mark*, 48.

anointing of the Holy Spirit (Mark 1:10–11; cf. Ps 2:7). God's voice in Mark 1:11 is a narrative device to confirm the identity of Jesus as the messianic Son of God. Also, both "being torn" of the heaven and the temple veil (Mark 1:10; 15:38; cf. Isa 63:19) and the recognition of Jesus as the Son of God (Mark 1:11; 15:39) form the *inclusio* of the whole narrative.[26] The following scene in Mark 1:12–13 is Jesus' first conflict. Though the temptation by Satan in Mark does not specify the detail, Jesus' authority over evil spirits in the later episodes indicates Jesus' victory over Satan (i.e., Mark 1:26, 34). His victory over Satan as the first conflict of Jesus indicates that the conflict between the kingdom of God and that of Satan is the major conflict Jesus will engage in the Markan narrative.[27] The presence of the Holy Spirit and the conflict with Satan also foreshadow that he will conquer Satan with the power of the Holy Spirit (Mark 3:22–27).

To which part of the Markan structure Mark 1:14–15 belongs is one of the major scholarly debates. And where one locates Mark 1:14–15 in the narrative structure of Mark is immensely significant, as we will demonstrate. Most scholars side with one of the two views; Mark 1:1–13 vs Mark 1:1–15 as prologue. The scholars who consider Mark 1:1–1:13 to be a prologue of Mark argue that we can observe both shift in setting (i.e., from the wilderness to Galilee) and shift in time (i.e., before and after John's arrest) in Mark 1:14.[28] However, Johnson, one of the most persuasive proponents of Mark 1:1–15 as prologue, counterargues that (1) the fact that Jesus came from Galilee (Mark 1:9) and went back to Galilee (Mark 1:14) weakens the shift in setting from wilderness to Galilee.[29] (2) Mark 1:14–15 recapitulates many key words from Mark 1:1–13 (i.e., εὐαγγέλιον, Ἰησοῦς, Ἰωάννης, Γαλιλαία, κηρύσσω, μετανοέω). Especially, the presence of the word εὐαγγέλιον in Mark 1:1 and 1:15 forms *inclusio*.[30] (3) "The temporal markers" in Mark 1:1–15 indicate that Mark 1:14–15

---

26. Lane, *Mark*, 576; Caneday, "Christ's Baptism," 71; Strauss, *Mark*, 72, 706.

27. Edwards, *Mark*, 74.

28. Lane, *Mark*, 39, 63; France, *Mark*, 54–59; Johnson, "Form and Function," 81; Matera, "Prologue," 15; Funk, *Poetics*, 223.

29. Also, see Guelich, *Mark*, 4; Hatina, *In Search of a Context*, 97.

30. Johnson, "Form and Function," 70–72. Also, Hatina, *In Search of a Context*, 99–100; Guelich, "Beginning of the Gospel," 7; Keck, "Introduction to Mark," 359–60.

is the climax of the prologue.³¹ (4) The parallelism exists between John (Mark 1:2–8) and Jesus (Mark 1:9–15).³²

Johnson's summary of the form of Mark 1:1–15 deserves our attention:

> I intend to demonstrate that Mark 1:1–15 consists of an opening heading (1:1) for the prologue, followed by a synkrisis of John (1:2–8) and Jesus (1:9–15). As Jesus comes to the forefront of the narrative, John retreats to the background. John's ministry begins with a prophetic announcement offered *ipsissima vox* of Isaiah (1:2–3) and culminates in a generalizing statement *ipsissima vox* of John (1:7–8). On the other hand, Jesus' ministry begins with his movement from Galilee to the wilderness (1:9) and ends with his return to Galilee (1:14). The climactic utterance of Jesus in 1:15 is likewise given *ipsissima vox* and serves to summarize the essential nature of Jesus' ministry by providing a proper closure to the prologue with direct points of contact with the material that precedes it.³³

In other words, according to Johnson, after the title (Mark 1:1), the implied author arranges the prologue in such a way that Old Testament prophetic announcement on salvation history has been fulfilled beginning with John who prepares the way of Jesus and finally in Jesus' proclamation of the kingdom of God (Mark 1:14–15; cf. Isa 52:7).³⁴

When we consider that the prologue is programmatic to the whole narrative of Mark, the climax of Mark (Mark 1:14–15) highlights that the

31. Johnson states, "In sum, then, we observe the following trajectory established by Mark's temporal markers: 1) Mark initiates his narrative with a starting point (ἀρχή); 2) the narration narrows to focus on Jesus (ἐγένετο ἐν ἐκείναις ταῖς ἡμέραις); 3) the climax of the unit is anticipated with the quasi-temporal break initiated by μετά δέ; 4) the first words of Jesus bring to fullness both God's appointed time and his approaching kingdom (πεπλήρωται and ἤγγικεν); and 5) the yet-untold drama is alluded to through the utterance of tandem imperatives awaiting actualization (μετανοεῖτε and πιστεύετε)." Johnson, "Form and Function," 96.

32. Johnson, "Form and Function," 89–90. Pesch also observes the thematic parallels between John (Mark 1:2–8) and Jesus (Mark 1:9–15); (1) prophetic affirmation (Mark 1:2–3 and 1:11), (2) preliminary ministry in the wilderness (Mark 1:4–6 and 1:12–13), and (3) preaching (Mark 1:7–8 and 1:14–15). Pesch, "Anfang des Evangeliums," 313–14. For other critique of Mark 1:1–13 as prologue, see Hatina, *In Search of a Context*, 100–102.

33. Johnson, "Form and Function," 81–82.

34. Note how "the good news" and God's reign (i.e., God's kingdom) are tied in both Isa 52:7 and Mark 1:14–15: "How beautiful on the mountains are the feet of those who bring *good news*, who proclaim peace, who bring good tidings, who proclaim salvation, who say to Zion, 'Your *God reigns*!'" (Isa 52:7 NIV, emphasis mine).

kingdom of God is an ideological point of view on the whole Markan narrative.[35] We do not need to differentiate the ideological view of Jesus (i.e., God) from that of the narrator (i.e., Jesus) as Malbon does because the kingdom of God is fulfilled in Jesus.[36] Thus, the kingdom of God that Jesus inaugurates sets the interpretive framework of the entire narrative. As the following structural analysis will exhibit, the kingdom of God as interpretive framework, that is, an ideological point of view, includes not only eschatology (i.e., eschatological rule of God through the conflict with the kingdom of Satan) but also Christology (i.e., the identity of Jesus) and discipleship.[37]

Mark 1:16—8:21

Since this section does not contain any quotations and allusions that this study examines, I will briefly summarize the result from my analysis on the Markan narrative structure. I outline the subsections of the first major section of the Markan narrative (Mark 1:16—3:35; 4:1–34; 4:35—8:21) for the following reasons: (1) Mark 4:1 sets a boat as a spatial shift demarcating 4:1—8:21 from 1:16—3:35. (2) However, the boat as an instrument of sea-crossing begins with Mark 4:35. Second, in a macro-level of Markan structure, Mark 4:1–34 constitutes one of the two major teaching blocks that provide the interpretive lens to the whole Markan narrative.[38] I will focus on analyzing Mark 1:16–45; 2:1—3:6; 3:7–3:35; 4:1–34; 4:35—6:44; 6:45—8:10; and 8:11–21.

---

35. As for the kingdom of God as an ideological point of view, see Hatina, *In Search of a Context*, 90–135.

36. Malbon claims that "in the Gospel of Mark the tension between the narrator's point of view and Jesus' point of view enables the implied author to present a Jesus whose focus is always on God, even though the narrator keeps focusing on Jesus." Malbon, *Mark's Jesus*, 257.

37. Similarly, Guelich argues, "Mark's gospel about Jesus Messiah, Son of God, however, inherently involves eschatology, Christology, and discipleship. To single out one of these three as primary not only distorts the gospel but distorts Mark's Gospel." Guelich, *Mark*, xl.

38. Boring, *Mark*, 111; France, *Mark*, 182. The other major teaching block is Mark 13:3–37. Van Iersel notes that Mark uses the same word (κάθημαι) that indicates the teaching in Mark 4:1 and 13:3. Thus, he concludes that two teaching blocks in a way have similar function in Markan narrative. Van Iersel, "Concentric Structures," 86. See also Boring, *Mark*, 111, France, *Mark*, 182.

Mark 1:16—3:35

Mark 1:16-45: The first episode after the prologue begins with the call of the (four) disciples (Mark 1:16-20). The calling scene emphasizes Jesus' kingdom authority and the cost of discipleship."[39] The series of episodes after the calling of the four disciples (Mark 1:21-45) occurs around Capernaum. These episodes highlight Jesus' ministry of the teaching, healing, and exorcism that manifest the arrival of God's kingdom through Jesus' authority.[40] The leper story in Mark 1:40-45 functions as a bridge to Mark 2:1—3:6 that contains "the issue of the Jewish law" (Mark 2:6-7, 16, 18, 24; 3:3-4).[41]

Mark 2:1—3:6: The unit contains the series of five episodes that deals with the conflict between Jesus and religious leaders about healing, eating, and fasting (Mark 2:1-12, 13-17, 18-22, 23-28; 3:1-6).[42] Joanne Dewey demonstrates admirably how the unit is structurally marked by chiasm.[43] The literary analysis of the structure of the five conflicts draws the following conclusions. First, the five conflicts are in essence about Jesus' authority vs the authority of Jewish religion. Second, the eschatological nature of the kingdom Jesus brings (i.e., Jesus brings new age that is incompatible with the old age) authorizes Jesus' authority over sin, association with sinners, fasting, and the Sabbath.[44] Third, the callous heart of the religious leaders not only blinds them to recognize Jesus as the inaugurator of the kingdom of God but also induces the conflict with Jesus to escalate. Thus, the series of conflicts builds up to the climax when it reaches to the final episode (Mark 3:1-6).[45] And especially, Mark 3:1-6 foreshadows the ensuing conflicts with religious leaders that culminate in the death of Jesus.

---

39. Strauss, *Mark*, 85.

40. Strauss, *Mark*, 94; France, *Mark*, 116-17; Edwards, *Mark*, 60; Guelich, *Mark*, 79; Stein, *Mark*, 110; Marcus, *Mark 1-8*, 208-9; Boring, *Mark*, 71.

41. Stein, *Mark*, 104. Also, Strauss, *Mark*, 109.

42. Lane, *Mark*, 91; Dewey, *Markan Public Debate*, 110-30, 181-97; Marcus, *Mark 1-8*, 212-14, 218; Moloney, *Mark*, 60; Boring, *Mark*, 73-74; Stein, *Mark*, 112-13; Strauss, *Mark*, 117.

43. Dewey, *Markan Public Debate*, 110-7.

44. Considering that the center of the chiastic structure often provides the overarching theme, the message of Mark 2:18-22 is the axis of rest of the conflict episodes. Bain, "Literary Surface Structures," 78.

45. Dewey, *Markan Public Debate*, 117-19; van Iersel, *Mark*, 59-60.

Mark 3:7–35: The changes of setting (i.e., sea) and characters (i.e., the crowd) indicate Mark 3:7–12 as a new unit. As a transitional summary statement,[46] Mark 3:7–12 highlights the ministry of Jesus that manifests the arrival of the kingdom in Mark 1:20–45. The second calling of the disciples in Mark 3:13–19 shows that they are called to extend Jesus' mission to usher in the kingdom of God (Mark 3:14–15). Mark 3:20–35 is a typical intercalation of Markan narrative (A: Mark 3:20–21. B: Mark 3:22–30. A': Mark 3:31–35). The conflict between Jesus and the teachers of the law from Jerusalem (B) is inserted into the story of the conflict between Jesus and his family (A and A'). A–B–A' structure of Mark 3:20–35 presents that the teachers of the law and Jesus' family do not understand that Jesus ushers in the kingdom of God. By opposing Jesus, they side with Satan.[47] The other side of the coin is that only those who do the will of God belongs to the kingdom of God, thus becomes the true family of Jesus.[48] The section provides the clear "interpretive lens" for the rest of the Markan narrative.[49]

Mark 4:1–34

The shift in spatial setting (i.e., from a house to a seashore in Mark 4:1 and from a seashore to the sailing of a boat in Mark 4:35–36) and the framing with the word, "παραβολή" in Mark 4:2 and 4:34 set the unit apart from the neighboring passages.[50] Many scholars agree on the subdivisions of Mark 4:1–34 (Mark 4:1–2; 3–9; 10–12; 13–20; 21–25; 26–32; 33–34).[51] Introduced by the setting (Mark 4:1–2), the parable in Mark 4:3–9 addresses the responses to the kingdom message Jesus brings.[52] The framing by Jesus' call to listen (ἀκούω) in Mark 4:3 and 4:9 signifies Jesus' urgent request for the hearers to engage and receive what is told.[53] Mark 4:10–12 talks about the purpose of the parables: the revelation of

---

46. Guelich, *Mark*, 142–44; Collins, *Mark*, 211.
47. Edwards, *Mark*, 126.
48. Strauss, *Mark*, 172. See also, Stein, *Mark*, 189.
49. Shively, *Apocalyptic Imagination*, 10.
50. van Iersel, "Concentric Structures," 85.
51. Gnilka, *Markus*, 155–92; Dupont, "Transmission," 206; France, *Mark*, 187; Donahue and Harrington, *Mark*, 143.
52. Stein, *Mark*, 202; Bock, *Mark*, 172–73.
53. Edwards, *Mark*, 128–30; Bock, *Mark*, 174.

THE STRUCTURE AND THE PURPOSE OF MARK   35

the secret of the kingdom of God to the insiders who "hear in faith"[54] and the concealment of it to the outsiders because of their stubborn and unbelieving heart as Isaiah prophesied (Isa 6:9).[55] The interpretation of the parable of the seed and soil is followed in Mark 4:13–20. In conclusion, the response to the word of the kingdom of God Jesus brings will determine one's destiny.

Mark 4:21–25 consists of two parabolic sayings (Mark 4:21–23; 4:24–25). By the repetition of the theme of revelation and concealment with the exhortation to listen, the narrator stresses the importance of hearing in faith. Mark 4:25–32 presents two parables that emphasize that the kingdom of God is either "hidden" or "unrecognized" but will "come with power" eventually.[56] Mark 4:1–34 ends with the conclusion (Mark 4:33–34). As Mark 4:1–2 begins with Jesus' teaching in parables, Mark 4:33–34 ends with Jesus' saying in parables (i.e., *inclusio*).[57] Also, the conclusion recapitulates the key motif of the whole unit: the revelation to the insiders and the concealment to the outsiders in parables (Mark 4:34).

Mark 4:35—8:26

Sun Wook Kim suggests two-cycle structure (Mark 4:35—6:44; 7:45—8:10) based on Malbon's sea and land as the spatial framework[58] and Kelber's argument that Jesus' ministry across the sea of Galilee as bridging the gulf between Jews and gentiles in Mark 4:35—8:10.[59] According to Kim, Mark 8:11–21 concludes the two cycles.[60] Thus, Kim claims that the geographical movement from the west to the east demonstrates Jesus' expanded mission from Jews to gentiles that breaks down the "boundaries of ethnicity, gender, and class."[61] Adopting Kim's structure, I analyze the narrative structure of Mark 4:35–8:26 as following.

Mark 4:35—6:44 (The first cycle): The first cycle deals with Jesus' ministry around the Sea of Galilee, focusing mainly on the west side of

54. Bock, *Mark*, 175; Edwards, *Mark*, 131; France, *Mark*, 196; Stein, *Mark*, 205.
55. Edwards, *Mark*, 130–33; Marcus, *Mark 1–8*, 306. France, *Mark*, 199–200; Bock, *Mark*, 175.
56. France, *Mark*, 212.
57. van Iersel, "Concentric Structures," 85.
58. Malbon, "Jesus of Mark," 369.
59. Kelber, *Kingdom in Mark*, 62–63; Kim, "Jesus' Missional Movement," 226.
60. Kim, "Jesus' Missional Movement," 233–34.
61. Collins, *Mark*, 241.

the Sea (Jewish region).⁶² Mark 4:35—5:43 is a series of episodes that reveals Jesus' authority over "nature" (Mark 4:35-41), "demons" (Mark 5:1-20), "disease," and "death" (i.e., the intercalation of Jairus—the hemorrhaging woman—Jairus stories; Mark 5:21-43).⁶³ Nothing can prevail against the power of God's kingdom.⁶⁴ Mark 6:1-6a treats the lack of faith in his hometown that deters Jesus from proclaiming and manifesting the arrival of God's kingdom.⁶⁵ The people of Jesus' hometown are foil to the characters who demonstrated their faith in the previous episode (the hemorrhaging woman and Jairus; Mark 5:21-43). Mark 6:6b-30 is another intercalation where Herod and John's story is sandwiched by the commission of Jesus' disciples (Mark 6:6b-13; 6:14-29; 6:30).⁶⁶ The disciples continue and expand Jesus' mission to proclaim the kingdom of God and manifest the kingdom power.⁶⁷ The insertion of Herod and John's story functions to elucidate the nature of the disciples' mission.⁶⁸ In Mark 6:31-44, Jesus is portrayed as the messianic shepherd king who teaches the crowd about the kingdom of God and provides their needs (Mark 6:34, 39-44). Jesus and his kingdom contrast with Herod and his kingdom.⁶⁹

Mark 6:45—8:26 (The second cycle and transition): The shifts in spatial setting (the Sea of Galilee) and characters (only Jesus and the disciples) are evident in Mark 6:45-52. Like the first sea miracle (Mark 4:35-41), Jesus exercises his divine power over the nature and teaches the disciples about who he is. The disciples' fear and hardened heart signify that they are unable to understand that "the kingdom of *God* is

---

62. Mark 5:1-20 is the exception. The episode happens in the gentile territory.

63. Ernst, *Markus*, 148; Moloney, *Mark*, 98; Stein, *Mark*, 239; Iverson, *Gentiles in Mark*, 23-24; Bock, *Mark*, 184; Strauss, *Mark*, 204.

64. Ernst, *Markus*, 148; Moloney, *Mark*, 98.

65. Stein, *Mark*, 284.

66. Edwards, *Mark*, 176; Donahue and Harrington, *Mark*, 200; Moloney, *Mark*, 118-19; Boring, *Mark*, 167; Collins, *Mark*, 314; Miller, "Intercalation Revisited," 178; Strauss, *Mark*, 257.

67. Stein, *Mark*, 290-91; Miller, "Intercalation Revisited," 186-87; Strauss, *Mark*, 253.

68. Edwards, *Mark*, 177. The conflict is between the kingdom of God represented by John and the kingdom of Satan represented by Herod. Thus, the implied author of Mark forecasts that Jesus would share the same destiny with his forerunners. Guelich, *Mark*, 328; Moloney, "Mark 6:6b-30," 660. Edwards, *Mark*, 189; Stein, *Mark*, 308; Karakolis, "Narrative Funktion," 154; Strauss, *Mark*, 267-68.

69. Edwards, *Mark*, 189-90.

manifesting itself in the words and deeds of Jesus."[70] Mark 6:53–56 briefly depicts how Jesus manifests the kingdom power through the miracles of healing in a summary fashion. Mark 7:1–23 concerns the controversy over the defilement issue between Jesus and the religious leaders. Jesus condemns the hypocrisy of his opponents by quoting the Scriptures: they deserted the commandments of God to keep the tradition of men (Mark 7:6–13; Isa 29:13). In the second part of the unit (Mark 7:14–23), Jesus abrogates "the touch defilement" from the tradition of the elders (i.e., food).[71] Jesus' declaration signifies the nullification of the barrier between Jews and gentiles and therefore justifies Jesus' mission to gentiles.[72]

Mark 7:24–30 changes the setting to the region of Tyre. Mark 7:24–30 portrays the Syrophoenician woman as a foil to the religious leaders and, to a certain extent, to the disciples in the previous episode (Mark 7:1–23).[73] The kingdom of God is available, regardless of Jews or gentiles, for "all those who respond in repentance and faith."[74] Mark 7:31–37 presents Jesus' further gentile ministry beyond Tyre, especially in Decapolis. The second feeding miracle in Mark 8:1–9 brackets the second cycle just as the first feeding miracle did. In conclusion, the structure of two cycles shows that both Jews and gentiles are the members of God's kingdom in Jesus.[75]

Mark 8:10–13 shifts the setting as Jesus and his disciples sail to Dalmanutha. The Pharisees continue to refuse to acknowledge the sign of the kingdom of God in Jesus' teaching and deeds by requesting a sign from heaven.[76] Mark 8:13–21 is the final boat scene that concludes the two cycles.[77] The spiritual dullness of the disciples shown in the previous

70. Moloney, *Mark*, 135.

71. Mueller, "Cleansing the Common," 183.

72. Boring, *Mark*, 196.

73. Edwards, *Mark*, 216; Bock, *Mark*, 229. She is a "model disciple" who perceives the parable and humbly asks the crumb of the kingdom benefit. Iverson, *Gentiles in Mark*, 57. As for the contrast between the disciples and the woman, see Williams, *Other Followers*, 121, 124.

74. Strauss, *Mark*, 317. See also France, *Mark*, 299; Edwards, *Mark*, 222; Stein, *Mark*, 355.

75. Malbon's comment is to the point. "The duality of the Markan Jesus' technique reflects the twofoldness of the Markan implied author's convictions: Jesus is Messiah for both Jews and Gentiles." Malbon, "Narrative Criticism," 47.

76. Moloney, *Mark*, 159. In other words, the Pharisees deny the heavenly authority of Jesus' words and deeds. Edwards, *Mark*, 235; France, *Mark*, 311; Strauss, *Mark*, 338.

77. Donahue and Harrington consider Mark 8:14–21 as a "culmination to the first major section of the whole Gospel (1:1–8:21)." Donahue and Harrington, *Mark*, 254.

two boat scenes culminates in Mark 8:13–21. The episode connects bread motif with the conflict with the Pharisees in Mark 8:13–21. The disciples should not be outsiders like the Pharisees and Herod, who have the hardened heart toward the kingdom Jesus brings (Mark 8:17–18). Mark 8:22–26 (i.e., opening the eyes of a blind man) frames the middle section of the Markan narrative with Mark 10:46–52.[78] Also, each of them is a transitional episode (i.e., Mark 8:22–26, from the first part of Mark to the second part, and Mark 10:46–52, from the second part to the third part of the Markan narrative).[79] Mark 8:22–26 both demonstrates Jesus' kingdom work by the healing of the blind man and foreshadows the disciples' full awareness of Jesus who inaugurates God's kingdom.

Mark 8:27—10:52

Mark 8:27—10:45 contains the three set of three structural framework: (1) the prediction of the passion, death, and the resurrection of Jesus (Mark 8:31; 9:30–32; 10:32–34), (2) the failure of the disciples (Mark 8:32–33; 9:33–34; 10:35–37), and (3) Jesus' instruction on discipleship (Mark 8:34–9:1; 9:35–10:31;10:38–45).[80] Interwoven into this framework are the revelation of Jesus' identity from Peter's confession (Mark 8:27–30), transfiguration (Mark 9:2–13), and the exorcism from deaf and mute boy (Mark 9:14–29). The whole section centers around Jesus' true identity and the true meaning of discipleship with a special emphasis on Jesus' suffering, death, and resurrection.[81] However, just as the other sections of Mark, the middle section closely connects the Christology and discipleship to eschatology (i.e., the kingdom of God).

Mark 8:27—9:1 is marked by the identical setting (Caesarea Philippi; Mark 8:27) and characters (Jesus and his disciples; Mark 8:27). The episode is pivotal in that it begins Jesus' series of overt revelations

---

78. Stein, *Mark*, 386.

79. Perrin, *New Testament*, 239.

80. Stein, *Mark*, 386. While specific verses may be different, many commentators recognize the identical three cyclic patterns. See Lane, *Mark*, 293; Donahue and Harrington, *Mark*, 265; Moloney, *Mark*, 172; France, *Mark*, 320; Boring, *Mark*, 231; Collins, *Mark*, 397; Strauss, *Mark*, 370.

81. Boring, *Mark*, 232; Morrison, *Turning Point in Mark*, 37. The emphasis on Jesus' suffering, death, and resurrection anticipates the full revelation of God's kingdom in Jesus' passion and resurrection. Lane, *Mark*, 294.

concerning his identity and his role "in the divine plan of God."[82] Also, the episode starts a series of Jesus' explicit instructions on discipleship to his disciples.[83] Peter's confession of Jesus as the Messiah (Mark 8:29) is connected to the theme of the progressive understanding of the disciples in Mark 8:22–26.[84] Peter's confession rightly identifies Jesus as the Messiah, the anointed king, who will bring the anticipated kingdom. However, the role of messiahship that Jesus will assume is different from what Peter expects. God ordained Jesus to suffer, die, and resurrect to bring the kingdom of God (Mark 8:31).[85] Jesus' rebuke on Peter reveals the cosmological nature of the conflict between Peter and Jesus: Peter's opposition to Jesus' death and resurrection represents the conflict between the kingdom of Satan and that of God (cf. Mark 3:22–27).[86] Peter, in spite of his right confession, fails to understand Jesus' true identity and mission. Jesus' death is the will of God to accomplish the inauguration of God's kingdom. Jesus' revelation on his mission leads to his teaching on discipleship to his disciples and the crowd: just as Jesus' death on the cross leads to his resurrection, the disciples are to follow his path to gain life. One must be willing to die for Jesus and the message he brings (Mark 8:34–38).[87] Mark 9:1 ends the episode and connects it with the following episode, Mark 9:2–14.[88] Jesus' prediction on the foretaste of the coming of God's kingdom in power (Mark 9:1) indicates the proleptic advent of God's kingdom manifested in Jesus' transfiguration (Mark 9:1–8).[89]

The specific description of the shift in time ("after six days") in Mark 9:2 implies that the incident in Mark 9:2–13 is the sequel of Mark 8:28—9:1.[90] Jesus' transfiguration, the presence of Elijah and Moses with Jesus on the mountain, and the heavenly confirmation of Jesus' divine

---

82. Boring, *Mark*, 232.

83. Boring, *Mark*, 231.

84. Moloney, *Mark*, 166.

85. Note the divine δεῖ in Mark 8:31. Jesus' passion and resurrection fulfills God's purpose to bring God's kingdom.

86. Boring, *Mark*, 242.

87. Jesus as the eschatological judge in Mark 8:38 and the coming of the God's kingdom in power in Mark 9:1 corroborate the inseparability of Jesus and the kingdom of God. Lane, *Mark*, 312.

88. Lee, *Transfiguration*, 10.

89. For the view of the transfiguration as the proleptic coming of God's kingdom, see Pesch, *Markusevangelium 8,27–16,20*, 67; Evans, *Mark 8:27–16:20*, 29; Stein, *Mark*, 410–11; Strauss, *Mark*, 376.

90. Stein, *Mark*, 416.

sonship manifest the proleptic coming of God's kingdom.[91] In addition, the voice of God both reveals Jesus' identity as the royal and divine Son of God and commands the disciples to listen to Jesus' words about his destiny and their destiny (Mark 9:7; 8:31–38; cf. Ps 2:7).[92] Thus, the two episodes share the common themes of the kingdom of God, Jesus' identity, and discipleship.[93] Mark 9:8–13 has a transitional setting ("coming down from the mountain"; Mark 9:9). The conversation between Jesus and the disciples derives from the transfiguration experience. The episode focuses on the meaning of Jesus' death and resurrection in relation to John the Baptist. Just as the Scripture was fulfilled in what happened to John the Baptist, the returned Elijah, Jesus' suffering and resurrection is ordained by the Scriptures (Mark 9:11–13).[94] Thus, Mark 9:8–13 shares Jesus' passion and resurrection motif with Mark 8:31–38.[95] Jesus' passion and resurrection is the divine necessity (Mark 9:11–13; cf. Mark 8:31) before the coming of God's kingdom in power (i.e., Jesus' second coming, Mark 9:8–9).[96]

Mark 9:14–29 forms one episode demarcated by the setting (down the mountain where the other disciples were; Mark 9:14) and the characters (the twelve disciples, crowd, teachers of the law, epileptic boy and his father, and Jesus). The episode concludes "a series of encounters between Jesus and his fragile disciples (Mark 8:32—9:29)."[97] In light of the major themes—Jesus' passion and discipleship—of the middle section (Mark 8:28—10:45), the episode functions to show the unbelief of the generation that will reject Jesus and the need for faith on the part of the disciples.[98] The episode contains at least three different conflicts: the disciples vs the teachers of the law, Jesus vs the unbelieving generation (i.e., the entire group including the disciples), and Jesus vs the demon. The conflict between the disciples and the teachers of the law is not specifically depicted but seems to derive from the inability of the disciples to drive out demon (Mark 9:14). The disciples' lack of faith leads to the conflict

---

91. Stein, *Mark*, 420.

92. Edwards, *Mark*, 268; Boring, *Mark*, 262; Strauss, *Mark*, 386.

93. Another shared motif is the disciples' failure (i.e., Peter as the representative of the disciples) in Mark 8:32 and 9:5–6.

94. Boring, *Mark*, 263.

95. Edwards, *Mark*, 272.

96. Bock, *Mark*, 252; Strauss, *Mark*, 387.

97. Moloney, *Mark*, 183.

98. Strauss, *Mark*, 392.

between Jesus and the entire group (i.e., Jesus' rebuke on the unbelieving generation; Mark 9:19).[99] After seeing the demon-possessed boy and hearing his father's plea, Jesus challenges the little faith of the boy's father (Mark 9:20–21). One needs to believe that Jesus has the authority to bind the strong one, Satan (Mark 9:22–23). Jesus' conflict with the demon manifests once again how the stronger one, Jesus, brings God's kingdom by binding Satan (Mark 9:25–27). In a house where Jesus usually reveals the mystery of the kingdom of God to the insiders, Jesus instructs the disciples to bind the Satan by depending not on their power but God's power (i.e., prayer; Mark 9:28–29).[100] In a nutshell, the episode stresses that faith is a prerequisite to be a partaker of God's kingdom.

Mark 9:30—10:31 is the second cycle of Jesus' passion prediction, the disciples' failure, and Jesus' teaching about discipleship. Mark 9:30–50 is marked by the change in setting (Galilee, especially Capernaum) and the characters (Jesus and the disciples). Jesus predicts his passion and resurrection (Mark 9:31). The disciples fail to understand Jesus' words (Mark 9:32). Their argument over who is the greatest in the kingdom clearly shows their failure to understand Jesus' prediction (Mark 9:33–34).[101] The conflict among the disciples becomes the opportunity for Jesus to teach about "the way of the kingdom of God" (Mark 9:33–34).[102] The disciples need to be humble servants rather than to be served in God's kingdom (Mark 9:35–37). John's report about stopping an unknown exorcist (Mark 9:38) generates another series of Jesus' teachings on discipleship in the kingdom of God (Mark 9:39–50). We can summarize Jesus' teaching on discipleship in Mark 9:35–50 as the self-sacrificial servanthood eligible for the kingdom of God.

Mark 10:1–31 consists of three different episodes that deal with divorce (Mark 10:1–12) and the positive and the negative aspects in relation to entering the kingdom of God (Mark 10:13–16; 10:17–31).[103] The three episodes are closely related to Mark 9:30–50 since they apply the theme of what is required to the disciples for the kingdom of God in specific areas of life.[104] The changed setting (Judea and across the Jordan)

---

99. Hooker, *Mark*, 223; Witherington, *Mark*, 267; Stein, *Mark*, 433; Bock, *Mark*, 256; Strauss, *Mark*, 397.

100. Boring, *Mark*, 275–56; Edwards, *Mark*, 281; Strauss, *Mark*, 400–1.

101. Boring, *Mark*, 280.

102. Strauss, *Mark*, 408.

103. Strauss, *Mark*, 436.

104. Boring, *Mark*, 284.

and character (crowds and Pharisees) in Mark 10:1–2 indicate the new unit (Mark 10:1–12). In Mark 10:1–12, Jesus challenges the accepted norm of divorce in Judaism and demands the disciples for the radical commitment to marriage union, "restoration of God's original design in the kingdom inaugurated by Jesus."[105] In Mark 10:13–16, the conflict between the parents of the children and the disciples leads to another conflict between Jesus and the disciples (Mark 10:13–14a). Confronting the disciples who look down on the insignificant ones (i.e., children), Jesus teaches the disciples the importance of children-like attitude, that is, the humble dependence on God to enter God's kingdom (Mark 10:14b–16).[106] The rich man in Mark 10:17–31 is a foil to the one who has a child-like attitude (Mark 10:14–15).[107] In spite of his observance on God's commandments, his love for money more than God prevents him from entering God's kingdom (Mark 10:17–25). Entering the kingdom of God (i.e., the eternal life) is only possible by God (Mark 10:26–27). Eternal life is for those who are willing to surrender everything for Jesus and the gospel (Mark 10:28–31).[108]

Mark 10:32–45 forms the third cycle of the passion prediction–failure–discipleship teaching. The setting ("on the way up to Jerusalem") and the response of some characters ("Jesus was going ahead" and "the disciples were astonished while those who followed were afraid") in Mark 10:32 portend that the climax of Jesus' mission is approaching.[109] Also, the fact that Mark 10:32–34 is "the most detailed of the three" passion predictions indicates the climactic function of the third prediction (Mark 10:32–34).[110] However, the request of two disciples, James and John, betrays their failure to understand the significance of Jesus' passion prediction. They are so preoccupied with Jesus' enthronement as the

---

105. Moloney, *Mark*, 196. For the similar view, see also France, *Mark*, 388–89.

106. Edwards, *Mark*, 307; Boring, *Mark*, 290; Bock, *Mark*, 271; Strauss, *Mark*, 432–33.

107. Evans, *Mark*, 91; France, *Mark*, 399; Stein, *Mark*, 466. To a certain extent, despite their failure, the disciples who left everything for Jesus are also the foil to the rich man (Mark 10:28).

108. The word, eternal life (ζωὴν αἰώνιον) in Mark 10:17 and 30 brackets the episode. "To follow Jesus is to enter into eternal life." Bock, *Mark*, 277. Also, Jesus and the gospel (of the kingdom of God) are inseparably related to each other (cf. Mark 8:35). Stein, *Mark*, 473.

109. France, *Mark*, 410.

110. Strauss, *Mark*, 451.

king in Jerusalem and their positions in his kingdom (Mark 10:35-40).[111] Their audacious request triggers the conflict among the disciples and the ensuing teaching of Jesus on discipleship (Mark 10:41-45); in contrast to the worldly kingdom that demands service from others, the kingdom of God is characterized by servant leadership (Mark 10:42-44).[112] The basis of Jesus' teaching on servanthood leadership is Jesus' mission to serve and redeem people by giving his life (Mark 10:45). Therefore, the third cycle (Mark 10:32-45) "serve[s] as the climax" of Mark's middle section (Mark 8:22-10:52) and "summarize[s] the sacrificial mission" of Jesus.[113]

Mark 10:46-52 frames the central section of Mark (Mark 8:27—10:45) with Mark 8:22-26.[114] The changed setting (Jericho) and characters (Jesus, many people including the disciples, and Bartimaeus) set Mark 10:46-52 apart. The conflict arises when many people rebuke Bartimaeus's cry to Jesus (Mark 10:48). However, the conflict is resolved when Jesus invites the insignificant one in the eyes of the world to himself (Mark 10:49; cf. Mark 10:14-15). Bartimaeus's cry for mercy and his determination demonstrate his faith that Jesus honors with salvation (Mark 10:47-52). The narrative presents Bartimaeus, who follows Jesus on the way to Jerusalem as a foil to other disciples.[115] The episode epitomizes the emphasis of the first and the middle sections of Mark (Mark 1:16—10:45): (1) the arrival of God's kingdom to the one who approaches Jesus with faith (cf. Mark 2:2-4; 5:24-27), (2) the countercultural value of God's kingdom and discipleship (i.e., the least likely one enters the kingdom of God and he follows Jesus; cf. Mark 10:17-31).[116]

---

111. Pesch, *Markusevangelium*, 2:155-56; Evans, *Mark*, 116; Stein, *Mark*, 484.

112. Edwards, *Mark*, 325; France, *Mark*, 419; Stein, *Mark*, 486-86; Strauss, *Mark*, 458.

113. Strauss, *Mark*, 449.

114. Mark 10:46-52 is also "transitional" in geography (from on the way to Jerusalem to Jerusalem) and content (from Jesus' teaching on discipleship to his confrontation with the religious leaders in Jerusalem). Schweizer, *Markus*, 214; Perrin, *New Testament*, 155-58.

115. Kingsbury, *Conflict in Mark*, 25-26; Marshall, *Faith*, 124, 139; Williams, *Other Followers*, 164.

116. Williams, *Other Followers*, 152-66. Many commentators recognize the discipleship motif in Mark 10:52. Evans, *Mark*, 134; France, *Mark*, 425; Moloney, *Mark*, 211; Stein, *Mark*, 497; Strauss, *Mark*, 472.

Mark 11:1—16:8

The third section of the Markan narrative (Mark 11:1—16:8) transpires in Jerusalem and in the vicinity of Jerusalem. The third section consists of Jesus' entry into Jerusalem and the confrontation with Jerusalem establishment (11:1—12:44), his teaching discourse (13:1—37), his passion (14:1—15:47), and the resurrection (16:1—8). Many commentators divide the third section into Mark 11–13 (Jesus and the temple) and Mark 14–16 (the passion and the resurrection).[117] While Mark 13 contains Jesus' discourse about the temple, it also foreshadows Jesus' passion, teaches about discipleship, and anticipates his second coming. Moreover, as aforementioned, Mark 13 and Mark 4:1–34 share the same structural marker (κάθημαι in Mark 4:1 and 13:3) and the function with Mark 4:1–34 (i.e., the two teaching blocks are situated in the middle of first and the third sections to serve as the interpretive framework for the readers).[118] Therefore, we regard Mark 13 as the disparate part of the third section of Mark.[119]

Mark 11:1—12:44

Mark 11:1–11 depicts Jesus' entry into Jerusalem. The spatial setting (Jerusalem and near Jerusalem) sets the unit apart from the previous section (i.e., on the way to Jerusalem). Jesus' riding on a colt and entering into Jerusalem clearly indicate that he is fulfilling Zechariah's prophecy about "the coming of Israel's messiah to Jerusalem" (Mark 11:1c–11b; cf. Zech 9:9).[120] The crowds' shout ("Blessed is the coming kingdom of our father David"; Mark 10:10a) that echoes Bartimaeus's cry ("Son of David"; Mark 10:47–48) narratively functions to confirm that Jesus, the Davidic

---

117. Lane, *Mark*, 390; Moloney, *Mark*, 215–16; Edwards, *Mark*, 333; Stein, *Mark*, 499; Strauss, *Mark*, 475.

118. van Iersel, "Concentric Structures," 86; Boring, *Mark*, 111, France, *Mark*, 182, 427.

119. Gray's structural analysis is to the point. He states, "Thus Mark 13 continues the motif of the temple found in Mark 11–12, while at the same time it looks forward to the story of Jesus that follows in Mark 14–15. Mark 13 plays a pivotal role in Mark's narrative by bridging the story of the temple's end with that of the end of Jesus." Gray, *Temple in Mark*, 10.

120. Strauss, *Mark*, 477. Lane, *Mark*, 393–94; Boring, *Mark*, 315; Stein, *Mark*, 503–4. "Rejoice greatly, Daughter Zion! Shout, Daughter Jerusalem! See, your king comes to you, righteous and victorious, lowly and riding on a donkey, on a colt, the foal of a donkey" (Zech 9:9 NIV).

Messiah, brings God's kingdom that was anticipated by Scriptures (Ps 118:25–26).[121] Jesus' thorough examination on the temple courts (Mark 11:11) anticipates his condemnation on the temple and its establishment in the following episodes (Mark 11:12–13:2).[122]

Mark 11:12–25 consists of the sandwich structure—A (11:12–14; the curse on the fig tree), B (11:15–19; the temple purification and condemnation), and A' (11:20–21; the dried fig tree)—with the accompanying conclusion (11:22–25; Jesus' teaching).[123] Jesus' cursing on the fig tree and its withering serve as an enacted parable on the temple purification and condemnation (Mark 11:12–14; 11:20–21).[124] Just like the fig tree bears no fruit, the temple fails to function its role as the house of prayer for the all nations (Mark 11:17; cf. Isa 56:7; Jer 7:11). Thus, just as the withered fig tree even from the root, Jesus' temple purification and condemnation signify the judgment on the temple and its establishment, which signals "the eschatological inbreaking" of God's kingdom inaugurated by Jesus (Mark 11:15–19).[125] Jesus' authority and the plot to kill Jesus by the temple establishment foreshadow a series of confrontations between Jesus and the religious leaders who challenge Jesus' authority in the following episodes. Accompanied by the intercalation, Mark 11:22–25 presents the characters of the new community of Jesus that will replace the temple order. The members of the kingdom of God composed of Jews and gentiles who believe in Jesus will be characterized by faith, prayer, and forgiveness.[126]

Mark 11:27—12:44 transpires in Jerusalem courts. Situated between Jesus' condemnation of the temple and his prophecy about the destruction of the temple (Mark 13:1–2), Mark 11:27—12:44 reveals the necessity of the temple destruction: the religious leaders do not submit to Jesus and his kingdom message. The series of conflicts between Jesus and the religious leaders dominates the section. Despite the religious leaders' challenge to denigrate Jesus' authority, Jesus silences them with

---

121. Donahue and Harrington, *Mark*, 324; Boring, *Mark*, 316; Strauss, *Mark*, 482. Though God's kingdom Jesus brings is totally different from the expectation of the crowds, Mark 11:1–11 clearly depicts the return of the king and his kingdom. Boring, *Mark*, 316.

122. Evans, *Mark*, 147.

123. Donahue and Harrington, *Mark*, 330–31; Stein, *Mark*, 508;

124. France, *Mark*, 439; Strauss, *Mark*, 492.

125. Gray, *Temple*, 43. The word, ὁ καιρὸς in Mark 11:13 indicates the time of the kingdom of God inaugurated by Jesus (cf. ὁ καιρὸς in Mark 1:15). Gray, *Temple*, 33–34.

126. Dowd, *Payer*, 45–55; France, *Mark*, 448; Boring, *Mark*, 318

the God-given authority (Mark 11:27—12:34).[127] After confounding the scribes' interpretation about the Messiah as David's son (Mark 12:35–37), Jesus contrasts their hypocritical religion with a widow's true religion (Mark 12:38–44).[128] Throughout the section, Jesus manifests himself as the inaugurator of God's kingdom with his authority that condemns the unbelief of the religious leaders. Also, the stories of a scribe and a widow function as foils to these religious leaders who are hostile to the coming of God's kingdom in Jesus.[129]

Mark 11:27—12:12 is a self-contained unit signaled by *inclusio* ("the chief priests, the teachers of the law, and the elders") in Mark 11:27 and 12:12. The unit is connected to Mark 11:1–25 because the Sanhedrin members (the chief priests, the teachers of the law, and the elders) challenge Jesus' authority for his entry and temple actions.[130] Jesus' counter-question concerning the authority of John the Baptist brings the narrative back to the prologue: God sent John to prepare the way for Jesus to bring God's kingdom (Mark 1:2-11). The religious leaders' unwillingness to answer the question divulges their unwillingness to acknowledge the coming of God's kingdom manifested in Jesus' authority.[131] Thus, their response condemns them as false leaders and reveals Jesus' authority from God. The Sanhedrin's response leads to Jesus' parable about God's plan in his redemptive history (Mark 12:1–12). The parable places these rebellious leaders and Jesus as both the continuation and the culmination of God's dealing with Israel.[132] Following their predecessors, the religious leaders of Israel will "refuse to submit to Jesus, God's Son, or to respond to his proclamation of the kingdom of God" (Mark 12:7-8).[133] However, in spite of and through the rebellion of the religious leaders (i.e.,

---

127. The series of conflicts with the religious leaders about Jesus' authority echoes the previous series of the conflict in Mark 2:1–3:6. Strauss, *Mark*, 502. Just as the previous conflict, Jesus' authority reveals that Jesus is the inaugurator of God's kingdom.

128. Moloney, *Mark*, 229.

129. A scribe is not far from God's kingdom (Mark 12:34). A poor widow's dedication is a good example of discipleship for God's kingdom addressed in Mark 10 (Mark 12:41–44).

130. Moloney, *Mark*, 230; Strauss, *Mark*, 504–5.

131. Edwards, *Mark*, 354; Gray, *Temple*, 57–58.

132. The parable is retrospective of how God's messengers are persecuted by the leaders of Israel. It is also proleptic of what the religious leaders (the successors of the leaders of Israel in the past) would do to God's beloved son, Jesus, and the subsequent consequences (God's judgment on the religious leaders and handing over the right of God's people from Israel to the messianic community).

133. Strauss, *Mark*, 516.

crucifixion), God will hand over the vineyard (i.e., the people of God) to Jesus and his disciples (Mark 12:9).[134] God will make the rejected stone (i.e., the rejected Son) as the cornerstone of "the eschatological temple" that replaces the Jerusalem Temple (Mark 12:11; cf. Ps 118:22–23).[135] God establishes his kingdom in "the reversal of human values and expectation" (Mark 12:11; cf. Mark 10).[136] The religious leaders understood the meaning of the parable. But instead of accepting God's kingdom through repentance and faith in Jesus, they sought to enact the parable (Mark 12:12).[137]

Mark 12:13–44 poses the three different groups that challenge Jesus' authority. The first group is the unlikely allies of the Pharisees and the Herodians (12:13–17).[138] Their entrapping question about paying a tax to Caesar fails to invalidate Jesus' heavenly authority.[139] Jesus' answer reveals not only his God-given authority but also provides the principle for "living as members of the kingdom of God" in the world.[140] The second group that confronts Jesus is the Sadducees (12:18–27). In response to their intriguing question that claims no resurrection by utilizing the Scriptures (i.e., levirate marriage; Deut 25:5–10), Jesus refutes their argument in a chiastic manner (Mark 12:18–27): A–No knowledge of the Scriptures. B–No knowledge of God's power. B'–God's power to resurrect the dead and their angel-like existence. A'–God of the living not of the dead (Exod 3:1–22).[141] The episode once again demonstrates Jesus' messianic authority. The Sadducees' blindness to see God's kingdom power manifested in the words and deeds of Jesus precludes them from understanding God's power (i.e., the resurrection) and the Scriptures.[142]

---

134. Evans, *Mark*, 337; Donahue and Harrington, *Mark*, 339, 342; Boring, *Mark*, 332; Marcus, *Mark 8–16*, 813–14; Strauss, *Mark*, 517.

135. Gray, *Temple*, 76. See also Boring, *Mark*, 332; Strauss, *Mark*, 517–18.

136. France, *Mark*, 464.

137. Edwards, *Mark*, 361.

138. They were sent by Sanhedrin (Mark 11:27; 12:12). Though their political interests were different (i.e., the Pharisees are anti-Romans while the Herodians are pro-Romans), Jesus' popularity threatened their stability and, thus, made them allies (cf. Mark 3:6). Moloney, *Mark*, 235, Edwards, *Mark*, 362; Stein, *Mark*, 543; Strauss, *Mark*, 523.

139. Jesus' answer aroused the amazement of his opponents, which proves his heavenly authority and wisdom. Stein, *Mark*, 547; Strauss, *Mark*, 526.

140. Stein, *Mark*, 548.

141. Garland, *Mark*, 470; Boring, *Mark*, 339–40; Strauss, *Mark*, 530.

142. Strauss, *Mark*, 535–36.

The third group that has the conflict with Jesus is οἱ γραμματεῖς ("the teachers of the law"; Mark 12:28–44). Mark 12:28–44 is divided into the dialogue between Jesus and one of the teachers of the law (12:28–34), Jesus' correction on the teaching of the teachers of the law (12:35–37), Jesus' condemnation on the teachers of the law (12:38–40), and Jesus' praise on the poor widow's devotion to God as a foil to the teachers of the law (12:41–44). Interestingly, in chiastic structure, the first and the last stories (12:28–34 and 12:41–44) present positive characters (i.e., foil to the teachers of the law), while the second and the third stories (12:35–37 and 12:38–40) shed negative light on the teachers of the law. Mark 12:28–34 consists of one teacher of the law's question (12:28), Jesus' answer (12:29–31), a teacher of law's affirmative response (12:32–33), and Jesus' proclamation on him close to enter the kingdom of God (12:34). This conversation between the teacher of the law and Jesus silences any more question, thus proving Jesus' authority and wisdom (12:34).[143] The episode also demonstrates that whoever accepts Jesus and his message is fit for the kingdom of God regardless of their background.[144]

Mark 12:35–37 poses Jesus' teaching that discredits the authority of the teachers of the law. Quoting Ps 110:1, Jesus teaches that the messiah is more than the son of David. By stressing messiah's transcendent status, Jesus reveals his messianic identity. He is not the messiah who will restore the Davidic kingdom as his contemporary Jews anticipate.[145] Instead, he is the Messiah, the Son of God, who will bring the eschatological kingdom for all nations through his suffering, resurrection, ascension, and second coming.[146]

While Jesus discredits the scriptural interpretation of the teachers of the law in Mark 12:37–40, he condemns them based on their hypocritical lifestyle in Mark 12:38–40. Their pursuit of status and honor and their exploitation of the most vulnerable covered by ostentatious piety contrast with the kingdom values for the discipleship in Mark 10.[147] Their hypocritical lifestyle, especially as religious leaders who are supposed to lead people to God, deserves the severe punishment from God (Mark 12:40).[148] Mark 12:41–44 is connected to Mark 12:37–40 by the widow

---

143. Stein, *Mark*, 564.
144. Moloney, *Mark*, 242. Strauss, Mark, 544, 546.
145. Stein, *Mark*, 572; Boring, *Mark*, 348;
146. Stein, *Mark*, 570; Moloney, *Mark*, 244; Strauss, *Mark*, 552.
147. Fleddermann, "Warning," 66; Stein, *Mark*, 575.
148. Edwards, *Mark*, 379.

character (Mark 12:40, 42).[149] The devotion of a poor widow contrasts her with not only many rich people who "parade large sums" (Mark 12:42) but also the teachers of the law who parade "their religiosity" (Mark 12:38-40).[150] Moreover, located at the end of a series of confrontations with the religious leaders, the episode of the poor widow functions as a foil to the opponents of Jesus.[151] To enter God's kingdom, one must give one's whole life to the will of God (Mark 8:34—9:1; 10:35-40).[152] But the religious leaders do not relinquish what they have nor perceive the will of God, the good news of the kingdom of God ushered in by Jesus.

Mark 13:1-37

Mark 13:1-37 is the transitional section: (1) It concludes the theme of the judgment on the temple in Mark 11-12 with the prophecy on the temple destruction. (2) It anticipates God's vindication of Jesus with the prophecy on the coming of the Son of Man. While scholars disagree on the structure of Mark 13, they generally agree that Mark 13 deals with the destruction of Jerusalem temple and the coming of the Son of Man.[153] Mark 13:1-4 sets the setting for Jesus' teaching in Mark 13:5-37. The spatial setting ("Mount of Olives opposite the temple"; Mark 13:3) augurs the dreadful fate of the temple (i.e., its destruction).[154] In response to Jesus' announcement on the destruction of the temple, some disciples ask two questions: the time of the destruction and the sign of the destruction (Mark 13:2-4). Jesus' answer to their questions is framed by two cognate verbs of λέγω (λέγειν in Mark 13:5 and προείρηκα in Mark 13:23).[155] An "elegant inclusion" concerning the warning against false messiahs in

---

149. Stein, *Mark*, 573; Strauss, *Mark*, 554.

150. Moloney, *Mark*, 247. The poor widow is also a foil to the rich man was not able to "give up all for the kingdom of God." Strauss, *Mark*, 556.

151. Moloney, *Mark*, 248. The location of the poor widow episode functions also as a foil to all the opponents of Jesus in Mark 11:27–12:44. Moloney, *Mark*, 248.

152. Moloney, *Mark*, 247-48.

153. Stein, *Commentary on Mark 13*, 24. The limit of the space does not allow us to examine different views on the structure of Mark 13 in detail. See Stein, *Mark*, 584-85; Stein, *Jesus*, 24-25; Sloan, *Mark 13*, 2-4.

154. Moloney, *Mark*, 253.

155. Stein, *Jesus*, 72.

Mark 13:5–6 and 22–23 reinforces the demarcation of Mark 13:5–23 as a distinct unit.[156]

Framed by the warning against the false messiahs (Mark 13:5–6 and 21–23), Mark 13:7–20 is divided into the warning about the time before the end (i.e., the destruction of the temple; Mark 13:7–13) and the warning about the end (Mark 13:14–20).[157] The time before the destruction of the temple is characterized by natural and political upheavals as the birth pangs of the end (Mark 13:7–8). Also, the time before the end will be the time of persecution for the believers in Christ (Mark 13:9–13).[158] The warning about the destruction of the temple (Mark 13:14–20) is signaled by the sign of the temple destruction ("When the abomination of the desolation stands where it should not be"; Mark 13:14; cf. Mark 13:4) in the pattern of Dan 9:27.[159] The narrative aside ("Let the readers understand"; Mark 13:14b) alerts the readers to pay attention to the ensuing warnings concerning the destruction of the temple (Mark 13:14c–20).[160]

The shift in temporal setting ("in those days after that tribulation"; Mark 13:24a) preceded by adversative conjunction, ἀλλά, and the coming of the Son of Man marks Mark 13:24–27 as the unit concerning the Parousia.[161] The allusions to Isa 13:10; 34:4(LXX); Joel 2:10; and Dan 7:13 in Mark 13:24–25 indicate that the coming of the Son of Man will be the fulfillment of the eschatological day of the Lord (i.e., either judgment or salvation according to one's relationship with Jesus). Mark 13:28–30 and Mark 13:31–37 are the concluding "parabolic clarifications" of the whole discourse in Mark 13:5–37.[162] The former refers to the certainty of the destruction of the temple within Jesus' generation, while the latter points

---

156. Moloney, *Mark*, 249. A–Warning to watch out (βλέπετε) (13:5b), B–Many who come in my name will lead astray (πλανήσουσιν) (13:6), B'–Many false messiahs and prophets will appear to lead astray (ἀποπλανᾶν) (13:22), A'–Warning to watch out (βλέπετε) (13:23). See also, Stein, *Mark*, 593; Strauss, *Mark*, 566.

157. France, *Mark*, 508–9; Stein, *Mark*, 593, 598; Strauss, *Mark*, 575.

158. Jesus' warning for the believers to watch out and his promise of the eternal life to those who persevere frame the persecution of the believers (Mark 13:9, 13).

159. Lane, *Mark*, 466; Moloney, *Mark*, 261; Stein, *Mark*, 602; Strauss, *Mark*, 577.

160. Strauss, *Mark*, 580.

161. Gnilka, *Markus*, 200; Pesch, *Markusevangelium*, 2:302; Stein, *Mark*, 612–15; Strauss, *Mark*, 589–92.

162. Strauss, *Mark*, 593. Mark 13:28–31 contains the parable of the fig tree while Mark 13:32–39 does the parable of the house owner's return.

to the uncertainty of the timing of the Son of Man's coming and the need to be alert for his coming.¹⁶³

In conclusion, Mark 13:1-37 can be divided into Introduction (Mark 13:1-4), A (Mark 13:5-23; the destruction of the temple), B (Mark 13:24-27; the coming of the Son of Man), A' (Mark 13:28-30; the destruction of the temple), B' (Mark 13:31-37; the coming of the Son of Man).¹⁶⁴ In the entire Markan narrative, alongside Mark 4, Mark 13 functions to provide the teaching about the kingdom of God inaugurated by Jesus: the destruction of the temple confirms the coming of the eschatological kingdom of God in Jesus and the coming of the Son of Man consummates the kingdom of God. What is required to the disciples of Jesus is watchfulness.¹⁶⁵

Mark 14:1—16:8

Mark 14:1—16:8 is the last section of the Markan narrative that shows how Jesus' predictions of his passion and resurrection (Mark 8:31; 9:31; 10:33-34) are fulfilled. One can partition the section according to the events and the main characters into Mark 14:1-72 (the events that lead to crucifixion; Jesus, the disciples, and the religious leaders) and Mark 15:1-47 (the events that lead to crucifixion and burial; Jesus, the Roman authority, and other followers of Jesus), and Mark 16:1-8 (the resurrection scene; the female disciples and the angel).¹⁶⁶

Mark 14:1-72: Mark 14:1-11 is an intercalation that contains two episodes: the plot to arrest and kill Jesus (A: Mark 14:1-2; A': Mark 14:10-11) and the anointing of Jesus (B: Mark 14:3-9). The chronological

---

163 The word ταῦτα (Mark 13:29, 30) is the interpretive key to understand Mark 13:28-31 to be about the destruction of the temple. The word ταῦτα also appears in the disciples' question (Mark 13:4). They all point to the destruction of the temple. Lane, *Mark*, 479-80; Witherington, *Mark*, 348-49; France, *Mark*, 538, 540; Stein, *Mark*, 618-19; Strauss, *Mark*, 594. Also, the phrase, ὅταν ἴδητε appears in Mark 13:14 and 29 and they both are concerning the abomination of desolation, thus, the destruction of the temple. France, *Mark*, 538; Stein, *Mark*, 618-19; Strauss, *Mark*, 594. As for Mark 13:32-37, περὶ δὲ (Mark 13:32) clearly indicates the shift of subject. France, *Mark*, 541; Stein, *Mark*, 621; Strauss, *Mark*, 595.

164. Lane, *Mark*, 466, 474-75, 478, 481-82; Witherington, *Mark*, 340; Stein, *Mark*, 584; Strauss, *Mark*, 566; Sloan *Mark 13*, 143.

165. Note the repeated use of second person imperative verbs of watchfulness such as βλέπετε (Mark 13:5, 9, 23, 33), ἀγρυπνεῖτε (Mark 13:33), and γρηγορεῖτε (Mark 13:35, 37).

166. Moloney, *Mark*, 276-78.

setting ("two days before the Passover and the Festival of Unleavened Bread"; Mark 14:1) marks Mark 14:11 as one unit.[167] Though the conflict does not exist in Mark 14:1–2 and 10–11, the plot of the religious leaders gains the momentum by Judas's betrayal. In Mark 14:3–9, the conflict arises when the anointing of a woman on Jesus was rebuked by some of those who are present in the dinner at the home of Simon the leper (Mark 14:3–5). Jesus resolves the conflict by affirming her action (Mark 14:6–9). Her action, according to Jesus, will be remembered as an example of self-sacrificial love and preparation for the atoning death of Jesus that will inaugurate the kingdom of God. Her action poses a stark contrast with that of the religious leaders and Judas in the sandwich structure.[168]

Mark 14:12–31 is marked by temporal setting ("On the first day of the Festival of Unleavened Bread"; Mark 14:12) and the characters (the twelve disciples). Mark 14:12–16 (the preparation of Passover meal) introduces Passover meal events (Mark 14:17–31). Just like Mark 11:1–6, Mark 14:12–16 reveals Jesus' sovereignty over arranging Passover meal.[169] Mark 14:17–21 (Jesus' prediction of Judas's betrayal) and Mark 14:26b–31 (Jesus' prediction of the disciples' fallaway and Peter's denial) frame Mark 14:22–26a (Passover meal).[170] The two predictions of Judas's betrayal and the disciples' failures contrast with Jesus' new covenant of redemption symbolized by the bread and blood in Eucharist. Despite the human failures, Jesus will inaugurate God's kingdom, which will be consummated in the eschatological messianic banquet (Mark 14:25).[171] Mark 14:12–31 also highlights God and Jesus' sovereignty over all things that lead to his crucifixion, resurrection, and second coming (Mark 14:13–16; 18–21; 22–25; 27–28; 30).[172] Jesus clearly avers that what he will undergo fulfills the Scriptures (Mark 14:21, 27; cf. Zech 13:7).

The shift of spatial setting ("Γεθσημανὶ," Mark 14:32) marks Mark 14:32-52 as one narrative unit. The unit contains the two events: Jesus' prayer (Mark 14:32–42) and his arrest (Mark 14:43–52). The conflict in

---

167. In the passion narrative, chronological setting plays an important role to distinguish the disparate unit from other units (Mark 14:1, 12; 15:1, 25, 34, 42; 16:1).

168. France, *Mark*, 547–48; Edwards, *Mark*, 411; Stein, *Mark*, 629; Bock, *Mark*, 337; Strauss, *Mark*, 610.

169. Evans *Mark*, 373–74; Moloney, *Mark*, 283; Boring, *Mark*, 388; Edwards, *Mark*, 419; Bock, *Mark*, 340.

170. Strauss, *Mark*, 616.

171. Stein, *Mark*, 656.

172. Stein, *Mark*, 656; Strauss, *Mark*, 628.

Mark 14:32–42 occurs between Jesus and the disciples,[173] while in Mark 14:43–52, the conflict arises between Jesus and his opponents (Mark 14:43–49). However, both events consistently contrast Jesus with his disciples:[174] in Mark 14:32–42, Jesus overcomes the temptation to avoid the hour and the cup of suffering with his submission to God's will in his prayer (Mark 14:36), while the disciples fail to be watchful in their prayer (Mark 14:34, 37–38, 40–41; cf. Mark 13:5, 9, 23, 35–37).[175] In Mark 14:43–52, Jesus surrenders himself to the hands of the opponents according to the will of God (i.e., the fulfillment of the Scriptures; Mark 14:49) while his disciples either betray him or flee from him.[176] Mark 14:32–53 also consistently portrays God and Jesus' sovereignty over all the events leading to Jesus' crucifixion in order to inaugurate the kingdom of God (Mark 14:36; 48–49).[177]

Mark 14:53–72 is another sandwich structure. Jesus' trial in Mark 14:55–65 is intercalated by Mark 14:54 and Mark 14:66–72.[178] Mark 14:53 places the spatial setting in the house of the high priest and introduces the Sanhedrin, the opponents of Jesus. Mark 14:54 places Peter in the courtyard of the high priest, thus presenting Jesus' Jewish trial (Mark 14:55–65) and Peter's denial (Mark 14:66–72) simultaneously. In the conflict between Jesus and the Sanhedrin (Mark 14:55–65), the narrator highlights that the witnesses' charges against Jesus were false and contradictory (Mark 14:56–59). Jesus' affirmative answer to the question of the high priest (i.e., Jesus is the Messiah, the Son of God) echoes Mark 1:1. Jesus' public revelation of his identity at the Jewish trial ends the messianic secret motif as he is about to fulfill his messianic mission at the cross.[179] Jesus' further proclamation, as the Son of Man at the right hand of God who will come to judge, reveals that he is the heavenly messianic

---

173. i.e., the threefold failure of the disciples and Jesus' rebuke, Strauss, *Mark*, 632.

174. van Iersel, *Mark*, 432; Boring, *Mark*, 395.

175. Moloney, *Mark*, 290; Stein, *Mark*, 666; Strauss, *Mark*, 630. The "hour" and "cup" are related to God's kingdom in Mark (Mark 13:32; 10:38). Moloney, *Mark*, 289–90.

176. Stein, *Mark*, 675. Strauss, *Mark*, 640.

177. Evans, *Mark*, 418, 426–27; Stein, *Mark*, 665–66, 675.

178. Donahue and Harrington, *Mark*, 426; Moloney, *Mark*, 300–1.

179. Jesus' identity as Messiah, the Son of God, is informed only to *the implied readers* in Mark 1:1. His identity is known to *his disciples* in Mark 8:29 and 9:7. His identity is now revealed to *his opponents* in Mark 14:62.

figure who will consummate God's kingdom (Mark 14:62; cf. Pss 80:18; 110:1; Dan 7:13).[180]

His response provokes the charge of blasphemy and suffering (Mark 14:63–65). Mark 14:66–72 depicts Peter's threefold denial of Jesus. The contrast between Jesus and Peter is evident. Jesus does not deny his identity and consequently suffers because of his confession. However, Peter denies his identity as Jesus' disciple in order to avert suffering.[181] Therefore, Mark 14:53–73 continues to demonstrate how Jesus faithfully accomplishes his mission—the inauguration of God's kingdom—through his passion while even his leading disciple, Peter, fails to keep his oath to follow Jesus (Mark 14:29, 31).

15:1–47: The whole narrative escalates to the climax and denouement in Mark 15 as events lead to his crucifixion, death, and burial. Throughout all the events in Mark 15, God's sovereign purpose to inaugurate his kingdom through the death of Jesus is evident as everything unfolds according to Jesus' prediction and according to the Scriptures (i.e., the Davidic lament psalms). The change of the setting in Mark 15:1—time ("very early in the morning") and place (from the house of the high priest to the praetorium of Pilate)—and the shift in characters signal Mark 15:1–20a as the new unit. The first scene is Pilate's hearing on Jesus (Mark 15:1–5), where the conflict between Jesus and the Sanhedrin continues. The scene portrays Jesus as the king of the Jews, the motif that runs through Mark 15:1–32.[182] Jesus' acknowledgment of his kingship evokes the different understanding about the kingdom between Jesus and Pilate (and Jews).[183] "King of the Jews," asked by Pilate, has a "political connotation."[184] But, in the Markan narrative, Pilate's question ironically confirms "Jesus' messianic identity."[185] The second scene is the question to the crowds about releasing either Jesus or Barabbas (Mark 15:6–15a). The conflict arises between Pilate who seemingly desires to release Jesus and the crowd who desires to have Jesus crucified (Mark 15:9–14). The

---

180. Thus, the confession of Jesus as the messianic Son of God and the coming son of Man in Mark 14:62 serves as "the climax to the portrait of Jesus" throughout the whole Markan narrative. Donahue and Harrington, *Mark*, 428.

181. Boring, *Mark*, 410; Stein, *Mark*, 693.

182. France, *Mark*, 628. "King of the Jews" is the gentile expression, while "king of Israel" (Mark 15:32) is the Jewish term. Thus, they are synonymous. Evans, *Mark*, 478; Boring, *Mark*, 418–19; Stein, *Mark*, 699.

183. Evans, *Mark*, 484; Stein, *Mark*, 703.

184. Edwards, *Mark*, 458–59.

185. Strauss, *Mark*, 680.

scene highlights the guilt of the religious leaders and the crowd (i.e., Jews) for crucifying Jesus, their king.[186] In the third scene, the Roman soldiers mock Jesus as the king of the Jews (Mark 15:16–20a). Their mocking continues to portray Jesus as the Messiah, the king of the Jews and ironically announces the truth that Jesus is the suffering Messiah.[187]

Mark 15:20b–39 depicts the crucifixion and the death of Jesus. The shift in the spatial setting from the praetorium to Golgotha marks the new unit. The first scene (Mark 15:20b–25; cf. Ps 22:18) purely focuses on how the crucifixion was performed.[188] The second scene (Mark 15:26–32) emphasizes the ironic revelation of the truth about Jesus.[189] The litany of charge and mocking against him in Mark 15:26–32 ironically proclaim the truth about Jesus (i.e., the king of the Jews in Mark 15:26, the one who will destroy the temple and build the new temple by his death and resurrection in Mark 15:29, his redemptive death to save others in Mark 15:31, and Messiah and the king of Israel in Mark 15:32).[190] In the third scene (Mark 15:33–39), Markan narrative reaches the climax (i.e., the death of Jesus). The eschatological darkness (cf. Amos 8:9) and Jesus' cry of dereliction quoting Ps 22:1 illustrate the foretaste of the eschatological event Jesus' death will bring[191] and the depth of abandonment laid upon Jesus on the cross (Mark 15:33–34). However, Jesus' cry is not the mere expression of despair because Jesus' death ends the darkness (Mark 15:33) and he is vindicated by resurrection (Mark 16:1–8).[192] Mark continues the mocking motif of the passersby who do not understand the significance of Jesus' death on the cross (Mark 15:35–36; 15:29–30; cf. Pss 22:7–8; 69:21). The whole narrative reaches the climax in Jesus' death (Mark 15:37–39). The significance of Jesus' death is expressed by God, who tears apart ("ἐσχίσθη," the divine passive) the temple veil, which indicates the end of the old age characterized by the temple.[193] Also, it signifies that the access to God is available through the death of Jesus (Mark 15:38; cf.

---

186. Hooker, *Mark*, 369.

187. Donahue and Harrington, *Mark*, 439–30; Moloney, *Mark*, 316; Boring, *Mark*, 425.

188. Moloney, *Mark*, 318.

189. Moloney, *Mark*, 321; France, *Mark*, 639.

190. Strauss, *Mark*, 697.

191. Allison, *End of the Ages*, 36–39.

192. Boring, *Mark*, 430.

193. France, *Mark*, 657–58; Brown, *Death of the Messiah*, 1099–109.

Mark 1:10a).[194] A gentile Roman centurion, the human counterpart to God, confesses Jesus as the Son of God (Mark 15:39). Considering that Mark 15:38–39 forms the bookend with Mark 1:10–11, we can say that the confession of a Roman centurion, on a narrative level, affirms Jesus' messianic sonship and his mission to bring God's kingdom.[195]

Mark 15:40–47 concerns the burial of Jesus. The episode functions as a bridge between Jesus' passion and resurrection.[196] The presence of the female disciples in Mark 15:40–41 and 15:47 frame the episode.[197] Also, the female disciples motif in Mark 15:47 is linked to Mark 16:1 and thus bridges to the resurrection episode in Mark 16:1–8.[198] Mark 15:42–46 depicts Jesus' burial initiated by Joseph of Arimathea.[199] Joseph is a foil to the disciples who were supposed to bury Jesus[200] and wait for the full manifestation of God's kingdom in Jesus' resurrection and second coming (Mark 15:43).

Mark 16:1–8: Mark 16:1–8 is the denouement of the entire narrative of Mark. The shift in the temporal setting ("διαγενομένου τοῦ σαββάτου"; Mark 16:1) marks the new unit. The main character of the episode is the female disciples. They are portrayed as the faithful witnesses of Jesus' death, burial, resurrection (Mark 15:40—16:8).[201] Their encounter with the young man, the angelic epiphany, generates the shock to the female disciples (Mark 16:5).[202] The young man announces Jesus' resurrection (Mark 16:6) and affirms that Jesus will encounter the disciples in Galilee and restore them (Mark 16:7–8; cf. Mark 14:28). Gripped by the awe and fear because of the encounter with the angel and his message, the female

---

194. Stein, *Mark*, 717–18; Strauss, *Mark*, 72.

195. Moloney, *Mark*, 330; Strauss, *Mark*, 705. Caneday argues that the baptism of Jesus ("anointing" of the king) and his crucifixion ("enthronement" of the king and the "climax" of the narrative) forms *inclusio*. Caneday, "Christ's Baptism," 71–76. While his evidence of parallel catchwords between Mark 1:1–13 and 15:33–41 is coerced to a certain extent, he is right that the crucifixion of Jesus manifests clearly Jesus' identity as the suffering Messiah, the Son of God, and his mission to bring God's kingdom even to gentiles. Caneday, "Christ's Baptism," 76.

196. Donahue and Harrington, *Mark*, 456; Moloney, *Mark*, 332.

197. France, *Mark*, 661.

198. France, *Mark*, 661.

199. The story of Pilate and the centurion (Mark 15:44–45) is intercalated into Joseph's burial story (Mark 15:43 and 46). Donahue and Harrington, *Mark*, 456.

200. Williams, *Other Followers of Jesus*, 190; Moloney, *Mark*, 334.

201. Strauss, *Mark*, 707.

202. Evans, *Mark*, 536; France, *Mark*, 678–79; Collins, *Mark*, 795–96; Strauss, *Mark*, 718.

disciples obey to go to the disciples (Mark 16:8).[203] Therefore, the Gospel of Mark ends with the fulfillment of Jesus' predictions (i.e., resurrection, Mark 8:31; 9:31; 10:33–34, and the encounter with the disciples, Mark 14:28) and the obedience of the female disciples. The ending of Mark is the fitting denouement of the entire Markan narrative: Jesus, the messianic Son of God, inaugurated the kingdom of God by his death and resurrection. He will encounter his disciples so that they may witness to all nations that Jesus is the usher of God's kingdom (Mark 16:7).

Conclusion

Having attempted to identify the structure of Markan narrative, we note the following observations: (1) The prologue (Mark 1:1–1:15) is programmatic for the whole narrative. Jesus' identity as the Messiah, the Son of God, and his mission to bring the kingdom of God are tied together. This study has evinced that the whole narrative has in mind the kingdom of God as an ideological point of view. (2) Mark 1:16—3:35 demonstrates mainly Jesus' kingdom authority manifested in his ministry of teaching and deeds. The major conflict of the narrative is between the kingdom of God represented by Jesus and his followers and the kingdom of Satan represented by Satan and his followers (Mark 3:22–30). The conflict escalates especially when the religious leaders confront Jesus' kingdom authority in his words and deeds (i.e., Mark 2:1—3:6). The motif of insiders and outsiders also develops since Mark 3:32.

(3) Mark 4:1–34 is the disparate unit of Jesus' discourse on the kingdom of God. The parables of the kingdom of God in Mark 4:1–34 are teachings of Jesus, and they provide the interpretive framework for Mark 1:16—8:21, that is, the persevering faith as the criteria for the insiders and the outsiders of the kingdom of God. (4) Mark 4:35—8:21 continues Jesus' kingdom authority. At the same time, the series of episodes exhibits how faith distinguishes the insiders from the outsiders in relation to the kingdom of God. The expansion of Jesus' mission across the Sea of Galilee by boat further demonstrates that the kingdom of God Jesus brings is not bound by specific groups (i.e., Jews vs gentiles; male vs female; the

---

203. The silence and fear of the female disciples should not be viewed as the response of their disobedience but the natural response of shock to the angelic epiphany. Collins, Mark, 799–800. For the further detailed arguments that defend the obedience of the female disciples, see Hurtado, "Women, the Tomb," 427–50; Aernie, "Cruciform Discipleship," 779–97.

privileged vs the underprivileged) but for those who come to Jesus in repentance and faith (Mark 1:15).

(5) Mark 8:27—10:44 reveals Jesus' identity once again as the messianic Son of God. However, his messiahship is fundamentally tied to his passion and resurrection. The disciples are taught and shown to follow the way of their suffering Messiah to participate in the kingdom he inaugurates. (6) Jesus reaches his final destiny (i.e., Jerusalem) in Mark 11. Mark 11–12 depicts how Jesus fulfills the Scriptures concerning the coming of the eschatological anointed king, the Messiah, to inaugurate God's kingdom. The condemnation of the Jerusalem establishment that will be culminated in the destruction of the temple is inevitable, as they oppose the coming king and his kingdom.

(7) Mark 13, just as Mark 4:1–34, is the other distinctive teaching discourse of Markan narrative that provides the interpretive framework for Mark 11–16. While Mark 4:1–34 focuses on the present aspect of God's kingdom, Mark 13 stresses on the future aspect of the kingdom that culminates in the destruction of the temple and the Parousia. The disciples are warned to be watchful and persevere, which foreshadows the passion narrative in the following section. (8) Mark 14:1—16:8 is devoted to the passion and the resurrection of Jesus. The divine necessity of Jesus' suffering, death, and resurrection is evident throughout the section. While Mark 14 pays attention to the relationship between Jesus and the disciples, Mark 15 focuses on how Jesus, the king of the Jews, brings God's kingdom ironically by his death. Jesus' death clearly manifests that he is the messianic Son of God (Mark 15:38–39). After reaching the climax in Jesus' death in Mark 15, the narrative ends with the resurrection scene (the denouement; Mark 16:1–8). Mark 16:1–8 shows Jesus' vindication by the resurrection and anticipates the restoration of the disciples.

In summary, Markan narrative identifies Jesus as the messianic Son of God (Mark 1:1, 10–11; 8:29; 9:7; 14:61–62; 15:38–39). Jesus' identity is fundamentally bound by his mission to bring the kingdom of God in Markan narrative. The major conflict in the narrative is between the kingdom of God and the kingdom of Satan, represented by the conflict between Jesus (and his followers) and Satan (and all who follow Satan by opposing Jesus, especially the religious leaders and Judas Iscariot). The disciples are the followers of Jesus by default. They often falter in their step to follow Jesus, but the narrative never portrays their failure to be irreversible (i.e., Mark 14:28; 16:7). As a foil to the religious leaders and the wavering disciples, the narrator presents many minor characters, the other followers of Jesus, who exemplify discipleship and the kingdom value. They embody the kingdom value to follow Jesus such as the persevering faith, humility, and self-sacrifice that Jesus himself demonstrates in his mission. Jesus' messianic sonship is most vividly exhibited in his death. From the beginning to the end, the divine necessity motif demonstrated in allusions and quotations of the Scriptures and Jesus' predictions and fulfillment concerning his suffering and resurrection colors the entire narrative.

THE PURPOSE OF THE GOSPEL OF MARK

According to Adam Winn, Markan scholarship has identified the purpose of the Gospel of Mark in five different avenues: (1) historical, (2) theological, (3) pastoral, (4) evangelistic, and (5) social-political.[204] While each approach has its own merits and foibles, our focus on the narrative of Mark prohibits us from evaluating them.[205] Only one caveat to each approach would suffice for our purpose. No matter what approach one takes to draw the purpose of Mark, one must pay careful attention to the narrative of Mark. Therefore, even though identifying the purpose of Mark on the narrative level may be limited to the narrative of Mark without considering the factors outside of the text such as historical and sociopolitical factors, it would at least suggest the road map for any approach to identify the purpose of Mark further than the narrative level. Unfortunately, almost every approach tends to focus on either a certain part of Mark or certain theological theme to reach the desired conclusion. Instead, having analyzed the structure of Mark meticulously, we will identify the purpose of Mark that fully reflects the narrative of Mark.

Having examined the narrative structure of the Gospel of Mark, I find four key threads that weave the entire Markan narrative. First, the

---

204. Winn, *Purpose of Mark*, 5–41.

205. Readers may refer to Winn, *Purpose of Mark*, 5–41; Roskam, *Purpose of Mark*, 2–14. For the readers who are interested in the resources of each approach on the purpose of Mark, here we suggest some samples of literature for each approach. I heavily depend on Adam Winn in suggesting the following bibliographies. Winn, *Purpose of Mark*, 7–41. For historical purpose, see Taylor, *Mark*, 131–32; Hengel, *Studies in Mark*, 1–30. For theological purpose, Evans, *Mark*, lxxix–lxxx; Stein, *Mark*, 35–37; Marxsen, *Mark the Evangelist*. For pastoral purpose, see Kee, *Community of the New Age*; Lane, *Mark*, 12–17. For evangelistic purpose, Gundry, *Mark*, 5–15; Williams, "Apology for the Cross," 109–10. As for sociopolitical purpose, see Roskam, *Purpose of Mark*; Horsley, *Hearing the Whole Story*; Winn, *Purpose of Mark's Gospel*.

narrative consistently portrays who Jesus is. Starting from the title (Mark 1:1), the whole narrative highlights Jesus as the Messiah, the Son of God. John the Baptist prepares his coming, and the voice from God confirms that he is the Messiah, the Son of God (Mark 1:11; 9:7). His messiahship is affirmed also by other characters such as demons (Mark 3:11; 5:7), Peter (Mark 8:29), Roman centurion (Mark 15:38), and even Jesus' human opponents verbally (Mark 14:61; 15:2, 12, 18, 32).[206] Not only the verbal affirmation, but also Jesus' ministry in his life and death manifests that Jesus is the Messiah, the Son of God: his teaching, miracles, temple action, passion, and resurrection reveal his messiahship.

Second, the discipleship motif also runs through the whole narrative. Since the calling of the four disciples in Mark 1:16–20, the whole narrative has Jesus' disciples in mind. They are identified as insiders of God's kingdom despite their temporary failures and are called to follow Jesus and extend his mission by witnessing Jesus and his kingdom. Even though their presence is not visible since Mark 15, Jesus exemplifies what discipleship should be like in his passion. Besides, many minor characters who represent other followers of Jesus serve as the examples of discipleship throughout the narrative. The implied restoration of the disciples at the end of the narrative (Mark 16:7) also adds to the discipleship motif.

Third, I demonstrated how the kingdom of God motif penetrates the entire narrative as the ideological point of view of Markan narrative. We have observed how Jesus' identity (the messianic Son of God) is inseparable from Jesus' mission (inaugurating God's kingdom). Jesus' entire ministry (i.e., his coming, baptism, teaching, miracles, suffering, death, and resurrection) solely focuses on inaugurating God's kingdom. Also, we have noticed that Jesus' example and teaching of discipleship center on God's kingdom. Since discipleship is defined to follow Jesus, just as Jesus' identity is tied to Jesus' mission (the coming of God's kingdom), discipleship and his mission are interconnected.

Fourth, we have observed that the whole Markan narrative demonstrates the fulfillment of the Scriptures: Mark 1:1–15 is replete with the quotation and allusions to show that Jesus' coming as the Messiah, the Son of God who proclaims the good news of God's coming kingdom fulfills the Scriptures. The following narrative shows how this programmatic prologue is fulfilled: (1) Jesus' kingdom authority as the Messiah who brings God's kingdom penetrates through Mark 1:16–10:45. (2) People's

---

206. Though Jesus' human opponents did not intend, they ironically reveal that Jesus is the Messiah.

response to God's kingdom brought by Jesus fulfills the Scriptures (i.e., Mark 4:12; Isa 6:9–10). (3) The divine necessity of Jesus' passion and resurrection that fulfills the Scriptures is repeatedly addressed by Jesus (Mark 8:31; 9:11–13; 14:21, 27, 49). (4) Jesus' entry to Jerusalem as the Davidic Messiah, the destruction of the temple, and building the new temple fulfill the Scriptures (Mark 11:1–11, 17; 12:11; 13:14). (5) Jesus' enthronement at the right hand of God and his future coming as the Son of Man are according to the Scriptures (Mark 12:36–37; 13:26; 14:62). (6) Jesus' passion fulfills the Scriptures, especially many Davidic lament psalms (Mark 14:34, 55; 15:24, 29–30, 34). These are only representative examples on how Markan narrative emphasizes the fulfillment motif.

The four overarching themes in Markan narrative lead us to propose the purpose of Mark, on the narratival level, as follows: the implied author of Mark intends (1) to inform the implied readers of Jesus' identity as the messianic Son of God; (2) to help his readers to understand that Jesus has brought the kingdom of God in his coming and ministry, especially in his death and resurrection; (3) to encourage the implied readers to enter God's kingdom by following Jesus as they persevere and prepare for his second coming, the consummation of God's kingdom; and finally (4) to ensure that the Scriptures have been fulfilled in all these matters and to urge the readers to participate in God's salvation history. Therefore, the purpose of Mark is thoroughly rooted in Jesus' identity (Christology), his mission (eschatology), discipleship, and the fulfillment of the Scriptures.[207]

CONCLUSION

We briefly reviewed the different approaches to the structure of Markan narrative and pursued to apply narrative criticism (i.e., setting, plot, character, rhetoric) to identify the structure of Mark. In summary, we propose Mark 1:1—8:21, Jesus' ministry in Jerusalem—[Mark 8:22–26, transition]—Mark 8:27–10:45, on the way—[Mark 10:46–52,

---

207. As for the purpose of Mark, many scholars tend to treat eschatology in the future aspect of God's kingdom, especially the destruction of the temple and the Parousia in Mark 13. For example, see Marxsen, *Mark the Evangelist*, 75–94, 107; Winn, *Purpose of Mark's Gospel*, 150–52. However, we consider eschatology as God's eschatological establishment of his kingdom in Jesus as the fulfillment of his words in the mouth of his prophets. In that sense, eschatology includes both the present aspect of God's kingdom (i.e., Jesus' ministry on the earth) and the future aspect of God's kingdom (i.e., God's kingdom manifested since Jesus' ascension until his second coming).

transition]—Mark 11:1—16:8, Jesus' ministry in Jerusalem as the structure of Markan narrative on a macro level. On a micro level, we suggest the following: 1:1–15 (Prologue), 1:16–45 (the calling of the disciples and manifestation of the kingdom power in Jesus' teaching and actions), 2:1—3:6 (five conflicts between Jesus and the religious leaders), 3:7–35 (the second calling of the disciples, kingdom ministry, insiders and outsiders of the kingdom), 4:1–34 (revealing and concealing of the secret of God's kingdom), 4:35—6:44 (Jesus' ministry around the Sea of Galilee: the first cycle), 6:45—8:21 (Jesus' ministry around the Sea of Galilee: the second cycle), 8:27—10:45 (the prediction on Jesus' passion, death, and resurrection and teaching on discipleship), 11:1—12:44 (Jesus' entry into Jerusalem and the confrontation with the temple establishment), 13:1–37 (his second teaching discourse on the temple destruction and the Parousia, 14:1—15:47 (his passion), and 16:1–8 (the resurrection).

The study of the structure of the Markan narrative and the purpose of Mark suggest that Jesus' identity, Jesus' mission, and discipleship are closely interrelated. Jesus' identity as the messianic Son of God signifies that Jesus is the king who will inaugurate the kingdom of God. His kingship is manifested in his authoritative words and deeds and climaxes in his suffering, death, and resurrection. Discipleship is closely bound to Jesus' words and deeds. The disciples are the members of God's kingdom and they must follow the way of their king, Jesus. Finally, the Markan narrative consistently demonstrates that these three inseparable themes, Jesus' identity as the messianic Son of God, his ministry to ushering in God's kingdom, and the participation in God's kingdom by following Jesus by faith, are according to the Scriptures. The following chapters will focus on Mark's use of the four psalms and see what significance they make in light of the narrative structure and the purpose of Mark.

3

PSALM 2 IN MARK

BEFORE WE DELVE INTO Mark's use of Ps 2, it would be useful to review the methodological assumptions that the book holds. In chapter 1, we concluded that NT authors seem to have the hermeneutical axiom that presupposes that God who spoke in the OT continues to speak in light of the Christ event. Thus, they are willing not only to apply the meaning of the OT but also extend and deepen it. Applying this hermeneutical axiom to the use of Psalms in Markan text, we will investigate how the author of Mark applied, extended, and deepened the meaning of Psalms, as well as for what purpose he did it.

To reach this goal, first, in light of the existence of diverse textual variants of Psalms, I will compare Mark's citation of Ps 2:7 with that of the different text-types instead of assuming that the LXX is the *vorlage* text of Mark's citation. Second, I will examine the whole context of Ps 2 to see if Mark has the whole context in mind by using Ps 2:7. Third, I will explore the function of Ps 2 in the canonical context of the Psalter and other OT texts to see if the canonical context sheds any light on Mark's use of Ps 2. Fourth, I will examine the interpretation of Ps 2 (i.e., the royal and Davidic messiahship) in Second Temple literature to find out how the interpretation of Mark's contemporaries might have influenced Mark's use of Ps 2. Finally, I will investigate how and for what purpose Mark uses Ps 2:7 in the immediate context of Mark and in light of the whole narrative of Mark. In the process, I will examine the three basic criteria (lexical, thematic, and structural parallels) to verify the citation of Mark as the allusion to Ps 2:7.

TEXTUAL FORM OF PSALM 2:7 IN MARK

We concur with many scholars that Mark 1:11 and 9:7 contain clear allusion to Ps 2:7. Here we provide first of all the comparison of the text form of Ps 2:7 in the MT and LXX with the two occurrences of the possible Ps 2:7 allusion in Mark 1:11 and 9:7.[1]

MT	LXX	Mark 1:11	Mark 9:7
אֲסַפְּרָה אֶל חֹק יְהוָה אָמַר אֵלַי בְּנִי אַתָּה אֲנִי הַיּוֹם יְלִדְתִּיךָ	διαγγέλλων τὸ πρόσταγμα κυρίου κύριος εἶπεν πρός με υἱός μου εἶ σύ ἐγὼ σήμερον γεγέννηκά σε	καὶ φωνὴ ἐγένετο ἐκ τῶν οὐρανῶν· σὺ εἶ ὁ υἱός μου ὁ ἀγαπητός, ἐν σοὶ εὐδόκησα.	καὶ ἐγένετο νεφέλη ἐπισκιάζουσα αὐτοῖς, καὶ ἐγένετο φωνὴ ἐκ τῆς νεφέλης· οὗτός ἐστιν ὁ υἱός μου ὁ ἀγαπητός, ἀκούετε αὐτοῦ.
I will declare Yahweh's decree. He said to me. "**You are my son.** Today, I have begotten you."	Proclaiming the Lord's command. Lord said to me. "**You are my Son.** Today, I have begotten you."	And there was a voice from heaven. "**You are my** beloved **Son.** I am pleased with you."	And a cloud overshadowed them. And there was a voice from the cloud. "He **is my** beloved **Son.** Listen to him."

The chart above shows that God's saying ("You are my Son. Today, I have begotten you") in Ps 2:7 of the LXX is identical with the MT, even to the word order. Mark 1:11 seems to follow the LXX, except that the Markan text has changed word order with an additional ὁ ἀγαπητός. The citation of Ps 2:7 in Mark 9:7 is identical with that of Mark 1:11, except that οὗτός ἐστιν is used instead of σὺ εἶ. But considering the different narrative contexts—the hearer of God's voice is Jesus in Mark 1:11, while it is Jesus' disciples that hear God's voice in Mark 9:7—one can easily understand the reason for the change. Also, the fact that Mark 1:11 and Mark 9:7 are the only scenes that God speaks in the entire Gospel and

---

1. All translations are mine unless indicated otherwise. The three commonly used editions of the LXX (i.e., OG) are "the Cambridge Septuagint, Rahlfs's provisional edition, and the Göttingen edition." Cox, "Septuagint," 92. Of these, the Göttingen edition is the critical edition and is, according to Troyer, "the best text to use when quoting the OG of specific books." The Göttingen critical edition is the best text to use when quoting the OG of specific books. Troyer, "Septuagint," 110. All the LXX texts used in this book are based on Rahlfs's Göttingen edition, Rahlfs, *Psalmi*. As for the LXX of Psalms, Rahlfs's provision edition and Gottingen edition are virtually identical. Bucker, "Observations," 355.

that both of them have the lexical and structural parallels (i.e., ὁ υἱός μου ὁ ἀγαπητός and subject+verb word order) validate that Mark 1:11 and 9:7 share the same OT citations. Since the LXX and MT have the identical text for the cited portion of Ps 2:7 in Mark, it is difficult to decide which text-type Mark follows. Therefore, we need to examine both the LXX and MT text of the whole Ps 2 to see how the wider context of Ps 2 may affect the citation of Ps 2 in Mark.

THE INTERPRETATION OF PSALM 2

Sitz im Leben and Structure

Before we tackle the detailed interpretation of Ps 2, it would be wise to review the different hermeneutical approaches to the *Sitz im Leben* of Ps 2. First, traditionally, interpreters have sought to find the *Sitz im Leben* of the psalm in the history of Israel, such as David's or his descendant's enthronement,[2] or the coronation of the postexilic characters like Zerubbabel or one of Hasmonean rulers.[3] Second, Gunkel and Mowinckel proposed the cultic interpretation of Ps 2.[4] Third, many scholars who hold the predictive or messianic approach view Ps 2 basically as the prediction of a future messiah (i.e., Jesus) because of various reasons.[5] As we interpret the text of Ps 2, we will both utilize the above approaches eclectically

---

2. As for David as the anointed king in Ps 2, see Calvin, *Psalms*, 9; Perowne, *Psalms*, 113. As for those who view Davidic line of the kings as the messiah, see Longman, "Messiah," 18.

3. Sam Janse, '*You Are My Son*,' 29–35; Treves, "Two Acrostic Psalms," 81–85. Oancea does not specify the person but postulates the date of the psalm during the time of Ptolemaic rule. Oancea, "Psalm 2," 173–74.

4. Gunkel thinks that the lofty language of the psalm is too unrealistic for the Judean kingdom. Rather, Judean poets adopted the cultic poetry of Egyptian and Babylonian empires to describe the Judean kingdom. Gunkel and Begrich, *Psalms*, 112–17. Mowinckel finds the origin of the psalm in Israel's preexilic coronation festival. Mowinckel, *Psalm Studies*, 580.

5. (1) Some scholars hold this approach because they do not find any correspondence between Ps 2 and Israel's history. Phillips, *Psalms in Hebrew*, 6–12. (2) Some of them recognize the historical context of the psalm (i.e., Davidic covenant and the coronation of the Davidides in Israel's history) and yet find the ultimate fulfillment in Jesus Christ because of the psalm's exalted language (i.e., the begotten Son of God and the possession of the ends of the earth). Calvin, *Librum Psalmorum*, 46; Gerstenberger, *Psalms: Part 1*, 49. (3) Those who propose the postexilic dating of the psalm tend to consider the psalm to be messianic. Zenger, "Wozu tosen die Völker," 507–8; Bons, "Psaume 2," 151–53.

and evaluate them. We will treat another popular approach—the canonical interpretation—after probing the text of Ps 2, since this interpretation treats the wider context than Ps 2 itself.

As for the structure of Ps 2, I adopt the commonly accepted ABB'A' structure according to the four strophes of the psalm: A (vv. 1–3)—The rebellion of the nations against the LORD and his messiah; B (vv. 4–6)—YHWH's response: the declaration to install his anointed king; B' (vv. 7–9)—The king's rule over the nations; A' (vv. 10–12)—exhortation to the nations to serve YHWH and to submit to his messiah.[6]

Exegesis

Psalm 2 is one of the royal psalms that emphasize God's rule through his messiah. A (vv. 1–3) starts with "why," the question of surprise not caused by the worry about the rebellion of the nations but by the certainty of God's sovereign power and the vanity of their presumptuous rebellion (v. 1).[7] Verse 2 vividly describes their opposition and the target (YHWH and

---

6. Many scholars adopt ABB'A' structure. See Auffret, *Literary Structure*, 30; Hossfeld and Zenger, *Psalmen 1–50*, 49; Goldingay, *Psalms. Volume 1*, 96; Fokkelman, *Major Poems*, 55; VanGemeren, *Psalms*, 89. Though the word *messiah* literally means "anointed (one)," the definition of messiah relates to the concept of messiah that is beyond the mere semantic study of the term. Hays, "Response to Daniel I. Block," 59–60. Scholars are not in one accord concerning the definition of messiah. For instance, one the one hand, Collins and Rose see messiah as the eschatological kingly figure. Collins, *Scepter and the Star*, 11; Rose, *Zemah and Zerubbabel*, 23. On the other hand, Charlesworth and Roberts consider the term messiah to be applicable to other figures also, such as priests and prophets. Also, they view and the temporal reference not as future but present. Charlesworth, *Messiah*, xv; Roberts, "Messianic Expectations," 31–51. Being conscious of these various opinions in reference to the "sociological role" and "temporal reference," Boda suggests that messiah in the Old Testament refers to kings, priests, and prophets who "are consecrated to an office or role within Israel." And as for the temporal reference, he argues that even though the "'messianic' figures may have referred to 'present' figures in their 'original' historical settings, they may have been taken up to encourage future hope in a later era." Boda, "Figuring the Future," 38–40. As for messiah in Psalter, Block points out that the term is only related to a Davidic king. Block, "My Servant David," 40–41. Therefore, we may define the term, *messiah in Ps 2 as an eschatological Davidic king who is the object of future hope*. The fact that Ps 2 functions as the introduction to the whole Psalter, as the exegesis will demonstrate, corroborates the proposed definition of messiah in Ps 2. In this study, we will lowercase a messiah figure (i.e., messiah) but capitalize when we refer to Jesus (i.e., Messiah) because of our recognition of Jesus' unique messiahship as we will demonstrate. See Kutsko, *SBL Handbook of Style*, 33.

7. Kraus, *Psalms 1–59*, 127.

his messiah). By the word of the foreign kings and rulers, verse 3 climaxes their plot to rebel against the rule of YHWH and his anointed king.

B (vv. 4–6) "parallels and contrasts with" A (vv. 1–3).[8] Verses 4–5 describes God's responses and verse 6 closes God's response with his "actual words."[9] God's heavenly reign (v. 4) contrasts with the earthly kings (v. 2). God's initial response to the rebellion of the earthly kings is mockery and laughter due to their foolish and ridiculous plot (v. 4).[10] Then YHWH speaks in his anger that causes the earthly kings and rulers to be terrified.[11] Verse 6 specifies God's word against the rebellious ones: the installation of his king on Zion, the holy mountain. Thus, God's word about the installation of God's messiah is the expression of God's anger, and it terrifies the earthly kings.[12] The installation of God's messiah on Zion where God's presence dwells reminds of God's covenant with David to establish Davidic kingdom (2 Sam 7:5–16).[13]

B' (vv. 7–9) continues and specifies God's decree about the installation of his messiah. But while God's decree is proclaimed directly to the rebellious earthly rulers in Ps 2:6, God's anointed king reiterates God's decree, that is, the installation of his kingship and its effect in B' (vv. 7–9). Many scholars rightly consider 2 Sam 7:14 as the background of the sonship language in Ps 2:7, when YHWH makes the covenant with David that God would be like a father to his descendants.[14] While it is not likely that Ps 2:7 expresses literal begetting of the Messiah by YHWH, it seems

---

8. Goldingay, *Psalms 1–41*, 99.

9. Goldingay, *Psalms 1–41*, 99.

10. Ross, *Psalms: Volume 1 (1–41)*, 205; VanGemeren, *Psalms*, 93.

11. Ross, *Psalms 1–41*, 205–6; Goldingay, *Psalms 1–41*, 99; VanGemeren, *Psalms*, 94.

12. Peter C. Craigie, *Psalms 1–50*, 66; Ross, *Psalms 1–41*, 206.

13. VanGemeren, *Psalms*, 94.

14. "I will be a father to him. And he will be a son to me." (2 Sam 7:14). Ross, *Psalms 1–41*, 207; Goldingay, *Psalms 1–41*, 100; Kraus, *Psalms 1–59*, 131. They see the sonship and begetting language as metaphorical rather than literal. Furthermore, some scholars consider the following verses (Ps 2:8–9) as the rights given to an adopted son, the practice witnessed in ancient Near Eastern document. Mowinckel, *Psalms in Israel's Worship*, 54, 65; Kraus, *Psalms 1–59*, 131–32; Ross, *Psalms 1–41*, 207; Goldingay, *Psalms 1–41*, 100–1. But probably begetting language is influenced by Egyptian practice of "the physical engenderment of the Egyptian king by the deity." Roberts, "Whose Son," 153. John J. Collins evidences some examples of the Egyptian inscriptions that contain the parallel of "the formula, 'you are my son, today, I have begotten you.'" Collins and Collins, *Kings and Messiah*, 13.

that begetting motif signifies more than adoption.[15] Thus, we agree with Gerhard von Rad that the decree of Ps 2:7 resembles the Egyptian royal protocol that a god bestows to a new king at his enthronement.[16] Also, we regard begetting language as the figurative expression that connotes that the deity endows "a divine nature" to the king at the time of coronation (i.e., "today" Ps 2:7b).[17]

Psalm 2:8–9 continues God's decree. The privilege of the anointed king as God's son accompanies the proclamation of his enthronement. God as the ruler of the whole world promises that his messiah will inherit all the nations (v. 8).[18] Verse 9 explicates how the messiah will rule. According to Masoretic text, he will *break* (תְּרֹעֵם) the earthly rulers of the nations with an iron rod, which parallels nicely with the following line ("You will smash them like a potter's vessel").[19]

A' (vv. 10–12) is the conclusion of the psalm. The speaker is the psalmist. In light of God's installation of his anointed king who will rule all the nations with the authority to judge them, the kings and rulers of the earth are warned to be wise and be instructed (v. 10). The specific instructions to escape from the anger of YHWH are given in verses 11 and 12a. First, they are commanded to serve (i.e., "worship") and rejoice—"'give a (cultic) shout of joy'"—with fear (v. 11).[20] "Kiss the Son" signifies submission to God's anointed king (v. 12a).[21] Otherwise, they will incur God's anger (v. 12a). Thus, the psalm once again confirms that God's rule is exercised through the rule of his messiah. To submit to the anointed king is to submit to YHWH. God's anger results in their destruction

---

15. Craigie, *Psalms*, 67. As for coronation as figurative birthing, see also Grund, "Aus Gott geboren," 112–13; Collins and Collins, *Kings and Messiah*, 20–21.

16. von Rad, "Das Judäische Königsritual," 211–16.

17. Craigie, *Psalms*, 67. Collins rightly points to the metaphorical nature of "begetting" language, and yet, that indicates "a closer kinship between king and god than is conveyed by 'adoption.'" Collins and Collins, *Kings and Messiah*, 22.

18. Kraus, *Psalms 1–59*, 132; VanGemeren, *Psalms*, 95–96; Ross, *Psalms 1–41*, 209.

19. תְּרֹעֵם בְּשֵׁבֶט בַּרְזֶל כִּכְלִי יוֹצֵר תְּנַפְּצֵם: (Ps 2:9 MT). However, Septuagint uses the word "shepherd" (ποιμανεῖς) instead of "break."

20. Ross, *Psalms 1–41*, 211–12.

21. The Masoretic text of Ps 2:12a, נַשְּׁקוּ־בַר is different from other ancient versions except the Syriac, thus, is considered as a *crux interpretum*. The scholars who support the Masoretic text view בַר as an Aramaism since the command is given to the foreign nations. Craigie, *Psalms*, 64; Ross, *Psalms 1–41*, 198. Delitzsch also proposes that בַר פֶּן is used to avoid the dissonance (פֶּן בֵּן). Delitzsch, *Psalms*, 98. Septuagint has δράξασθε παιδεία ("receive instruction").

because of the imminent judgement of YHWH (v. 12b).[22] Therefore, the earthly rulers are called to decide between serving and perishing.[23] The psalm ends with the promise of the blessing to those who take refuge (i.e., trust) in God (or possibly in the king, v.12c).

Ancient Variants

Having mentioned that the target text, the citation of Ps 2:7b, is attested by both the MT and LXX, we are obliged to compare the text of Ps 2 in the MT with that of the LXX. Since we provided the major differences in the footnotes above, here we will focus on the implications. First, despite some minor differences, Ps 2 texts of the MT and LXX basically offer the same interpretation. Second, the LXX seems to reveal more sapiential tendency than the MT (i.e., δράξασθε παιδεία in Ps 2:12a and ἐξ ὁδοῦ δικαίας in 2:12b).[24] The LXX's sapiential translation results in more explicit reading of Pss 1 and 2 as unity.[25] Second, the LXX seems to demonstrate the eschatological interpretation. For instance, unlike the MT, the LXX uses the temporal conjunction (ὅταν ἐκκαυθῇ ἐν τάχει ὁ θυμὸς αὐτοῦ, "when his anger burns promptly," Ps 2:12b), which may point to "the coming, final judgment."[26] Third, contrary to Schaper's argument, we cannot find the messanization tendency in the LXX.[27]

Even though the date of the Targum on the Psalm is difficult to pin down, it seems to be written sometime in the first century CE.[28] Thus, we will examine the Targum of Psalms in this chapter and the following chapters of this book to see if it sheds any light on the interpretation of

---

22. While the MT simply states דָּרֶךְ ("way"), the LXX specifies it by translating ἐξ ὁδοῦ δικαίας ("from a right way"). Also, the MT has a causal conjunction כִּי ("because"), but the LXX has a temporal conjunction ὅταν ("when").

23. Goldingay's comment aptly catches the wordplay of the Hebrew text (Ps 2:12). He states, "The nations are being invited to choose whether they 'perish' (*ābad*) or 'serve' (*ābad*)." Goldingay, *Psalms 1–41*, 103.

24. Maiberger, "Verständnis von Psalm 2," 89.

25. Willgren, *Formation*, 160.

26. Janse, *You Are My Son*, 39.

27. Schaper, *Eschatology*, 72–76. Cox, "Schaper's Eschatology," 295, 301; Collins, "Interpretation of Psalm 2," 55.

28. Janse, *You Are My Son*, 46. As for the other ancient versions, Aquila, Theodotion, and Symmachus are excluded since they are regarded to be translated after the date of the Gospel of Mark. Brock, "Bibelübersetzungen I.2," 163–72.

the given Psalms.²⁹ The Targum of Ps 2:7 clearly underplays the unique father-son relationship between YHWH and his anointed king ("You are *as dear to me as a son to a father, pure as though I had created you this day*").³⁰ The following begetting language found in Hebrew and Greek texts are likewise changed into creation motif in order to downplay the possible divine nature of the king.³¹ One may speculate that the Targum of Ps 2:7 is the reaction to the Christian interpretation that considers Ps 2:7 as the evidence of Jesus' divinity, if the Targum of Ps 2 was written after the New Testament.³² If it was written before the writing of the New Testament, it may reflect one of Jewish interpretive traditions (i.e. the Pharisaic interpretation) that guards against the interpretation of the literal divine sonship of messiah.

PSALM 2 IN THE CANONICAL CONTEXT OF THE PSALTER AND OTHER OT TEXTS

Recently scholars have an increased interest in interpreting Ps 2 in its canonical context. First, they focus on the location and the function of Ps 2 as the first royal psalm in "the final shape" of Psalms.³³ Gunkel's classification of the royal psalms is widely accepted by the scholars.³⁴ However, it is Wilson who identified the function of the royal psalms in the final shape of the Psalter. Wilson argues that the three royal psalms (Pss 2; 72; 89) are arranged "at the seams" of the major books of the Psalter.³⁵ According to Wilson, YHWH's covenant with David (Ps 2) is handed down

---

29. Beale, *Handbook*, 117. Targum originally was oral Aramaic interpretation of the Hebrew texts read in Jewish synagogues in Palestine. Later it was gradually written and became a part of Rabbinic literature. Even though, no one knows the exact date of each psalm in Targum, the final form of the Targum of Psalms was written much later than first century CE. Chilton, "Rabbinic Literature," 419.

30. Stec, *Targum of Psalms*, 30.

31. Janse, *You Are My Son*, 48.

32. Midrash Tehillim II. 9 has very similar wording with the Targum of Ps 2:7. Oancea, "Psalm 2," 177.

33. Kim, "Message of Psalm 2," 4.

34. Gunkel classifies certain psalms (Pss 2; 18; 20; 21; 45; 72; 101; 110; 132; 144) into the category of royal psalms that *entirely* concern with Israelite kings. Gunkel and Begrich, *Introduction*, 99. His successors accept Gunkel's classification of the royal psalms but either modify or expand Gunkel's royal psalms. For Gunkel's influence on the scholarship, see Crim, *Royal Psalms*, 7–11.

35. Wilson, "Royal Psalms," 87.

to his offspring in petition form (Ps 72). However, the Davidic covenant failed in exile, and Israel yearns for the restoration of the covenant (Ps 89). Thus, Books IV and V are "the later addition" to the first three books of Psalms in response to the plea to God in Ps 89. God's answer to the plea of the exiled community is not a human Davidic king but YHWH who will rule directly as the king (i.e., YHWH Malek in Pss 94–99).[36]

While agreeing with Wilson about the strategic location of the royal psalms in the Psalter, some scholars question Wilson's argument on the failure of Davidic covenant and the absence of Davidic messiah motif in Books IV and V. They correctly observe that the hope for a Davidic king reappears in Books IV and V (i.e., Pss 110; 132; 144).[37] Thus, in view of Wilson and other scholars who modified his argument, we concur with those who propose that the ideal theocratic rule through a Davidic messiah frames the entire Psalter.

Second, more and more scholars are convinced that Pss 1 and 2 function as the unified introduction of the Psalter to present the main theme of the whole book of Psalms.[38] They propose the following evidences to support their argument: (1) Neither Pss 1 and 2 has a superscription.[39] (2) The blessing formula in Pss 1:1 and 2:12 forms an *inclusio*.[40] (3) Many verbal parallels are found in Pss 1 and 2.[41] (4) The two psalms share the motif of the two ways—the one that leads to life and the other to death (Pss 1:6; 2:11–12).[42] (5) The occasions of Pss 1 and 2 as a unified intro-

---

36. Wilson, "Royal Psalms," 95. See also Wilson, *Editing*, 214–28; Wilson, "Structure," 229–46.

37. Kim, "Psalm 110," 94–138; Grant, "Psalms," 108–9. Krusche, *Göttliches*, 439–40.

38. Hossfeld and Zenger, *Psalmen I*, 45; Cole, "Integrated Reading," 75–88; Grant, *King as Exemplar*, 20–39; Whiting, "Psalms 1 and 2," 246–62; deClaissé-Walford, Jacobson, and Tanner, *Book of Psalms*, 59. Many modern interpreters used to think that Ps 1 focuses on the individual piety characterized by Torah, while Ps 2 deals with the kingship of God's messiah. Willis, "Psalm," 392–93; Cohen, *Psalms*, 3–5; Gillingham, "Messiah," 209–37.

39. Cole, "Integrated Reading," 77, Janse, *You Are My Son*, 22; Whiting, "Hermeneutical Lens," 249.

40. Cole, "Integrated Reading," 77; Janse, *You Are My Son*, 22.

41. i.e., "Sitting" (Pss 1:1 and 2:4) and the combination of "perish" and "way" (Pss 1:6 and 2:12). Jansen, *You Are My Son*, 22; Whiting, "Hermeneutical Lens," 250.

42. Janse, *You Are My Son*, 22; Oancea, "Psalm 2," 176; Botha, "Ideological Interface," 189–203.

duction are found in Second Temple literature,[43] patristic literature,[44] and rabbinic tradition.[45] (6) The verbal parallels between 1) Pss 1 and 2; and 2) Josh 1 and Deut 17 suggest that Pss 1 and 2 as a unified entity present the ideal royal figure, who subjugates his enemies by adhering to "the Deuteronomic command for the king (Deut. 17.18–20)."[46] Thus, all the evidences above convince us that one should interpret Pss 1 and 2 as the unified introduction to the whole Psalter that envisions coherently "the king as exemplary Israelite and human who is fully reliant on God and God's instruction."[47]

In a nutshell, we postulate the implication of the canonical interpretation of Ps 2 as follows. First, while the postexilic Israel did not have a Davidic king in reality, they continued to hope for "the consummation of God's kingship" through a Davidic messiah.[48] Psalm 2 as the introduction of the whole Psalter reflects this eschatological expectation of a Davidic messiah. Second, Pss 1 and 2, as a unified introduction of the whole Psalter, helps us to understand that the theme of the Psalter is the rule of God consummated through his anointed king. Torah that the exemplary king is reliant on is not simply "the law" but "instruction" and the word of YHWH as the way of his rule.[49] Therefore, Pss 1 and 2 function as the gospel to listeners of the Psalter to submit to the rule of God through his anointed king.[50]

So far, we have stated the relationship between Ps 2 and Ps 1, 2 Sam 7, Josh 1, and Deuy 17. Here we will briefly examine the intertextual

---

43. The Qumran literature 4Q174 I.14–19 cites Pss 1 and 2 together, which seems to indicate that the Qumran community considers them to be unified. Brownlee, "Psalms 1–2," 321–36.

44. Maiberger, "Verständnis von Psalm 2," 85.

45. Maiberger, "Verständnis von Psalm 2," 86. Streett corroborates the point (5) by identifying "complementary connections"—the combination of wisdom and kingship motifs—in Pss 72–73; 89–90; 107–10 that Wilson considers to be the seams between the individual books of the Psalter. Streett, *Vine*, 62.

46. Cole, "Integrated Reading," 80. Grant's argument that Pss 1 and 2 present the king as an exemplar for the readers also supports Cole's thesis. Grant, *King*, 20–63. Grant finds the combination of "Torah-Kingship" theme in Pss 18–21 (book I) and 118–19 (book V). Grant, *King*, 71–188.

47. Streett, *Vine*, 63.

48. Childs, *Introduction*, 517. The eschatological and messianic tendency of the Psalter is in tune with other prophetic books and the milieu of the Second Temple period. Childs, *Introduction*, 518; Streett, *Vine*, 66.

49. Kraus, *Theology of Psalms*, 161–62.

50. Kim, "Gospels," 1–36.

relationship between Ps 2 and other Old Testament passages. The Psalter witnesses several allusions to Ps 2: (1) Ps 59:8 ("But You, O Yahweh, laugh [תִּשְׂחַק] at them. You deride [תִּלְעַג] all the nations") is a clear allusion to Ps 2:4 ("The One who sits in heavens laughs [יִשְׂחָק]. The Lord derides [יִלְעַג] them").[51] (2) Psalm 149 clearly corresponds to Ps 2, with the thematic link between YHWH's kingship and the defeat of the rebellious nations.[52] (3) Some scholars suggest also that Isa 49:3 (וַיֹּאמֶר לִי עַבְדִּי־אָתָּה "He said to me, you are my servant"; Isa 49:3) contains the allusion to Ps 2:7 (אָמַר אֵלַי בְּנִי אַתָּה "He said to me, you are my Son"; Ps 2:7).[53] Interestingly, none of the allusions to Ps 2 in this section contain royal messianic concepts. As we will see, it is rather Second Temple literature that witnesses a messianic motif.

PSALM 2 IN SECOND TEMPLE LITERATURE

Psalm 2 is not cited frequently in Second Temple literature. Nevertheless, some Second Temple texts throw light on how early Judaism interpreted Ps 2. Among Dead Sea Scrolls, 4Q Florilegium (=4Q174) preserves a "Midrash on 2 Samuel and Psalms 1–2."[54] The midrash on 2 Sam 7 and Pss 1–2 are closely related. Both consistently use the scriptural quotations that are prophetic in nature.[55] The "thematic link" between 2 Sam 7 and Ps 2 in 4Q174 would be "oppression by enemies"[56] In corollary, a mi-

---

51. Tate, *Psalms 51–100*, 97–98; Wilson, *Psalms Volume 1*, 851; Goldingay, *Psalms 42–89*, 217; Ross, *Psalms 42–89*, 328; Gillingham, *Journey*, 10. Psalm 59 is David's prayer for God to deliver the righteous from the wicked enemies. By alluding to Ps 2:4, the psalmist places the situation in the right perspective: YHWH who is sovereign over the world power mocks those who threaten the righteous. Ross, *Psalms 42–89*, 328.

52. Wittman, "'Let Us,'" 56–57; Tucker and Grant, *Psalms Volume 2*, 1027–28. YHWH is the king of Zion (149:2) who executes the saving victory (149:4) by punishing the nations and the peoples, and by binding their kings and nobles (149:7–8). While Ps 149 does not have a royal messianic ideology as Ps 2, the kingship of God and God's punishment on the disobedient foreign nations are parallel with Ps 2. Gillingham, *Journey*, 11.

53. Westermann, *Jesaja*, 169; Janse, *You Are My Son*, 16–17. Gillingham, *Journey*, 11. The key question is whether the servant is "a royal or a prophetic figure." If Ps 2 is alluded to as some suggested, Isa 46:1–6 seems to point to a prophetic character with royal elements. Janse, *You Are My Son*, 17.

54. Milgrom, "Florilegium," 248.

55. i.e., 2 Sam 7:11c–12b, 13b–14a; Amos 9:11a; Isa 8:11; Ezek 37:23a; Pss 1:1; 2:1–2; Dan 12:10; 11:32b. Brooke, *Exegesis at Qumran*, 167–68.

56. 4Q174 I, 7–11 and I, 18–II, 2. Mason, "Interpretation," 81.

drash on Ps 2 equates the nations that oppose the anointed one with the unfaithful Israel that stands against the faithful Qumran community (the chosen ones of Israel). We can also find other possible allusions to Ps 2 in 4Q246. 4Q246 contains the expressions "the Son of God," and "the Son of the Most High," which may have originated from Ps 2:7 or 2 Sam 7:14.[57] But the fragmentary nature of the text deters us from being conclusive.

Pseudepigraphic literature offers more evident examples of the messianic interpretation of Ps 2 than Qumran literature. *Psalms of Solomon* 17 is a "plea for deliverance" from the foreign enemy (i.e., Pompey) through a Davidic messiah.[58] God's eternal kingship frames the entire psalm (*Pss. Sol.* 17:1, 46).[59] The psalmist clearly alludes to Ps 2:9 in describing his victory over the Roman invaders ("to smash the arrogance of sinners like a potter's jar"; "To shatter all their substance with an iron rod"; *Pss. Sol.* 17:23b–24a). The psalmist pictures the messianic rule characterized by righteousness and the wisdom of God, possibly according to the instruction to a king in Deut 17 (*Pss. Sol.* 17:32–36).[60]

The allusions and echoes to Ps 2 extend beyond Ps 2:9. Janson points out many words of Ps 2 are found also in *Psalms of Solomon* 17, especially in 17:21–30.[61] Going beyond the mere verbal correspondence, we notice many thematic parallels between the two psalms.[62] In addition, we may consider that the description of Deuteronomic kingship and the emphasis on the wisdom of the king motif in *Psalms of Solomon* 17 are related to the sapiential tendency in Pss 1–2 as unity.

We can draw the following conclusions from the ample parallels between *Psalms of Solomon* 17 and Ps 2 and the intertextual interplay in *Psalms of Solomon* 17: (1) the interplay of 2 Sam 7, Ps 89, and Ps 2 clearly indicates that the author of *Psalms of Solomon* 17 interpreted the messiah of Ps 2 as a Davidic messiah.[63] (2) The psalmist emphasizes that Davidic

57. Janse, *You Are My Son*, 53.
58. Collins, "Interpretation," 56.
59. Sloan, "Understanding," 49.
60. Collins, "Interpretation," 58.
61. i.e., ἄρχοντας ("rulers," 22), ἔθνη ("nations," 22, 24, 25, 29), κληρονομίας ("inheritance," 23), λαοὺς ("peoples," 29, 30), δουλεύειν ("to serve," 30), and τὸν ζυγὸν ("yoke," 30), Janse, *You Are My Son*, 55–56.
62. i.e., messiah's judgment on ἄρχοντας λαοῦ (*Pss. Sol.* 17:22–24, 36. Cf. Ps 2:9), Jerusalem/Zion as the holy place (*Pss. Sol.* 17:14, 22, 30. Cf. Ps 2:6), Lord's anointing, and the establishment of the Davidic king, who is the heir of the nations (*Pss. Sol.* 17:21–24, 32, 34, 37–39, 42; Cf. Ps 2:6–8). Janse, *You Are My Son*, 64–65.
63. Sloan, "Understanding of the Psalms," 50–51.

messianic kingship originates from and depends on God's kingship.[64] (3) He exercises judgment not only on gentile nations but also the sinful Jewish rulers (*Pss. Sol.* 17:22–25, 36).[65] (4) Like the interpretation of Ps 2 in LXX and the canonical reading of Pss 1 and 2 as unity, messiah is portrayed as the sapiential and eschatological figure.[66] (5) However, messiah is not depicted as son of God.[67]

The *Similitudes of Enoch* also has two allusions—"Kings of the earth" (*1 En.* 48:8a) and "For they have denied the Lord of Spirits and his Anointed One." (*1 En.* 48:10d)—to Ps 2:2 ("The kings of the earth take their stand and conspire against Yahweh and his anointed").[68] The background of the allusion is the heavenly tribunal, where Danielic son of man is affirmed as the judge of the unrighteous earthly kings and rulers and as the savior and vindicator of the righteous ones (*1 En.* 46–49). The two allusions to Ps 2:2 form an *inclusio* in *1 Enoch* 48:8–10 that predicts the judgment of the kings of the earth and the strong (i.e., rulers) who oppose God and his Anointed One before the righteous ones.[69] Thus, the allusion to Ps 2:2 in *1 Enoch* 48:8–10 assumes the scheme of Ps 2: God anoints his messiah, who will judge the kings of the earth and the mighty ones of the land.[70] While "Davidic lineage" is not clearly specified, the allusions to Ps 2 and Isa 11 (*1 En.* 48:8, 10; 49:1–4) indicate a "Davidic messiah" who is also a preexistent (*1 En.* 48:6; 62:7) and supernatural eschatological figure (*1 En.* 51:3; 55:4; 61:8; 62:2; 69:29).[71]

We may conclude concerning the interpretation of Ps 2 and its interpretive history before Mark as follows. First, Ps 2 is the royal psalm about God's installation of his anointed king who will rule all the nations with the authority to judge them. The kings and rulers of the earth are warned to submit to God's rule exercised through the messiah's rule. The intimate relationship with the Davidic covenant in 2 Sam 7 identifies the

---

64. Collins, "Interpretation," 58.
65. Trafton, "What Would David Do," 170.
66. Janse, *You Are My Son*, 65–66.
67. Janse, *You Are My Son*, 65–66; Collins, "Interpretation," 58.
68. Nickelsburg and Vanderkam, *1 Enoch 2*, 174, 176; Janse, *You Are My Son*, 72. The other name of *the Similitudes of Enoch* is the Book of Parables (*1 En.* 31–71). *1 Enoch* 49 belongs to the second parable (*1 En.* 45–57). The translation is cited from Nickelsburg and VanderKam, *1 Enoch*.
69. Nickelsburg and Vanderkam, *1 Enoch 2*, 174.
70. Collins, "Interpretation," 60–61.
71. Collins, "Interpretation," 60.

anointed king with a Davidic messiah. Second, the MT and the LXX are virtually same with minor differences. All ancient variants, including the Targum, envision the rule of an eschatological Davidic messiah. Third, the canonical context of the Psalter reveals that Ps 2, in tandem with Ps 1, is the gateway to the whole Psalter. They portray the ideal Davidic king who relies on God and his Torah. This canonical context of Ps 2 reflects the postexilic Jewish community's hope for the consummation of God's kingdom through a Davidic messiah. However, the allusions to Ps 2 in other OT texts do not have royal messianic connotation. Fourth, Second Temple literature also witnesses an eschatological messianic motif in its interpretation of Ps 2. Though the fragmentary nature of Dead Sea Scrolls deters us from making a definitive conclusion, a thematic link between 2 Sam 7 and Ps 2 in 4Q174 implies the possible interpretation of a Davidic messiah. 4Q174 also applies the rebellion of gentile nations motif in Ps 2 to the Jewish opponents of the anointed one. The Pseudepigrapha attests more evident allusions of Ps 2. *Psalms of Solomon* 17 clearly demonstrates an eschatological Davidic messiah who rules with wisdom and dependence on God. Like 4Q174, *Psalms of Solomon* 17 sees the possibility of the Jewish opponents. Also, the allusion to Ps 2:2 in *1 Enoch* 48:8–10 also views the anointed one as the Davidic messiah. All the allusions to Ps 2 in Second Temple literature both anticipate the future fulfillment[72] and combine other OT texts to portray the messianic motif. It will be interesting to see what correlations the interpretation of Ps 2 in the context of Old Testament and Second Temple literature may have with Mark's use of Ps 2. Keeping these findings in mind, we now turn to Mark's use of Ps 2.

PSALM 2 IN MARK

Psalm 2 in Mark 1:11

In the narrative structure of Mark, Jesus appears as the main character on the scene in Mark 1:9–11. Before Jesus' first appearance, the narrator informs who Jesus is through the witnesses of the Scriptures and of John the Baptist: he is the Messiah, the Son of God (Mark 1:1), the Lord of the new exodus (Mark 1:2), and the stronger one who will baptize with the Holy Spirit (Mark 1:7–8). As we have observed in the narrative structure

---

72. Hurtado, "Christological Interpretation," 83. He states, ". . . it is noteworthy that we have evidence that Psalm 2 in particular was read as predictive of various eschatological developments." Hurtado, "Christological Interpretation," 82.

of Mark, these descriptions of Jesus' identity are not about the disparate aspects of who Jesus is but are interrelated. Mark 1:9–11 introduces the anticipated coming of Jesus with the heavenly witness to who Jesus is. Heaven is torn. The Holy Spirit comes upon him. The voice from heaven confirms him as the Son of God.

Jesus' baptism by John in Mark 1:9–11 is laden with multiple allusions to Old Testament. First, the heaven being torn and the coming down of the Holy Spirit on Jesus in Mark 1:10b (εἶδεν σχιζομένους τοὺς οὐρανοὺς καὶ τὸ πνεῦμα ὡς περιστερὰν καταβαῖνον εἰς αὐτόν "He saw *the heaven torn open* and the Spirit *come down* on him like a dove") allude to Isa 63:19b (לוּא־קָרַעְתָּ שָׁמַיִם יָרַדְתָּ "If only you would *tear open the heavens* and *come down*") in the MT.[73] Isaiah pleads with God to look down on the miserable situation of Israel (Isa 63:15–18) and to restore his kingly rule by tearing apart the heavens and coming down to save his people (Isa 63:19b MT=64:1 LXX). Mark 1:10 alludes that God's tearing heaven and the descent of the Holy Spirit on Jesus is the answer to Isaiah's prayer for the new exodus.[74] God's kingly rule, that is, his "eschatological work of deliverance," has begun through Jesus.[75]

Second, Mark 1:11 (καὶ φωνὴ ἐγένετο ἐκ τῶν οὐρανῶν· σὺ εἶ ὁ υἱός μου ὁ ἀγαπητός, ἐν σοὶ εὐδόκησα "And there was a voice from heaven, 'You are my beloved Son, in you I am pleased.'"), the heavenly voice to Jesus, is generally considered to evoke three allusions to the Hebrew Scriptures (Ps 2:7; Isa 42:1; Gen 22:2, 12, 16).[76] The conflated Scriptural allusions have affinity to Mark's Jewish contemporary interpretive method that juxtaposed seemingly unrelated Scriptures to elicit the theological understandings for its "eschatological community."[77] The first part of God's voice in Mark 1:11 (σὺ εἶ ὁ υἱός μου) is the allusion to Ps 2:7.[78] In addition to the verbal parallel we noticed in the beginning of the chapter, the

---

73. Marcus, *Way of the Lord*, 48–49; Gundry, *Mark*, 48, 51; Hays, *Gospels*, 17–18.

74. Bauckham, *Who Is God*, 93–95.

75. Hays, *Gospels*, 18.

76. Even though some scholars, such as Bousset, Cullmann, and Jeremias, contend for Isa 42:1 as the only allusion in Mark 1:11, their argument is successfully refuted by other scholars. See Bousset, *Kyrios Christos*, 97–98; Cullman, *Christology*, 66; Jeremias, s. v., 'παῖς θεοῦ,' *TDNT*; Marshall, "Son of God," 326–36; Rowe, *God's Kingdom*, 249; Hatina, "Embedded Scripture," 86–87; Janse, *You Are My Son*, 106–7.

77. Kee, "Function," 181.

78. Matera, *Kingship*, 77; Marcus, *Way of the Lord*, 69–72; Rowe, *God's Kingdom*, 248–9; France, *Mark*, 80, Collins, *Mark*, 150; Cho, *Royal Messianism*, 85–89; Botner, *Jesus*, 52.

structural parallel (i.e., God speaks to Jesus, his Son) clearly points to its allusion to Ps 2:7. The allusion to Ps 2:7 in Mark 1:11 demonstrates that Jesus is the eschatological Davidic messiah that Israel has awaited.[79] Just like the anticipation of some of the contemporary Jewish literature concerning the eschatological Davidic messiah, Mark portrays Jesus as the Davidic messiah who will bring "the eschatological victory" over God's enemies.[80] According to the pattern of Ps 2, Mark affirms that Jesus is enthroned as the Messiah who will actualize God's rule through his victory over Satan and his followers. The following Markan narrative—Jesus' messianic authority manifested in his deeds and words such as exorcism, miracles, the teaching of God's kingdom, the judgment on rebellious religious leaders—demonstrates that Jesus is the Messiah who executes his kingly authority to bring about God's kingdom.[81]

Some scholars argue that Mark's wording in Mark 1:11 may indicate that Jesus is beyond the anticipation of Ps 2:7 and that of Mark's contemporary interpreters: Mark 1:11 changes the word order of LXX (i.e., from υἱός μου εἶ σύ to σὺ εἶ ὁ υἱός μου), thus emphasizing "the naming" of Jesus as "God's Son," while the *Vorlage* text of Ps 2:7 stresses on choosing "the addressee" as a son.[82] It implies that the allusion to Ps 2:7 in Mark 1:11 does not point to the appointment of Jesus to be God's Son.[83] Rather, the heavenly voice is the confirmation of Jesus' status as God's Son.[84] The identical allusion to Ps 2:7 in Mark 9:7 corroborates that the heavenly voice is not the appointment.[85] However, we must remember that Mark may have used another Greek text that has a different word order from the LXX. Also, the changed word order itself does not necessarily endorse the interpretation that God confirms Jesus' sonship, since it can have other connotations (i.e., the emphasis on Jesus as the anointed Son). Therefore, we cannot ascertain Jesus' preexistent sonship from the word order itself.

---

79. Hays, *Gospels*, 48; Cho, *Royal Messianism*, 85; Botner, *Jesus Christ*, 85–88.
80. Marcus, *Way of the Lord*, 61.
81. Hays, *Gospels*, 48; Botner, *Jesus Christ*, 88–89; Cho, *Royal Messianism*, 86–88.
82. Marshall, "Son of God," 333. Also, Kampling, *Israel*, 56; Gundry, *Mark*, 49.
83. Kampling, *Israel*, 56; Rose, *Theologie*, 143.
84. Boring, *Mark*, 46; France, *Mark*, 82–83; Johansson, "Jesus and God," 38, Boring and France note that the absence of "today I have begotten you" may indicate that Jesus was already Messiah.
85. Boring, *Mark*, 46; Johansson, "Jesus and God," 38.

The other scriptural allusions color the unique character of Jesus' messiahship. "The beloved one" (ὁ ἀγαπητός) alludes to Gen 22:2, 12, 16, when God calls Abraham to sacrifice his son, Isaac.[86] The word ἀγαπητός connotes "only," corresponding to the Hebrew word יָחִיד, of Gen 22:2, 12, 16 in the MT. The allusion to Gen 22 may adumbrate that Jesus has the unique filial relationship with God. Mark already indicated Jesus' divine status in Mark 1:2–3: God's conversation partner, "you" (σου) in Mark 1:2, is identical with "Lord" (κυρίου) in Mark 1:3.[87] In view of Mark 1:2–3, the allusion to Gen 22 may indicate that Jesus is not a mere human but the divine Son.[88] Furthermore, it is quite probable that Mark intends to imply Jesus' suffering with the expression υἱὸν ἀγαπητόν because both the "beloved son" in Gen 22 and υἱὸν ἀγαπητόν in Mark 12:6 share the same motif, the death of the beloved son, in their immediate contexts.[89] If so, Mark may indicate Jesus' suffering from the beginning of the gospel.

The last scriptural allusion in Mark 1:11 (ἐν σοὶ εὐδόκησα) is from Isa 42:1(רָצְתָה נַפְשִׁי) "[in whom] my soul is pleased"). The disparate translations of Isa 42:1 in different ancient versions may cause one to hesitate to verify the allusion.[90] However, Chilton confirmed the Deutero-Isaianic

86. Ruckstuhl, "Jesus," 205; Guelich, *Mark*, 34; Kampling, *Israel*, 57; van Iersel, *Mark*, 101; Strauss, *Mark*, 73. Some scholars contend that ἀγαπητός alludes to Isa 42:1. For instance, Marcus argues that ἀγαπητός has the "close linguistic relationship" with ἐκλεκτός (Isa 42:1) and that ἀγαπητός is a "reflection" of Isa 42:1 that is alluded in Mark 1:11 (ἐν σοὶ εὐδόκησα). Marcus, *Way of the Lord*, 52. But even Watts who is keen on finding Isaianic connection with Mark questions the close linguistic relationship between ἀγαπητός and Isa 42:1. Watts, *Isaiah's New Exodus*, 113. As Marcus himself acknowledges, the verbal and linguistic parallels between Gen 22 and ἀγαπητός are obvious. While Marcus is suspicious of the thematic correspondence between the two, we would argue that Mark intentionally uses ἀγαπητός to emphasize Jesus' unique relationship with God as God's only Son. Bauckham, *Who Is God*, 96. τὸν υἱόν σου τὸν ἀγαπητόν (Gen 22:2); τοῦ υἱοῦ σου τοῦ ἀγαπητοῦ (Gen 22:12); τοῦ υἱοῦ σου τοῦ ἀγαπητοῦ (Gen 22:16).

87. ". . . ἰδοὺ ἀποστέλλω τὸν ἄγγελόν μου πρὸ προσώπου σου, ὃς κατασκευάσει τὴν ὁδόν σου· φωνὴ βοῶντος ἐν τῇ ἐρήμῳ· ἑτοιμάσατε τὴν ὁδὸν κυρίου, εὐθείας ποιεῖτε τὰς τρίβους αὐτοῦ" (Mark 1:2–3).

88. Some scholars argue that Mark 1:11 attests to Jesus' "filial self-consciousness" as God's divine Son. Rowe, *God's Kingdom*, 249. The expression ὁ υἱός (μου) ὁ ἀγαπητός in Mark 1:11 may imply that Jesus is the Son who obeys God even to his death. Markan narrative points to that direction: the other occurrences in Mark 9:7 and 12:6 are embedded in the story that anticipate Jesus' suffering and death. Hays, *Gospels*, 42–43. Also, when we consider the narrative context of Gen 22 and the contemporary interpretation of Jewish literature of Mark, Isaac is depicted as obedient son who "effects atonement." Hatina, "Embedded Scripture," 88–92. We will further develop this idea when dealing with Mark 9:7 and 12:6.

89. Blank, "Sendung," 38; Kampling, *Israel*, 57; Strauss, *Mark*, 73.

90. MT: "In whom my soul is pleased," רָצְתָה נַפְשִׁי, LXX: "My soul accepted him,"

background behind Mark 1:10–11 by comparing the similarities between the Targum of Isa 41:8–9, 42:1, and 43:10, such as "the direct address of 41:8, 9, the references to the spirit in 42:1, and the messiah in 43:10."[91] Mark already showed that the gospel Jesus brings is the fulfillment of the new exodus that the prophet Isaiah prophesied (Mark 1:1–3, 10). So, the link between Ps 2:7 and Isa 42:1 may indicate that Jesus is the messianic Servant who will inaugurate "Yahweh's sovereign universal rule over the nations."[92] In addition, Bauckham suggests that we should read so-called Deutero-Isaiah (Isa 40–55) as a whole rather than interpret individual texts.[93] If we agree with him, we should interweave the use of the servant motif throughout Isa 40–55 rather than interpret each servant passage separately. If so, the allusion to Isa 42:1 in Mark 1:11 may imply the suffering and exaltation of Jesus (cf. Isa 53).[94] If the heavenly voice at the baptism of Jesus is programmatic for the entire Markan narrative, as we will propose, it will strengthen the possibility that the allusion to Isa 42:1 implies Jesus' suffering and exaltation as the Isaianic servant figure. Apart from the servant motif, the connection between ἀγαπητός and εὐδόκησα intensifies God's inseparable unique relationship with Christ in Mark 1:11.[95]

To summarize, Mark's use of Ps 2:7 in Mark 1:11 emanates the multivalent nuances in conjunction to other scriptural allusions. Mark presents Jesus as the eschatological Davidic Messiah who will inaugurate God's rule by defeating the enemy as the rest of the narrative demonstrates. But at the same time, he is more than a mere human figure. The allusions to Gen 22 and Isa 42:1 point to Jesus' unique relationship with God. Therefore, the heavenly voice confirms Jesus as the unique Messiah who will usher in God's kingdom. Moreover, the heaven being torn open and the descent of the Spirit in Mark 1:10 augment the motif of God's

---

προσεδέξατο αὐτὸν ἡ ψυχή μου, Theodotion and Symmachus: "My soul delights in," εὐδόκησεν ἡ ψυχή μου.

91. Chilton, *Galilean Rabbi*, 128–30. Targum of Isaiah 41.8–9: "But You, Israel, my servant Jacob *in* whom *I am pleased* . . . 'You are my servant, I *am pleased with* you and I will not cast you off.'" Targum of Isaiah 42.1: "Behold my servant, . . . my chosen in whom my *Memra is pleased*; I will put my *Holy Spirit* upon him . . ." Targum of Isaiah 43.10: ". . . my servant *the Messiah* with whom I *am pleased* . . ." Chilton, *Isaiah Targum*, 80–81, 84.

92. Watts, *Isaiah's New Exodus*, 115.

93. Bauckham, *Jesus and the God*, 33–37.

94. See Strauss, *Mark*, 73, for the similar logic and conclusion.

95. Kampling, *Israel*, 58; Rose, *Theologie*, 144–46; Bauckham, *Who Is God*, 98.

reign. Furthermore, the use of ἀγαπητός and εὐδόκησα not only stresses the intimate and unique relationship between God and Jesus but also implies Jesus' vicarious suffering. We may investigate further how Ps 2:7 in Mark 1:11 functions in the entire narrative. In order to do that, we need to first observe the other use of Ps 2:7 in Mark 9:7 to which we now turn.

Psalm 2 in Mark 9:7

As we examined in chapter 2, the transfiguration section falls into the middle section of the whole Markan narrative that focuses on discipleship in relation to Jesus' identity and God's kingdom. In Mark 8:27—9:1, Jesus redefines his messiahship as suffering Messiah whom the disciples must follow and reaffirms that he is the inaugurator of God's kingdom in which the faithful disciples will partake. The following transfiguration confirms Jesus' words that some of the disciples will see the proleptic coming of God's kingdom powerfully manifested (Mark 9:1).[96] While the various interpretations exist concerning when God's kingdom in power would come (Mark 9:1), the parallels between Mark 8:28—9:1 and Mark 9:2–13 seem to indicate that Mark intends to point to Jesus' transfiguration as the coming of God's kingdom in power (Mark 9:1).[97] The frequent references to the disciples in the episode (Mark 9:2, 4, 6, 7, 8) evidently exhibit that the transfiguration transpires for the disciples in Mark.[98] The basic plot consists of Jesus' ascension to a high mountain with his three disciples, his transfiguration and conversation with Moses and Elijah, Peter's offer to build three booths for them, and finally the heavenly voice that climaxes the episode (Mark 9:2–8).[99]

96. Wenham and Moses, "Some Standing," 149.

97. Morrison persuasively presents the linguistic, thematic, and synthetic correspondences between Mark 8:27—9:1 and Mark 9:2–13. Morrison, *Turning Point*, 117–27.

98. Stein, *Mark*, 416.

99. Kee, "Transfiguration," 139; Similarly, Öhler states that the heavenly voice is the climax of the transfiguration episode because it functions to interpret the previous event. Öhler, "Verklärung," 213. The transfiguration episode has generated diverse scholarly opinions regarding its genre and meaning. Some scholars proposed it was an interpolated resurrection account. The earliest proponent of the view is believed to be J. Wellhausen. Wellhausen, *Evangelium Marci*, 71. Some of Wellhausen's followers are Bultmann, *Synoptic Tradition*, 259–61; Robinson, "Jesus," 5–37. But this theory is refuted persuasively by others. See Fossum, *Image*, 71–94. The second group of scholars propose Jesus' changed status in transfiguration. For example, Burkett, "Transfiguration," 411. But this view does not stand when we consider that the heavenly

Mark 9:2–7 is replete with OT allusions and echoes. First of all, many scholars observe echoes from Exod 24 and 34. Johansson's summary represents their observations: "1) The six days (Mark 9:2; Exod 24:16); 2) three witnesses (Mark 9:2; Exod 24:1, 9); 3) ascent of the mountain (Mark 9:2; Exod 24:9,12–13); 4) transfiguration (Mark 9:2–3; Exod 34:29); 5) God's presence in clouds (Mark 9:7; Exod 24:15–16, 18); 6) God speaking (Mark 9:7; Exod 24:16)."[100] On the basis of the multiple echoes of Exod 24 and 34, as well as the interpretive tradition of Jewish literature that portrays Moses as divine and kingly figure, Marcus proposes Jesus in Mark 9:2–8 as a new Moses.[101] In addition, the majority of the scholars propose Deut 18:5 (αὐτοῦ ἀκούσεσθε) as the allusion of ἀκούετε αὐτοῦ in Mark 9:7. If Deut 18:5 is the allusion to Mark 9:7, the text presents Jesus as the prophet like Moses whom the disciple must listen to.[102] However, while one cannot deny the echoes from Exod 24 and 34, some of the seemingly similar echoes we find between Exod and Mark 9:2–9 accounts are more distant than they look.[103] Also, the transfiguration of Jesus does not

---

announcement—Jesus is his Son—in Mark 9:7 is identical with Mark 1:11 and that what is changed is only the addressees of the heavenly voice from Jesus to his three disciples. The third group argues for epiphanic character (i.e., a manifestation of deity) of the story. Of this group, Lohmeyer and others find the similarity between the transfiguration and Hellenistic myth. i.e., Lohmeyer, "Verklärung," 185–215; Collins, "Mark and His Readers," 90–92; Moss, "Transfiguration," 69–89. But Jesus does not disguise himself as human and later reveals his divine identity in Mark as the Hellenistic myth does. Other scholars rather observe the parallel with Jewish apocalyptic literature. They pay attention to how prophetic figures like Moses and Elijah are regarded as heavenly beings in Jewish contemporary literature. For instance, Marcus presents Jesus as "a New Moses" with divine and kingly character. Marcus, *Way of the Lord*, 84–92. But rather, Moses and Elijah seem to represent as the eschatological characters who confirm the role of Jesus who fulfills eschatological anticipation of God's kingdom. Also, Mark seems to present Jesus a "new Sinai theophany." Johansson, "Jesus and God," 129–30. The section will explore and defend the view that the transfiguration portrays Jesus a new Sinai theophany.

100. Johansson, "Jesus and God," 126. See also Marcus, *Way of the Lord*, 82; Stegner, "Use of Scripture," 114–17; Wypadlo, *Verklärung*, 28–39.

101. Marcus, *Way of the Lord*, 80–92. Also, France, *Mark*, 353.

102. Lane, *Mark*, 321; Stegner, "Use," 119; Bock, *Mark*, 251; Kee, "Transfiguration," 146; Lee, *Transfiguration*, 35. Lee, however, admits that Mark describes Jesus beyond the eschatological Prophet-like-Moses.

103. For instance, Tàrrech observes the differences between them as following: "Moses ascends the mountain with three (Aaron, Nadab, and Abihu) but also with the seventy elders of Israel (Exod 24.1, 9) and with Joshua (24.13); the cloud does not cover the mountain when Jesus is transfigured; in contrast to Moses, Jesus descends from the mountain with his face unchanged: he has not spoken with God; rather, it is God who has spoken about him to the disciples after his appearance was changed." 155. Tàrrech,

correspond to Moses, as we will argue further.[104] Moreover, Mark has already dissociated Jesus from being identified with the prophetic figures (Mark 6:14–15; 8:28).[105]

The echoes of Exodus and the appearance of Moses and Elijah signify three things in Mark 9:2–8. First, Moses and Elijah seem to appear as eschatological characters. Their eschatological character is witnessed by "Jewish eschatological tradition."[106] However, Mark presents Jesus as the main character of the episode.[107] Even though Peter ignorantly desires to pay equal homage to three of them (Mark 9:5–6), the narrative explicitly depicts the centrality of Jesus. It is Jesus whose appearance is metamorphosed (Mark 9:2–3). The heavenly voice recognizes Jesus as God's beloved Son whose voice the disciples should listen to (Mark 9:7). Only Jesus is seen after the heavenly voice (Mark 9:8). Therefore, Moses and Elijah's presence with Jesus (Mark 9:4) functions to highlight Jesus as the one who fulfills eschatological anticipation of God's kingdom.

Second, the presence of Moses and Elijah on a high mountain clearly reverberates their encounters with God on Mount Sinai (Exod 24:15–18; 34:4–8; 1 Kgs 19:8–18).[108] Third, in corollary, the differences between theophanic experience of Moses and Elijah on Mount Sinai and what happened in Mark 9:2–5 strongly point to Jesus' divine identity: (1) Jesus' transfiguration takes place without any indication of the encounter with God. However, Moses' facial reflection of God's glory happened after his encounter with God (Exod 34:28–30).[109] (2) Moses and Elijah encounter Jesus and speak (συλλαλέω) with him on Mount of Transfiguration while they encountered YHWH and spoke with him on Mount

---

"Glory," 155. See also, Gundry, *Mark*, 475–76; Fossum, *Invisible God*, 76–78; Öhler, "Verklärung," 202–4; Johansson, "Jesus and God," 126.

104. Öhler, "Verklärung, " 214; Steichele, *leidende Sohn Gottes*, 173, 178.

105. Hooker, " Elijah," 62–63.

106. Kee, "Transfiguration," 144–47. See also Evans, *Mark*, 36; Marcus, *Mark 8–16*, 632–33.

107. Lane, *Mark*, 317. Wypadlo argues that the reversed order of the three characters (Elijah-Moses-Jesus-Jesus-Moses-Elijah, Mark 9:4–5) underlines the centrality of Jesus. Wypadlo, *Verklärung*, 167. Some scholars suggest the priority of Elijah to Moses in light of the Elijah-Moses order in Mark 9:4 (i.e., Marcus, *Mark 8–16*, 637). However, if we consider the reversed order, what Mark intends does not seem to be the importance of Elijah over Moses as an eschatological figure, but the centrality of Jesus.

108. Marcus, *Mark 8–16*, 632

109. Collins, *Mark*, 417; Johansson, "Jesus and God," 131.

Sinai (i.e., συλλαλέω in Exod 34:35).[110] Therefore, the differences indicate that the transfiguration manifests Jesus' "divine glory" that he "shares with the Father" (cf. "when he comes in the glory of his Father with the holy angels"; Mark 8:38) and that Moses and Elijah's encounter with Jesus is another form of theophany.[111]

Second, the allusion to Ps 2:7 appears in Mark 9:7. We have already observed that Mark 9:7 is virtually the identical phrase with Mark 1:11 (οὗτός ἐστιν ὁ υἱός μου ὁ ἀγαπητός "He is my beloved Son") in the beginning of this chapter. The only difference is that Mark 9:7 uses the third person (οὗτός ἐστιν) instead of the second person (σὺ εἶ; Mark 1:11). However, it is totally understandable as the listeners of the heavenly voice are Jesus' disciples. In addition, the introductory wording of Mark 9:7 ("the voice from the cloud") is very similar to Mark 1:11.[112] Therefore, Mark 9:7 has the clear allusions to Ps 2:7 and Gen 22. The almost exact wording not only confirms the allusions but also indicates that the significance of the allusions to Ps 2:7 and Gen 22 in Mark 1:10 are transposed into Mark 9:7: Jesus is the Davidic Messiah who will inaugurate God's eschatological kingdom. And the text once again reveals Jesus' divine filial relationship with God the Father to the disciples. Also, the implication of Jesus' suffering derived from "beloved son" fits in the immediate context of Mark 9:7: the transfiguration and the heavenly voice are God's revelation to the disciples who do not understand Jesus' suffering messiahship, and Mark 9:7 is situated in the midst of the motif of Jesus' suffering (Mark 8:31-38; 9:9-12). Peter's proposal to build three booths proves wanting as the heavenly voice reveals Jesus' true identity.[113] The disciples need to listen to Jesus.

Third, ἀκούετε αὐτοῦ in Mark 9:7 may allude to YHWH's command to the Israelites to listen to himself or his angel (of the Lord).[114] We have

---

110. Johansson, "Jesus and God," 129–30. Also, Wypadlo, *Verklärung*, 146–47.

111. Johansson, "Jesus and God," 130, 132. See also Hooker, "Elijah," 60; Hurtado, *Mark*, 145; Lee, *Transfiguration*, 44–45.

112. Öhler, "Verklärung," 212.

113. Peter did not recognize Jesus' superiority to Moses and Elijah. His presumptuous suggestion to build three booths may have derived from his thought of Jesus as the messianic king, Elijah as an eschatological high priest, and Moses as a prophet in a restored Israel. Bauckham, *Who Is God*, 99–100.

114. Exod 15:26; Lev 26:14–27; Jos 3:9; 1 Sam 15:1; Ps 81:11–13; Isa 46:3, 12; 48:12; 49:1; 51:1, 7; 55:2; Jer 34:14; 35:15; Ezek 3:7; 20:39. Johansson, "Jesus and God," 138; Johansson and others also suggest the possible allusion to God's command to listen to the angel of the Lord in Exod 23:21. Johansson, "Jesus and God," 136; Juncker, "Jesus,"

already rejected the idea that Deut 18:5 is the allusion to ἀκούετε αὐτοῦ in Mark 9:7.[115] As aforementioned, Jesus is not portrayed as a prophetic figure in the Markan narrative (i.e., Mark 8:28).[116] Especially, the heavenly voice calls Jesus as "my Son," not the prophet, in Mark 9:7.[117] Instead of the unlikely parallel between Deut 18:5 and Mark 9:7, the more probable allusion is YHWH's command for Israelites to listen to himself or his angel, which fits better when we consider that Mark 9:2–8 presents a "'new Sinai' theophany."[118] Indeed, Mark's gospel shows that Jesus speaks with the authority beyond the prophet that can only equate with God's authority (Mark 4:1–20; 7:14, 15, 19; 10:29; 13:31).[119] Even in the immediate context of Mark 9:2–8, Jesus demands the disciples to keep his words for their life (Mark 8:34–38). As Marcus puts it, "Listening to Jesus is like listening to God."[120]

In light of its immediate context and multifaceted OT allusions, how are we to interpret the heavenly voice in Mark 9:7? In response to the misconceived understanding of Jesus' messiahship by the disciples, Jesus corrects it with the prediction of suffering and resurrection with the implication for discipleship (Mark 8:31–38). Jesus reveals the divine glory he shares with the Father in transfiguration. The presence of Moses and Elijah confirms that the transfiguration is a new Sinai theophany that manifests proleptically the powerful advent of the eschatological kingdom of God (Mark 9:1). Followed by Peter's wrong response to the transfiguration, the heavenly voice climaxes the transfiguration event by confirming that Jesus is God's beloved Son. He is the Messiah who is beyond the eschatological royal messiah that Peter and his Jewish contemporaries anticipated. In its immediate context, the command for the

---

381–82; Lee, *Transfiguration*, 29.

115. Apart from Johansson, a group of other scholars also question Deut 18:5 as the allusion to Mark 9:7. Here are some samples listed by Johansson. Steichele, *Leidende Sohn Gottes*, 173, 178; Gundry, *Mark*, 461; Öhler, "Verklärung," 214.

116. Evans is open to the possibility of echoing Deut 18:15 in Mark 9:7. He concludes that it "would be consistent with the popular opinion earlier expressed in 8:28 that Jesus was "one of the prophets." Evans, *Mark*, 38. However, the Markan narrative clearly indicates that Jesus is not one of the prophets (Mark 8:38–39).

117. Öhler, "Verklärung," 214; Johansson, "Jesus and God," 135.

118. Johansson, "Jesus and God," 130, 138.

119. Johansson, "Jesus and God," 136–38; Boring, "Markan Christology," 451–71.

120. Marcus, *Way of the Lord*, 92. See also Watts, "Mark," 188.

disciples to listen to Jesus functions to affirm Jesus' words about suffering, the resurrection, and discipleship (Mark 8:31-38).[121]

The transfiguration event finishes with the disciples seeing Jesus alone, accompanied by the messianic secrecy (Mark 9:8-9). While the transfiguration clearly marks the revelation of Jesus' identity in tandem with the kingdom power in the middle of the Markan narrative, Jesus' mission and the full revelation of his identity still await the crucifixion and resurrection. Even the disciples who have experienced the theophany do not fully understand what they witnessed until the resurrection. However, the heavenly voice they heard plays the key role in the framework of the whole narrative of Mark, as we will explore further.

Psalm 2 in the Markan Narrative

Having examined the use of Ps 2:7 in the baptism and transfiguration of Jesus, now we need to synthesize the function of Ps 2:7 in the entire narrative of Mark. First, the passages that contain two allusions to Ps 2:7 (Mark 1:9-11; 9:2-8) with the passage around the Roman centurion's confession (Mark 15:34-39) which includes an echo of Ps 2:7 provide the basic framework of the whole narrative.[122] The two allusions are situated strategically in the prologue and the center of the narrative. The Son of God confession by the centurion is at the end of the narrative. The three of them share the Elijah motif, heavenly sign, and the announcement of Jesus' sonship as the following table of Bauckham illustrates.[123]

Mark 1:1-11	Mark 9:2-8	Mark 15:34-39
Baptism	Transfiguration	Death
By John	with Moses and Elijah	Elijah does not come
heavens rent (σχιζομένους)	overshadowing cloud	temple veil rent (ἐσχίσθη)

---

121. Edwards, *Mark*, 268; Strauss, *Mark*, 386.

122. Bauckham, *Jesus*, 263; Bauckham, *Who Is God*, 90. Other scholars also notice the threefold revelation of the Son of God. Some of them suggest the chiastic structure (A-B-A'). Myers, *Binding*, 391; Witherington, *Mark*, 398; Caneday, "Christ's Baptism," 78.

123. The table is simplified from the original table of Bauckham. Bauckham, "Markan Christology," 34. See also Bauckham, *Jesus*, 263-64. The similar parallels are observed by Myers, *Binding*, 390-91.

"You are my Son, the Beloved, with you I am well pleased"	"This is my Son, the Beloved; listen to him!"	"Truly this man was the Son of God"

Though the confession of Son of God by the Roman centurion (Mark 15:39) is not an allusion to Ps 2:7, it functions as an equivalent revelation of Jesus' sonship: (1) Jesus' messianic kingship is repeatedly shown in the immediate context of the centurion's confession (Mark 15:18, 26, 32). (2) We have already noticed that Mark 1:11 and 15:39 frames the entire narrative through *inclusio*.[124] Therefore, the series of revelations of Jesus' sonship climaxes in the centurion's confession. Mark portrays Jesus's sonship as it is disclosed to Jesus only in Mark 1:11. The revelation is extended to the disciples in Mark 9:7. And finally Jesus' sonship is revealed to the gentile centurion who proclaims it to "the world" after the death of Jesus.[125]

Second, according to our study, Mark uses Ps 2:7 with the wider context of Ps 2 in mind. As we have examined, Ps 2 demonstrates the two-tier kingship: the kingship of God and the kingship of his messiah. God's rule is accomplished through his anointed king. And the messiah will subjugate his opponents and establish God's kingdom. Mark's narrative also parallels the wider context of Ps 2:7. In the prologue, after the confirmation of Jesus' messiahship in Mark 1:11, the proclamation of the kingdom of God by Jesus in Mark 1:15 attests that Jesus is the messianic king who has come to inaugurate God's rule. Jesus' ensuing ministry of words and deeds manifests God's rule. Mark clearly shows that Satan and human opponents of Jesus (i.e., Jewish religious leaders) oppose God and his kingdom. In the center of Markan narrative, Jesus' messiahship is clearly confessed by Peter's confession. The revelation of Jesus' sonship confirms Jesus' messiahship and yet at the same time corrects Jewish understanding of Jewish militant messianic expectation with suffering and the resurrection motif. As the following narrative shows, Jesus' way to plunder Satan is by the cross and the resurrection (cf. Mark 3:23–27). However, the transfiguration clearly reveals that the kingdom of God Jesus brings is the eschatological fulfillment. The last revelation

124. Many scholars notice *inclusio* format in Mark 1:10–11 and 15:38–39. Some of the parallels are heaven being torn apart (σχίζω), the identification of Jesus as God's Son, and the parallel between the Spirit (πνεῦμα) in Mark 1:10 and Jesus' breathing out (ἐκπνέω). See Juel, *Master*, 34; Caneday, "Christ's Baptism," 72; Bauckham, *Who Is God*, 91–92.

125. Bauckham, "Markan Christology," 35.

of Jesus' sonship also affirms the messianic kingship of Jesus. The narrative ironies indicate Jesus is the messianic king. The heavenly signs and the confession of the Roman centurion confirm that Jesus is the Son of God (Mark 15:33, 38–39). The death on the cross is the victory over the enemy (i.e., Satan and his followers) to bring God's kingdom. The burial by Joseph Arimathea who awaits God's kingdom and the resurrection thereafter also indicate that Jesus' death on the cross is not failure but the fulfillment of the advent of God's kingdom in Jesus (Mark 15:43—16:7).

Third, Mark juxtaposes the allusion to Ps 2:7 with other allusions in such a way that the composite allusions portray Jesus as the Son of God beyond the traditional understanding. Jesus is not only the eschatological Davidic Messiah but also the divine Son of God who dies vicariously to usher in God's kingdom. The allusions to Gen 22 and Isa 42:1 added to Ps 2:7 elicit the unique characteristics of Jesus' sonship. Jesus not only fulfills the eschatological anticipation of Davidic Son of God (Ps 2:7) but also is the unique and only Son (Gen 22) who gives himself to establish God's kingdom (Isa 42:1; cf. Isa 53): Both the "beloved son" in Gen 22 and Mark 12:6 share the same motif, the death of the beloved son, in their immediate contexts. Also, Isa 42:1 should be read as a part of Deutero-Isaiah, which envisions the vicarious death and exaltation of the Servant (Isa 53) that coheres with the Markan narrative. Furthermore, we should note that Mark 15:39, which forms the framework of the Markan narrative with two Ps 2:7 allusions, comes right after Jesus' vicarious suffering. While we cannot be sure what the Roman centurion meant by confessing the Son of God, God's rending the temple veil and the built-up connotation of the term, the Son of God, in the narrative (Mark 1:11; 3:11; 5:7; 8:38; 9:7; 12:6; 13:32; 14:36) seem to support that his confession implies Jesus' divine sonship.[126] Finally, we must also notice that the allusion to Isa 64:1 ("heaven being torn apart" Isa 63:19b MT) is used with that of Ps 2:7 in the beginning and the end of the narrative. The allusion affirms that Jesus fulfills the anticipation of the new exodus. Therefore, Mark juxtaposes the new exodus motif with Jesus' sonship of Ps 2 in such a way that they strengthen the overarching theme of Mark that Jesus ushers inthe kingdom of God.

---

126. Bauckham, "Markan Christology," 34. Bauckham states Jesus' death that induces the centurion's confession as following: "The point of his radical identification with those who suffer and die in God's absence is actually the climax of the revelation of his divine identity . . . it is his self-identification with the godforsaken in his death that finally brings a human being to recognize his divine identity." Bauckham, *Jesus*, 266.

CONCLUSION

Mark specifically alludes to Ps 2:7 in Mark 1:11 and 9:7 that functions as the key framework of the whole narrative in combination with Mark 15:39. The close proximity between the three occurrences of the Son of God above and the kingdom of God language in the immediate context (Mark 1:15; 9:1; 15:43) clearly shows that Jesus' identity (i.e., the Messiah, the Son of God) and the kingdom of God are interconnected and serve as the overarching themes of Mark. Also, the revelation of Jesus' sonship to the disciples in Mark 9:7 is connected to discipleship, another overarching theme.

Having observed Ps 2 in its original context and in its Jewish interpretive tradition, we conclude that Mark takes the context of Ps 2:7 into account (God's rule through his messiah and his victory over the rebellious rulers and nations) and appropriates it just as his contemporary interpreters did. For example, Mark replaces Satan and the disobedient Jewish rulers with the rebellious rulers and the nations in Ps 2 just as his Jewish contemporaries did. Also, Mark's composite use of scriptural citations with Ps 2:7 resembles that of his contemporaries. Moreover, as his contemporary Jewish interpreters anticipated the coming of the eschatological Davidic messiah, Mark views Jesus as its fulfillment.

However, his use of Ps 2:7 goes beyond the original context of Ps 2 and the interpretive tradition of his contemporaries as he juxtaposes the allusion to Ps 2 with other Old Testament allusions (Gen 22; Isa 42:1). First, Jesus is not the militant messiah but the suffering Messiah. While the suffering Messiah motif stands out from the middle section around the transfiguration, Mark sowed its seed in the composite allusions in Mark 1:11 as the part of the framework of the narrative. However, the motif is explicit when Jesus revealed his identity and mission to the disciples. The echo of Ps 2:7 in the centurion's confession after Jesus' death climaxes the suffering Messiah motif.[127] Thus, the suffering Messiah motif is progressively revealed alongside with Jesus' messianic sonship.

Second, the allusions to Isa 64:1 and 42:1 in Mark 1:10–11 and 15:38 juxtaposed with the allusion to Ps 2:7 interweaves the new exodus with the kingdom of God through the Messiah. They share the theme of the

---

127. Hays argues that the centurion's confession answers the question of who "the Son of God" is by echoing Ps 2. He says, "The Gentile outsider, the soldier who had been the tool of 'the kings of the earth' to plot the death of the LORD's anointed, now joins the heavenly voice in naming Jesus, the crucified Messiah, as God's true Son." Hays, *Gospels*, 96.

coming of the eschatological rule of God, which forms the overarching theme of Mark. Their location in the beginning and the end of Mark corroborates their importance in the Markan narrative.

Finally, Mark employs his typical narrative skill in such a way that he adumbrates the divine sonship of Jesus in allusion to Ps 2:7 in Mark as he does in the rest of Markan narrative.[128] The allusion to Gen 22 indicates Jesus' unique filial relationship with God the Father. The immediate context of Mark 1:11 and 9:7, where the beloved Son appears, indicates that Jesus is not a mere human but the divine being (Mark 1:2–3 and 9:2–8). However, Mark never explicitly expresses Jesus' divine identity but only alludes to it as he does in other parts of his narrative (i.e., the authority to forgive sin in Mark 2:5–11 and many miracles that allude to YHWH's acts from Old Testament in Mark 4:39; 6:37–44; 48–49; 7:37; 8:6–10).

---

128 According to Chester, "whereas for much of the twentieth century the dominant view was that high Christology represented something that emerged relatively late and under Gentile or pagan influence, more recently it has been seen as coming about at an early stage and within a Jewish setting." Chester, "High Christology," 22. Just as his evaluation, more and more scholars propose that the high Christology originated from the early stage of the Christianity. For example, Richard Bauckham argues that Jesus is different from God the Father, but Jesus is worshiped by the early Christians as the equal being with God the Father because Jesus shares the divine identity, such as "God's unique sovereignty over all things" and "God unique activity of creation." According to Bauckham, the "divine identity" is fundamental to Jewish monotheism, which distinguishes God from other intermediary beings such as angels. Bauckham, *Jesus*, 18–31. Larry Hurtado is another major proponent of high Christology. His focus is how the early Christians started to worship Jesus. According to Hurtado, "God's principal agent" who worked on behalf of God could be a precedent for Jesus. But what makes Jesus unique is that, unlike other principal agents, he became the object of worship that only God could receive. Hurtado, *Lord Jesus Christ*, 47. But, the NT witnesses to Jesus show that Jesus has the divine identity greater than any angelic being. Also, Jewish monotheism should embrace broader aspects than the worship. Bauckham, "Devotion," 188–93. See also Gathercole, *Preexistent Son*, who especially claims how "I am" sayings evidence Jesus' divine status. As for Mark, the major proponent of the high Christology is Johansson. See Johansson, "Jesus and God." As for the opposing view, see Kok, "Marking a Difference," 102–24. While I am sympathetic with the efforts to find Jesus' divine identity in Mark, I must admit that Mark does not explicitly identify it as the author of the John's Gospel does. It seems that, for some reason, Mark does not overtly pronounce Jesus' divine identity. Yet, there are multiple allusions and adumbrations in Mark that witness Jesus' divine nature (i.e., the authority to forgive sin, many miracles that allude to YHWH's act in Old Testament, Jesus' messiahship beyond Davidic messiah, etc.). Therefore, it appears that it is Mark's narrative artistry to present Jesus' divine nature with allusions and implications instead of direct elucidation.

4

Psalm 118 in Mark

In the previous chapter, we have observed how Mark uses Ps 2:7 at the key junctures of Mark (i.e., the beginning, the center, and the end) as the skeleton of the Markan structure. Mark's use of Ps 2:7 underscores that Jesus is the eschatological Davidic Messiah who will bring God's kingdom and conquer his enemies by his suffering on the cross. In this chapter, we will examine how Mark uses Ps 118 at other key junctures (Jesus' entry into Jerusalem in Mark 11:9–10 and the parable of the wicked tenants in Mark 12:10–11) of the Markan narrative. This chapter will demonstrate that Mark uses Ps 118 in such a way that Jesus brings God's kingdom as the Davidic Messiah, and the kingdom he brings will be the new exodus and the beginning of the new temple.

Mark's Gospel identifies two clear quotations from Ps 118. The first quotation, Ps 118:25–26, is located in Mark 11:9–10, the end of Jesus' entry into Jerusalem where he will fulfill his threefold prediction about his death and resurrection (Mark 8:31–32; 9:30–31; 10:32–34). The second quotation, Ps 118:22–23, is found in Mark 12:10–11, the end of the parable of the wicked tenants, as Jesus' answer to the Jewish leaders who challenged his authority to cleanse the temple. This chapter will examine Mark's use of Ps 118:25–26 and 22–23 and discuss how the passages function in the narrative structure of Mark. Just like the previous chapter, this research will investigate (1) the textual form of the quotations, (2) the interpretation of Ps 118, (3) Ps 118 in the canonical context of the Psalter and in other OT texts, and (4) Ps 118 in the Second Temple literature before we delve into Mark's use of Ps 118 in the Markan narrative.

TEXTUAL FORM OF PSALM 118 IN MARK

In the first quotation from Ps 118(117):25–26, Mark uses a mixture of Hebrew and Greek texts as shown in the chart below.

Psalm 118:25–26 (MT)	Psalm 117:25–26 (LXX)	Mark 11:9–10 (NA 28)
הוֹשִׁיעָה נָּא (Ps 118:25a) בָּרוּךְ הַבָּא בְּשֵׁם יְהוָה (Ps 118:26a)	σῶσον δή (Ps 117:25a) εὐλογημένος ὁ ἐρχόμενος ἐν ὀνόματι κυρίου (Ps 117:26a)	ὡσαννά· εὐλογημένος ὁ ἐρχόμενος ἐν ὀνόματι κυρίου·(Mark 11:9b) ὡσαννά (Mark 11:10b)
Save! We pray (Ps 118:25a) Blessed is the one who comes in the name of Yahweh! (Ps 118:26a)	Save! Indeed (Ps 117:25a) Blessed is the one who comes in the name of the LORD (Ps 117:26a)	Save! We pray. Blessed is the one who comes in the name of the LORD (Mark 11:9b) Save! We pray. (Mark 11:10b)

Ὡσαννά (Mark 11:9b, 10b) is the Greek transliteration of הוֹשִׁיעָה נָּא (Ps 118:25a). Εὐλογημένος ὁ ἐρχόμενος ἐν ὀνόματι κυρίου (Mark 11:9b) agrees verbatim with Ps 117:26a (LXX). Compared with the Hebrew text, the Greek text seems to be the literal translation of the Hebrew text (Ps 118:26a).

Psalm 118:22–23 (MT)	Psalm 117:22–23 (LXX)	Mark 12:10–11 (NA 28)
אֶבֶן מָאֲסוּ הַבּוֹנִים הָיְתָה לְרֹאשׁ פִּנָּה: מֵאֵת יְהוָה הָיְתָה זֹּאת הִיא נִפְלָאת בְּעֵינֵינוּ:	λίθον ὃν ἀπεδοκίμασαν οἱ οἰκοδομοῦντες οὗτος ἐγενήθη εἰς κεφαλὴν γωνίας παρὰ κυρίου ἐγένετο αὕτη καὶ ἔστιν θαυμαστὴ ἐν ὀφθαλμοῖς ἡμῶν	λίθον ὃν ἀπεδοκίμασαν οἱ οἰκοδομοῦντες οὗτος ἐγενήθη εἰς κεφαλὴν γωνίας·παρὰ κυρίου ἐγένετο αὕτη καὶ ἔστιν θαυμαστὴ ἐν ὀφθαλμοῖς ἡμῶν
The stone that the builders rejected has become the cornerstone. This is from the Lord. It is wonderful in our eyes.	The stone that the builders rejected has become the cornerstone. This is from the Lord and is wonderful in our eyes.	The stone that the builders rejected has become the cornerstone. This is from the Lord and is wonderful in our eyes.

As for the second quotation, Ps 118(7):22–23 in Mark 12:10–11, the reader finds that Ps 117:22–23 (LXX) agrees with Mark 12:10–11 verbatim. The Greek text is the literal translation of the Hebrew text except for the use of demonstrative pronouns. On the one hand, by adding οὗτος, the Greek text emphasizes that the rejected stone became the cornerstone, while the Hebrew text does not have any equivalent demonstrative pronouns. On the other hand, the Hebrew text has an additional demonstrative pronoun, הִיא, while the Greek text uses only one demonstrative pronoun, αὕτη, with a connective conjunction, καί. Therefore, the two quotations of Ps 118 utilized in Mark are virtually the same as the LXX translation, except the Hebrew transliteration included the word ὡσαννά. At the same time, the LXX text of the quotations is similar to the corresponding Hebrew text. Therefore, this research will pay close attention to both the LXX and the MT texts in the following section.

INTERPRETATION OF PSALM 118

Sitz im Leben and Structure

Psalm 118 is the last psalm of the so-called "Egyptian Hallel" (Pss 113–18), which speaks about the exodus from Egypt motif.[1] Psalm 118 was sung at the end of Passover meal as the Jews drank "the fourth cup of celebratory wine."[2] Interpreters have proposed diverse views on the origin and genre of the psalm, such as a liturgy of individual thanksgiving,[3] annual coronation ritual of the Davidic king,[4] the thanksgiving psalm of the returnees from the exile,[5] some events occurred during Hellenistic period,[6] and finally, the Davidic king who leads the procession to give thanks to YHWH after military victory.[7]

Regardless of the identity of the psalmist, scholars tend to agree that the psalm may have been originally used for the liturgical temple

---

1. Vaillancourt, "Psalm 118," 721. According VanGemeren, "The Hallel psalms are found in three separate collections: the 'Egyptian Hallel' (113–118), the 'Great Hallel' (120–136), and the concluding Hallel psalms (146–150)." VanGemeren, *Psalms*, 831. See also deClaissé-Walford, Jacobson, and Tanner, *Psalms*, 864.

2. deClaissé-Walford, Jacobson, and Tanner, *Psalms*, 864.

3. Gunkel, *Psalmen*, 504–11; Drijvers, *Psaumes*, 192; Haglund, *Historical Motifs*, 45.

4. Mowinckel, *Psalms*, 180–81; Sanders, "New Testament," 180–85; Eaton, *Kingship*, 129–30.

5. Kalt, *Psalms*, 451; Goulder, *Psalms*, 182–91.

6. Berder, *Pierre*, 80–89.

7. They argue that the psalmist is the Davidic king because the language of the psalm (i.e., vv. 10–12) may imply YHWH's deliverance of Israel from the military assault of the neighboring nations. Dahood, *Psalms III*, 155; Allen, *Psalms 101–150*, 123; Tucker and Grant, *Psalms*, 676.

procession, just as Pss 15 and 24 were in the early stages of Israel's history.[8] Later, the postexilic community might have weaved the older pieces of the psalm into its present form to express thanks to YHWH in reflecting God's deliverance in the past and hope for his deliverance once again in their dire situation.[9] Though the psalmist is an individual, the psalm is sung in a communal context to invoke thanks for God's past salvation and hope for his continuous salvific acts for his people.[10] The basic structure of Ps 118 can be divided into four areas: (A) introduction–call to praise God (v. 1) with antiphonal responses (vv. 2–4); (B) thanks for God's salvific acts in the past (vv. 5–18) with two interludes (vv. 8–9 and vv. 15–16); (C) praise and supplication inside the temple (vv. 19–28); and (D) the conclusion—the call to praise God (v. 29).

Exegesis

In A (vv. 1–4), the psalmist urges Israel, more specifically the house of Aaron (i.e., the priests) and those who fear YHWH (i.e., the worshiping community), to confess YHWH's everlasting covenantal faithfulness.[11] In B (vv. 5–18), the psalmist explains YHWH's faithfulness to his covenant. First, verses 5–7 are the summary of the psalmist's experience of God's salvation and inferences from it.[12] When the psalmist cried to YHWH out of הַמֵּצַר (literally "the distress", here in the context of a military war), YHWH answered by delivering him.[13] Verses 8–9 generalize the psalmist's personal inference derived from his experiences in verses 6–7:[14] "It is better to take refuge in YHWH than to trust in humans" (v. 8), or (even) "in leaders" (v. 9).

---

8. Kraus, *Psalms 60–150*, 394–96; deClaissé-Walford, et al., *Psalms*, 864.

9. Kraus, *Psalms 60–150*, 394–96; Tucker and Grant, *Psalms*, 676; Ross, *Psalms 90–150*, 444.

10. Tucker and Grant, *Psalms*, 676.

11. The house of Aaron and those who fear YHWH seem to be the subgroups of Israel in a liturgical context. We can find the same usage in another Egyptian Hallel, Ps 115:8–10, 12–13. Also, Psalms 15:4; 22:23–24 attest that those who fear YHWH may refer to the Israelite worship community. Sander, "Bringing," 172–73.

12. Goldingay, *Psalms 90–150*, 356.

13. Vaillancourt, "Psalm 118," 724.

14. Goldingay, *Psalms 90–150*, 357; Tucker and Grant, *Psalms*, 679.

The psalmist offers a more detailed account of his distress and YHWH's salvation in verses 10–18.[15] All the nations pose a fierce threat on the psalmist to the point he cannot escape by his own strength.[16] However, the psalmist defeats his enemies with YHWH's help (vv. 10–12).[17] Verses 13–14 are thematically parallel with verses 10–12, as they look at the enemy's attack and YHWH's salvation. Verse 14 is an extended description of YHWH's help in verse 13.[18] Quoting Exod 15:2a, the psalmist likens his experience of God's salvation from the nations to God's salvation of Israel from the Egyptian army.[19] The threefold repetition of "Yahweh's right hand" that is lifted and does a valiant thing (vv. 15b–16) communicates the mighty saving act of God, just as he did to the Egyptian army (Exod 15:6a, 6b, 12).[20] After the interlude in verses 15–16, the psalmist ends the account of his distress and salvation with his resolution and the "theocentric understanding of suffering" (vv. 17–18).[21]

Praise and supplication transpire inside the temple (vv. 19–28).[22] Verses 19–21 are the psalmist's praise as he enters the gate of the temple. As one of the righteous who experienced the deliverance of God, the psalmist enters the temple gate and praises YHWH's saving act.[23] Verses 22–25 are praise from the worshipers concerning what God has done to the psalmist (vv. 22–24) and their supplication (v. 25). The section begins with the proverbial saying, "The stone that the builders rejected has become the cornerstone" (v. 22).[24] The imagery derives from how a stone

---

15. Goldingay, *Psalms 90–150*, 358.

16. Estes, *Psalms 73–150*, 391.

17. While interpreters differ in their interpretation of the verb, מוּל ("cut off"), most agree that the phrase connotes victory over the psalmist's enemy by God's help. Kraus, *Psalms 60–150*, 397–98; VanGemeren, *Psalms*, 854; Goldingay, *Psalms 90–150*, 358; deClaissé-Walford, et al., *Psalms*, 867–68; Estes, *Psalms 73–150*, 391.

18. Goldingay, *Psalms 90–150*, 359; Ross, *Psalms 90–150*, 451.

19. Kraus, *Psalms 60–150*, 398; VanGemeren, *Psalms*, 854–55; Goldingay, *Psalms 90–150*, 358; Ross, *Psalms 90–150*, 451; Tucker and Grant, *Psalms*, 681; Estes, *Psalms 73–150*, 392. Compare Ps 118:14 (עָזִּי וְזִמְרָת יָהּ וַיְהִי־לִי לִישׁוּעָה) with Exod 15:2 (עָזִּי וְזִמְרָת יָהּ וַיְהִי־לִי לִישׁוּעָה).

20. Tucker and Grant, *Psalms*, 681.

21. Kraus, *Psalms 60–150*, 398; See also, Tucker and Grant, *Psalms*, 682.

22. The shift also moves from the first-person confession of the psalmist (vv. 5–18) to the voices of several participants of the temple liturgy (vv.19–28) such as the psalmist, priests, and the worshiping congregation. Tucker and Grant, *Psalms*, 682.

23. Hossfeld and Zenger, *Psalms 3*, 328; Tucker and Grant, *Psalms*, 683; Estes, *Psalms 73–150*, 394.

24. Kraus, *Psalms 60–150*, 400; Ross, *Psalms 90–150*, 453; Tucker and Grant, *Psalms*,

not valued by builders could be used as an important part of another building in ancient Israel.[25] The saying is analogous to the experience of the psalmist as the representative of Israel, who was saved and exalted by God after having been disregarded and almost destroyed by the great nations.[26] The worshiping community recognizes that YHWH has done this wondrous act (נִפְלָאת) of salvation,[27] and the people rejoice over it, as Israel did in Exod 15 (vv. 23–24).[28] Followed by the praise for YHWH's salvific work in the past, the worshipers desperately ask YHWH to do the wonerous salvific work once again so that they may prosper (v. 25).[29] Therefore, this prayer reflects the urgent desire of the postexilic community for YHWH's intervention.[30]

Verses 26–28 are the combination of the announcement of blessing (v. 26) and the responsive praise of those who are blessed (vv. 27–28). The priests pronounce YHWH's blessing on the psalmist (i.e., "the one who is coming") and the worshipers led by the psalmist (i.e., plural "you," v. 26).[31] The shared confession from both the worshipers and the psalmist that "Yahweh is God" (vv. 27a; 28a) suggests Exod 15:2[32] Just as Israel did

---

683. The LXX (λίθον ὃν ἀπεδοκίμασαν οἱ οἰκοδομοῦντες οὗτος ἐγενήθη εἰς κεφαλὴν γωνίας (Ps 117:22 LXX) is very similar to MT except that λίθον is referred to again by the demonstrative pronoun, οὗτος. Thus, it emphasizes the rejected stone as the cornerstone. Some scholars contend that the stone is not the cornerstone but the keystone. For example, see Cahill, "Not a Cornerstone," 345–57. Whether the stone is the cornerstone or keystone, it is evident in the context that the rejected stone becomes the most important part of a building.

25. Goldingay, *Psalms 90–150*, 362; Ross, *Psalms 90–150*, 453; Tucker and Grant, *Psalms*, 683–84.

26. Goldingay, *Psalms 90–150*, 362; Ross, *Psalms 90–150*, 453; Estes, *Psalms 73–150*, 394–95.

27. Berlin, "Critical Notes," 568.

28. Tucker and Grant, *Psalms*, 684.

29. The literal translation of Ps 118:25 MT, "Please, Yahweh, save! We pray. Please, Yahweh, make (us) prosper! We pray," clearly exhibits the desperateness of the postexilic community. LXX is less dramatic than MT (ὦ κύριε σῶσον δή ὦ κύριε εὐόδωσον δή), but still demonstrates their urgency.

30. Mark, *Meine Stärke*, 268; James, "Narrow Straits," 185; Ross, *Psalms 90–150*, 455; Tucker and Grant, *Psalms*, 685.

31. Goldingay, *Psalms 90–150*, 363; Estes, *Psalms 73–150*, 396. Estes notes, "In several biblical passages coming in a person's name means to come with designated authority from that person." Thus, he argues, "If the psalmist is the Davidic king, then he is the Lord's designated representative in Zion." Estes, *Psalms 73–150*, 396.

32. Tucker and Grant, *Psalms*, 685–86. Psalm 118:27b ("bind the festival offering with cords to the horns of the altar") appears to indicate the readiness of the "thanksgiving offering." Estes, *Psalms 73–150*, 396.

in Exod 15:2, the psalmist confesses that YHWH is his God whom he praises for salvation.[33] The psalm concludes with verse 29, "Give thanks to Yahweh, for he is good, and his covenantal faithfulness is forever."

In conclusion, the psalm's theme is the psalmist's praise to YHWH's covenantal faithfulness, that is, salvation from his distress. The prevalent military imageries throughout the psalm strongly indicate that the psalmist is portrayed as the Davidic king.[34] Thus, it is likely that the psalm was composed originally before the exile but later used by the postexilic community in their worship.[35] The psalm conveys the picture of the Davidic royal figure leading a procession (i.e., the nation of Israel) to the temple for thanksgiving (vv. 19–28; cf. vv.1–4).[36]

Ancient Variants

As for the witness of Ps 118 among ancient translations other than the MT, the most noticeable feature in the LXX is the tendency to harmonize a certain text with Ps 118.[37] However, the harmonization tendency does not affect our interpretation of Ps 118 significantly. Despite the presence of many variant readings in the LXX, we do not find any variant reading that may influence the use of Ps 118 in Mark meaningfully.

The Targum of Ps 118 provides more specific interpretation in several passages.[38] The most striking feature of the Targum of Ps 118 is found

---

33. Mark, *Meine Stärke*, 494.

34. McKelvey, "Messianic Nature," 46–49; Vaillancourt, *Psalm 118*, 725. Jamie Grant lists five "textual indications" that support the identity of the psalmist as Davidic king: (1) the military battle as the context of the deliverance, (2) the refusal to trust in princes, that is, foreign rulers (v.9), (3) the hostility of the nations (i.e., military conflict, vv. 10–12), (4) the "representative nature" of the psalmist, and (5) the association of the blessing formula (v. 26a) with "kingship in the OT." Grant, *King*, 127–28.

35. Dahood, *Psalms 101–150*, 156; Kraus, *Psalms 60–150*, 394–96; Tucker and Grant, *Psalms*, 676; Ross, *Psalms 90–150*, 444; Vaillancourt, "Psalm 118," 725.

36. Vaillancourt says, "In light of the communal element in vv.1–4, it is clear from the outset—in addition to vv. 19–28—that the deliverance recounted in vv. 5–18 is an occasion for national celebration. This is the first hint that the narrator is likely to be viewed as the Davidic king, for what other individual within Israel could experience a crisis and deliverance that would affect the entire community so directly?" Vaillancourt, *Multifaceted Saviour*, 142.

37. Constant, "Psaume 118," 33.

38. For instance, it is the psalmist's sin that pushed him hard (Ps 118:13). The gate of YHWH is translated as "the gate of the house of sanctuary of the LORD" (Ps 118:20). Stec, *Targum of Psalms*, 209–11. The following citations of the Targum of Ps 118 are from Stec's translation.

in verses 22–29. The paraphrased translation of the Targum clearly places David at center stage. The Aramaic word, טליא ("the youth" or "boy"; Ps 118:22) appears to be derived from "the Hebrew wordplay" between אֶבֶן ("stone") and בֵּן ("son").[39] The Targum not only replaces the stone that the builders rejected with David but also confirms his kingship (Ps 118:22). The names of the characters who praise antiphonally also support the idea that the Targum of Ps 118:22–29 celebrates "David's role in the building up of the kingdom and in the preparing the building of the temple."[40] Therefore, the Targum of Ps 118 evidences one example of the Jewish hermeneutical tradition in the first century that relates Ps 118 to the Davidic messiah.[41]

In conclusion, despite the diverse interpretations concerning the identity of the psalmist, we argue that the Davidic king is the most plausible figure. Psalm 118 portrays how the Davidic king experienced God's salvation from his enemies and enters the gate of the temple with the song of victory. The comparison among the various ancient versions of Ps 118 yields the conclusion that there are not significant differences in the text. However, it is noticeable that Targum clearly identifies the psalmist as the Davidic messiah. Therefore, we can tentatively conclude that Ps 118 describes the Davidic messiah who has experienced the salvation from his enemies that alludes to the exodus. He now enters the temple with the worshiping community. The psalm seems to reflect the postexilic community's anticipation for the coming of an eschatological messianic figure like David who will lead them toward the new exodus by saving them from their oppression. The ultimate goal is to worship YHWH in the temple.

PSALM 118 IN OTHER OT TEXTS

Psalm 118 has several intertextual links to other Old Testament texts.[42] However, due to the limit of the scope of this paper, this research cannot

---

39. Hatina, *In Search of a Context*, 322.
40. Hatina, *In Search of a Context*, 322.
41. Brunson, *Psalm 118*, 41.
42. Readers who are interested in the full list of the Old Testament intertexts to Ps 118 are advised to refer to Vaillancourt's book. He helpfully provides the table that lists related "key word links" in "the [w]ider Book of Psalms" and "the [w]ider Hebrew Bible" to Ps 118. Vaillancourt, *Multifaceted Saviour*, 197–99.

treat all the Old Testament intertexts in this section.⁴³ This research has already observed some texts from Exodus in the exegesis of Ps 118. According to Vaillancourt, those texts from Exodus are most frequently related to Ps 118.⁴⁴ This confirms that the exodus motif is predominant in Ps 118. Also, Ps 118 has some Exodus intertexts that overlap with Isaiah intertexts (i.e., יָהּ in Ps 118:5, 14, 17, 18, 19; Exod 15:2; 17:16; Isa 12:2; 26:4 and עָזִּי וְזִמְרָת יָהּ וַיְהִי־לִי לִישׁוּעָה in Ps 118:14; Exod 15:2a; Isa 12:2b). These Isaiah intertexts (Isa 12:2 and 26:4) are related to each other and convey the new exodus motif that is connected to the Davidic messiah motif.⁴⁵ Therefore, it appears that Ps 118 reappropriated Exodus and Isaiah texts to express the exodus and the new exodus motifs in tandem with the Davidic messiah motif.

---

43. Though Vaillancourt's list is quite exhaustive, some of the key words he suggests are not contextually linked. Therefore, this writer only utilized some of the Old Testament texts from his list that are contextually relevant to Ps 118.

44. i.e., Exod 33:19 (טוֹב, Ps 118:1, 29), 9:6–8, 20, 26–27, 35; 18:1, 8–9, 12, 21, 25 (three worshiping groups, Ps 118:2, 3, 4), 15:2; 17:16 (יָהּ, Ps 118:5, 14, 17, 18, 19), 15:2a (עָזִּי וְזִמְרָת יָהּ וַיְהִי־לִי לִישׁוּעָה, Ps 118:14), 16:16; 18:7 (אֹהֶל, Ps 18:15), 15:6, 12 (יָמִין, Ps 18:15, 16), 14:8, 16; 15:2; 17:11 (רוּם, Ps 118:16, 28), 15:11 (פֶּלֶא, Ps 118:23), 14:13 (הַיּוֹם עָשָׂה יְהוָה, Ps 118:24), 13:21 (אוֹר, Ps 118:27) from Vaillancourt, *Multifaceted Saviour*, 197–99.

45. First, Isa 12 is connected to Isa 11:11–16 by the same temporal phrase: "in that day" (בַּיּוֹם הַהוּא, Isa 11:11; 12:1). The context shows it is the eschatological day of the new exodus. Motyer, *Isaiah*, 127; Smith, *Isaiah 1–39*, 279–80. Smith pays attention to the "linguistic connection between the praise of Isaiah 12 and the Israelites' song in Exod 15. Smith, *Isaiah 1–39*, 280–81. Another בַּיּוֹם הַהוּא in Isa 11:10 links the new exodus motif to the vision of the Davidic messiah's reign in Isa 11:1–10. Motyer, *Isaiah*, 125; Smith, *Isaiah 1–39*, 275. Second, Isa 26:1–6 is the song about YHWH's kingdom established in "Zion/Jerusalem" after his judgment on earthly rulers (cf. 24:21–25:12). Hibbard, *Intertextuality*, 124. While Isa 26:1–6 does not have a clear quotation from Exod 15 like Isa 12:2, there are some common motifs and intertextual clues among Exod 15, Isa 12, and 26:1–6: (1) Isa 26 is an "eschatological song, much like 12:ff" (i.e., בַּיּוֹם הַהוּא, Isa 12:1,4; 26:1). Childs, *Isaiah*, 190. (2) Isaiah 26:1–6 shares many lexical correspondences with Isa 12:1–6. i.e., יְשׁוּעָה (Isa 12:2,3; 26:1), בָּטַח (Isa. 12:2; 26:3, 4), עַז (Isa. 12:2; 26:1), נִשְׂגָּב (Isa. 12:4; 26:5), Hibbard, *Intertextuality*, 129. (3) Especially, the fact that the archaic word יָהּ is used frequently in Exod 15 and is only found in Isa 12:2 and 26:4 corroborates the correlation among Exod 15, Isa 12, and Isa 26:1–6. Isaiah 38:12 witnesses consecutive occurrences of יָהּ (i.e., יָהּ יָהּ). However, the double use of יָהּ seems to derive from a "scribal error" (i.e., Scribes inadvertently read יְהוָה as יָהּ יָהּ because they were confused between י and ה). Roberts, *First Isaiah*, 481; NET notes, Isa 38:11. There are additional evidences that support the idea that Isa 12 and 26 are intertexts of Ps 118: (1) Ps 118, Isa 12, and Exod 15 share some common themes. Constant, "Psaume 118," 135–36. (2) There is a close linguistic correspondence between Isa 26:2 and Ps 118:19–20. Hibbard, *Intertextuality*, 126.

Finally, we examine the Old Testament links to our target text, Ps 118:22–23, 25–26. First, we witness another Davidic messiah motif in Ps 118:26a, הַבָּא בְּשֵׁם יְהוָה ("the one who comes in the name of Yahweh"), which alludes to אָנֹכִי בָא־אֵלֶיךָ בְּשֵׁם יְהוָה ("I am coming to you in the name of Yahweh") in 1 Sam 17:45, where David is coming to Goliath to save Israel in the name of YHWH.[46] Just as David delivered Israel in the name of YHWH (1 Sam 17:45), the Davidic king comes in the name of YHWH with victory (Ps 118:26).[47]

Second, some scholars propose a parallel between Zech 4:7 and Ps 118:22.[48] Zechariah 4:6b–10 is a prophecy about Zerubbabel rebuilding the second temple. While scholars do not agree on the meaning of הָאֶבֶן הָרֹאשָׁה (Zech 4:7)—whether it is a capstone that completes the temple rebuilding or a cornerstone laid as a temple foundation—the same expression used for building imagery clearly corresponds to Ps 118:22.[49] If Ps 118:22 alludes to Zech 4:7, considering the theme of the temple rebuilding in Zech 4, Ps 118:22 could relate to the temple building.

PSALM 118 IN THE CANONICAL CONTEXT OF THE PSALTER

Having examined the text of Ps 118 and other related texts in Old Testament, we must see if the conclusions we have drawn so far would cohere with the broader canonical context of the psalm. Examining the canonical context of the psalm helps us overcome the atomistic interpretation of the psalm and may shed further light on the use of the psalm in Mark. In chapter 3, we observed that (1) Pss 1–2 serve as the introduction to the

---

46. Out of thirty occurrences of the phrase בְּשֵׁם יְהוָה in Old Testament (i.e., 1 Sam 17:45; 20:42; 1 Kgs 18:32; 22:16; 2 Kgs 2:24; 5:11; 1 Chron 21:19; 2 Chron 18:15; 33:18; Ps 20:7; 116:4, 13, 17; 118:10, 11, 12, 26; 119:55; 129:8; Isa 50:10; Jer 11:21; 26:9, 16, 20; 51:16; Joel 3:5; Amos 6:10; Zeph 3:9, 12; Zech 13:3), only 1 Sam 17:45 and Ps 118:10, 11, 12, 26 indicate the victory over the enemy by God's help. Apart from 1 Sam 17:45 and Ps 118, the verbs of other occurrences are such as "speak," "call," "prophesy," "trust" (in the name of YHWH).

47. We have already observed that Ps 118:10–12 expresses how Davidic king defeats his enemy by God's help. And Ps 118:26a is the praise of the worship community for the Davidic king who comes after the victory against his enemy by God's help (Ps 118:10–12). Therefore, both 1 Sam 17:45 and Ps 118 have either David or Davidic king as the subject of the victory.

48. Berder, *Pierre*, 135–40; Stead, *Intertextuality*, 179; Hossfeld and Zenger, *Psalm 3*, 242.

49. Peterson, *Behold*, 70–71.

whole Psalter, and (2) the two-tier kingship of YHWH and Davidic king continues from the beginning to the end of the Psalter. With these two observations in mind, in this chapter, we will focus on (1) the intertexts of Ps 118 in the Psalter, (2) Book V of the Psalter (Pss 107–50), especially Pss 107–18, (3) the Egyptian Hallel (Pss 113–18).

Psalm 118 in the Entire Psalter

As for the key word links in the wider book of Psalms suggested by Vaillancourt, three things emerge: (1) There are many other Psalms that share the common key words of praise and thanks with Ps 118.[50] This is not surprising since Ps 118 is a thanksgiving psalm. (2) The three worshiping groups in Ps 118:2, 3, 4 appear in Ps 135:19–20. The similar context—the exodus story and the anticipation of the new exodus—shared by Ps 135 and Ps 118 is probably the reason why these psalms have the same worshiping groups.[51] (3) The context of צֶדֶק in Ps 118:19 ("the gate of righteousness") is a metaphorical expression about entering God's sanctuary after he delivers the psalmist (and God's people). Many Davidic psalms relate צֶדֶק to God's deliverance (i.e., Pss 4:2; 7:9; 9:4; 17:1, 15; 18:21, 25; 35:24, 27; 37:6; 40:10), which corroborate that the psalmist of Ps 118, who enters the gate of righteousness after experiencing God's salvation, is the Davidic king.

Book V of the Psalter

In the previous chapter, we have briefly argued that the Davidic king motif does not disappear in Book V (Pss 107–50). This section will defend the argument in detail. Many proposals on the structure of Book V may be divided into two kinds. Some scholars analyze the structure of Book V according to the locations of הוֹדוּ and הַלְלוּ־יָהּ.[52] The other group

---

50. i.e., הוֹדוּ in Pss 118:1; 30:35; 33:2; 97:12; 100:4; 105:1; 106:1; 118:1, 29; 136:1, 2, 3, 26, חַסְדּוֹ לְעוֹלָם in Pss 118:1, 2, 3, 4, 29; 100:5; 106:1; 136, et al; 138:2. from Vaillancourt, *Multifaceted Saviour*, 197.

51. Psalms 114–15, where the same three worshiping groups appear (i.e., Ps 115:9–13), also have a similar context (i.e., the exodus story and the anticipation of the new exodus).

52. Wilson, "Shaping," 78–79; Kratz, "Tora Davids," 26; Allen, *Psalms 101–150*, 75–76, 80.

of scholars eclectically structure Book V.[53] In the midst of the diverse views on the structure of Book V, Wilson's advice deserves attention. Wilson rightly warns that any proposals about the macro structure of the Psalter should result from a rigorous "analysis of the psalms in question in terms of their linguistic, thematic, literary, and theological links and relationships."[54] As for the analysis of the macro structure of Book V, Michael K. Snearly's book *The Return of the King* is an excellent example that follows Wilson's advice.[55]

Snearly recognizes that Book V is the continuation of the literary structure of the whole Psalter. He rightly argues that Pss 1–2 are the introduction of the whole Psalter.[56] He identifies the key words *king*, *Torah*, and *Zion* in Pss 1–2, which recur and form the main message in Book V. According to him, "[T]hey picture the ideal ruler of God's people."[57] Based on his criteria that demonstrate "the links between neighboring passages,"[58] Snearly analyzes the structure of Book V as follows: (1) Pss 107–18 consistently proclaim that YHWH's covenantal faithfulness (חֶסֶד) to the Davidic kingship is eternal (עוֹלָם) (2).[59] The similarities among Ps 1, Deut 17:14–20, and Ps 119 strongly suggest that Ps 119 represents an ideal Davidic king who abides by the Torah.[60] Therefore, just as Pss 107–18, Ps 119 testifies to "the re-emergence of the ideal Davidic ruler within the storyline of Psalms."[61] (3) Psalms 120–37 highlights that YHWH has not forsaken his Davidic king on Zion (cf. Ps 2).[62] (4) As the conclusion of Book V, Pss 138–45 reverberate the two-tier kingship of YHWH and

---

53. i.e., Zenger, "Composition," 98; Grant, *King*, 243.

54. Wilson, "Understanding," 48.

55. Snearly, *Return of the King*.

56. Snearly, *Return of the King*, 88.

57. Snearly, *Return of the King*, 94.

58. His five criteria are as follows: "(1) key-word links; (2) distant parallelism (e.g. *dis legomena*, parallelism of syntactical constructions, *inclusion*); (3) common superscriptions; (4) common theme; and (5) structural parallels." Snearly, *Return of the King*, 37.

59. Snearly, *Return of the King*, 117–26. Snearly evidences the unity of Pss 107–18 with the double *inclusio* (הֹדוּ לַיהוָה כִּי־טוֹב כִּי לְעוֹלָם חַסְדּוֹ, Pss 107:1; 118:1, 29) and how the key linking words, חֶסֶד and עוֹלָם, unite the Pss 107–18. See also Davis, "Contextual Analysis," 8; Crutchfield, "Circles of Context," 84. As for the relationship of the eternal covenant with the Davidic king, see Grant, *King*, 128–29.

60. Snearly, *Return of the King*, 137–39.

61. Snearly, *Return of the King*, 139.

62. Snearly, *Return of the King*, 153–54.

Davidic king and the submission of foreign rulers in Pss 1–89.⁶³ Finally, Pss 146–50 are the conclusion to the whole Psalter because the climatic praise of Pss 146–50 (i.e., הַלְלוּ־יָהּ superscriptions) and their similarities with Pss 1–2 indicate that the unit (Pss 146–50) concludes the Psalter's storyline: "The story of a heavenly king and his earthly representative who form a people in the midst of a hostile world and extend their kingdom over the unruly nations."⁶⁴

As the subtitle of his book reveals, Snearly concludes that the editorial activity of the Psalter, especially the arrangement of Book V, reflects the messianic expectation of Jewish community in Second Temple period.⁶⁵ His thesis corroborates that of Mitchell and others, who argue against Wilson in that Book V clearly manifests the reemergence of the Davidic messiah who will rule the nations from Zion as God's vice-regent.⁶⁶ In the midst of no Davidic king during Second Temple period, the message of the Psalter reflects that the postexilic Jewish community anticipated the advent of a Davidic messiah who would demonstrate YHWH's rule.⁶⁷

Egyptian Hallel (Pss 113–18)

We have observed that Pss 107–18 consistently proclaim that YHWH's covenantal faithfulness (חֶסֶד) to the Davidic kingship is eternal (עוֹלָם). Many scholars notice the unity among Pss 113–18.⁶⁸ As a unified group of psalms, the Egyptian Hallel exhibits a messianic hope interwoven into the exodus (and the new exodus) motif.⁶⁹ There are numerous lexical and

---

63. Snearly, *Return of the King*, 155–60, 168–69.

64. Snearly, *Return of the King*, 181. See also, Wilson, "Shape" 132–33; Zenger, "Fleisch," 1–27.

65. Snearly, *Return of the King*, 189–95.

66. Mitchell, *Message*, 78–79; Kim, "Psalm 110," 94–138.

67. Childs, *Introduction*, 517; Mitchell, *Message*, 87–88; Waltke and Yu, *Old Testament Theology*, 890; Snearly, *Return of the King*, 190. In light of this broader context of Ps 118 and the historical background of the editorial activity of the Psalter, Vaillancourt's statement is accepted: "It is easy to see how key phrases from Psalm 118—such as 'the coming one' (v. 26) and 'the rejected stone' (vv. 22–24)—along with its images—especially a royal figure of salvation who led the jubilant victors into YHWH's presence with thankful song—could have all been cast forward as typologically prophetic oracles about the coming Davidic messiah." Vaillancourt, "Psalm 118," 728.

68. Schröten, *Entstehung*, 111. See also, Prinsloo, "Šeʾôl," 756; Trublet, "Approche canonique," 356–63; Prinsloo, "Unit Delimitation," 232–63; Hayes, "Unity," 148–51.

69. While Ps 113 starts with a general praise of YHWH, the basis of the praise—the reversal of the "fortunes of people and the nations"—derives from Hannah's song that

thematic parallels between Pss 113–17 and Ps 118.⁷⁰ As a unified unit, Pss 113–18 coherently interweave the exodus (and the new exodus) and the Davidic Messiah motifs.

Psalm 118 concludes the unit that clearly manifests God's *hesed* in his past salvation and anticipates this salvation within the dire situation of the postexilic community. It is the Davidic messiah who will consummate God's salvation of his people. However, the scope of God's people is not limited to Israel but extends to all nations who wait for God's salvation. Also, "a spatial story suggestive of a climactic movement from captivity to Jerusalem to the house of the Lord to the sanctuary to the altar"⁷¹ in the Egyptian Hallel appears to indicate "the sanctuary on Zion as goal

---

expects God's salvation through his Messiah. Crutchfield, "Circles of Context," 185. Psalms 114–15, when read together, proclaim God's presence in his "creation of Israel" in the past and in the present when he seems to be distant. Sander, "Bringing," 160. There are many textual witnesses of Pss 114–15 as one unit. (i.e., Codex Leningradensis, Aleppo Codex, LXX, Vulgate, Peshitta). See more examples and the arguments to defend the unified delimitation of Pss 114–15 in Prinsloo, "Psalms 114 and 115," 197–200; Sander, "Bringing," 160–223. Just as he saved Israel from bondage in Egypt, YHWH will show his *hesed* by saving them in the present oppression by foreign nations that worship worthless idols. Sander, "Bringing," 177. Thus, Pss 113–15 as a whole show the reversed fortune of God's people through the Davidic messiah, that is, the new exodus for the postexilic community. In Ps 116, the individual psalmist praises YHWH for delivering him from life and death situations. The psalm contains many allusions to Davidic psalms (i.e., Ps 116:1–3 and Ps 18:3–6, which parallels 2 Sam 22:5–6; Ps 116:8–9 and Ps 56:14; Ps 116:11a and Ps 31:23; and Ps 116:16 and Ps 86:16). Hossfeld and Zenger, *Psalms 3*, 216; Estes, *Psalms 73–150*, 378. These many allusions seem to indicate that Ps 116 intentionally portrays the Davidic messiah who is saved by YHWH and gives thanks to God. Psalm 117 is the universal call to praise YHWH for his eternal *hesed*. Situated just before Ps 118, which is the culmination of an Egyptian Hallel, Ps 117 reminds us that God's eternal *hesed* is not only for Israel but also for all who fear him. Psalm 118 is the "climactic conclusion" of the Egyptian Hallel. Vaillancourt, *Multifaceted Saviour*, 167. See also Balhorn, *Telos des Psalters*, 201–2; Prinsloo, "Contextual," 409.

70. Some of the lexical parallels are as follows: (1) חֶסֶד (Pss 115:1; 117:2; 118:1, 2, 3, 4, 29), (2) three groups of people who are called to praise YHWH (Pss 115:9–13; 118:2–4), (3) "distress" (Pss 116:3; 118:5), (4) "YH" (Pss 113:1, 9; 115:17, 18; 116:19; 117:2; 118:5, 14, 17, 18, 19), (5) עֹזֵר (Pss 115:9, 10, 11; 118:7, 13). Vaillancourt, *Multifaceted Saviour*, 197. As for the thematic parallels, Crutchfield suggests "the praise of God" (Pss 113:1–3; 118:28–29), "his sovereignty over the nations" (Pss 113:4–6; 118:6–7; 10–12), the reversal of the fortunes of the rejected (Pss 113:7–9; 118:22–24), Exodus motif (Ps 114 and Exodus allusions in Ps 118), "trust in God" (Pss 115:1–11; 118:6–9), "God's blessing on those who fear him" (Pss 115:12–18; 2–4, 19–21), "God's gracious deliverance from his servant from death" (Pss 116; 118:17–18), and "a call to the nations to admire God's character" (Pss 117; 118:1–4, 29). Crutchfield, *Psalms*, 54.

71. Prinsloo, "Šeʾôl," 755.

of the Exodus"[72] (and the new exodus). Therefore, the temple is another key motif of the Egyptian Hallel. As the culmination of the Egyptian Hallel, Ps 118 clearly manifests the three key motifs—the Davidic messiah, the new exodus, and the temple.

PSALM 118 IN SECOND TEMPLE LITERATURE

The Dead Sea Scrolls include five manuscripts that contain parts of Ps 118: 11Q5 (=11QPs^a), 11Q6 (=11QPs^b), 4Q84 (=4QPs^b), 4Q87 (=4QPs^e), and 4Q173a (=4Q173 frg. 5 *olim*).[73] First, of the five manuscripts that include Ps 118 in the Dead Sea Scrolls, 11Q5, 11Q6, and 4Q87 have the identical arrangement of the Psalters.[74] While the fragmentary nature of the manuscripts deters from a conclusive judgment, the arrangement of the Psalters in these manuscripts indicates a possible liturgical use, according to the solar calendar with a strong Davidic emphasis.[75] Having already identified the Davidic messiah motif and its liturgical nature in Ps 118, it is not odd to see that these manuscripts contain Ps 118. Second, the similar arrangement of 4Q84 with that of MT, especially the extant Pss 113–18 (i.e., Hallel Psalms) and the location of Ps 118 at the end of the manuscript may indicate that Ps 118 may have been viewed at least as the conclusion of the Hallel Psalms.[76] Third, the quotation of Ps 118:20 in 4Q173a may signify the return of the righteous ones (i.e., the Qumran community) to a purified temple. However, the fragmentary status of 4Q173a inhibits readers from being certain. Apart from the witnesses of

---

72. Zenger, "Composition," 92.

73. Finally, 4Q173a (=4Q173 frg. 5 *olim*) witnesses the quotation of a part of Ps 118:20. Flint, *Dead Sea Psalms*, 220.

74. Of 11Q5, fragment E consists of Ps 118:25–29 followed by parts of Ps 104, 147, and 105 in order. Sanders, *Dead Sea Psalms*, 160–65. Also, 11Q5 16 is equivalent to Ps 118:1, 29, 15, 16, 8, 9, 1, 29 in MT with an additional phrase, "(It is) better to take refuge in Yahweh than trust in a thousand people." Charlesworth, and Rietz, *Dead Sea Scrolls*, 159. Second, 11Q6 and 4Q87 are similar to 11Q5. 11Q6 and 11Q5 are "two copies of the same composition." Martínez and Tigchelaar, "Psalms Manuscripts from Qumran," 75. 4Q87 contains 118:29 and has virtually the same arrangement with 11Q5, namely, Psalms "118–104–[147]–105–146." Flint, "Psalters at Qumran," 147. Therefore, we may deduce the same conclusion about the use of Ps 118 in 11Q6 and 4Q87 with that of 11Q5.

75. Brunson, *Psalm 118*, 87–88.

76. 4Q84 preserves Ps 118:1–3, 6–11, 18–20, 23–26, and 29. Skehan, "Psalm Manuscript," 313–22. The manuscript seems to generally follow the order of MT except that Pss 104–11 are missing. Flint, "Psalters at Qumran," 147.

the Dead Sea Scroll, there is little use of Ps 118 in Second Temple literature before New Testament.[77]

To summarize, we may conclude the following points for Ps 118 in the Old Testament and the interpretive history of Ps 118. First, Ps 118 depicts God's salvation for the Davidic king from his enemies that alludes to the exodus and the king's entrance into the temple with the victory. Among the ancient variants of Ps 118, the Targum clearly presents the psalmist as the Davidic messiah. Overall, the psalm seems to reflect the expectation of the postexilic community for the coming of an eschatological Davidic messiah to save them (i.e., the new exodus) so that they may worship YHWH in the temple.

Second, the canonical context of Ps 118, such as the intertext of the Psalter, Book V of the Psalter, and Egyptian Hallel, consistently expresses

77. Some scholars consider the witness of rabbinic literature in the use of Ps 118 in the New Testament. For example, quoting Longenecker (". . . while changes due to development or differing circumstances cannot be denied, this desire to preserve the traditional—barring other considerations—minimizes the severity of the problem") and his Jewish professor Rabbi Novak, Vaillancourt argues that a lot of the content of rabbinic literature "date to the NT period and the century prior." Vaillancourt, "Psalm 118," 730. Due to the multiple witnesses of Ps 118 from rabbinic literature, it would be worthwhile to make brief comments about them that may shed light on the interpretation of Ps 118 in Mark here on the assumption that they possibly derive from the tradition of Second Temple Judaism. First, Ps 118 as the part of Hallel Psalms was sung at the major Jewish festivals such as the feasts of Tabernacles (*m. Sukk.* 3.9; 4.5), the Weeks, Passover (*m. Pesah.* 5.5–7), and Hannukah (*b. Šabb*). Solomon Zeitlin, "The Hallel: A Historical Study of the Canonization of the Hebrew Liturgy," *The Jewish Quarterly Review* 53 (1962): 22; Sanders, "Hermeneutic Fabric," 179. We may highlight three things about Ps 118 sung at these Jewish Festivals: (1) At the feast of Tabernacles, the people would cite Ps 118:25 ("Save us, we pray, O Yahweh!") while waving palm or willow branches. (2) At Hanukkah, when Jews commemorated the dedication of the temple, Ps 118 was sung since Ps 118:27 is related to the temple. (3) Psalm 118, as the part of the Hallel Psalms, was sung at the Passover dinner possibly because both Ps 118 and the Passover have a clear exodus motif. Brunson, *Psalm 118*, 57–62, 77–78. Second, the Rabbinic literature reveals that Hallel Psalms, especially Ps 118 are interpreted messianically and eschatologically. Brunson, *Psalm 118*, 22; Snodgrass, *Stone*, 84; Kwon, "Psalm 118," 72. Jeremias proposes the possibility that, "The interpretation given to Ps 118:24–29 in the Midrash has influenced the accounts of the Triumphal Entry even down to details." Jeremias, *Eucharistic Words*, 258. Second, having examined the entry to Ps 118 in *Midrash Tehillim* which holds many oral traditions that may be dated to the time of the New Testament and even before, Vaillancourt argues that Ps 118 is related to "Sukkoth, the exodus, and the vision of the end of captivity for Israel in Isaiah 12." Vaillancourt, "Psalm 118," 730–31. Thus, with a Davidic motif in the Ps 118 of the Targum, the themes of the anticipation of God's deliverance, the temple, the end of captivity, and the Jewish festivals may explain the background of Ps 118 in the Gospel of Mark. These witnesses of early Judaism seem to cohere with some New Testament witnesses, which will be investigated in the section, the use of Ps 118 in Mark.

the return of the Davidic messiah, who will bring God's kingdom as the vice-regent of YHWH. Especially, Ps 118 is the culmination of Egyptian Hallel in that (1) the Davidic messiah will consummate God's salvation of his people (i.e., Israel and all nations who wait for God's salvation), and (2) the theme of the new exodus culminates in Ps 118 as the Egyptian Hallel proceeds spatially from captivity to Jerusalem to the house of the Lord to the sanctuary to the altar. Thus, the sanctuary on Zion becomes the goal of the new exodus.

Third, the OT intertexts of Ps 118 also witness the Davidic messiah, the new exodus, and the temple motifs. Fourth, the extant Second Temple literature on Ps 118 (i.e., Dead Sea Scrolls) is meager and fragmentary to give a definitive verdict on the nature on their interpretation on Ps 118. But at the very least, they seem to attest the strong Davidic emphasis. Having observed the interpretive history of Ps 118 before Mark, now we will turn to Mark's use of Ps 118. We will pay attention to how our findings so far, especially the Davidic messiah, the new exodus, and the temple motifs may relate to Mark's use of Ps 118 in the narrative structure of Mark's Gospel. At the same time, we will see how these motifs contribute to the ideological view of Mark, that is, Jesus' inauguration of God's kingdom.

PSALM 118 IN MARK

The previous sections on Ps 118 exhibit that Ps 118 anticipates the coming of the Davidic messiah, who will bring about God's kingdom that is closely connected the temple and the new exodus experience. We will now focus on the two passages where Ps 118 are quoted and will see how Mark uses the citations of Mark in light of the narrative structure of Mark. Especially, we will see how Mark develops the three motifs—Davidic messiah, temple, and the new exodus—of Ps 118 to show that Jesus ushers in God's kingdom.

Psalm 118:25–26 in Mark 11:9–10

Mark 11:1–11 is pivotal in that it is the beginning of Jesus' final ministry in Jerusalem where the temple is located (Mark 11–16).[78] The

---

78. According to Gray, the quick pace of Markan narrative changes to more detail in Mark 11:1–11, which serves to "highlight the importance of Jesus' entry and presence

temple motif permeates Mark 11–15, as we will see later. Mark uses two scriptural allusions (Gen 49:9–10; Zech 9:9–10) and one quotation (Ps 118:25–26) as the interpretive framework for Jesus' entry into Jerusalem in Mark 11:1–11.[79] These scriptural allusions and quotation are interrelated in such a way that they portray Jesus' entry into Jerusalem as the eschatological Davidic Messiah's coming to usher in God's kingdom.

First, Mark's allusions to Gen 49:11 (LXX) and Zech 9:9 (LXX) in Mark 11:1–7 indicate that Jesus is the eschatological Davidic Messiah. Before he enters Jerusalem, Jesus commands two of his disciples to go to the village, untie a colt, and bring it from there.[80] "A colt tied" (πῶλον δεδεμένον) in Mark 11:2b may allude to Gen 49:11a ("tying his colt to the vine," δεσμεύων πρὸς ἄμπελον τὸν πῶλον αὐτοῦ), a part of Gen 49:10–11 that has been regarded as the prophecy about the eschatological Davidic king in Jewish literature (i.e., Num 24:17; Q252 1–4).[81]

Mark 11:1–7 alludes to Zech 9:9 (LXX). In Zech 9:9, the inhabitants of Jerusalem are called to rejoice because YHWH, the Divine Warrior who conquered Israel's oppressors and restored the Jerusalem temple (Zech 9:1–8), installs his earthly king, the Davidic messiah.[82] The description of the king as righteous, saved, and riding on a foal exhibits that he is the Davidic messiah.[83] The description of the king coming to

---

in Jerusalem and its temple." Gray, *Temple*, 11.

79. Krause, "One Who Comes," 147.

80. "Go into the village ahead of you. As soon as you enter it, you will find a colt tied upon which no one has ever sat. Unite it and bring it" (ὑπάγετε εἰς τὴν κώμην τὴν κατέναντι ὑμῶν, καὶ εὐθὺς εἰσπορευόμενοι εἰς αὐτὴν εὑρήσετε πῶλον δεδεμένον ἐφ' ὃν οὐδεὶς οὔπω ἀνθρώπων ἐκάθισεν· λύσατε αὐτὸν καὶ φέρετε; Mark 11:2).

81. Botner summarizes the five main points of Heinz Kuhn and Joseph Blenkinsopp, who representatively argue for this view, as follows: "(1) The repetition of the lexeme πῶλος, "colt," always modified by the perfect passive particle 'tied' (11:2, 4) or 'untied' (11:2, 4, 5); (2) the presence of syntactic double entendre, 'the Lord/its master has need of it [ὁ κύριος αὐτοῦ χρείαν ἔχει],' perhaps subtly raising the question of the colt's true owner; (3) the concentric structure of the pericope, placing emphasis on the action of untying the colt; (4) the widespread assumption that Gen 49:9–11 is about a future son of David . . . , and (5) the narrative location of Jesus' instructions to his disciples, just after he has been heralded 'son of David' (10:47–48) and just before the festal shout, "Blessed is the coming kingdom of our ancestor David' (11:10)." Botner, *Jesus Christ*, 147–48. See Kuhn, "Reittier Jesu," 82–91; Blenkinsopp, "Oracle of Judah," 55–64. As for those who follow their view, see Matera, *Kingship*, 71–72; Lane, *Mark*, 395–96; Pesch, *Markusevangelium*, 2:179; Krause, "One Who Comes," 141–53; France, *Mark*, 431, Cho, *Royal Messianism*, 27–28, 44, 95.

82. Boda, *Zechariah*, 562–64.

83. Boda, *Zechariah*, 567–70.

Jerusalem riding on a new foal (ἐπιβεβηκὼς ἐπὶ . . . πῶλον νέον, Zech 9:9b) corresponds to Jesus coming to Jerusalem sitting upon a foal no one ever sat on (πῶλον . . . ἐφ' ὃν οὐδεὶς οὔπω ἀνθρώπων ἐκάθισεν [Mark 11:2b] and φέρουσιν τὸν πῶλον πρὸς τὸν Ἰησοῦν . . . καὶ ἐκάθισεν ἐπ' αὐτόν [Mark 11:7]).[84] The fact that Zech 9:9–10 has the inner-biblical allusions to Gen 49:10–11 and Ps 72:8, where Davidic messiahship is clearly depicted, helps scholars understand why Gen 49:11 and Zech 9:9 are alluded to in Mark 11:1–7.[85] Therefore, the two scriptural allusions signify the eschatological Davidic nature of Jesus' entry into Jerusalem.

Second, as Jesus enters Jerusalem, the shout of the crowds from Ps 118:25–26 clearly demonstrates Jesus as the eschatological Davidic Messiah (Mark 11:9–10). The crowds appropriately respond to Jesus' symbolic enactment[86] of the coming of the Davidic messiah.[87] The actions of the crowds—spreading their clothes and branches—in Mark 11:8 seem to have an overtone of welcoming the royal messiah.[88] Just as the Jews recited Ps 118 at the time of Sukkot and Passover, these crowds cried out Ps 118 when they welcome Jesus' entry into Jerusalem.[89] The cry of the crowds (Mark 11:9b–10) is structured chiastically:[90]

---

84. Catchpole, "Triumphal Entry," 324; Krause, "One Who Comes," 149–50; France, *Mark*, 429; Evans, *Mark*, 142; Collins, *Mark*, 518; Marcus, *Mark 8–16*, 772; Cho, *Royal Messianism*, 95–96; Botner, *Jesus Christ*, 150; Sloan, *Zechariah in Mark*, 59–60. Furthermore, Sloan suggests that (1) the "'rejoicing' and 'proclaiming'" of Zech 9:9 match the crowd's shout (ἔκραζον) in Mark 11:9. Sloan, *Zechariah in Mark*, 59.

85. Boda, *Zechariah*, 568–69, 573; Sloan, *Zechariah in Mark*, 59–60; According to Krause, the phrase "your king is coming to you" (מַלְכֵּךְ יָבוֹא לָךְ) in Zech 9:9 is a "direct interpretation" of "until Shiloh comes" (עַד כִּי־יָבֹא שִׁילֹה) in Gen 49:10. Krause, "One Who Comes," 147.

86. As for Jesus entering Jerusalem on a foal as a symbolic act, I agree with Juho Sankamo, who argues, "Jesus' riding is thus to be seen as a prophetic symbol; an act in accordance with a prophetic paradigm. Through Jesus' entry the kingdom of God was ushered into the city and challenged it to realize the eschatological moment and visitation." Sankamo, "Jesus' Entry," 35.

87. Hatina, *In Search of a Context*, 305–24; Brunson, *Psalm 118*, 109; Botner, *Jesus Christ*, 152–53.

88. Sanders, "Hermeneutic Fabric," 179; Brunson, *Psalm 118*, 106; Hatina, *In Search of a Context*, 313. They all refer to Jehu's anointing as a king in 2 Kings 9:13 as the allusion to spreading clothes.

89. Scholars debate the time of Jesus' entry between Sukkot and Passover. Regardless of the exact timing, it seems that the crowd who welcomed Jesus may have considered his entry into Jerusalem as the fulfillment of the hope of Jews who had sung Ps 118 and yearned for the coming of the Davidic messiah who would save them.

90. France, *Mark*, 433; Hatina, *In Search of a Context*, 315. While the parallel passages in other Gospels (Matt 21:9; Luke 19:38; John 12:13) depict the acclamation of the

A: ὡσαννά

    B: εὐλογημένος ὁ ἐρχόμενος ἐν ὀνόματι κυρίου

    B': εὐλογημένη ἡ ἐρχομένη βασιλεία τοῦ πατρὸς ἡμῶν Δαυίδ

A': ὡσαννὰ ἐν τοῖς ὑψίστοις

The cry of ὡσαννά ("save, we pray" in A and A') frames the proclamation of the blessing of the coming Davidic messiah. In the original context of Ps 118:25, the cry of *hosanna*, followed by the praise for YHWH's salvific work in the past, was the desperate request of the postexilic community for YHWH to do a wondrous salvific work once again. In Jewish tradition, this cry for salvation continued. The crowds in Mark might have understood that the coming of Jesus served as an answer to their long-waited cry for salvation.[91]

The other quotation from Ps 118:26 appears in a blessing formula (B). The one who comes in the name of the Lord (ὁ ἐρχόμενος ἐν ὀνόματι κυρίου), the allusion to David who delivered Israel in the name of YHWH (1 Sam 17:45), clearly represents the Davidic messiah who comes in the name of YHWH (i.e., by the help of YHWH) to bring victory for the community in Ps 118:26.[92] The acclamation of the crowds in Mark affirms that Jesus is the anticipated Davidic Messiah who will deliver them with YHWH's authority. B' not only functions as the parallel with B in the chiastic format, but also, it is the interpretation of B.[93] The coming of the Davidic messiah for salvation signifies the advent of the Davidic messiah's rule. This section reveals the link between Ps 118:26 and Zech 9:10. Just as Zech 9:10 envisions "the ideal reign of the Davidic king," B' (the interpretation of Ps 118:26) proclaims "the coming kingdom 'of our father, David.'"[94] The crowd's welcome of Jesus as the anticipated messiah who brings the messianic kingdom sheds light on another aspect of his identity in the Markan narrative. Their acclamation serves as the climax

---

crowds as the cry for the coming of the royal figure, only Mark uses a chiastic structure.

91. Therefore, Cho rightly comments, "In OG Psalm 117:26, the king is to be blessed as the divine medium of deliverance, as 'the one who comes in the name of the Lord.' So 'the kingdom of our father David' is in keeping with the theme of God's dominion both in OG Psalm 117 and in Mark." Cho, *Royal Messianism*, 93.

92. We have noticed that Ps 118:10–12 repeatedly describes that the psalmist, the Davidic king, defeats his enemy "in the name of YHWH", which corroborates that Ps 118:26 is the allusion to 1 Sam 17:45.

93. Botner, *Jesus Christ*, 152.

94. Sloan, *Zechariah in Mark*, 59–60.

of Jesus' entry as the eschatological Davidic Messiah. However, Jesus' messiahship and the kingdom Jesus brings surpass their understanding as the ensuing narrative more explicitly demonstrates.[95]

The allusion to Zech 9:9–10 and the quotation of Ps 118:25–26 in Mark 11:9–10 demonstrate not only the Davidic messiah motif but also the temple motif. The background of Zech 9:9–10 is the restoration of the temple by the Divine Warrior, YHWH. Therefore, the entrance of the Davidic messiah into Jerusalem, and his ideal rule, presuppose the restoration of the temple. Similarly, Ps 118's spatial movement is towards the temple. The Davidic messiah leads in a "song of victory" into the temple.[96] This temple motif is significant in Mark 11. Jesus, the Davidic Messiah, enters Jerusalem where the temple is located as the fulfillment of Gen 49:9–10, Zech 9:9–10, and Ps 118:25–26. However, Mark does not quote Ps 118:26b ("We bless you from the house of Yahweh") because, as the following Markan narrative shows, the temple establishment who are supposed to welcome him as Messiah reject him.[97] Therefore, instead of coming with the triumphal victory into the temple in the pattern of Zech 9 and Ps 118, Jesus enters the temple for inspection (Mark 11:11), which is followed by cleansing and judgment in Mark 11:15–17.[98] The following section of Ps 118:22–23 in Mark 12:10–12 further develops this temple motif to which we now turn.

---

95. Hatina, *In Search of a Context*, 310–11.

96. Vaillancourt, "Psalm 118," 735.

97. Ironically, it is the crowds who welcome Jesus instead of the priests who were supposed to bless him. Brunson, *Psalm 118*, 109; Cho, *Royal Messianism*, 97; Botner, *Jesus Christ*, 153–54. According to Hatina, the silence of the priests serves as a "prolegomenon to the ensuing conflict" in Markan narrative. Hatina, *In Search of a Context*, 316.

98. Watts, holding to Isaiah's new exodus motif with a Malachi quotation as the overarching paradigm for the entire Markan narrative, views Jesus' entry into Jerusalem as "Yahweh's warrior march" according to the pattern of the Isaianic new exodus motif. Watts, *Isaiah's New Exodus*, 304–8. However, Mark 11:1–11 speaks to the coming of the Davidic messiah. See Hatina, *In Search of a Context*, 302. If there is a new exodus motif, it should derive from Ps 118, not Isaiah in Mark 11:1–11. For example, the anticipated salvation of YHWH through the Davidic messiah the crowds are crying out for may be considered as the new exodus, though it is not evident if that was Mark's intention in Mark 11:1–11.

Psalm 118:22–23 in Mark 12:10–12

Mark 12:10–11 is Jesus' quotation of Ps 118:22–23. It serves as the conclusion of his parable spoken to the Jerusalem temple establishment (the chief priests, the teachers of the law, and the elders, οἱ ἀρχιερεῖς καὶ οἱ γραμματεῖς καὶ οἱ πρεσβύτεροι) in Mark 12:1–12. The quotation of Ps 118:22–23 in Mark 12:10–11 serves not only as the conclusion of the parable but also, with Mark 12:12, as the conclusion of the conflict between Jesus and the religious leaders which begins in Mark 11:27.[99] Therefore, it is worthwhile to examine how previous episodes are related to and lead to the parable and the conclusion in Mark 12:1–12.

The series of conflicts between Jesus and the Jewish religious leaders (Mark 11:27—12:27) is triggered by Jesus' temple demonstration (Mark 11:15–17). After stopping the temple activities, Jesus announces judgment on the temple by quoting Isa 56:7 (LXX) and alluding to Jer 7:9 (LXX). God's intention for the eschatological temple is to restore the proper function of the temple as the place of worship for the Jews and the gentiles as envisioned by Solomon's prayer (Isa 56:3–7; 1 Kgs 8:42–43, LXX).[100] However, as unfaithful Judah and religious leaders who naively trusted in the "security of temple" without repenting of their sin resulted in the announcement of the destruction of the temple (Jer 7:4–10), the temple establishment's hostility toward the coming kingdom of God via the Messiah (i.e., Jesus) inevitably leads to Jesus' condemnation of the temple.[101]

Mark's narration of the religious leaders' intent to kill Jesus (Mark 11:18) divulges that they understood Jesus' actions and conceived them as a threat to their authority. Therefore, the Jewish leaders challenged Jesus' authority for such actions (Mark 11:28). Instead of answering their question directly, Jesus asks if John's baptism is from heaven (i.e., God) or not (Mark 11:29–30). This question harkens back to the scriptural quotations (Mal 3:1 and Isa 40:1) in the prologue of Mark that affirm the heavenly origin of John's mission to prepare the way of Jesus. If the priests recognized that John was an eschatological messenger sent before

---

99. Iverson, "Jews, Gentiles," 316.

100. Cho, *Royal Messianism*, 155–57; See also, Marcus, *Way of the Lord*, 121; Alvarez, "Temple Controversy," 141–42.

101. Telford, *Temple*, 163; Barrett, "House of Prayer," 13–20; Cho, *Royal Messianism*, 143–46. Mark's enacted parable of the withered fig tree that forms the intercalation (A–B–A') reinforces the theme of the judgment on the temple in Mark 11:15–17.

YHWH's coming for the judgment (Mal 2:17–3:5), especially for the purification of the priests (Mal 3:2), they would have accepted the baptism of Jesus.[102] Yet, their refusal to answer Jesus' question reveals they do not submit to the arrival of God's kingdom through Jesus anticipated by the Scriptures, preached by John (Mark 1:2–15) and manifested in Jesus' authority to condemn the temple.[103]

Mark 12:1–12 consists of a parable (Mark 12:1–9), Jesus' rhetorical question with the quotation of Ps 118:22–23 (Mark 12:10–11), and the Sanhedrin's reaction (Mark 12:12). While Jesus initially did not respond as they questioned his authority, the parable of the wicked tenants and the following quotation of Ps 118:22–23 answer their question.[104] Jesus is God's beloved Son who will be rejected but vindicated as the cornerstone of the new temple. In corollary, the temple and the temple establishment will be destroyed.[105]

Jesus' parable adopts the typical imageries in Israel's history to address how Jesus' death and resurrection will culminate in salvation-history. The parable alludes to Isa 5:1–7 linguistically and thematically.[106]

---

102. If the religious leaders had acknowledged the heavenly origin of John's origin, they may have been aware of Mal 3:1–4, which anticipates the coming of the messenger (i.e., Elijah-like messenger, that is, John the Baptist) before the coming of YHWH, that is, the messenger of YHWH to the temple. To see the messenger of YHWH as Jesus, see Clendenen, "Messenger," 81–102. Whether the religious leaders understood Jesus as the messenger of YHWH or not, John's baptism was to prepare the hearts of the people for Jesus (Mark 1:4–8). Cho argues, "Mal 3:1 implies a warning to the Jerusalem priests: the eschatological messenger would prepare the way of Yahweh's return to the temple so as to purge the sons of Levi . . . in order for 'the gospel of Jesus the messiah' to represent the comfort proclaimed in OG Isa 40, Yahweh's return to Zion must be preceded by the priests' appropriate response to the message of John." Cho, *Royal Messianism*, 114. While John's ministry and Jesus' judgment on the temple establishment may be foreshadowed by the quotation of Mal 3:1 in the prologue, it is questionable that the priests' positive response to John was a prerequisite for the gospel to represent the comfort in Isa 40. Hellerman claims that John's baptism for "the forgiveness of sins outside the normal avenues of the centralized sacrificial system was to essentially call into question the ongoing validity of that system for the procurement of divine forgiveness." Hellerman, "Authority of Jesus," 226. Even if readers do not accept his claim at face value, if John's ministry followed the pattern of the prophecy of Mal 2:17–3:5, his call to repent and the baptism for the forgiveness of sins would definitely include the religious leaders in Jerusalem.

103. Edwards, *Mark*, 354; Gray, *Temple*, 57–58.

104. Rowe, *God's Kingdom*, 272.

105. Marcus, *Way of the Lord*, 123–24.

106. Despite some obvious differences between the parable of the wicked tenants in Mark 12 and the parable of the vineyard in Isa 5 (i.e., the recipients of the judgment—the vineyard in Isa 5 vs the tenants in Mark 12—are different), the two parables are

Though the tenants and their judgments are not present in Isa 5:1–7, Mark 12 alludes to God planting the vineyard (i.e., Israel) in Isa 5:1–2. Also, the punishment on the tenants due to their unfaithfulness to God reverberates God's judgement on the vineyard because of their covenantal unfaithfulness in Isa 5:3–7. Also, the vineyard owner's repeated sending of his servants to the tenants and the tenants' rebellion to the vineyard owner by persecuting his servants echo the rebellion of Israel's religious leaders against God by persecuting his prophets throughout Israel's history.[107]

The vineyard owner's sending his beloved son (υἱὸν ἀγαπητόν; Mark 12:6) echoes his voice at Jesus' baptism (Mark 1:11) and on Mount of Transfiguration (Mark 9:7). Thus, Jesus is identified as the beloved son in Markan narrative who will bring the kingdom of God. Also, his death by the tenants and the transfer of the inheritance followed by the punishment on the tenants proleptically forecast the rest of the Markan narrative (Mark 12:7–9). Therefore, the parable is unique in that it "effectively condenses the plot of Mark's gospel into a miniature."[108] By sharing the parable in light of salvation history, Jesus not only demonstrates his authority but also prophesies the consequences of the conflict between himself and the religious leaders.[109]

---

closely related. (1) Many observe the linguistic correspondences between the two. Eight Greek words are either identical or almost identical between Mark 12 and Isa 5:1–2 (LXX)—ἀμπελών, φυτεύω, περιτίθημι, φραγμός, ὀρύσσω, οἰκοδομέω, πύργος, ὑπολήνιον (προλήνιον). Taylor, *Mark*, 473; Marcus, "Polemic," 224; Iverson, "Jews, Gentiles," 308. (2) They share the common theme of judgment as the consequence of transgression. Both of them are juridical parables. Cho, *Royal Messianism*, 168. See also, Fuhrmann, "Use of Psalm," 70.

107. Compare Mark 12:2–6 with 2 Chr 36:14–16 ("Furthermore, all the leaders of the priests and the people became more and more unfaithful, following all the detestable practices of the nations and defiling the temple of the LORD, which he had consecrated in Jerusalem. The LORD, the God of their ancestors, sent word to them through his messengers again and again, because he had pity on his people and on his dwelling place. But they mocked God's messengers, despised his words and scoffed at his prophets until the wrath of the LORD was aroused against his people and there was no remedy" NIV). Cho, *Royal Messianism*, 172. See also Kloppenborg, *Tenants*, 220. Scholars also notice the echo of Gen 37:20 in Mark 12:7. Marcus, *Mark 8–16*, 803; Kloppenborg, *Tenants*, 220. As for the different interpretive options on the parable, see Snodgrass, "Recent Research," 187–216.

108. Kloppenborg, *Tenants*, 220.

109. Klyne Snodgrass summarizes the significance of the parable as follows: "This parable is of the utmost significance for understanding Jesus and his mission. [It] stands as a threat to the Jewish authorities, but in doing so it stresses the authority of the son, who like the prophets, brings a message from God, but who, unlike the prophets, stands

However, without the quotation of Ps 118:22–23, the parable is not complete. The quotation concludes the parable by explaining and applying it.[110] According to Fuhrmann, just as the parable concerns "both the rejection of the son and the judgment of the tenants," the quotation deals with the "rejection" and the "vindication" of the stone, which implies the "judgment" on the builders.[111] The widely accepted wordplay between son (בֵּן) and stone (אֶבֶן) in Hebrew also corroborates that the quotation is the application of the parable.[112] Moreover, the word, טליא ("the youth" or "boy") in the Targum of Ps 118:22 may derive from the wordplay between son (בֵּן) and stone (אֶבֶן) in Hebrew.[113] This wordplay is perfectly suitable in that (1) the word, son, in Mark has a messianic connotation as seen in chapter 3, and (2) in the original context of Ps 118, stone is the Davidic messiah figure.

Another reason for using Ps 118:22–23 as the conclusion of the parable is the temple motif. Several factors point to the strong temple theme in Ps 118:22. First, as observed in the section of the Old Testament intertexts of Ps 118:22–23, the cornerstone alludes to the texts related to the temple.[114] Second, the context of Ps 118:22–23 is the liturgy inside the

---

in a unique relation to God and is the final messenger. Rejection of him is disastrous in that one loses participation in God's Kingdom and faces judgment." Snodgrass, *Parable*, 112.

110. "At the heart of the question about the place of the quotation is the issue of the relation of *meshalim* to their *nimshalim*, of the parable narratives to their applications or explanations. Too often NT scholars have ignored such explanations as later additions, but the effectiveness of a parable often depends upon its *nimshal*. In fact, David would never have known Nathan's parable was against him without the explanatory *nimshal* (2 Sam 12:1–7)." Snodgrass, "Recent Research," 203. Snodgrass derives the idea from Stern. Stern, "Jesus' Parables," 66–67.

111. Fuhrmann, "Use of Psalm 118:22–23," 68–71. Similarly, Rowe argues that the use of Ps 118:22–23 refers to "both rejection *and* vindication." Rowe, *God's Kingdom*, 271. Scholars also pay attention to the meaning of Jesus' rhetorical question, "Have you not read the Scripture before?" (Mark 12:11a). According to the paraphrase of Daube, it means, "Surely you have read this or that text, so you ought to understand its import, or but you do not seem to understand its import." Daube, *New Testament and Rabbinic Judaism*, 432–33. It is the rebuke to the hardened heart of the religious leaders, one of the typical motifs of Mark.

112. The following list of scholars who acknowledge the wordplay is derived from Cho, *Royal Messianism*, 174. Black, "Christological Use," 11–14; Milavec, "Mark's Parable," 307–8; Trimaille, "La Parole," 253; Evans, *Jesus and His Contemporaries*, 403–4; Brooke, "Use of Scripture," 287; France, *Mark*, 463; Collins, *Mark*, 548.

113. Hatina, *In Search of a Context*, 322.

114. This research concludes that the parallel between Zech 4:7 and Ps 118:22 may indicate the temple building in Ps 118:22. Some scholars argue "the builders" is

temple. As the Davidic messiah proceeds inside the temple, he praises the Lord's salvation from his enemies. Indeed, the Markan parable in Mark 12:1–9 foreshadows how the temple establishment would reject Jesus by leading him to the crucifixion and how God would vindicate Jesus by destroying the temple (and the temple establishment) and handing over the vineyard (the people of God) to others (the messianic community).[115] Therefore, the quotation of Ps 118:22 in Mark 12:10 clearly portrays Jesus as the "cornerstone of the new temple."[116]

Psalm 118:23 integrates the new exodus motif with the Davidic messiah motif. In combination with the temple motif and the Davidic messiah motif, Ps 118 culminates in the (new) exodus motif that runs through the Egyptian Hallel. Many allusions to Exod 15 in Ps 118 can be observed. פלא in Ps 118:23 alludes to Exod 15:11 (עֹשֵׂה פֶלֶא), God's wonerous deliverance of Israel from Egypt. Likewise, God saved the Davidic messiah from his enemies in Ps 118. The fact that Ps 118 re-appropriated the Exodus texts and Isaiah texts that convey both the new exodus motif and the Davidic messiah motif corroborates that Ps 118:23 signifies the new exodus through the Davidic messiah.[117] The quotation of Ps 118:23 in Mark 12:11 connects the new exodus motif to Jesus' vindication typologically: Jesus' vindication (i.e., resurrection) from the rejection by the builders (i.e., crucifixion) is God's marvelous new exodus through the Davidic Messiah.[118]

---

traditionally considered as the symbolic word for "the religious leaders" in Jewish literature. Marcus, *Way of the Lord*, 125; Snodgrass, "Recent Research," 204; As for relevant Jewish texts, see Derrett, "Stone," 64–65; Evans, *Mark*, 238. If builders in Ps 118:22 indicate the religious leaders, it may reinforce the temple language of Ps 118:22–23.

115. Evans, *Mark*, 337; Donahue and Harrington, *Mark*, 339, 342; Boring, *Mark*, 332; Marcus, *Mark 9–16*, 813–14; Strauss, *Mark*, 517. It is interesting to observe that just as the religous leaders function as the Messiah's enemy in the use of Ps 2 in Mark, they serve the same role in the use of Ps 118 in the Markan narrative.

116. Marcus, *Way of the Lord*, 121. See also Gray, *Temple*, 76; Boring, *Mark*, 332; Strauss, *Mark*, 517–18.

117. As aforementioned, Ps 118 has some Exodus intertexts that overlap with Isaiah intertexts (i.e., יָהּ in Ps 118:5, 14, 17, 18, 19; Exod 15:2; 17:16; Isa 12:2; 26:4 and עָזִּי וְזִמְרָת יָהּ וַיְהִי־לִי לִישׁוּעָה in Ps 118:14; Exod 15:2a; Isa 12:2b). These Isaiah intertexts (Isa 12:2 and 26:4) are related to each other and convey both the new exodus motif and the Davidic messiah motif.

118. Fuhrmann, *Use of Psalm*, 75. R. D. Aus suggests a typological connection between Exod 15:17 and Mark 12:7. According to Aus, the inheritance (κληρονομία) language in the parable of the wicked tenants echoes inheritance (κληρονομία) in Exod 15:17 ("Bring them in and plant them in the mountain of your inheritance, in your ready habitation, which you, O Lord, have prepared, the sanctuary, O Lord, which your

In tandem with the parable, Ps 118:22–23 in Mark 12:10–11 forecasts not only the rejection and vindication of Jesus but also their significance (i.e., the judgment on Messiah's enemies and the creation of the new messianic community). Psalm 118:22–23 in Mark 12:10–11 shows that the enemies of the Messiah encompass all who oppose his kingdom (i.e., the religious leaders). In the canonical context of Ps 118, we observed how Ps 118 both unifies and culminates the Egyptian Hallel. And Ps 118 as the part of the Egyptian Hallel was often sung at the major Jewish feasts, such as the Sukkot and the Passover, by Mark's contemporary Jews.[119] Therefore, it is quite possible that Mark would consider the canonical context (i.e., Egyptian Hallel) of Ps 118 and indicate that the worshiping community that follows the Davidic messiah extends beyond Israel (i.e., Ps 117); thus, the beneficiaries of the kingdom Jesus brings extend to all the people who welcome him by faith (i.e., the new messianic community).

Mark 12:12 ends both the conflict between Jesus and the Sanhedrin that started in Mark 11:27 and the parable that began in Mark 12:1. The Sanhedrin's knowledge of the parable does not change their mind. Their hardened hearts accomplish the purpose of the parable for the outsiders

---

hands have made ready," the translation of LXX), and both occurrences of inheritance refer to the temple. Aus, *Wicked Tenants*, 18–36. Several commentators point out that the sanctuary in Exod 15:17 indicates the future temple. Sana, *Exodus*, 82; Stuart, *Exodus*, 360–61; Durham, *Exodus*, 209. On the one hand, according to Exod 15:17 (LXX), inheritance refers to temple. On the other hand, as for the parable of the wicked tenants, inheritance signifies the ownership of the vineyard (i.e., Israel, that is, God's people). Therefore, one cannot equate inheritance in Mark 12:9 with the temple. However, in light of the context of the parable in Mark 12:1–9, the temple is inextricably connected to the inheritance. The temple signifies YHWH's kingship among his people. In other words, it is his ownership of Israel (i.e., vineyard). As tenants take care of the vineyard for its owner, the temple establishments were supposed to lead Israel to the proper worship of YHWH (i.e., the proper function of the temple). In light of the salvation-historical typology, the conflict over the inheritance in the parable refers to the conflict over the authority over the temple that signifies the kingship of YHWH. Therefore, Aus's argument seems plausible enough to consider another typological connection between Exod 15 and Mark 12:1–11 in terms of the temple motif. Aus's argument prompts scholars to consider the combination of the temple and the kingship motifs that connect Exod 15, Ps 118, and Mark 12:1–11. In Exodus, the ultimate purpose for bringing Israel to the land is to worship YHWH in the temple so that YHWH may reign as their king forever (Exod 15:18). Childs, *Exodus*, 252. In Ps 118, the Davidic messiah brings praise to the temple where the heavenly king, YHWH dwells. In Mark 12;1–11, though the word, king is not used, the language of the vineyard owner, his beloved son (i.e., the inheritor), and Ps 118:22–23 imply both the kingship and temple motifs.

119. Sanders, "Hermeneutic Fabric," 179; Vaillancourt, "Psalm 118," 732.

of God's kingdom (i.e., the quotation of Isa 6:9–10 in Mark 4:11–12).[120] Though they leave Jesus temporarily, they enact their desire to arrest him by sending other people to trap him (Mark 12:13) and collaborating with Judas Iscariot (Mark 14:10–11, 43–46). Therefore, Mark 12:12 exhibits that the parable of the wicked tenants with the quotation of Ps 118:22–23 has a pivotal function (i.e., the enacted parable) in the rest of the Markan narrative.

Psalm 118 in the Markan Narrative

So far, this research has examined how Ps 118:22–23 and 25–26 highlights three motifs—the Davidic messiah, the temple, and the new exodus—in its immediate context of the Markan narrative. This section will investigate the function of Ps 118 in the broader context of the Markan narrative. While Ps 2 functions as the framework of the whole Markan narrative, Ps 118 focuses on how Jesus fulfills the role of the Davidic Messiah who comes to the temple and accomplishes the new exodus through his death and resurrection to bring about God's kingdom.

First, Ps 118:25–26 portrays Jesus as the Davidic Messiah in the Markan narrative. The allusion to Ps 2:7 in Mark 1:11 and 9:7 previously implied Jesus as the Davidic Messiah, as examined in chapter 3. However, Jesus' messiahship was kept secret until Peter's confession. It was only when Jesus' journey to Jerusalem was almost complete that his identity as the Davidic Messiah came to light (Mark 10:47–48).[121] Unlike others, Jesus does not silence Bartimaeus's cry ("Son of David, have mercy on me"; Mark 10:47–48). Thus, Mark 10:46–52 prepares "the way" for the entry of the Davidic Messiah into "the city of David."[122] As Jesus enters Jerusalem, he intentionally prepares his entry as the Davidic Messiah, as alluded by the Scriptures (Gen 49:11 and Zech 9:9), and this motif climaxes in the shout of the crowds (Ps 118:25–26 in Mark 11:9–10). Thus, the quotation of Ps 118:25–26 functions as the climax of the Davidic motif in the Markan narrative. Jesus fulfills the prophecy of the Scriptures concerning

---

120. Berder opines how the Sanhedrin's response exemplifies Isa 6:9–10 in Mark 4:11–12. "Mc 12, 12 présente une illustration originale du principe énoncé par Jésus en Mc 4,11–12, faisant appel à Is 6,9–10. Les auditeurs de la parabole entendent et ne comprennent pas, ou, plus exactement ici, comprennent mais agissent comme s'ils ne comprenaient pas." Berder, *Pierre*, 291.

121. Cho, *Royal Messianism*, 90–91.

122. Botner, *Jesus Christ*, 146. See also Cho, *Royal Messianism*, 90–92.

the anticipated eschatological messiah coming to the temple.[123] The cry "hosanna" forebodes Jesus' role as the Messiah who will save his people and establish his kingdom, though the way he will achieve salvation and the kingdom he brings will be beyond human expectation.

Second, the two citations of Ps 118:25-26 and 22-23 function as the scriptural witnesses to the temple motif in Mark 11:1—12:12. Watts proposes a chiastic structure around the two quotations in Mark 11:1—12:12.

Jesus, the 'triumphant' Davidic king (Ps 118:25-26) (11:1-11)
> Cursing of the fig-tree (11:12-14)
>> Jesus' Temple demonstration (Isa 56:7/Jer 7:11) (11:15-19)
> Withered fig-tree, and mountain-moving (11:20-25)

Jesus, the rejected but vindicated Davidic king (Ps 118:22-23) (11:27—12:12)[124]

This proposed structure highlights how Mark uses two quotations of Ps 118 around the quotation of the temple destruction (Isa 56:7; Jer 7:11). With the help of Watts's chiastic structure, the role of Ps 118 in the temple motif in Markan narrative can be viewed as follows: Jesus enters Jerusalem as the Davidic king who is coming to the temple according to the Scriptures (Gen 49:11; Zech 9:9; Ps 118:25-26). However, the arrival of the king and the kingdom he brings are not welcomed by the temple establishment. Therefore, the temple ought to be destroyed (Isa 56:7; Jer 7:11), which is further elaborated in Mark 13. Instead, God builds the new temple by laying the cornerstone through Jesus' rejection and vindication (Ps 118:22-23). Jesus' vindication (i.e., the resurrection) from the builder's rejection (i.e., crucifixion) is also the fulfillment of God's marvelous new exodus through the Davidic messiah (Ps 118:22-23).[125]

Third, Ps 118:22-23 serves as the scriptural witness not only to the temple motif in Mark 11:1—12:12 but also to Jesus' death and resurrection motif that pervades the second half of Mark. Jesus' death and resurrection were forecasted by three predictions (Mark 8:31-32; 9:30-31;

---

123. Ådna, *Jesu*, 88; Botner, *Jesus Christ*, 145.

124. Watts, "Psalms," 32.

125. This writer does not agree with Watts's statement that "Psalm 118's particular connection with the new exodus restoration of the Temple" coheres with Isaiah's new exodus motif." Watts, "Psalms," 35. Rather than follow the pattern of Isaiah's new exodus motif, the relationship between the exodus motif and the temple motif in Ps 118:23 seems to allude to that of Exod 15.

10:32–34) that structure the middle macro-section of Mark's narrative. Of these predictions, the first contains an echo to Ps 118:23. The word ἀποδοκιμάζω in the first prediction (Mark 8:31) appears elsewhere only in Mark 12:10 in the Markan narrative, and both refer to Jesus' death caused by the Sanhedrin.[126] The prediction about the rejection of Jesus by the Sanhedrin in Mark 8:31 and 12:10 is fulfilled specifically in Mark 14:5—15:1. However, the theme of rejection and vindication through the cornerstone of the temple penetrates Mark 11–16. The parable of the fig tree and the temple demonstration (Mark 11:12–26), the confrontation between Jesus and the religious leaders around the temple (Mark 11:27—12:44), the teaching about the temple destruction (Mark 13), Jesus' trial before the Sanhedrin (Mark 14:53—15:1), and his death on the cross (Mark 15:29, 38) are inseparably interrelated to the rejection and vindication of Jesus and the temple motif. Jesus' resurrection (Mark 16) can be viewed as the fulfillment of being the cornerstone of the temple. In addition, the reversal of the fortune and the salvation that generate the wonder in Ps 118:22–23 indicate that Jesus' death and resurrection are the new exodus.

In conclusion, Mark strategically uses Ps 118 in the Markan narrative and highlights Jesus as the Davidic Messiah who comes to the temple for salvation (Ps 118:25–26) by becoming the cornerstone of the new temple through his rejection and vindication (Ps 118:22–23). Each quotation of Ps 118 serves not only as the climax in its immediate context but also as the climax of the key juncture in the entire narrative: (1) Jesus, as the Davidic Messiah, enters Jerusalem and the temple to accomplish his mission to initiate God's kingdom (Ps 118:25–26). (2) Along with the parable, Jesus predicts his rejection and vindication, which impregnate the destruction of the temple and the beginning of the new temple (Ps 118:22–23). Thus, the quotation and the parable forecast that Jesus fulfills the role of the Davidic Messiah who brings salvation (i.e., the new exodus) by becoming the cornerstone of the new temple through his death and resurrection. (3) This section serves as the beginning of the climax of the entire Markan narrative. Also, Jesus' prediction of his death and resurrection in the context of the temple motif functions as the blueprint for the climax of the Markan narrative (Ps 118:22–23).

---

126. Breytenbach, "Markusevangelium," 215–16; Watts, "Psalms," 34; Cho, *Royal Messianism*, 175.

CONCLUSION

Psalm 118 is a psalm with multifaceted imageries. The psalm speaks of the Davidic messiah who has experienced an exodus-like salvation from his enemies (Ps 118:1–18). He brings a song of victory with other worshipers into the temple (Ps 118:19–21). He becomes the foundation of the new temple through his rejection and vindication, thus manifesting God's wonderous salvation (Ps 118:22–23). The postexilic community anticipates the coming of the Davidic messiah in YHWH's name to save them (Ps 118:25–26). Thus, the psalm begins and ends with the praise of the psalmist and the worshiping community (Ps 118:1–9, 27–29). The psalm emanates several diverse themes—the Davidic messiah, the new exodus, and the temple—that are corroborated by the canonical contexts of Ps 118 such as the Book V of the Psalter, the Egyptian Hallel (Pss 113–18), and other OT intertexts. Though Second Temple literature on Ps 118 is meager and not substantial, at the least, the extant literatures consistently witness to the Davidic messiah motif in Ps 118.

Mark uses Ps 118 in a strategic location of his narrative so that Ps 118 serves as the climax of the Davidic Messiah motif and blueprint of the latter part of the Markan narrative (i.e., Mark 12–16). The three themes of Ps 118—the Davidic messiah, the new exodus, and the temple—function as the key motifs of the Markan narrative. First, the quotation of Ps 118:25–26 portrays Jesus as the Davidic Messiah. There is an escalation of the Davidic messiah motif from the allusion to Ps 2:7 (Mark 1:11 and 9:7) to the cry of Bartimaeus (Mark 10:47–48). They prepare the way for the Davidic Messiah's entry to Jerusalem. As he enters, the theme of the Davidic messiah reaches a climax with two allusions (Gen 49:11 and Zech 9:9) and finally with the quotation of Ps 118:25–26 in Mark 11:9–10.

Second, the chiastic structure, with the two citations of Ps 118:25–26 and 22–23 and the composite citation of Isa 56:7 and Jer 7:11 (Mark 11:1—12:12), highlight the temple motif as one of the central themes of Mark 11–16. In the Markan narrative, Mark stresses that (1) Jesus' entry to Jerusalem fulfills the coming of the Davidic messiah to the temple, (2) Jesus' demonstration in the temple fulfills the judgment on the temple, and (3) Jesus' death and resurrection fulfill the rejection and vindication of the stone as the cornerstone of the new temple.

Finally, Ps 118:22–23 functions as the scriptural witness to Jesus' death and resurrection motif that permeates the second half of Mark. Jesus' death and resurrection motif already runs through the middle section of the Markan narrative via the three predictions (Mark 8:31–32; 9:30–31; 10:32–34). Moreover, the presence of echo to Ps 118:22 (i.e., ἀποδοκιμάζω; Mark 8:31) in the first prediction (Mark 8:31) connects the death and resurrection motif by the quotation of Ps 118:22–23 in Mark 12:10–11. The quotation of Ps 118:22–23 in Mark 12:10–11 forecasts Jesus' death and resurrection in tandem with the temple motif. Also, the reversal of the fortune and the salvation that arouse the wonder communicate the new exodus motif (Ps 118:23).

In conclusion, Mark's usage of Ps 118 shows that his narrative has the context of Ps 118 in mind. Mark appropriates Ps 118 in such a way that Jesus is coming to Jerusalem as the Davidic Messiah to accomplish the mission of bringing about God's kingdom through the judgment of the temple and creating the new temple. However, Jesus accomplishes his mission through his death and resurrection, the new exodus for all who trust in him.

5

Psalm 110 in Mark

THE PREVIOUS CHAPTER EXAMINED how Mark used two quotations of Ps 118 at the key junctures (e.g., Jesus' entry into Jerusalem and the parable of the wicked tenants) in the Markan narrative. Thus, Mark's use of Ps 118 highlights Jesus' coming to Jerusalem as the Davidic Messiah who brings about God's kingdom through the judgment of the temple and creating the new temple. Also, Mark appropriated Ps 118 to stress the new exodus motif in the Markan narrative.

This chapter will explore how Mark uses two citations of Ps 110 at other key places in his narrative (i.e., Mark 12:35–37 and Mark 14:61). Psalm 110 is considered one of the key OT texts cited in the New Testament. Psalm 110 functions as the scriptural fulfillment of Jesus' enthronement and vindication as king. Also, Mark's use of Ps 110 shows that Jesus is the Melchizedek-like priest-king who will inaugurate the kingdom of God.

Mark, like many other NT writers, uses only Ps 110:1 in the narrative.[1] Psalm 110:1 appears when Jesus quotes it in contrast to the scribes' teachings in Mark 12:35–37. Later, Jesus alludes to Ps 110:1, Dan 7, and Ps 80 in Mark 14:61–62 at his trial. This section will explore the importance of Ps 110:1 in the narrative structure of Mark. For that purpose, this chapter will investigate first the textual form of the citations to compare the Markan text with the MT and LXX. Then, we will explore the original context of Ps 110, the canonical context of the Psalter and other Old Testament texts, and witness of Second Temple literature to

---

1. The only exception is the book of Hebrews, where Ps 110:4 is also used.

see how the interpretation history of Ps 110 may have influenced Mark's use of Ps 110.

TEXTUAL FORM OF PSALM 110 IN MARK

The following chart shows the textual form of Ps 110:1 in Mark in comparison to the Hebrew and Greek texts.

Hebrew	LXX	Mark 12:36	Mark 14:62
לְדָוִד מִזְמוֹר נְאֻם יְהוָה לַאדֹנִי שֵׁב לִימִינִי עַד־אָשִׁית אֹיְבֶיךָ הֲדֹם לְרַגְלֶיךָ׃	τῷ Δαυιδ ψαλμός εἶπεν ὁ κύριος τῷ κυρίῳ μου κάθου ἐκ δεξιῶν μου ἕως ἂν θῶ τοὺς ἐχθρούς σου ὑποπόδιον τῶν ποδῶν σου	αὐτὸς Δαυὶδ εἶπεν ἐν τῷ πνεύματι τῷ ἁγίῳ· εἶπεν κύριος τῷ κυρίῳ μου· κάθου ἐκ δεξιῶν μου, ἕως ἂν θῶ τοὺς ἐχθρούς σου ὑποκάτω τῶν ποδῶν σου.	ὁ δὲ Ἰησοῦς εἶπεν· ἐγώ εἰμι, καὶ ὄψεσθε τὸν υἱὸν τοῦ ἀνθρώπου ἐκ δεξιῶν καθήμενον τῆς δυνάμεως καὶ ἐρχόμενον μετὰ τῶν νεφελῶν τοῦ οὐρανοῦ.
A Psalm of David. **Yahweh said to my lord, "Sit at my right hand until I make your enemies a footstool for your feet."**	A Psalm of David. **LORD said to my lord, "Sit at my right hand until I make your enemies a footstool for your feet."**	David himself said in the Holy Spirit, **"LORD said to my lord, 'Sit at my right hand until I put your enemies under your feet.'"**	And Jesus said, "I am. And you will see the Son of Man **sitting at the right hand of the Powerful One** and coming with the clouds of heaven."

It is evident that Ps 109:1 (LXX) is the literal translation of Ps 110:1 (MT). Mark 12:36 is almost identical with Ps 109:1 (LXX), except that (1) Mark 12:36 says, "David himself said in the Holy Spirit," instead of the superscription. Mark 12:36 recognizes Davidic authorship but also considers Ps 110:1 as David's prophetic oracle. (2) The definite article ὁ is absent in Mark 12:36. (3) Mark 12:36 uses ὑποκάτω instead of ὑποπόδιον. The similarity with Ps 8:7 (ὑποκάτω τῶν ποδῶν αὐτοῦ, LXX) leads readers to opine that Mark 12:36 is influenced by Ps 8:7.[2]

As for Mark 14:62, the phrase ἐκ δεξιῶν καθήμενον τῆς δυνάμεως corresponds with κάθου ἐκ δεξιῶν μου in Ps 109:1(LXX). Mark 14:62 uses καθήμενον instead of κάθου due to the context, and τῆς δυνάμεως is the circumlocution for YHWH according to the custom of Greek-speaking

---

2. Breytenbach, "Markusevangelium," 212–13; Botner, *Jesus Christ*, 167n85.

Judaism.³ Acknowledging his messiahship, Jesus identifies himself (i.e., the Son of Man, the favored self-designation of Jesus) with David's lord (i.e., the Davidic Messiah) enthroned at the right hand of God in Ps 110:1. Thus, the phrase clearly alludes to Ps 110:1. Since the LXX and Hebrew have the identical text for the cited portion of Ps 110:1 in Mark, it is essential to examine both the LXX and Hebrew text of the whole Ps 110 to determine if the wider context of Ps 110 may affect the citation of Ps 110 in Mark.

INTERPRETATION OF PSALM 110

Sitz im Leben and Structure

Psalm 110 is a notoriously difficult psalm that generates various proposals concerning its *Sitz im Leben*. Therefore, this research will draw from the most convincing conclusions about the date, author, and setting. Several different periods for the date of the psalm have been proposed such as the preexilic period, early Persian era, and rule of the Hasmoneans.⁴ However, it is likely that the psalm originated in the early preexilic period.⁵ Concerning the author of the psalm, scholars generally suggest either David or a cultic prophet of the preexilic era. The superscription and the final form of Ps 110 advocate Davidic authorship.⁶

Scholars postulate different ideas about the setting of the psalm such as a "royal coronation," "annual New Year Festival," "a real battle," purely "eschatological and messianic" psalm,⁷ and the Ark's return to Jerusalem

---

3. Breytenbach, "Markusevangelium," 210–11. According to Breytenbach, τῆς δυνάμεως has a military connotation, and "the messiah, the Son of God will come with the ruling power of God to judge the high priest and the whole Sanhedrin." Breytenbach, "Markusevangelium," 212.

4. See Goldingay, *Psalm 90–150*, 292 and 13–16 for bibliographic information on the different proposals about the dating of Ps 110. The primary reason some scholars date the psalm during the postexilic period is their presupposition that the royal and priestly functions are separated in the Israelite monarchy. Granerød, *Abraham and Melchizedek*, 188.

5. "Most scholars opt for the period of the monarchy, generally in its early stages." Allen, *Psalm 101–150*, 83. See also Corley, "Psalm 110," 70; Hengel, "Sit at My Right Hand," 176n117.

6. Vaillancourt, *Multifaceted Saviour*, 93.

7. Allen, *Psalm 101–150*, 83. See the bibliographies for the different views on the setting in Allen, *Psalm 101–150*, 83.

by David,[8] among others.[9] The similarity with Assyrian prophetic oracles attests that Ps 110 is a psalm of royal coronation.[10] In addition, the similarity with "Egyptian iconography" concerning a "real co-enthronement of the addressee" confirms that the setting of Ps 110 is the enthronement.[11] Regarding structure of Ps 110, most scholars agree that the psalm basically consists of "two divine oracles in verses 1 and 4, each followed by amplifications."[12] While agreeing with the two-part structure, Hilber argues one must consider the whole psalm as one divine oracle.[13] Thus, it is best to adopt Waltke's structure, as he followed Hilber in exegeting Ps 110.[14]

Exegesis

The superscription (v. 1aa) indicates that the author and the speaker of Ps 110 is David. The expression נְאֻם יְהוָה (v. 1ab) introduces the psalm as a prophetic oracle to David's lord (לַאדֹנִי) mediated through David, the prophetic figure.[15] The authority of David's lord is confirmed by the divine citation, "Sit at my right hand while I make your enemies your

---

8. Delitzsch, *Psalms*, 3:186–87.

9. More suggestions about the *Sitz im Leben* are proposed by Johnson, "Hermeneutical Principles," 430.

10. Waltke and Houston, *Psalms*, 498; Hilber, *Cultic Prophecy*, 78.

11. Hossfeld and Zenger, *Psalms 3*, 148. Waltke asserts, "David probably composes his royal prophecy to be sung by cultic functionaries at the coronation ceremony of his heirs, hoping that in the end of salvation history a final successor of his would fulfill and consummate his prophecy." Waltke and Houston, *Psalms*, 518.

12. Estes, *Psalms 73–150*, 340. See also, Allen, *Psalms 101–150*, 85.

13. Hilber reasons, "A shift between first person divine speech and third person reference of the deity" is not uncommon in Old Testament prophetic writings (i.e., Isa 3:1–4; Amos 3:1–7; Mic 1:3–7) and Assyrian oracles. Therefore, he rightly contends one must consider Ps 110 as one divine oracle with two subdivisions. Hilber, "Psalm CX," 359.

14. Waltke and Houston, *Psalms*, 501.

15. Vaillancourt, *Multifaceted Saviour*, 95. According to Vaillancourt, נְאֻם יְהוָה is "'an almost completely fixed technical expression . . . [occurring in] prophetic oracles,' and is 'used exclusively of divine speaking.'" Vaillancourt, *Multifaceted Saviour*, 95. The word, אדֹנִי always refers to a human figure differentiated from a divine being, אֲדֹנָי (i.e., v. 4). Vaillancourt, *Multifaceted Saviour*, 96. However, it is indistinguishable in LXX since the word κύριος is used for both. By referring to the addressee as his lord, David acknowledges the authority of his seed, the eschatological future messiah over him. Ross, *Psalms, 101–150*, 346.

footstool" (v. 1b).¹⁶ Sitting at the right hand of YHWH signifies the co-enthronement of David's lord with YHWH, "while at the same time the divine being is presented as the ultimate king."¹⁷ By sitting at the right hand of YHWH, David's lord is elevated to the highly honored position with authority and functions as the vice-regent of YHWH.¹⁸

The king's co-enthronement with YHWH transpires "until" YHWH makes the enemies of David's lord a footstool. Making the king's enemies as his footstool signifies their complete subjugation to him.¹⁹ Therefore, Ps 110:1c connotes that the king's rule will continue and experience "the turning point" (i.e., until) of his rule at the time of the total subjection of his enemies.²⁰

Verses 2–3 are the prophetic reflection of verse 1. The divine declaration to enthrone the king at the right hand of YHWH (v. 1b) is followed by the specific command for the king to rule (רדה) in the midst of his enemies (v. 2b).²¹ Verse 3 continues the motif of the king's rule. The king rules by engaging a holy war against his enemies with the help of his voluntary army.²² YHWH enables the king's reign as he empowers the

---

16. שֵׁב לִימִינִי עַד־אָשִׁית אֹיְבֶיךָ הֲדֹם לְרַגְלֶיךָ (Ps 110:1 MT)

17. Vaillancourt, *Multifaceted Saviour*, 97; Hossfeld and Zenger, *Psalms 3*, 147. Hay notices some ancient parallels such as Egyptian iconographies and an Ugaritic text to sitting at the right hand of YHWH. According to Hay, sitting at the right hand "signified divine honor and sometimes worldly authority and power." Hay, *Glory at the Right Hand*, 52–53.

18. Perowne, *Psalms*, 304.

19. Estes, *Psalms 73–150*, 342; Goldingay, *Psalms 90–150*, 294; Ross, *Psalms 90–150*, 347–48.

20. Ross, *Psalms 90–150*, 348.

21. YHWH's command to the king to rule is empowered by sending the mighty scepter to the king (מַטֵּה־עֻזְּךָ v. 2a). "Your mighty scepter" symbolizes power from YHWH to strike the enemies of the king. "From Zion" (מִצִּיּוֹן) indicates the temple where YHWH dwells is the center of his reign. Goldingay, *Psalms 90–150*, 294.

22. עַמְּךָ נְדָבֹת בְּיוֹם חֵילֶךָ ("your people free offerings in the day of your power," v. 3a) represents that the king's people offer themselves voluntarily to fight the battle for their king. Allen, *Psalms 101–150*, 86. While scholars are not in agreement in accepting the MT text, בְּהַדְרֵי־קֹדֶשׁ in verse 3b, it seems that there is no obvious reason to reject MT text. Brown, "Royal Performance," 96. Therefore, the voluntary army of the king is described symbolically as attired with holiness in accordance with the holy war for the king. The phrase מֵרֶחֶם מִשְׁחָר ("from the womb of the dawn"), being very symbolic, generates various interpretations. Despite its diverse interpretations, the expression seems to relate to the strength of the king and his army. The final phrase of verse 3, לְךָ טַל יַלְדֻתֶיךָ ("dew of your youth is for you") engenders different interpretive options. The phrase has many textual variants. The LXX (ἐξεγέννησά σε) rewords יַלְדֻתֶיךָ as a verb ("I have begotten you") and omits לְךָ טַל. Peshitta, Origen, and many Hebrew manuscripts

king to rule in the midst of the enemy. YHWH will raise up the willing and mighty army of the king, and they will fight to ensure his rule.

Verses 4–7 are the second part of the divine oracle that starts with the divine citation (v. 4). The divine citation is preceded by the phrase נִשְׁבַּע יְהוָה וְלֹא יִנָּחֵם ("Yahweh swore. He will not change his mind," v. 4a). The implication of the oath formula is significant. It ascertains that what God says about the king, that is, his identity as an eternal priest-king, is irrevocable.[23] The divine citation, אַתָּה־כֹהֵן לְעוֹלָם עַל־דִּבְרָתִי מַלְכִּי־צֶדֶק: ("You are a priest forever in the manner of Melchizedek," v. 4b)[24] is the second divine appointment for David's lord. He is not only the co-enthroned king with YHWH but also the eternal priest. Having been appointed as a king already (v. 1), his additional status as a priest explains why the description "in the manner of Melchizedek" is attached to David's lord in verse 4 (cf. Gen 14:18–20).[25]

The uniqueness of Ps 110:4 is not that a priest-king figure did not exist before or after Melchizedek until the prophecy of Ps 110:4 appears (i.e., Adam, David).[26] Rather, the peculiarity of the priest-king in Ps 110:4

---

also follow LXX's verbal rewording. Kraus, *Psalms 60–150*, 344; VanGemeren, *Psalms*, 815. The verbal rewording ("I have begotten you") of LXX and many other textual variants seem to result from an over-assimilation of the text to Ps 2, motivated by the similarity between Ps 110 and Ps 2. Allen, *Psalms 101–150*, 81; Defani, "Psalm 109," 247. The MT text ("dew of your youth for you") may represent "the absolute power" of the king's army. Goldingay, *Psalms 90–150*, 295; Tucker & Grant, *Psalms*, 593. As a result, verse 3 supports the idea of the king's reign.

23. Kraus, *Psalms 60–150*, 351; Ross, *Psalms 90–150*, 354; Vaillancourt, *Multifaceted Saviour*, 104–5.

24. I follow Hossfeld and Zenger and Vaillancourt's translation "in the manner of." Hossfeld and Zenger, *Psalms 3*, 143; Vaillancourt, *Multifaceted Saviour*, 86.

25. Vaillancourt, *Multifaceted Saviour*, 105. A group of scholars who do not see the clear role distinction between a priest and a king (i.e., David) rightly claim that, like many other ancient Near Eastern kings of his day, David as a king played the role of a priest (i.e., "patron" and "a high priest"), i.e., Hays, "Response to Daniel I. Block," 66–68. Kraus argues that David and his offspring performed diverse priestly roles (1 Sam 13:9; 2 Sam 6:13–14, 17–18; 24:17; 1 Kgs 8:14,16; Jer 30:21). Kraus, *Psalms 60–150*, 351. Merrill not only mentions David's priestly roles (i.e., 2 Sam 6 presents how he as a king wore a priestly robe, "offering sacrifice and issuing priestly benedictions") but also the appointment of his sons as "priests" (2 כֹּהֲנִים, Sam 8:18). Merrill, "Royal Priesthood," 60. Merrill also points out that the punishment on King Uzziah derives from infringing on the task assigned only to Aaronic priests (i.e., burning incense) but not necessarily involving in other priestly roles (i.e., presiding over a cult). Merrill, "Royal Priesthood," 61.

26. According to Hamadi, Adam was God's vice-regent to establish God's kingdom by ruling over creation and "perpetuate the divine image through procreation." Adam also served as a priest to *serve* and *keep* the garden of Eden, an "archetypal sanctuary"

is that he is the ultimate fulfillment of the scriptural anticipation of a priest-king in the manner of Melchizedek ("priest *forever* in the manner of Melchizedek"; Ps 110:4b).[27] According to Emadi, Melchizedek is the mediator of the Abrahamic covenant.[28] The Davidic covenant (2 Sam 7) succeeds the Abrahamic covenant to bless all nations.[29] David serves as a pattern for the ultimate priest-king in Ps 110.[30] As a result, YHWH appoints David's lord as the priest-king in the manner of Melchizedek in the pattern of David (i.e., the priest-king). Just as David became a mediator of the Abrahamic blessing like Melchizedek did, the eternal priest-king in Ps 110 will be a channel of Abrahamic blessing for all who follow him.[31]

Verses 5–7 function as another prophetic reflection on the divine oath in verse 4, just as verses 2–3 do concerning the divine command in verse 1.[32] Verse 5 corresponds to verse 1.[33] By switching the positions between verse 1 (i.e., David's lord sitting at YHWH's right hand) and verse 5 (i.e., YHWH sitting at David's lord's right hand) but reflecting the same thing, verse 5 highlights YHWH's "protection" and "support" to ensure the rule of David's lord.[34] At the same time, verse 5 illuminates the great closeness between God and the king from different perspectives.[35] Verse

---

where God resides and is worshiped. Emadi, "Royal Priest," 35, 42–43. As for David, see the previous footnote.

27. *Forever* emphasizes "the finality and immutability" of the Melchizedekian priesthood. Russell, "Royal and Priestly Contribution," 80.

28. Emad examines the connection between Gen 14:18–24 (i.e., Melchizedek's blessing on Abram) and 15:1–6 (i.e., God's confirmation on Abrahamic covenant) and concludes, "The solidarity between Melchizedek and Abraham hints at the type of priesthood that will be capable of mediating the blessings of the Abrahamic covenant to the nations." Emadi, "Priest Forever," 66–68.

29. Emadi, "Priest Forever," 68.

30. Merrill, "Royal Priesthood," 59; Emadi, "Royal Priest," 154–60.

31. Just as Melchizedek, the priest-king of Salem, blessed Abraham and, in corollary, his future descendants who are the recipients of Abraham's blessing, David as a priest-king in Jerusalem would bless Abraham's descendants (Israel). Emadi, "Royal Priest," 149–50; Routledge, "Psalm 110," 14.

32. Waltke and Houston, *Psalms*, 501; Vaillancourt, *Multifaceted Saviour*, 109.

33. While David's lord is told to sit at YHWH's right hand in verse 1, the Lord (i.e., YHWH) is at the right hand of David's lord in verse 5. However, in principle, they mean the same thing. Verse 5b (And the Lord will crush kings on the day of his anger) semantically matches verse 1b ("I make your enemies a footstool for your feet").

34. Vaillancourt, *Multifaceted Saviour*, 110; Goldingay, *Psalms 90–150*, 297; Ross, *Psalms 90–150*, 355.

35. Bail, "Psalm 110," 109–10.

6 elaborates upon how YHWH will crush the foes of David's lord.[36] Verse 7 describes YHWH's judgement on the nations through the priest-king, as illustrated by the human aspect of the priest-king (i.e., "drinking" and "lifting up his head").[37] The verse shows that David's lord is "the instrument of the judgment by Yhwh."[38]

Ancient Variants

Scholars generally agree that differences between the MT and LXX mainly derive from different readings of the Hebrew vowels that reflect "the stylistic, rhetorical or theological interests" of the LXX translator.[39] The following aspects of Ps 109 (LXX) signal that the translator interpreted the psalm messianically. First, the ambiguous use of the same word, κύριος, for both YHWH and David's lord (εἶπεν ὁ κύριος τῷ κυρίῳ μου) in Ps 109:1 (LXX) seems to be motivated by the translator's messianic

---

36. Vaillancourt, *Multifaceted Saviour*, 112. The context of Ps 110:5–6, especially the two accompanying prophetic perfect verbs, מָלֵא ("he will fill") and מָחַץ ("he will crush"), indicate that YHWH's judgment on the nations will be the expression of his just wrath. The verb, מָלֵא (he will fill) expects to be followed by the double-accusative form. Thus, several scholars prefer to emend the text by adding the word גְּוִיּוֹת ("valley") to MT. They suspect either homoioteleuton or homoioarcton. See Waltke and Houston, *Psalms*, 498n50; Corley, "Psalm 110," 58. NET notes on Ps 110:6. The word, ראשׁ (head) is singular in MT, while LXX has plural form (κεφαλάς). In spite of the seeming difference, if one takes the singular form of MT as the collective form, the meaning of MT and LXX seems identical. Goldingay, *Psalms 90–150*, 291; Vaillancourt, *Multifaceted Saviour*, 90.

37. Scholars propose different views on the subject of the third-person singular verbs in verses 5–7 such as Lord (i.e.), the priest-king, the shift of the subject from YHWH (vv. 5–6) to David's lord in verse 7, etc. See Hossfeld and Zenger, *Psalms 3*, 150–52; Brueggemann and Bellinger, *Psalms*, 480; Whybray, *Reading the Psalms*, 96; Barbiero, "Non-Violent Messiah," 3; Ross, *Psalms 90–150*, 357; Vaillancourt, *Multifaceted Saviour*, 114. This writer opts for the shift of the subject from YHWH (vv. 5–6) to David's lord (v. 7). Even though the subject of the third person singular verbs in Ps 110: 5b–6 can be either divine or human, the subject of the verbs in Ps 110:7 seems most likely a human figure.

38. Vaillancourt, *Multifaceted Saviour*, 114–15. It seems that "drinking water along the way" signifies YHWH's provision for his messiah in battle. VanGemeren, *Psalms*, 817; Waltke and Houston, *Psalms*, 511–12. "Lifting up his head" indicates the king will receive "honor and glory" after the final triumph. Ross, *Psalms 90–150*, 358; Corley, "Psalm 110," 61. As Waltke aptly comments, "In contrast to the abased kings whom he makes his footstool (v. 1), I AM's king holds his head high." Waltke and Houston, *Psalms*, 512.

39. Bons, "Septuaginta-Version," 123–24. See also Hossfeld and Zenger, *Psalms 3*, 141, 152. Ἡ ἀρχή seems to be the LXX translator's word choice that matches μετὰ σοῦ. Bons, "Septuaginta-Version," 131.

interpretation.⁴⁰ Second, in comparison to the MT (עַמְּךָ "your people," v. 3a) that highlights the king's voluntary army, the LXX translation, μετὰ σοῦ ἡ ἀρχὴ ("the dominion is with you," v. 3a) focuses on the king's power rather than the king's army.⁴¹ Third, the most drastic contrast between the MT and LXX is found in the translation of verse 3c (ἐκ γαστρὸς πρὸ ἑωσφόρου ἐξεγέννησά σε ("I have begotten you from the womb before the morning star"). Ἐξεγέννησά σε is almost identical to γεγέννηκά σε in Ps 2:7. The translation reflects the translator's interpretive choice to identify David's lord with the messianic son of God in Ps 2:7.⁴² Therefore, Ps 109 (LXX) reveals a messianic interpretation that reflects the "eschatological and messianic expectations" of the postexilic Jewish community.⁴³

The Targum not only recognizes the authorship of David but also considers that the divine oracle was addressed to David (v. 1).⁴⁴ The Targum interprets that the divine oracle in verse 1 was given to David to *wait* until the death of his predecessor, Saul, rather than to *command* his enthronement.⁴⁵ The typical Targumic emphasis on the Law appears throughout the psalm (vv. 1, 3, 7). Interestingly, another divine oracle in verse 4 does not mention the priesthood in the manner of Melchizedek but describes David as an eschatological prince ("prince for the worlds to come") because of his righteous character as king. The Targum clearly shows that some Jews during the Second Temple period considered David as the author of the psalm.⁴⁶ However, the Targum does not mention the priesthood. Instead, it stresses David as a rightful messiah and worldwide ruler.⁴⁷ The Targum of Ps 110 portrays a synthesis of both the historical and the eschatological David with the emphasis on the Law.⁴⁸

40. Defani, "Psalm," 248.

41. Corley, "Psalm 110," 62.

42. Defani, "Psalm," 247. If the phrase, πρὸ ἑωσφόρου, connotes the preexistent status, as some scholars suggest, it would indicate the heavenly origin of the messiah. Tilly, "Psalm 110," 167; Schaper, *Eschatology*, 102–03.

43. Schaper, *Eschatology*, 144. According to Schaper, Ps 109 (LXX) demonstrates the eschatological "messianic judgment." Schaper, *Eschatology*, 106–7.

44. The interpretation of the Targum of Ps 110 is based on Stec's translation. Stec, *Targum of Psalms*, 202–3.

45. Hay, *Glory at the Right Hand*, 30–31.

46. Chapter 2 proposed the possibility of the Targum of Psalms written before NT era.

47. "The LORD has sworn and will not relent, 'You are appointed as prince for the world to come, on account of the merit that you have been a righteous king.'" Stec, *Targum of Psalms*, 203.

48. von Nordheim, *Geboren*, 206.

To summarize, Ps 110 seems to originate from David's prophetic oracle about the enthronement of the future Messiah from his descendants. The messiah will be highly exalted as the vice-regent of YHWH and the eternal priest-king in the manner of Melchizedek. He will be the ultimate fulfillment of the Davidic covenant, which is also the continuation of the Abrahamic covenant. As the vice-regent of YHWH, he will subjugate his enemies with God's help. As for the ancient variants, the LXX shares the identical text with the MT, though rewording of some vowels exhibits the messianic interpretation of the postexilic Jewish community. The Targum recognizes Davidic authorship. It combines the historical David with the eschatological rule of David; however, it omits the priestly nature of Ps 110.

PSALM 110 IN THE CANONICAL CONTEXT OF THE PSALTER

Psalm 110 is considered as a royal psalm and belongs to a group of the psalms of David in Book V. Therefore, it is necessary to examine Ps 110 in light of its strategic arrangement and the relationship with other royal psalms and Davidic psalms. The royal psalms reflect God's covenant with David and his promise to establish David's dynasty forever (2 Sam 7:11b–16).[49] In view of the Davidic covenant, the royal psalms are strategically located to convey a specific message about "the Messiah's installation (Ps 2), kingdom morality (Ps 72), rejection (Ps 89), victory (Ps 110), reign (in Zion; Ps 132), and final eschatological battle and blessings (Ps 144)."[50]

The seeming rejection of the Davidic covenant and the hope for the restoration in Ps 89 is followed by the divine assurance of the installation and victory of the messiah in Ps 110.[51] In light of the strategic arrange-

---

49. Kim, "Speaker and the Addressee," 254.

50. Kim, "Speaker and the Addressee," 254.

51. This strategic arrangement of the royal psalms 89 and 110 is further buttressed by the following points: (1) Ps 101 in Book IV underscores the coming of a Davidic ruler. Dempster argues that Ps 101, a Davidic psalm, stresses "the ideal characteristics of a human king," which suggests that "a just *Davidic* monarch" will reign one day. Dempster, *Dominion and Dynasty*, 199. (2) Book 4 ends with psalms that cry for deliverance from the exilic community (Pss 105–6). Hossfeld and Zenger, *Psalms 3*, 102; Tucker and Grant, *Psalms*, 550. (3) Book V begins with a psalm that praises God's covenantal faithfulness (i.e., the salvation of the exile and the restoration of Davidic covenant) as an answer to the plea for deliverance and restoration. Book V begins with the historical psalm of God's covenantal faithfulness that is considered as "an answer

ment of royal psalms, it is not surprising that Ps 110 resembles Ps 2. As with Ps 1, Ps 2 functions as the introduction of the whole Psalter. Psalm 110 affirms the installation and the victory of the eschatological Davidic messiah. Thus, the images of the messianic king in Ps 110 identify David's lord as the messiah installed by YHWH to rule the nations with an iron scepter in Ps 2.[52] Furthermore, Ps 110 "expands the vision of the figure of salvation to a multifaceted king-priest portrayal."[53]

In its immediate context, Ps 110 becomes "the linchpin Psalm of the first seven psalms of book 5."[54] Psalms 107–9 convey an "anguished plea for deliverance."[55] Psalm 110 responds to the plea with God's deliverance.[56] Psalms 111–13 are praise to YHWH for his deliverance.[57] In

---

to the plea of the exiles." The reappearance of David in Pss 108–10 indicates the return of the king (i.e., Davidic ruler) in accordance with God's covenantal faithfulness (i.e., Davidic covenant; 2 Sam 7). Vaillancourt, *Multifaceted Saviour*, 121. See also Hossfeld and Zenger, *Psalms 3*, 102.

52. Vaillancourt lists the shared images of the king as follows: "If Zion is the place of the king's enthronement in Ps. 2.6, Yhwh sends forth the strength of David's lord from Zion in Ps. 110.2. And if the king acts in power to break the enemies of Yhwh with a rod of iron (Ps. 2.9), the figure of salvation in Ps 110 will act in power and will also have a willing army at his disposal who will fight alongside him in the strength of Yhwh (Ps. 110.2–3, 5–7). Further, the theme of wrath toward the enemies of Yhwh also occurs in Ps. 110.5 and in Ps. 2.5, 12." Vaillancourt, *Multifaceted Saviour*, 119–20. See also, Hossfeld and Zenger, *Psalms 3*, 144; Seybold, *Psalmen*, 437.

53. Vaillancourt, *Multifaceted Saviour*, 119.

54. Davis, "Psalm 110," 168.

55. Davis, "Psalm 110," 168.

56. Psalm 110 is the final psalm of the three David psalms (Pss 108–110) in the beginning of Book V. Framing Book V with the other Davidic psalms at the end of Book V, these Davidic psalms stress the restoration of the Davidic messiah in Book V. Hossfeld and Zenger, *Psalms 3*, 118; Tucker and Grant, *Psalms*, 565. Situated at the end of the tripartite Davidic psalms (Pss 108–110), Ps 110 functions as the answer to David's petition and praise for God's deliverance and anticipated victory against his enemies. Zenger, "Composition and Theology," 90; Vaillancourt, *Multifaceted Saviour*, 123.

57. Davis, "Psalm 110," 168. See also Vaillancourt, *Multifaceted Saviour*, 123. Many scholars propose that Pss 111–12 elaborate on YHWH and David's lord in Ps 110. They argue that just as Ps 110 demonstrates the close interaction between YHWH and David's lord in Ps 110, YHWH in Ps 111 and the human kingly figure in Ps 112 relate to each other. Robertson, *Flow of the Psalms*, 199; Davis, *Contextual Analysis*, 319. Their argument derives from the verbal, thematic and structural links between Pss 110–12. For instance, the keyword עוֹלָם that links Pss 110–13 supports the interconnectedness between these psalms. Snearly, *Return of the King*, 120–27. Lee notices the verbal and thematic links between Pss 111–12 (i.e., Ps 111:2, 3b, 4a, 5, 7 correspond to Ps 112:1, 3b, 6, 4, 9, 5 in order). Lee, "Psalm 110," 35. Davis suggests the three conceptual links between Ps 110 and Ps 111: "a gathering of people (110:3; 111:1), God's special relationship to His people (110:3; 111:9), and the defeat of nations (110:6; 111:6)." Davis,

conclusion, Ps 110 not only affirms the installation and victory of the eschatological Davidic messiah in Ps 2, but also expands the image of this salvific figure with a priest-king motif.

PSALM 110 AND OTHER OT TEXTS

The relationship between Ps 110 and other Old Testament texts can broaden the understanding regarding the significance of the quotation and allusion of Ps 110 in the Markan narrative. First, this research has discussed how Ps 110 relates to the Davidic covenant and the Abrahamic covenant. The eternal nature of God's appointment (Ps 110:4) clearly reverberates his covenant with David in 2 Sam 7.[58] The promise of priesthood in the manner of Melchizedek connects Ps 110 to Melchizedek's blessing on Abram in Gen 14:18–24 and God's confirmation of the Abrahamic covenant in Gen 15:1–11. As Emadi states, "The solidarity between Melchizedek and Abraham hints at the type of priesthood that will be capable of mediating the blessings of the Abrahamic covenant to the nations."[59]

The priest-king imagery of Ps 110:4 appears also in other Old Testament texts.[60] A more relevant text to Ps 110 is Zech 6:9–15.[61] Especially, Zech 6:13 anticipates the coming of the eschatological Davidic king who will also assume the priestly role ("It is he who will build the temple of the LORD, and he will be clothed with majesty and will sit and rule on his throne. And he will be a priest on his throne. And there will be harmony between the two"; Zech 6:13 NIV).[62] The motifs of the eschatological

---

"Psalm 110," 169.

58. Furthermore, the chronicler (1 Chr 28:5; 29:23), in light of the sonship of the Davidic kings promised in 2 Sam 7, describes Solomon's coronation as sitting on the throne of YHWH. Gese, *Zur biblishen Theologie*, 130.

59. Emadi, "Priest Forever," 66–68.

60. Though a clear allusive relationship to Ps 110 cannot be proved, several texts about David and his sons serving as a priest-king are interconnected with Ps 110 thematically (2 Sam 6:14, 18; 8:18; 1 Kgs 8:14, 55, 62–64).

61. Zechariah is told by YHWH to crown Joshua. However, the crowning of the high priest, Joshua, does not signify Joshua's coronation but symbolically represents the nature of the crowning of the coming Shoot (Zech 6:9–11). Petterson, *Behold*, 104–8. The Shoot indicates the eschatological descendant of David who will build the temple (Zech 6:12–13a; cf. Jer 33:15). Petterson, *Behold*, 108–9.

62. In contrast to some scholars who translates Zech 6:13b as "a priest beside his throne" (i.e., Davidic king), Daniel Block translates the MT as following: "And he shall sit and rule on his throne. And he will be a priest on his throne, and harmonious

rule of a Davidic priest-king on YHWH's throne and a perfect harmony between the Shoot and YHWH seem to fit well with Ps 110. These similarities between the two texts appear to show that Zech 6:13 at least echoes Ps 110. Yet, without clear lexical parallels, one cannot affirm that Zech 6:13 alludes to Ps 110. Apart from the above texts, Hengel suggests Dan 7:9–14 as a parallel OT text of Ps 110:1.[63] While some similarities exist, it is difficult to prove that these texts are dependent on Ps 110:1.[64] But as the parallel text, Dan 7:13 seems to influence Mark's appropriation of Dan 7:13 and Ps 110:1 in tandem in Mark 14:62. In summary, Ps 110 clearly alludes to Melchizedek in Gen 14 and is inseparably tied to the Abrahamic covenant. Psalm 110 also alludes to the Davidic covenant (2 Sam 7). Finally, it seems that Zech 6:13 reflects the Davidic priest-king in Ps 110:4.

PSALM 110 IN SECOND TEMPLE LITERATURE

While some scholars suggest a few texts in Second Temple Jewish literature that allude to Ps 110, these texts are insufficient to be considered as allusions to Ps 110. Therefore, there are no clear allusions to Ps 110 during the Second Temple period before the New Testament. For instance,

---

counsel will exist between them" (Zech 6:13b). He bases his translation on the syntactical reason that "the initial waw consecutive precludes a change in subject from the previous clause." Block, "My Servant David," 36. NIV, NLT, NASB, and some other scholars basically agree with his translation. See Baldwin, *Haggai, Zechariah, Malachi*, 136–37; Petterson, *Behold*, 104, 110. Some scholars rightly question the interpretation that regards "the two (שְׁנֵיהֶם, literally 'two of them')" as the two roles (i.e., a king and a priest) instead of two persons, i.e., Rose, *Zemah and Zerubbabel*, 60. Therefore, it would be more appropriate to consider that "his throne" refers to YHWH's throne, and שְׁנֵיהֶם refers to the LORD and the Shoot (who assumes both roles of a king and a priest). Petterson, *Behold*, 111. Petterson addresses a group of scholars who take this view such as Pusey, Baron, Higginson, Kline, and Jauhiainen. For a complete bibliography, see Petterson, *Behold*, 111n99.

63. Hengel, "Sit at My Right Hand," 180–84.

64. According to Hengel, both texts share the concepts of "the subjugation of the kingdoms of the world, the judgement over kings and peoples and the everlasting character of his dominion." See Hengel, "Sit at My Right Hand," 185. See also Hay, *Glory at the Right Hand*, 26. Hengel himself admits that Daniel lacks the enthronement motif and "the title 'lord' for the 'one like a human.'" That is, the Aramaic Text of Daniel does not say that the human figure "takes his place at the right hand of the Ancient of Days." See Hengel, "Sit at My Right Hand," 185. In Mark 14, Jesus alludes to both Ps 110:1 and Dan 7:13–14 and identifies himself as the Danielic Son of Man, who is at the same time the Davidic Messiah, sitting at the right hand of God. Yet, there is no clear evidence that Dan 7:9–14 relates to Ps 110:1 before NT period.

Hengel proposes a combination of Dan 7 and Ps 110:1 in the *Similitudes of Enoch* that envisions the elect one (i.e., the Son of Man) sitting on God's throne and judging at the last days (i.e., *1 En.* 51:3; 55:4; 61:8; 62:2).[65] While we acknowledge the thematic similarities between Ps 110:1 and these texts of the *Similitudes of Enoch*, the allusion is not specific enough to claim that they derive from Ps 110. Bauckham rightly questions why the *Parables of Enoch* does not use the phrase "at the right hand of God," as many New Testament allusions to Ps 110:1 do.[66] Therefore, the given texts in the *Parables of Enoch* "represent a parallel rather than a source."[67] However, the similarities between the two texts may explain why Mark appropriated Ps 110:1 and Dan 7:13 together in Mark 14:62.

A more likely allusion to Ps 110:1 is *Testament of Job* 33:3.[68] *Testament of Job* 33:3 is the answer to Elihu, who repeatedly questions the glory of Job's earthly throne (*T. Job* 32:1–12) as he laments over Job's losses. Job replies, "My throne is in the upper world and its splendor and majesty come from *the right hand of the Father*" (*T. Job* 33:3b). Furthermore, Job's claim for the eternal nature of his throne and kingdom is confirmed as angels take his soul to heaven.[69] Despite these lexical and thematic parallels that point to *Testament of Job* 33:3 as an allusion to Ps 110:1, the disputed dating of the book prevents readers from accepting the book as pre-Christian literature.[70] Moreover, as Hay admits, Job is "never described as a ruler or Messiah of Israel."[71]

Besides *Testament of Job* 33:3, a group of scholars propose that certain texts of Second Temple literature allude to Ps 110 in defense of the Hasmonean dynasty that held both the high priesthood and the kingship. For example, Hay suggests that *Testament of Levi* 8 and 18 allude to Ps 110

65. Hengel, "Sit at My Right Hand," 185.
66. Bauckham, *Jesus and the God of Israel*, 170.
67. Bauckham, *Jesus and the God of Israel*, 175.
68. Hay, *Glory at the Right Hand*, 22–23; Bauckham, *Jesus and the God of Israel*, 174.
69. Hay, *Glory at the Right Hand*, 23.
70. Hay claims scholars widely agree that the book dates "from the first century BCE or the first century CE." Hay, *Glory at the Right Hand*, 22. However, Hay's assertion does not have scholarly consensus. Opinions on dating range from 200 BCE to 200 CE. Waugh, "Testament of Job," 782. Since our focus is to see how the appropriation of Ps 110 the Second Temple literature might have influenced Mark's use of Ps 110, we exclude any literature after the time of Mark.
71. Hay, *Glory at the Right Hand*, 22. Similarly, Bauckham perceives that the allusion to Ps 110:1 in the *Testament of Job* 33:3 is used differently from Ps 110:1 (i.e., "individual heavenly reward") and admits that the book may "be a Christian work influenced by the New Testament." See Bauckham, *Jesus and the God of Israel*, 174.

to legitimize the Hasmonean rule.⁷² Supporting the proposal that *Testament of Levi* alludes to Ps 110 to defend the legitimacy of the Hasmonean rulers, deSilva argues that *Testaments of the Twelve Patriarchs*, of which *Testament of Levi* is a part, contains a great amount of pre-Christian Jewish content.⁷³ However, deSilva acknowledges, "The Testaments of the Twelve Patriarchs in its present form is a Christian text preserved within Christian communities."⁷⁴ Therefore, though it is possible, scholars are not certain that the texts of *Testament of Levi* 8 and 18 are pre-Christian.

According to Tilly, 1 Macc 14:41 describes the decision of the people's assembly that the Hasmonean Simon will be the eternal "ἡγούμενος καί ἀρχιερεύς ('leader and high priest') 'until a true prophet appears.'"⁷⁵ Tilly considers 1 Macc 14:41 to be an allusion to Ps 110:1, 4.⁷⁶ However, we are not sure if 1 Macc 14:41 alludes to Ps 110 or Gen 14:18–20. If this text alludes to or echoes Ps 110, it would be an example of how Ps 110 was used for the Hasmonean propaganda.⁷⁷ However, even if the allusive relationship stands, it does not have any bearing on the use of Ps 110 in Mark since the Hasmonean dynasty does not have any relationship with the Davidic dynasty.⁷⁸

Why are there no explicit quotations or allusions to Ps 110 that exist from Second Temple Jewish literature before the NT? Von Nordheim argues that the paucity of the trace on Ps 110 during the Hellenistic and Roman periods may have derived from the tension between the Hasmonean ruling party and their opponents (i.e., the Essenes), who did not approve the high priesthood of the Hasmonean rulers.⁷⁹ Von Nordheim's claim seems to explain the absence of any trace of Ps 110 in Dead Sea

---

72. Hay suggests that *Testament of Levi* 8:3 and the several phrases of *Testament of Levi* 18 are correlated to the Hasmoneans and allude to Ps 110 (i.e., "From henceforth become a priest of the Lord, you and your seed forever. And the first man anointed me with holy oil, and give to me the staff of judgment," *T. Levi* 8:3; cf. Ps 110:2. Of *T. Levi* 18, "... he shall *execute* a righteous *judgment*..." Ps 110:6; "And his *star* shall arise in heaven as of a king," Ps 110:3; "And he shall give power to His children to *tread upon* the evil spirits," Ps 110:1c). Hay, *Glory at the Right Hand*, 24–25. See also Brooke, "Psalms," 19; Von Nordheim, *Geboren*, 230–35.

73. deSilva, "Testaments," 21–68.

74. deSilva, "Testaments," 67.

75. Tilly, "Psalm 110," 161–62.

76. Tilly, "Psalm 110," 161–62.

77. In addition, Hay suggests a possible allusion to Ps 110 from 11Q Melchizedek (11Q13). Hay, *Glory at the Right Hand*, 27.

78. Tilly, "Psalm 110," 162.

79. Von Nordheim, *Geboren*, 272.

Scrolls.⁸⁰ However, the absence (or the paucity for some scholars) of Ps 110 in the Second Temple literature does not mean that the postexilic Jewish community does not consider Ps 110 messianically. LXX and Targum interpret Ps 110 with the Davidic messiah in mind.⁸¹ Bauckham suggests that the seemingly audacious claim on the heavenly throne in Ps 110 may have discouraged Second Temple Jews from using Ps 110 to avoid the possible infringement on their monotheistic beliefs.⁸² Though one cannot be certain about the reason, Bauckham's suggestion seems to have some truth in it.

In conclusion, Ps 110 was written by David concerning the messiah from his offspring who would follow his pattern (i.e., the priest-king). Yet, this Davidic messiah will be greater than David (i.e., his lord). His rule will be the ultimate fulfillment of the Abrahamic and Davidic covenants. Thus, Ps 110 not only affirms the universal rule of the Davidic messiah, the son of God with the subjugation of his enemies in Ps 2, but also consummates it with the divine oracles of the complete subjugation and the eternal priestly kingship. As for the ancient variants, LXX is virtually identical with MT, though rewording of some vowels shows the messianic interpretation of the postexilic Jewish community. Targum affirms Davidic authorship and mingles the historical David with the eschatological rule of David, even to the point that it replaces the priestly aspect in Ps 110:4 with the Davidic royal ruler.

The canonical context of Ps 110 shows that Ps 110 is the response to the plea for God's deliverance in Pss 107–9 followed by praise to YHWH for his deliverance in Pss 111–13. Psalm 110 both affirms the installation

---

80. Von Nordheim illustrates that the Aramaic version of the Testament of Levi does not allude to Ps 118. von Nordheim, *Geboren*, 272. Scholars generally agree that neither text (either quotation or allusion) nor pesharim on Ps 110 are found in Dead Sea Scroll. Bons, "Septuaginta-Version," 123.

81. Similarly, Hay cautiously judges, "It seems fair to suppose that in the NT era a messianic interpretation of Ps 110 was current in Judaism, although we cannot know how widely it was accepted." Hay, *Glory at the Right Hand*, 30. Juel is more positive about the prevalence of the messianic interpretation on Ps 110. He states that the citation of Ps 110:1 in Mark 12:35–37 "seems to presume the widespread agreement that the psalm speaks of the Davidic Messiah." Juel, *Messianic Exegesis*, 138n10.

82. Bauckham, *Jesus and the God of Israel*, 175. As for the absence of the allusion to Ps 110 in Second Temple literature, Bauckham contrasts it with the role of Ps 110 in the New Testament as follows: "The explanation of its role in early Christology, contrasted with its absence from Second Temple Jewish literature, is that, for early Christians, it said about Jesus what no other Jews had wished to say about the Messiah or any other figure: that he had been exalted by God to participate now in the cosmic sovereignty unique to the divine identity." Bauckham, *Jesus and the God of Israel*, 175.

and victory of the eschatological Davidic messiah in Ps 2 and expands the image of this salvific figure with a priest-king motif. Psalm 110 in other OT texts shows that Ps 110's close relationship to Melchizedek in Gen 14, the Abrahamic covenant, and the Davidic covenant (2 Sam 7). Also, Zech 6:13 seems to reflect the Davidic priest-king in Ps 110:4.

Finally, as for Ps 110 in Second Temple literature, a combination of Dan 7 and Ps 110:1 in the *Similitudes of Enoch* may derive from their similar features (i.e., the elect on sitting on God's throne and judging at the last days). It offers an example that Mark follows when he uses both texts in tandem in Mark 14:62. Other possible allusions to Ps 110 in Second Temple literature seem to be either not pre-Christian, or the Hasmonean propaganda with no relation to Davidic covenant, or the combination of both. The fact that no explicit quotations or allusions to Ps 110 in Second Temple Jewish literature before the NT exist may have been motivated by the tension between the Hasmoneans and those who did not approve the high priesthood of the Hasmonean rulers. Also, the fear to infringe on the Jewish monotheistic beliefs derived from the daring claim on the heavenly throne in Ps 110 may have deterred Second Temple Jews from using Ps 110. However, the absence or paucity of the allusions to Ps 110 does not mean that the postexilic Jewish community did not view Ps 110 messianically (i.e., LXX and Targum). With these outcomes in mind, we now turn to Mark's use of Ps 110.

PSALM 110 IN MARK

The previous sections have stated that Ps 110 not only affirms the universal rule of the Davidic messiah in the pattern of Ps 2 but also consummates it with the divine oracles of the complete subjugation and the eternal priestly kingship. We also observed Ps 110's close tie to Melchizedek in Gen 14, the Abrahamic covenant, and the Davidic covenant. We hardly find any allusions and echo to Ps 110 in Old Testament text and Second Temple literature except Zech 6:13 and a combination of Dan 7 and Ps 110:1 in the *Similitudes of Enoch*. However, their presence and Ps 110 in LXX and Targum clearly evidence that some postexilic community considered Ps 110 to be messianic. We also noticed that Zech 6:13 echoes the priest-king in Ps 110:4 and that a tandem of Dan 7 and Ps 110:1 in the *Similitudes of Enoch* may show why Mark combined Dan 7:13 with Ps 110:1.

This section will scrutinize the two passages where Ps 110 is appropriated by Mark. In Mark 12:35–37, Mark quotes Ps 110:1. In doing so, Mark not only corrects the popular understanding of the Davidic messiah, but also, he builds up the literary tension that will be finally resolved by the full revelation of Jesus' identity in Mark 14:61–62. In addition, Mark was conscious of the whole context of Ps 110. In corollary, Mark's use of Ps 110 relates to the dominant temple motif in the surrounding context of Mark 12:35–37.

As for Mark 14:61–62, this section will address how the literary tension created by the quotation of Ps 110:1 in Mark 12:35–37 is resolved. Mark appropriated Ps 110:1 in Mark 14:61–62 in such a way that Jesus' heavenly enthronement typologically fulfills the messiah's rule as the vice-regent of YHWH over his enemies. This section will also examine how the temple motif relates to Mark 14:61–62 and the allusion to Ps 110. In investigating the above aspects, this section will observe how the other composited Old Testament texts (Dan 7:13; Ps 80:18) interrelate to the allusion to Ps 110:1 and present a coherent idea about Jesus' identity. Finally, this section will synthesize the findings and suggest the role of Ps 110 in the light of the entire Markan narrative structure.

Psalm 110 in Mark 12:35–37

Mark 12:35–37 is the first pericope after a series of questions which began in Mark 11:28 with the challenge of Jesus' authority over the temple (Mark 11:28—12:27). This series is followed by one exceptional question that genuinely seeks Jesus' answer (Mark 12:28–34). Having silenced the challenges of his opponents (καὶ οὐδεὶς οὐκέτι ἐτόλμα αὐτὸν ἐπερωτῆσαι "Then no one dared to ask him anymore"; Mark 12:34 b), Jesus now challenges the authority of the teaching of the scribes. Joel Marcus suggests the following chiastic structure of the passage around the quotation of Ps 110:1:

12:35a	And Jesus answered and said, teaching in the Temple, A	
12:35b	"How do the scribes say that the Christ is the Son of David? B	
12:36a	David himself said in the Holy Spirit, C	
12:36b	"The Lord said to my lord, "Sit on my right D	
12:36c	until I put your enemies under your feet."'	

12:37a   David himself calls him 'lord'; C'
12:37b   and how is he his son?" B'
12:37c   And the large crowd heard him gladly A'[83]

According to Marcus, A/A' (the setting—Jesus' teaching in the temple court and the crowd's hearing) clearly frames the passage as Jesus' teaching. B/B' poses Jesus' questions about the scribes' teaching on the Christ as David's son.[84] Marcus parallels C with C', arguing that these explain the problem of the scribes' teaching: "Davidic sonship contradicts what 'David himself' said about the Messiah."[85] However, C and the first part of the quotation ("The Lord said to my lord") in D seem to correspond better to C'. Regardless of this minor variation from Marcus's suggestion, his suggested structure demonstrates well that the citation of Ps 110:1 is the center of the narrative structure: Ps 110:1 provides scriptural evidence for Jesus' teaching about the identity of the messiah.

Many have inquired about the nature of the scribal teaching and Jesus' rhetorical question.[86] Jesus' question seems to negate the implication of the scribal teaching (i.e., David is the father of the Christ): David who called the Christ as his lord cannot be the Christ's father. Therefore, the messiah cannot be David's son.[87] However, this logic contradicts the

---

83. Marcus, *Mark 8–16*, 849.

84. Marcus, *Mark 8–16*, 849. Hays proposes the literal translation of B' (πόθεν αὐτοῦ ἐστιν υἱός;) as "'Whence (πόθεν) [comes it that] he is *his* son?'" Hays, *Gospels*, 53. According to Hays, "Jesus' question should be heard as a challenge to explicate the logic of Psalm 110:1 itself: 'Where in this text do you see the idea that the Messiah is David's son?'" Hays, *Gospels*, 54.

85. Marcus, *Mark 8–16*, 849. The contrast between David's prophetic statement and the scribes' opinion highlights the inadequacy of the scribes' teaching. Breytenbach, "Markusevangelium," 206. See also Gundry, *Mark*, 718; Evans, *Mark*, 273.

86. For instance, Lindars claims that Mark inserted the pericope in the present location to reflect the post-Easter Christian community concerning Jesus' resurrection and exaltation demonstrated in Acts 2. Lindars, *New Testament Apologetic*, 46–47. Similarly, Loader argues that Mark 12:35–37 is the "product of later christological reflection" to compensate the insufficiency of Davidic son messiahship. Loader, "Christ at the Right Hand," 215. However, a group of scholars defend the authenticity of Jesus' saying. N. T. Wright defends it based on a criterion of "double similarity and dissimilarity." Wright, *Jesus and the Victory of God*, 507–9. Rowe points out that the use of Ps 110:1 does not necessarily imply that the resurrection has transpired. He further argues that Jesus may have used the psalm that contains the theme of vindication being "aware of his likely suffering and rejection." Rowe, *God's Kingdom*, 281. See also Bock, who defends the "authenticity of Jesus' use" of Ps 110:1 in Mark 12:25–37 and Dan 7:13 in Mark 14:62. Bock, *Blasphemy and Exaltation*, 220–33.

87. Gourgues, *Droite de Dieu*, 135; Marcus, *Way of the Lord*, 140; Breytenbach,

Davidic sonship of the messiah witnessed in the OT and Second Temple literature (i.e., 2 Sam 7:12–14; *Pss. Sol.* 17:21). Moreover, the Markan narrative clearly portrays Jesus as the Davidic Messiah (i.e., Mark 10:47–48; 11:1–11).[88]

Therefore, many interpreters rightly argue that Jesus does not negate his Davidic messiahship.[89] Rather, Jesus teaches that his messianic identity surpasses the Davidic messianism taught by the scribes.[90] Possibly Jesus' teaching on the messiah's identity is the corrective to the popular militant messianism in his days.[91] Instead of negating the Davidic messianism, Jesus redefines it with Ps 110:1.[92] Its full meaning still awaits to be known at this stage of the Markan narrative. Jesus will fully reveal his messianic identity through his suffering, resurrection, ascension, and the Parousia as Mark 14:61–62, where the other citation of Ps 110:1 appears, succinctly presents.[93] As a result, the quotation of Ps 110:1 in Mark 12:35–37 serves to build the literary tension that is resolved in Mark 14:61–62 when Jesus fully reveals his identity.[94]

"Markusevangelium," 207. Some scholars, thus, conclude that Jesus announced his Davidic messiahship. See Lohmeyer, *Markus*, 262–63.

88. Though these texts do not contain Jesus' verbal affirmation on his Davidic messiahship, Mark seems to indicate that Jesus identified himself with the Davidic Messiah. He did not silence Bartimaeus's cry of "the Son of David." Moreover, Jesus himself arranged Jerusalem entry in the manner of the Davidic Messiah as the cited Scriptures in Mark demonstrate (i.e., Gen 49:10–11; Zech 9:9; Ps 118:26). See Botner, *Jesus Christ*, 140–53.

89. Gourgues, *Droite de Die*, 135; Marcus, *Way of the Lord*, 151–52; Evans, *Mark*, 274–75; France, *Mark*, 283–85; Watts, *Psalms*, 36.

90. Hay, *Glory at the Right Hand*, 111; Lövestam, "Davidssohnfrage," 80; Evans, *Mark*, 276; Subrahmanian, *Synoptic Gospels*, 62–63. Some scholars suggest that Jesus follows the haggadic practice of juxtaposing two seemingly contradicting Scriptures (i.e., the messiah as David's son possibly from 2 Sam 7:12–14 and David's lord from Ps 110:1) and solving the alleged contradiction. See Juel, *Messianic Exegesis*, 142–43; Rowe, *God's Kingdom*, 280. According to them, the solution appears at the time of Jesus' resurrection and enthronement at the right hand of God. Juel, *Messianic Exegesis*, 144. See also a similar opinion for the narrative tension, Hay, *Glory at the Right Hand*, 114.

91. Hay, *Glory at the Right Hand*, 111; Kingsbury, *Christology of Mark's Gospel*, 113; Wright, *Jesus and the Victory of God*, 509; France, *Mark*, 484; Ahearne-Kroll, *Psalms of Lament*, 165–66.

92. Hays, *Gospels*, 55.

93. Hay, *Glory at the Right Hand*, 113–14; Evans, *Mark*, 276; Rowe, *God's Kingdom*, 284.

94. Hay explicates how Mark uses the two citations of Ps 110:1 for his narrative purpose. He states, "After 14.61–62, 12.35–37 adds nothing to the gospel in terms of theological doctrine. But, coming two chapters before the trial confession, the debate

Furthermore, the connection between the two citations of Ps 110:1 in the Markan narrative may explain why the allusion to Ps 8:6 (ὑποκάτω τῶν ποδῶν σου) is combined with Ps 110:1 in Mark 12:36. Psalm 8:4–6 shares the Son of Man motif with Ps 80:18 (MT) and Dan 7:13, the two other Old Testament allusions that are combined with Ps 110:1 in Mark 14:62b. All the Son of Man passages in Ps 8:4, Ps 80:18, and Dan 7:13 seem to convey the notion of both an Adamic and Davidic royal figure.[95] Therefore, Mark may have intentionally combined the allusions to Ps 110 and Ps 8 in Mark 12:36 as a literary device to indicate the connection to Mark 14:61–62, where Christ's exaltation (Ps 110:1) is combined with the Son of Man motif (Ps 80:18; Dan 7:13).[96] Or, the similarities in idea and sound between Pss 8:6 and 110:1 may have caused the merging of the wording in Mark 12:36.[97]

Even though Mark quotes only Ps 110:1, Mark appears to have the whole context of Ps 110 in mind to disclose Jesus' messiahship. Several factors support this argument. First, in the exegesis of Ps 110, Ps 110:1 is not only the introduction but the key divine command that governs the entire psalm. The enthronement of the messiah at the right hand of God and the subjugation of his enemies by the collaboration of YHWH and the king (and his armies) are key points of the psalm. In Mark 12:35–37, Jesus proleptically enacts the subjugation of his enemies by silencing his opponents and indicating that his God-given authority is "premised upon his own eschatological place at the right hand of God."[98]

Second, Mark's use of Ps 110 reflects that of Ps 2. Chapter 3 of this book explained that Mark's use of Ps 2:7 exhibits the key motifs of Ps 2, such as God's kingdom rule through his Messiah (i.e., Jesus) and

---

story adds drama and a measure of suspense. Just as the message of the Messiah's suffering is not fully stated early in the gospel but emerges only gradually, so also the meaning of his glory is brought out in stages (e.g., at Mark 9.1–8; 13:26–27; 14:28, 62; 16.7). The saying in 12.35–37 essentially raises a question about the superiority of the messiah to the son of David expected within Judaism, and the reader is left uncertain how that superiority is to be specified. So, Mark's dominant motive for including this saying about David's son was probably a literary one, that of creating a tension in the gospel not to be resolved before Jesus' trial." Hay, *Glory at the Right Hand*, 114.

95. Mays, "What Is a Human Being," 517–18; Tate, "Exposition on Psalm 8," 343–59; Streett, *Vine*, 34–35, 38, 112–13.

96. Breytenbach, "Markusevangelium," 212–13. The composited allusions of Pss 80, 110, and Dan 7 will be discussed in the section of Mark 14:61–62.

97. I had this idea from the dialogue with my dissertation supervisor, Andrew Streett.

98. Hays, *Gospels*, 56–57. See also Emadi, "Royal Priest," 199.

subjugation of his enemies (i.e., Satan and his followers such as the religious leaders). It is evident that Mark's use of Ps 2:7 has the whole context of Ps 2 in mind. Likewise, the quotation of Ps 110:1 in Mark 12:36 and the allusion to Ps 110:1 in Mark 14:62 show that Mark is conscious of the whole context of Ps 110—Jesus' authority as the Messiah who will be enthroned as the king "next to God himself," and that both he and YHWH will subjugate the Messiah's enemies.[99]

---

99. Rowe, *God's Kingdom*, 283. Thus, in the pericope, the scribes are among the Messiah's enemies. Marcus, *Way of the Lord*, 133–37. Even though Mark does not explicitly cite Ps 110:4, the context of Mark 12:35–37 seems to support the idea that he was aware of the entire psalm, including Ps 110:4. Just as Ps 110 expands the images of the messiah with the priest-king like Melchizedek, the use of Ps 110 in Mark extends Jesus' messianic roles with his "priestly authority." Watts, "Psalms," 39. As for Mark 12:35–37, it is one of several instances of the confrontation between Jesus and the Jerusalem temple authorities concerning Jesus' authority over the temple actions and sayings. Moreover, Mark, by stating that the setting of Mark 12:35–37 is the temple (Mark 12:35), seems to highlight that Jesus' teaching is related to the temple. Therefore, as Watts states, it might be that "Mark highlights Jesus' priestly role in teaching and safeguarding the sanctity of the sanctuary precisely because of Ps 110's Melchizedek association. If so, the citation implies both Jesus' priestly authority and, by virtue of its Melchizedekian character, that it supersedes that of the present Temple authorities (cf. Heb 7)." Watts, "Psalms," 39. The fact that "the person David describes as 'my lord' is the only scriptural figure outside of Melchizedek in Gen 14:18 explicitly designated as a priest-king" increases the possibility that Mark considered the priest-king motif by citing Ps 110:1 in Mark 12:36. Botner, *Jesus Christ*, 167. Also, David's lord in Ps 110:1 is the priest-king who fulfills the Davidic covenant and the Abrahamic covenant. By citing Ps 110:1, Mark, through the lips of Jesus, may imply that Jesus is the fulfillment of the anticipated prophetic oracle of David regarding the priest-king. So Emadi says, "In the city of David, in the temple, Jesus claims the highest authoritative offices the Old Testament had to offer: Davidic kingship and Melchizedekian priesthood. By virtue of his kingly authority and superior priesthood, he will render the temple, its leadership, and the entire Mosaic program null and void." Emadi, "Royal Priest," 199. Several scholars argue that Jesus' priestly role supports his identity as the priest-king in the manner of Ps 110 even before the citation of Ps 110 in the Markan narrative (i.e., the exorcism of an unclean spirit in Mark 1:21–28; 5:1–20; touching a person with unclean skin disease in Mark 1:40–45; the offer of forgiving sins in Mark 2:1–13; eating and healing on the Sabbath in Mark 2:23–28; 3:1–6; declaration of all foods to be clean in Mark 7:9). See Broadhead, "Christology," 21–34; Fletcher-Louis, "Jesus as the High Priestly Messiah: Part I," 155–75; Fletcher-Louis, "Jesus as the High Priestly Messiah: Part 2," 57–79; Emadi, "Royal Priest," 185–98. However, the suggested texts do not necessarily support Jesus' priestly role. As Emadi, who draws from the arguments of other scholars to build up his case, admits, "No single strand of evidence in Mark 1:1—8:26 proves that Mark intended to portray Jesus' ministry as a priestly ministry." Emadi, "Royal Priest," 185. His plea for the cumulative force of the accumulated texts begs the question. For a detailed argument against Jesus' priestly role in some of these passages, see Snow, *Daniel's Son of Man*, 69–71, 75–77.

In conclusion, by quoting Ps 110:1 in Mark 12:36, Jesus distinguishes himself from the popular understanding about the messiah. He is more than the son of David. At the narrative level, the quotation anticipates the full revelation of who the Messiah is in Mark 14:62. At the same time, confronting the teaching of the scribes, one major group of the temple establishment, Jesus reveals his authority over the temple. It seems that Mark was conscious of the whole context of Ps 110: Jesus is the priest-king who will bring the new temple order (Ps 110:4) in the context of a series of temple confrontations with the present temple establishment. Also, by silencing his opponents, Jesus figuratively subjugates his enemies (Ps 110). The ensuing narrative—condemnation of the temple establishment (i.e., the scribes; Mark 12:38–40), widow at the temple as a foil for the scribes (Mark 12:41–44), and the destruction of the temple followed by Jesus' coming at the Parousia in Mark 13—indicates that Jesus' citation is related to the new order of the temple.

Psalm 110 in Mark 14:61–62

After Jesus' teaching discourse about the temple destruction and his second coming in Mark 13, Mark 14 begins the passion narrative. One characteristic feature of Mark 14 at the level of the narrative structure is to contrast Jesus (and his exemplary followers, such as the woman at Bethany) with those who either oppose him (the Jewish religious leaders) or fail to follow him (i.e., the disciples). Mark 14 depicts chronologically how Jesus' arrest and trial are enacted. Starting from the conspiracy between Judas Iscariot and the religious leaders, Mark 14 escalates to the arrest and the trial that lead to Jesus' death. Yet, Jesus is sovereign in all the incidents and determines to accomplish his mission, bringing God's kingdom through his crucifixion (Mark 14:8, 21–25, 27–28, 49).

Mark 14:61–62 is a part of the trial scene by the religious leaders (Mark 14:55–65), which is intercalated by Peter's denial (Mark 14:54 and Mark 14:66–72). The key point of this sandwich structure is evident: Jesus does not deny his identity and consequently suffers because of his confession. However, Peter denies his identity as Jesus' disciple in order to avert suffering. Even when his own disciples denied him, Jesus could not deny who he was. Thus, Mark 14:61–62 (the full revelation of Jesus' identity) is the crux of Mark 14:53–72.[100]

---

100. Juel, *Messiah and Temple*, 117.

Mark 14:55–59

While Mark 14:55–59 stresses Jesus' innocence in the midst of the false and contradictory witnesses against him, the narrator selectively presents one ironic example which is false but has some truth in it ("We heard him say, 'I will destroy this temple made with hands, and in three days, I will build another not made with hands'"; Mark 14:58).[101] Jesus never said that he would destroy the Herodian temple and build a new temple.[102] However, the Markan narrative presents that Jesus' coming and mission will induce the destruction of the Jerusalem temple and the constitution of a new temple (i.e., Mark 13; 12:11–12).[103] Mark seems to choose this testimony to highlight the temple motif in the trial of Jesus.

Since Jesus' entry into Jerusalem, the temple is the ongoing motif that runs through the Markan narrative. Jesus' trial and death fulfill the rejection of the temple cornerstone in Mark 12:11. Similar to the false

---

101. Juel, *Messiah and Temple*, 117; van Iersel, *Mark*, 446.

102. Juel, *Messiah and Temple*, 122; Stein, *Mark*, 682; Moloney, *Mark*, 302–3; Strauss, *Mark*, 660; Snow, *Daniel's Son of Man*, 178. In contrast to Juel and others, Botner argues that ἄλλον ἀχειροποίητον ("another sanctuary not made with hands") refers to an eschatological heavenly sanctuary rather than a Christian community. He interprets the connotation of ἀχειροποίητον as "heavenly" from the encyclopedia of the Second Temple literature and other New Testament books. Botner, "Sanctuary in the Heavens," 310–34. Though his suggestion is another semantic possibility for the word, ἀχειροποίητον, the Markan narrative seems to support the Christian community as the meaning of "another sanctuary not made with hands." Mark 12:11–12 indicates that Jesus will be the foundation of the new temple by his death after the destruction of the present temple. Snow, *Daniel's Son of Man*, 125. The same concept is found in other New Testament books (1 Cor 3:16–17; Eph 2:20–22; 1 Pet 2:5). Some scholars argue that building a new sanctuary not made with hand in three days indicates Jesus' resurrected body because Jesus' prediction on the passion connects his resurrection with three days (Mark 8:31; 9:31; 10:34). Hooker, *Mark*, 359; Donahue and Harrington, *Mark*, 421; Stein, *Mark*, 685. While it has some exegetical validity, again the clear new temple motif in Mark 12:11–12 points to Jesus as the foundation of the new temple (i.e., the Christian community).

103. Juel, *Messiah and Temple*, 118; Donahue, "Temple," 69; France, *Mark*, 605; Boring, *Mark*, 412. Juel connects Mark 11:17 (the warning on the temple establishment), 12:1–12 (the parable of the wicked tenants), 13:1–2 (the prediction on the temple destruction), and 15:38 (the tearing of the temple veil at the time of Jesus' death) to Mark 14:58 and concludes, "Mark intends the charge at the trial to be viewed as true in some sense." Juel, *Messiah and Temple*, 138. Referring to the messianic community of Jesus' followers, Donahue says, "This community is to be the new *naos*, a substitute for the Temple destroyed proleptically in the ministry of Jesus and historically in the events of the Roman-Jewish War." Donahue, "Temple," 70–71. Similarly, Juel lists a group of scholars who view the "'temple not made with hands' refers to the Christian community." Juel, *Messiah and Temple*, 144–45.

charge in Mark 14:58, the mockery at the cross ("Aha! You who is going to destroy the sanctuary and build it in three days"; Mark 15:28) confirms how the temple motif is intimately related to Jesus' death. The tearing of the temple curtain (τὸ καταπέτασμα τοῦ ναοῦ) in Mark 15:38 is the culmination of the temple destruction motif in the false charge and mockery against Jesus (Mark 12:58; 15:29) and functions as God's vindication for Jesus.[104] As a result, the false charge in Mark 14:58 discloses the nature of Jesus' messiahship. Through his suffering and death, Jesus will bring about God's kingdom by ending the old temple and building the new temple. Then, it is not inadvertent that Mark narrates the temple charge as the part of Jesus' "trial whose point is that Jesus was condemned for his messianic claim."[105]

Mark 14:60–62

Psalm 80:18 in Mark 14:62: the allusion to Ps 80:18 in Mark 14:62b witnesses the Messiah's suffering and vindication and, thus, connects the other allusions, Ps 110:1 and Dan 7:13 in Mark 14:62b.[106] Psalm 80 was originally written as "a lament for the destruction of the Northern Kingdom of Israel" in order to "remind Yahweh of God's former blessing on the twelve tribes and to plead for restoration through the leadership of a Davidic king."[107] In the canonical context of the Psalter, the messianic connotation of Ps 80 was strengthened as it is connected with other eschatological royal psalms (i.e., Pss 2; 89l 110).[108]

Psalm 80:18 seems to evidence verbal, structural, and thematic parallels with Mark 14:62b. According to Streett, (1) besides the suggested

---

104. Juel, *Messiah and Temple*, 137–38. Juel observes that only three occurrences of the temple in Mark (Mark 12:58, 15:29, 38) have ναός instead of ἱερόν. All three occurrences relate to the destruction of the temple (and building of the new temple). Juel, *Messiah and Temple*, 128. See also France, *Mark*, 657–58; Brown, *Death of the Messiah*, 2:1099–109.

105. Juel, *Messiah and Temple*, 213.

106. Streett, *Vine*, 191

107. Streett, *Vine*, 46. Similarly, Kaiser states, "The psalmist pleads with Israel's covenant God, YHWH, who is also God over all creation and over mighty armies, to repeat with Joseph's descendants his restoration of Joseph from suffering. The agent of this restoration is to be the 'son of man,' the Messiah." Kaiser, "Messiah of Psalm 80," 93. As for the identification of the son of man with the Davidic messiah, see Hill, "Son of Man," 261–69; Ahn, "Equivocality of Psalm 80," 109–10.

108. Streett, *Vine*, 49. Some scholars view Ps 80 as one of the royal psalms. i.e., Jo, "Equivocality," 100–8.

verbal correspondence above, the "'son=Messiah=son of man' equation" is found in both Ps 80:16, 18 and Mark 14:61–62.[109] (2) The word order of Mark 14:62b is closer to Ps 80:18 than Ps 110:1.[110] (3) The oppression and vindication motif in Ps 80 corresponds to Jesus' imminent suffering (and death) and vindication in Mark 14:62 and its immediate context.[111]

Streett rightly argues that Ps 80 shares some elements with Ps 110 and Dan 7. First, the right hand of YHWH in both Ps 80:18 and 110:1 "communicates the idea that the king is God's viceregent, the representative of God's reign on earth."[112] Second, Dan 7 alludes to Ps 80. They agree verbally and conceptually—the beastly foreign nations and a royal figure, (one like a) son of man. Also, the sequences of events correspond to each other.[113] Few scholars recognize the allusion to Ps 80:18 due to the verbal correspondences between Ps 80 and two other texts such as "right hand" and "son of man." However, considering the above correspondences between Ps 80 and other texts, it seems natural for Mark to conflate the three texts.

Especially, because of Ps 80's shared motifs with other appropriated texts, Mark may have used Ps 80:18, the plea to God for deliverance through the messiah, as "the connecting text" between Ps 110:1 and Dan 7:13:[114] (1) Pss 80:18 and 110:1 are linked in their focus on "the son of man sitting at God's 'right hand.'" (2) By "son of man," Ps 80:18 connects to Dan 7:14 as it "introduces the notion of Jesus' coming with the clouds."[115] (3) Thematically, Ps 80 complements Ps 110 and Dan 7 with

---

109. Streett, *Vine*, 186. Jesus admits his identity as the Messiah, the Son of God, and refers to himself as the Son of Man, just as there is "the connection between 'son' and 'son of man' in Ps 80:16, 18." Streett, *Vine*, 186.

110. Unlike the parallel passages, Matt 26:64 and Luke 22:69 (τὸν υἱὸν τοῦ ἀνθρώπου καθήμενον ἐκ δεξιῶν and ὁ υἱὸς τοῦ ἀνθρώπου καθήμενος ἐκ δεξιῶν), τὸν υἱὸν τοῦ ἀνθρώπου is placed before ἐκ δεξιῶν in Mark 14:62b (τὸν υἱὸν τοῦ ἀνθρώπου ἐκ δεξιῶν καθήμενον), just as ἄνδρα is located directly before δεξιᾶς in Ps 79:18 (LXX). Streett, *Vine*, 186.

111. Streett, *Vine*, 187–88.

112. Streett, *Vine*, 85.

113. Streett finds the following correspondences in the sequence of events: "First, the beastly nations oppress and destroy (Ps 80:14; Dan 7:4–7). Second, God is called to act on the people's behalf in Ps 80:15–16, and in Dan 7:9–10 the Ancient of Days comes for judgment. Third, Ps 80:17 actually asks God to cause the nation's enemies to 'perish at the rebuke of your countenance,' and Dan 7:11 recounts the destruction of the fourth beast. Finally, Ps 80:18 asks God to be with the royal son of man God has strengthened, and Dan 7:13–14 describes the coming of a son of man who receives the kingship." Streett, *Vine*, 107–8.

114. Streett, *Vine*, 190.

115. Streett, "Marginal to Mainstream," 96.

the suffering-vindication motif, which is not clearly manifested in the other texts.[116]

In light of Ps 80's function as the connecting text, I agree with Streett that "Mark may see the story of Jesus as Messiah persecuted and destroyed by the authorities as representative of Israel, but ultimately vindicated, 'strengthened' (Ps 80:18b), and raised from the dead (Ps 80:19). Jesus' statement would then be understood as a prediction of his suffering and vindication."[117] Therefore, it seems that, citing Ps 80 alongside Ps 110 and Dan 7, Jesus predicts that his messianic identity will be revealed through his suffering, vindication through resurrection, and his coming as judge.

Psalm 110:1 in Mark 14:62: As aforementioned, the allusion to Ps 110:1 in Mark 14:62b is developed from the citation of Ps 110:1 in Mark 12:36–37. While the emphasis in the citation of Ps 110:1 in Mark 12:36–37 is on the messiah being greater than David, the citation in Mark 12:36–37 prepares for the full-blown appropriation of Ps 110:1 in Mark 14:62: Jesus will be sitting at the right hand of God exercising his authority as the Messiah, who rules and judges his enemies.

In appropriating Ps 110:1 in Mark 14:62, Mark seems to have the context of Ps 110 in mind. As the enthroned Messiah, Jesus will judge his opponents.[118] In the immediate context of Mark 14:62, his opponents are Jewish religious leaders. The verb ὄψεσθε ("You will see"; Mark 14:62), does not necessarily connote judgment but rather Jesus' vindication in the eyes of the Sanhedrin.[119] However, the use of Ps 110:1 and other appropriated texts indicate that Jesus' vindication will be followed by judgment on those who oppose him.[120] Furthermore, in light of the context of the Markan narrative, Jesus' declaration may imply his judgment on all his enemies including Satan and all who oppose the coming of God's kingdom through him.

The allusion to Ps 110:1 in Mark 14:62 also seems to indicate Jesus as the priest-king in the manner of Melchizedek: (1) The narrative connects Jesus as the new temple builder (Mark 14:54–59) to his declaration in Mark 14:62 where Ps 110 is alluded to and points to Jesus' priestly kingship.[121] Jesus will initiate a new worshiping community.

116. Streett, *Vine*, 188.
117. Streett, *Vine*, 188.
118. Hay, *Glory at the Right Hand*, 127–28.
119. Collins, *Mark*, 705.
120. Strauss, *Mark*, 656–57.
121. Watts, "Psalms," 40.

The new temple he will build is different from the present temple order. Confronted by the high priest of the present temple establishment, Jesus, alluding to Ps 110, may present himself as the Melchizedek-like priest-king.[122] (2) Other conflated texts (Ps 80:18 and Dan 7:13) that impregnate a royal priesthood motif bolster that Mark has a priest-king motif in mind. For instance, Streett is open to the possibility of a royal priestly motif in Ps 80 based on its similarity with Ps 110.[123] Crispin Fletcher-Louis demonstrates that one like a son of man in Dan 7 is a royal-priest figure evidenced by the OT, Ancient Near Eastern sources, and rabbinic literature.[124] If the cumulative force of the three royal-priesthood texts is combined in the declaration of Jesus at the trial, and if Jesus' declaration is narratively connected to his identity as the initiator of the new temple, then it is very likely that the royal-priest in Ps 110 was implied by Mark.[125]

Daniel 7:13 in Mark 14:62: the allusion to Dan 7:13 in Mark 14:62 complements the citations from Pss 80 and 110 by portraying Jesus' coming with clouds.[126] The background of Dan 7 is the persecution of Israel by Antiochus Epiphanes IV.[127] Daniel 7 envisions the eternal dominion of God's kingdom in relation to his saints who suffer from worldly kingdoms.[128] The similarities between the one like a son of man and the faithful saints suggest that the one like a son of man represents the faithful

---

122. Emadi argues, "I suggest that Jesus' priesthood—an office inseparable from the temple—is an underlying concept in the narrative function of the trial scene. How so? The irony of this final confrontation between Jesus and the religious authorities is that the high priest of Israel is the primary prosecutor in the case. The high priest appears to wield authority over Jesus, yet it is Jesus who is the true messianic priest and king—a fact substantiated by Jesus' self-referential appeal to Psalm 110 and Daniel 7 in Mark 14:62." Emadi, "Royal Priest," 200. See also Hamilton, *Clouds of Heaven*, 190.

123. Streett, *Vine*, 85.

124. Fletcher-Louis, "High Priest," 169–93. See also other scholars who accept the royal-priest kingship of one like a son of man in Dan 7:13. Emadi, "Royal Priest," 200; Hamilton, *Clouds of Heaven*, 190; Streett, *Vine*, 113.

125. In Ps 110 and the OT section of this chapter, I argued that Zech 6:12 anticipates that the Davidic priest-king would build an eschatological temple. If my argument is accepted, Zech 6:12 would support Jesus' temple building as the Davidic royal priest.

126. Compare the verbal parallels between Dan 7:13 (Theodotion) and Mark 14:62. ἐθεώρουν ἐν ὁράματι τῆς νυκτὸς καὶ ἰδοὺ μετὰ τῶν νεφελῶν τοῦ οὐρανοῦ ὡς υἱὸς ἀνθρώπου ἐρχόμενος ἦν καὶ ἕως τοῦ παλαιοῦ τῶν ἡμερῶν ἔφθασεν καὶ ἐνώπιον αὐτοῦ προσηνέχθη (Dan 7:13); ὁ δὲ Ἰησοῦς εἶπεν· ἐγώ εἰμι, καὶ ὄψεσθε τὸν υἱὸν τοῦ ἀνθρώπου ἐκ δεξιῶν καθήμενον τῆς δυνάμεως καὶ ἐρχόμενον μετὰ τῶν νεφελῶν τοῦ οὐρανοῦ (Mark 14:62).

127. Newsom and Breed, *Daniel*, 215.

128. Newsom and Breed, *Daniel*, 216; Hill, *Daniel-Malachi*, 129.

saints of YHWH (Dan 7:14, 27).[129] However, the figure distinguishes himself from the faithful saints in that his status is comparable to that of YHWH (Dan 7:14, 27).[130] The original context of the alluded text, Dan 7:13, is his approach to the Ancient of the Days in the heavenly temple so that he may be granted eternal dominion and a kingdom (Dan 7:13–14). Thus, by alluding to Dan 7:13, Jesus identifies himself with the one like a son of man, the heavenly royal figure, who, at the same time, seems to be an Adamic and messianic royal figure.[131]

Mark's appropriation of Dan 7:13 in Mark 14:62b not only expresses Jesus' heavenly royal status but also his authority to judge. Although the original context of Dan 7:13 does not depict the one like a son of man as the active executor of the judgment, the judgment of the fourth beast is associated with the one like a son of man.[132] Furthermore, "the Danielic son of man" in *1 Enoch* 37–71 and *4 Ezra* 13 executes the judgment on the enemies of Israel from the heavenly temple, which aligns with Mark's

---

129. The similarities between the one like a son of man and the faithful saints stand out when comparing Dan 7:14 with Dan 7:27. In Dan 7:14, authority, honor, and kingdom are given to the one like a son of man. Similarly, in Dan 7:27, kingdom, authority, and majesty of the earthly kings are given to the saints. As for the representative nature of the one like a son of man, Snow states, "Contemporary interpretations of the figure include the Messiah, an angelic or divine being, or faithful Israel. All three approaches recognize that the SM either represents or symbolizes the 'holy ones.'" Snow, *Daniel's Son of Man*, 37.

130. In Dan 7:14, all the nations serve the one like a son of man, and his dominion and kingdom are eternal. Similarly, in Dan 7:27, all rulers will serve and obey the Most High (i.e., YHWH), and his kingdom is eternal. Also, "coming with the clouds of heaven" underlines the "heavenly nature" of the one like a son of man. Goldingay, *Daniel*, 394. In addition, Streett suggests the following reasons for the difficulty to identify the one like a son of man with the faithful saints: "(1) The one like a son of man does not appear until after the fourth beast and the little horn are destroyed, while the saints of the Most High appear concurrently with it and are oppressed by it; and (2) the prima facie fact that the one like a son of man is described solely as glorious and majestic in direct contrast to the suffering of the saints." Streett, *Vine*, 169.

131. Street explicates, "The messianic identification makes sense of the description of the son of man's dominion under the Ancient of Days. It can also explain the parallel description of the people of the saints of the Most High since the king is representative of the nation. This seems to be the most straightforward way of explaining the features of the son of man. A few prominent interpreters also see Adamic/creation imagery in Dan 7 because of the mythological content of the vision, its cosmic scope, the human appearance of the son of man juxtaposed to the beasts, his dominion over the beasts, and the Adamic imagery already applied to the Israelite king in the OT. Thus, the author of the vision may present the son of man as a messianic figure drawn from some Davidic messianic sources but without actually intending him to be understood as a Davidic descendant." Streett, *Vine*, 112–13.

132. Snow, *Danielic Son of Man*, 162.

usage of the Danielic Son of Man.¹³³ Mark appropriated Dan 7:13 in two other sayings of an apocalyptic Son of Man (Mark 8:35–38; 13:24–27).¹³⁴ In both sayings, the coming of Son of Man betokens the judgment on those who do not follow him.¹³⁵ Both sayings point to Jesus' second coming.¹³⁶ Likewise, the allusion to Dan 7:13 in Mark 14:62b refers to Jesus' second coming for judgment.¹³⁷ Therefore, the allusion to Dan 7:13 in Mark 14:62b indicates that the high priest and other religious leaders who judge Jesus will be judged as the hostile, beast-like foreign kingdoms

---

133. Snow, *Danielic Son of Man*, 162. See also Marcus, *Way of the Lord*, 165–67. Snow, following Mona Hooker, considers all the occurrences of Son of Man in Mark to allude to Dan 7:13–14. However, as we will demonstrate shortly, it seems that only apocalyptic Son of Man passages are related to Dan 7:13–14.

134. Compare Mark 8:38b (ὁ υἱὸς τοῦ ἀνθρώπου ἐπαισχυνθήσεται αὐτόν, ὅταν ἔλθῃ ἐν τῇ δόξῃ τοῦ πατρὸς αὐτοῦ μετὰ τῶν ἀγγέλων τῶν ἁγίων and Mark 13:26 (καὶ τότε ὄψονται τὸν υἱὸν τοῦ ἀνθρώπου ἐρχόμενον ἐν νεφέλαις μετὰ δυνάμεως πολλῆς καὶ δόξης with Dan 7:13b Theodotion (ἰδοὺ μετὰ τῶν νεφελῶν τοῦ οὐρανοῦ ὡς υἱὸς ἀνθρώπου ἐρχόμενος ἦν). Though Mark 8:38b does not have the phrase "with clouds," his coming with the Father's glory and the holy angels seems to presuppose Son of Man's heavenly abode which fits well the context of the Dan 7:13. Similarly, Marcus avers, "The verbal relation of the three Markan passages to Daniel 7 (Daniel 7:13–14; Mark 8:38—9:1; 13:26; 14:62)." Marcus, *Way of the Lord*, 164.

135. Leim, "Glory of His Father," 229. For instance, Marcus points out that Jesus' saying about being ashamed of those who do not acknowledge him (Mark 8:38) connotes "eschatological judgment." Marcus, *Way of the Lord*, 166. Also, in Mark 13:24–27, Son of Man's coming in clouds (Mark 13:26) is connected to the judgment motif (Mark 13:24–25). Hays says, "The images of cosmic signs in Mark 13:24 and 25 (sun and moon darkened and stars falling) are derived from Isa 13:10, Joel 2:10, 3;15, and Isa 34:4 LXX. These cosmic portents signify "the day of the Lord," and, in Isaiah, they are specifically associated with God's judgment on Babylon and the pagan nations that have oppressed Israel. Mark's language echoes these passages, without citing them directly." Hays, *Gospels*, 58. In light of the Markan narrative, especially, if Mark 13:24–27 concerns the Parousia, which anticipates the gathering of the elect (Mark 13:27), it seems natural that this judgment motif is intended toward those who do not obey and follow Jesus.

136. As for Mark 8:38, see, for instance, Lane, *Mark*, 314, Gundry, *Mark*, 457. We have already argued that Mark 13:24–27 concerns the Parousia in chapter 2 of this book.

137. Hay, *Glory at the Right Hand*, 127–28; Matera, *Kingship*, 113; Boring, *Mark*, 414; Evans, *Mark*, 451; Donahue and Harrington, *Mark*, 423; Stein, *Mark*, 684. Some scholars consider the coming of Jesus in Mark 14:62b signifies the ascent to YHWH just as the original context of Dan 7:13. Wright, *New Testament and the People of God*, 291–97; Hays, *Gospels*, 61. Marcus correctly points out that, "[T]he direction of movement in Dan 7:13, however, is upward, into the heavenly throne room, whereas in Mark it seems to be downward, since 'sitting at the right hand of the Power' precedes 'coming with the clouds.'" Marcus, *Mark 8–16*, 1008. See also, Tödt, *Son of Man*, 38; Matera, *Kingship*, 110.

in Dan 7.[138] In conclusion, Jesus' saying in Mark 14:62 not only admits that he is the Messiah, the Son of God, but also predicts that his opponents will witness God's vindication on Jesus as he will suffer, resurrect, ascend, and finally return to judge those who oppose him, including the religious leaders.[139]

Mark 14:63–65

The pericope ends with the high priest's announcement of blasphemy and Jesus' suffering (Mark 14:63–65). The announcement of blasphemy from the high priest is understandable when one ponders the significance of Jesus' proclamation. From the perspective of the high priest, Jesus commits a grave affront by reversing the role of the judge and announcing the verdict on the high priest and, therefore, infringes on the prohibition in Exod 22:17 ("Do not blaspheme God or curse the ruler of your people" NIV).[140] The blasphemy announcement and the ensuing mockery on Jesus reveal a series of ironies. Jesus' opponents blaspheme him by condemning him as a blasphemer (Mark 14:63–64). They seem to have the upper hand by condemning and inflicting pain on Jesus, but they will be condemned and punished in the coming of Son of Man (Mark 14:64–65).[141] They ridicule Jesus to prophesy, but Jesus prophesies, and his prophecy is true (Mark 14:62, 65).[142]

Psalm 110 in the Markan Narrative

Mark 12:35–37, where the first citation of Ps 110 appears, is a part of the conflict between Jesus and the temple establishment concerning his authority over the temple. Since Mark 11:27, the temple authorities attempt to denigrate Jesus' authority because of the threat he brings. Jesus' entry into Jerusalem as the Davidic Messiah and his announcement of the judgment on the temple augmented by the parable of the wicked tenants

---

138. Marcus, *Way of the Lord*, 167. Marcus further evidences his argument with a verbal similarity between Jesus' enemies who stood up (ἀνίστημι) to oppose Jesus (Mark 14:57, 60) and the four evil gentile kingdoms and rulers who rose (ἀνίστημι) from the earth (Dan 7:17). Marcus, *Way of the Lord*, 169.

139. Marcus, *Mark 8–16*, 1016. See also, Juel, *Messianic Exegesis*, 145–46.

140. Bock, *Blasphemy and Exaltation*, 235–36; Cho, *Royal Messianism*, 189–90.

141. Cho, *Royal Messianism*, 190.

142. Moloney, *Mark*, 305–6.

must be a tangible menace to the temple establishment. However, Jesus silences their hostile and entrapping questions with God-given authority, thus, proving his authority over the temple. In Mark 12:35–37, Jesus initiates a counterattack on the temple establishment (i.e., the scribes) after rebutting a series of hostile questions. Thus, in the immediate context of Mark 12:35–37, the quotation of Ps 110:1 serves to defeat Jesus' opponents (i.e., the scribes) by countering their teaching that the Messiah is the son of David.

At the macro-narrative level, the quotation serves several purposes. First, it corrects the popular understanding of the messiahship and prepares for the full revelation of Jesus' messiahship. Jesus does not deny his Davidic messiahship, as seen in the previous chapter (i.e., Mark 10:47–49; 11:1–11). However, his messiahship is beyond what people, including the religious leaders, anticipate. Jesus is greater than David's son. He will sit at the right hand of God until God places his enemies under his feet (Mark 12:36). His heavenly enthronement and subjugation over his enemies will be enacted as the other citation of Ps 110:1 in Mark 14:62 shows. However, at this stage of the Markan narrative (Mark 12:35–37), it is only implied. Thus, the quotation of Ps 110:1 in Mark 12:36 builds up the literary tension that is finally resolved in Mark 14:62 when Jesus fully reveals the nature of his messiahship.

Second, the citation of Ps 110 corroborates that Jesus is the Messiah, the Son of God. As observed in chapter 3, the allusions and echo to Ps 2:7 serve as the skeleton of the Markan narrative and reveal that as the Messiah, the Son of God, Jesus will bring God's kingdom and subjugate his enemies (i.e., Satan and his followers) through his death and resurrection. Mark's awareness of the whole context of Ps 2 is evident. Mark seems to both affirm and expand the motif of Jesus as the Messiah, the Son of God with the use of Ps 110. Psalm 110 affirms the enthronement and the victory of the eschatological Davidic messiah motif of Ps 2 in the canonical context of the Psalter. Mark also appropriated Ps 110 with its whole context in mind (i.e., Jesus' enthronement as God's vice-regent and subjugation of his enemies such as the religious leaders). Therefore, Mark's use of Ps 110 affirms that Jesus is the Messiah, the Son of God, and expands with the idea that he is the priest-king in the manner of Melchizedek. Yet, Mark 12:35–37 is implicit and readers need to examine Mark 14:61–62 for the full-scale revelation.

Mark 14:61–62 is a part of Jesus' trial by the Sanhedrin (Mark 14:55–65). The scene is pivotal in the narrative in many aspects. First, it reconnects the temple motif after Mark 13 and foreshadows another temple motif (Mark 15:29, 38). Second, it recapitulates Jesus' identity as the Messiah, the Son of God (Mark 1:1) and links it to another title, the Son of Man. Third, Jesus' proclamation in Mark 14:62b both accomplishes the part of the passion prediction (i.e., arrest) and becomes the basis of another part of the anticipated passion. Jesus' confession is charged as blasphemy and leads to his death. Moreover, it forecasts his resurrection, ascension, and second coming. Indeed, Mark 14:61–62 is the climax of the Markan narrative.

Conflated with Ps 80:18 and Dan 7:13, Ps 110:1 plays the significant role in this pivotal text of the Markan narrative. First, the allusion to Ps 110:1 in Mark 14:62b is used to affirm Jesus' heavenly enthronement. Anticipated by the quotation in Mark 12:36, Jesus reveals that he will be God's vice-regent, sitting at the right hand of God in his heavenly throne. With the allusions to Ps 80:18 and Dan 7:13, the allusion to Ps 110:1 contributes to Jesus' prediction for his vindication through suffering, resurrection, ascension, enthronement, and the Parousia. Second, in corollary, the use of Ps 110 in Mark 14:62b impregnates the Messiah's authority to judge his enemies. Just as the quotation in Mark 12:36 functions to condemn the temple scribes, the allusion in Mark 14:62b indicates judgment on those who oppose him. The conflated allusion to Dan 7:13 corroborates the motif of judgment on his enemies. As aforementioned, Ps 110's shared motif with Ps 2 and Mark's use of the whole context of Ps 2 reinforce the possibility that Mark has the subjugation in mind in Mark 14:62b.

Third, Mark seems to intend to evoke the priest-king motif in his use of Ps 110 in Mark 14:62b. The immediate context intimately connects the new temple motif with Jesus' confession. Moreover, two other composited OT allusions all have the royal priest connotation. It seems that Mark presents Jesus as the priest-king of the new temple order (i.e., in the manner of Melchizedek). The significance of the priest-king of the new temple order is reinforced when one considers that Jesus' interlocutor is the high priest of the present temple order. Therefore, two uses of Ps 110 in the Markan narrative contribute to the ideological point of view of Mark. The use of Ps 110 affirms that Jesus is the Son of God, the Messiah who will inaugurate God's kingdom by subjugating his enemies. Also, the use of Ps 110 extends the understanding of Jesus' kingship. He will rule on his heavenly throne. As the priestly king, he will bring about the new temple order.

In conclusion, Mark uses Ps 110:1 as the first polemical counter-question on the temple establishment after a series of the confrontational questions to denigrate Jesus' authority over the temple. He also uses it at the trial scene that fully reveals Jesus' identity. The following points summarize Mark's appropriation of Ps 110: (1) It affirms Jesus' messiahship as the Son of God and presents his heavenly enthronement and subjugation of his enemies. In view of the whole context of the Markan narrative, just like the use of Ps 2, his enemies refer to not only human opponents but also spiritual ones (i.e., Satan and his followers). Just as Ps 110 consummates the themes of Ps 2 with complete subjugation, the use of Ps 110 in Mark seems to point to the complete subjugation of his enemies. (2) The use of Ps 110 presents Jesus as the priest-king who will inaugurate the new temple order that perfectly suits the temple motif in Mark 11–15. (3) The use of Ps 110 alongside other conflated OT texts contributes to disclose Jesus' identity and serves as the basis for his death, the climax of the Markan narrative. (4) Finally, the use of Ps 110 with other composited texts demonstrates the full picture of how God would realize his kingdom through his Son, Jesus (i.e., Jesus' death, resurrection, ascension for enthronement, and the Parousia).

CONCLUSION

This chapter argued that Ps 110 is David's prophetic psalm framed by two divine oracles: (1) the enthronement of Davidic messiah and (2) his identity as the priest-king in the manner of Melchizedek. The messiah from his offspring follows his pattern (i.e., the priest-king). Yet this Davidic messiah will be greater than David himself (i.e., his lord). His rule will be the ultimate fulfillment of the Abrahamic and Davidic covenants. In the canonical context of the Psalter, there is a close relationship between Pss 110 and 2. Therefore, Ps 110 not only affirms the universal rule of the Davidic messiah, the Son of God with the subjugation of his enemies in Ps 2, but also consummates it with the divine oracles of the complete subjugation and the eternal priestly kingship.

In relation to the OT besides the Psalter, Ps 110 is closely related to the Davidic (i.e., 2 Sam 7) and Abrahamic covenants (i.e., Melchizedek's blessing on Abram in Gen 14:18–24 and God's confirmation on the Abrahamic covenant in Genesis 15:1–11). Zechariah 6:12 conveys the concept of a priest-king who will build a new temple; this evokes Ps 110:4. Yet, there are no clear allusive texts to Ps 110. In Second Temple literature, the result is similar. Scholars suggest several texts, but none are convincing concerning their allusive relationship with Ps 110. The absence of a clear allusion to Ps 110 in the Second Temple period before the NT may either derive from the tension between the Hasmonean ruling party and their opponents who do not approve the high priesthood of the Hasmonean rulers or from the seemingly audacious claim on the heavenly throne in Ps 110, which may have discouraged Second Temple Jews from using Ps 110 to avoid a possible infringement on their monotheistic belief. However, the absence (or the paucity for some scholars) of Ps 110 in Second Temple literature does not mean that the postexilic Jewish community does not consider Ps 110 messianically. The LXX and Targum interpret Ps 110 with the Davidic messiah in mind. In addition, the similarities between Dan 7:13 and Ps 110:1 seem to be the reason why two texts are used in tandem in the *Similitudes of Enoch*. It can be also the reason why Mark used them together in Mark 14:62.

Though citing only Ps 110:1 twice in Mark 12:36 and 14:62, the two strategic locations of the Markan narrative (i.e., the first polemical counter-question on the temple establishment and the full revelation of Jesus' identity) seem to have the whole context of Ps 110 in mind. Also, Mark builds up the narrative tension by citing Ps 110:1 in Mark 12:36 and resolves it in Mark 14:62. The use of Ps 110 in Mark does the following: (1) Affirms Jesus' messiahship as the Son of God and presents Jesus' heavenly enthronement and subjugation of his enemies as the consummation of the themes of Ps 2; (2) suggests Jesus as the priest-king who will bring a new temple order in lieu of the temple motif in Mark 11–15; (3) reveals Jesus full identity and leads the narrative to the climax, the death of Jesus as it is combined with the allusions to Ps 80:18 and Dan 7:13; and (4) provides the comprehensive picture of how God's kingdom will be realized through Jesus (i.e., Jesus' death, resurrection, ascension for enthronement, and the Parousia).

6

Psalm 22 in Mark

IN THE PREVIOUS CHAPTER, I argued that Mark uses the citation of Ps 110 at the strategic locations of the Markan narrative (i.e., Mark 12:35–37; 14:61–62) to do the following: (1) show Jesus' messiahship as the Son of God, (2) present Jesus' heavenly enthronement and subjugation of his enemies, (3) introduce Jesus as the priest-king who brings the new temple order, (4) give the full picture of the realization of God's kingdom through Jesus (i.e., Jesus' death, resurrection, ascension for enthronement, and the Parousia), and finally, (5) disclose Jesus' full identity in combination with other allusions to Ps 80:18 and Dan 7:13. On the narrative level, the revelation of Jesus' full identity in Mark 14:61–62 leads to the climax of the Markan narrative—the crucifixion.

In this chapter, I will argue that Mark typologically uses the citations of Ps 22 (i.e., Ps 22:1, 7–8, 18) at the climax of Markan narrative, Mark 15:20b–39 (i.e., the crucifixion). Mark's typological appropriation of Ps 22 asserts that Jesus is both the Messiah and the Righteous Sufferer in the pattern of David. Just as David experiences suffering and humiliation in his struggles to establish a messianic kingdom, Jesus undergoes suffering and death to bring about God's kingdom. This chapter will also demonstrate that Mark has in mind the entire context of Ps 22 (i.e., lament and vindication) that aligns with his narrative structure (i.e., Mark 15:20b—16:7). As the previous chapters, this chapter will establish (1) the textual form of Ps 22 in Mark first. Then the chapter will explore (2) the interpretation of Ps 22, (3) Ps 22 in the canonical context of the Psalter and other Old Testament texts, and (4) Ps 22 in Second Temple literature to see the relationship between them and Mark's use of Ps 22. And finally, the chapter will investigate (5) Mark's use of Ps 22 in Mark 15 to know its significance in the Markan narrative.

TEXTUAL FORM OF PSALM 22 IN MARK

Mark 15 focuses on Jesus' suffering as a part of the passion narrative. Mark 15 evokes many scriptural quotations and allusions of lament psalms, such as Pss 22:1 (=22:2 MT=21:2 LXX; cf. Mark 15:34), 22:7-8 (=22:8-9 MT=21:8-9 LXX; cf. Mark 15:29-30), 22:18 (=22:19 MT=21:19 LXX; cf. Mark 15:24), and 69:21 (=69:22 MT=68:22 LXX; cf. Mark 15:35-36).[1] These lament psalms describe the psalmist's lament over his unjust affliction from his adversaries. As a result, the psalmist advocates God's cause and cries out for deliverance from God, which perfectly fits the context of Jesus' passion.[2] Of these, Ps 22 stands out, as it has the only quotation and the predominant allusions among all these lament psalms in Mark. I investigate further the quotation and three allusions of Ps 22 in Mark 15 below.

Psalm 22:2a (MT)	Psalm 21:2a (LXX)	Mark 15:34b
אֵלִי אֵלִי לָמָה עֲזַבְתָּנִי	ὁ θεός ὁ θεός μου πρόσχες μοι ἵνα τί ἐγκατέλιπές με	ελωι ελωι λεμα σαβαχθανι; ὅ ἐστιν μεθερμηνευόμενον· ὁ θεός μου ὁ θεός μου, εἰς τί ἐγκατέλιπές με
"My God, my God, why have you forsaken me?"	"O God, my God, attention to me. Why have you forsaken me?"	"Eloi, Eloi, lema sabakthani, which is translated, "my God, my God, why have you forsaken me?"

Scholars generally agree that ελωι ελωι λεμα σαβαχθανι is the transliteration of the Aramaic text of Ps 22:1 (i.e., אלהי אלהי למה שבקתני "my God, my God why have you forsaken me"), which corresponds to the MT verbatim.[3] It seems that Jesus was quoting the Aramaic text of Ps 22 that may have been available during his time.[4] Hays suggests Mark may

---

1. Moo, *Old Testament*, 285-86. In addition, Moo suggests that another lament psalm, Ps 41:9 (=41:10 MT=40:10 LXX) is alluded to in Mark 14:18.

2. Moo, *Old Testament*, 226-27, 231; Carey, *Jesus' Cry*, 140.

3. See Collins, *Mark*, 730-31; Brown, *Death of the Messiah*, 2:1052; Moo, *Old Testament*, 267-68.

4. I agree with Brown who argues, "From the discovery of the Qumran (11Q) Targum of Job we have clear evidence that Aramaic translations of some biblical books

have used the Aramaic quotation "to enhance the raw immediacy of the moment and to enhance the narrative's historical verisimilitude."[5] Mark's translation of the Aramaic text in Mark 15:34 reflects the wording of the LXX, even though some features of Mark's Greek translation indicate he remained closer to the Masoretic text: (1) The repetition of "my God" is identical to the MT while the LXX omits one possessive form. (2) The unique phrase, "attend to me" of the LXX is absent in both the MT and Mark 15:34.[6]

Psalm 22:19 (MT)	Psalm 21:19 (LXX)	Mark 15:24b
יְחַלְּקוּ בְגָדַי לָהֶם וְעַל־לְבוּשִׁי יַפִּילוּ גוֹרָל	διεμερίσαντο τὰ ἱμάτιά μου ἑαυτοῖς καὶ ἐπὶ τὸν ἱματισμόν μου ἔβαλον κλῆρον	καὶ διαμερίζονται τὰ ἱμάτια αὐτοῦ βάλλοντες κλῆρον ἐπ' αὐτὰ τίς τί ἄρῃ.
"They divide my **garments** among themselves and **for my clothing they cast a lot**."	"They divided my **garments** among themselves and **for my clothing they casted a lot**."	"And they divided his **garments casting a lot for them** (i.e., the garments) (to see) what each should take."

The allusive relationship of Mark 15:24b to Ps 21:19 (LXX) is evident. Both texts depict that the enemies of the protagonist divide and cast a lot on the garment of the suffering protagonist. The lexical and structural parallels are extensive except for some minor details: (1) The persons of the narrative are different. (2) Mark 15:24b uses the participle form of βάλλω instead of the aorist. (3) While Ps 21:19 (LXX) uses two similar words of "clothing" for each verb respectively (i.e., τὰ ἱμάτιά and τὸν ἱματισμόν), Mark 15:24b uses only τὰ ἱμάτια, and the second verb refers to it with αὐτά. Also, unlike Ps 21:19 (LXX), the prepositional phrase ἐπ' αὐτὰ is located after the verbal phrase. The wording of the MT is identical with the LXX.

---

were in existence several centuries before Jesus' time. If he used these words, there is no convincing reason that he could not have spoken them in Aramaic." See Brown, *Death of the Messiah*, 2:1053.

5. Hays, *Gospels*, 83. See Carey, *Jesus' Cry*, 151–53, for the different scholarly opinions on the topic.

6. Brown, *Death of the Messiah*, 2:1054.

Psalm 22:8–9 (MT)	Psalm 21:8–9 (LXX)	Mark 15:29–30
כָּל־רֹאַי יַלְעִגוּ לִי יַפְטִירוּ בְשָׂפָה יָנִיעוּ רֹאשׁ׃ גֹּל אֶל־יְהוָה יְפַלְּטֵהוּ יַצִּילֵהוּ כִּי חָפֵץ בּוֹ	πάντες οἱ θεωροῦντές με ἐξεμυκτήρισάν με ἐλάλησαν ἐν χείλεσιν ἐκίνησαν κεφαλήν ἤλπισεν ἐπὶ κύριον ῥυσάσθω αὐτόν σωσάτω αὐτόν ὅτι θέλει αὐτόν	Καὶ οἱ παραπορευόμενοι ἐβλασφήμουν αὐτὸν κινοῦντες τὰς κεφαλὰς αὐτῶν καὶ λέγοντες· οὐὰ ὁ καταλύων τὸν ναὸν καὶ οἰκοδομῶν ἐν τρισὶν ἡμέραις, σῶσον σεαυτὸν καταβὰς ἀπὸ τοῦ σταυροῦ.
"All who see me deride me. They open (the mouth in a derisory gesture) with lips. **They shake the head.** 'He trusts in Yahweh; let him deliver him; **let him save him,** for he delights in him!'"	"All who see me ridicule me. The spoke with lips. **They shook the head.** 'He hoped in the Lord. Let him deliver him. **Let him save him,** for he takes pleasure in him.'"	"And those who passed by reviled him **shaking their heads** and saying 'Aha! You who would destroy the sanctuary and build in three days, **save yourself** and come down from the cross!"

Lexically, two phrases, "shake a head" and "save one(self)," are parallel in Ps 21:8–9 (LXX) and Mark 15:29–30. Moreover, the thematic and structural parallels between the two texts corroborate that these phrases in Mark 15:29–30 are allusions to Ps 21:8–9 (LXX): (1) Both texts describe that the Righteous Sufferer is derided by his adversaries. (2) Both texts share the same structure: the enemies' ridicule—shaking heads—the direct speech of ridicule ("save one[self] from suffering"). The wording of the MT is virtually the same with the LXX. In conclusion, I believe that Mark used virtually the same lexemes with those of Ps 22 (LXX) when he appropriated Ps 22, except for the Aramaic quotation which is closer to the MT. However, I also notice that the Septuagint text considered to be appropriated by Mark is similar to the MT. Therefore, I will consider both the MT and LXX in the interpretation of Ps 22.

INTERPRETATION OF PSALM 22

Sitz im Leben and Structure

Psalm 22 is an "individual lament psalm" that utilizes liturgical praise.[7] Theoretically the superscription, לְדָוִד, can mean several things.[8] According to Waltke, "the preposition *lᵉ* ('of/for/by'?) with a proper name, David, usually means 'by.'"[9] However, for some interpreters, the psalmist's intense suffering does not seem to match David's life written in the Scripture, which causes them to question Davidic authorship.[10] Thus, they have proposed a king,[11] a postexilic suffering redactor of the Scripture,[12] Hezekiah, and Jeremiah as possible authors of the psalm, but none are convincing.[13] Some interpreters express the difficulty in identifying the specific author and setting.[14] However, our ignorance to such a unique affliction in David's life does not nullify the possibility of Davidic authorship. We do not know the entire experience of David's suffering.[15] In view of the strong witness of the superscript, it seems that Ps 22 describes David's personal experience hyperbolically.[16] Therefore, the setting and date of the psalm may be one of the difficult times in David's life (i.e., his flight from Saul and Absalom).[17] As for the structure, the psalm is

---

7. VanGemeren, *Psalms*, 235. Similarly, Craigie, *Psalms*, 198.

8. According to Bateman, לְדָוִד can mean "'by David,' 'for David,' 'concerning David,' or 'for a Davidic collection.'" Bateman, "Recipient of Psalm 110," 8.

9. Waltke and Houston, *Psalms*, 89. For Waltke's further proofs (i.e., "Antiquity and Reliability of Superscripts in General," "An Extensive Royal Interpretation," and "Historical Notices") to defend Davidic authorship, see Waltke and Houston, *Psalms*, 90–92. Willgren, from the perspective of the formation of the Psalter, states that the superscript serves as "the interpretive framework" that designates the author. Willgren, *Formation*, 193–94. Other interpreters who consider David as the author are Calvin, *Psalms*, 1:362; Delitzsch, *Psalms*, 1:307; Ross, *Psalms 1–41*, 527–28; VanGemeren, *Psalms*, 235.

10. Ross, *Psalms 1–41*, 527.

11. Kraus, *Psalms 1–59*, 293.

12. Stuhlmueller, "Psalm 22," 86–90.

13. Ross, *Psalms 1–41*, 527.

14. Goldingay, *Psalms 1–41*, 322–23.

15. Ross, *Psalms 1–41*, 527.

16. Delitzsch, *Psalms*, 1:306–07. Delitzsch and others see that David's unique afflictions become a type for Christ's suffering (antitype). David's hyperbolic language exceeds his "own experience and finds its fulfillment in Jesus Christ." Waltke and Houston, *Psalms*, 112. See also Delitzsch, *Psalms*, 1:307; Ross, *Psalms 1–41*, 527–28, 548–51.

17. Delitzsch, *Psalms*, 1:306–07.

divided by lament (vv. 1–21a) and praise (vv. 21b–31).[18] The psalmist's confession of trust (vv. 3–5 and 9–11) and cry for help (vv. 11a, 19–21a) are interspersed in between the lament section.[19] The following exegesis reflects this structure.

Exegesis

Verses 1–2 are the beginning of the psalmist's lament (vv. 1–21). The three consecutive questions (v. 1) highlight the psalmist's intense feeling of dereliction and alienation from God.[20] Verse 2 contrasts the psalmist's constant (i.e., day and night) seeking along with God's silence.[21] By stating "*my* God," the psalmist evokes his intimate covenantal relationship with God.[22] At the same time, he "accuses God of thus far not keeping covenant."[23] However, the seeming accusation is a rhetorical plea for God to act.[24] The psalmist now recalls God's covenantal faithfulness in response to his ancestors' *trust* (vv. 3–5). However, unlike his ancestors, the psalmist is deemed as public scum and mocked by the ungodly because of his *trust* in YHWH (vv. 6–8). They ridicule the psalmist's faith in God because God appears to desert the psalmist (v. 8).[25] Yet, the psalmist once again reminds himself of his relationship with YHWH from birth (vv. 9–10).

Verse 11 is transitional.[26] The reflection on the faith relationship with God in the past and the dire situation in the present motivates the psalmist to ask God to come and rescue him (i.e., "Do not be far from me," Ps 22:11a).[27] At the same time, verse 11b ("because trouble is near,

---

18. Kraus, *Psalms 1–59*, 293; VanGemeren, *Psalms*, 235; deClaissé-Walford, Jacobson, and Tanner, *Psalms*, 227.

19. See deClaissé-Walford, Jacobson, and Tanner, *Psalms*, 227; Gerstenberger, *Psalms, Part 1*, 108; Waltke and Houston, *Psalms*, 396–97.

20. VanGemeren, *Psalms*, 237; Ross, *Psalms 1–41*, 531.

21. Ross, *Psalms 1–41*, 531.

22. Calvin, *Psalms*, 1:357; Kraus, *Psalms 1–59*, 294; Waltke and Houston, *Psalms*, 399.

23. Waltke and Houston, *Psalms*, 399.

24. Waltke and Houston, *Psalms*, 400; Goldingay, *Psalms 1–41*, 325.

25. Craigie, *Psalms*, 199.

26. Waltke and Houston, *Psalms*, 403.

27. Waltke and Houston, *Psalms*, 403; Wilson, *Psalms*, 416–17; VanGemeren, *Psalms*, 240.

because there is no one to help") introduces the long lament section (vv. 11b–18).[28] The lament consists of two cycles (vv. 12–15 and vv. 16–18). Each circle depicts the fearful attack from animal-like enemies ("encircling bulls," "devouring lions," and "scavenging dogs," vv. 12–13, 16)[29] and the psalmist's personal experience of suffering (vv. 14–15b, 17–18).[30] Between the two circles, the psalmist identifies God as the ultimate causer of his imminent death.[31] In this way, the psalmist expresses his misery and sense of abandonment from God (v. 15c, "You lay me in the dust of death"). Having depicted his affliction from his enemies without anyone to help, the psalmist once again petitions God to come and rescue him (vv. 19–21).[32]

Verse 21c ("You answered me") is transitional to the praise section (vv. 22–31).[33] After the series of imperatives plea for his deliverance, the psalmist is confident that God will save him.[34] The first part of the section regarding the praise is the psalmist's thanksgiving in the covenantal community (vv. 22–26).[35] In the second part of the section (vv. 27–31), the psalmist extends his praise for God's salvation to all nations.[36] The psalmist envisions that all the nations will turn to YHWH and worship him (vv. 27, 29–30a). The basis of his confidence is YHWH's universal kingship and salvation which people will share with the next generation (vv. 28, 30b–31).

Ancient Variants

Psalm 21 (LXX) generally corresponds to Ps 22 (MT), with some exceptions. Several features are markedly different from the MT that deserve

28. Goldingay, *Psalms 1–41*, 331.
29. Waltke and Houston, *Psalms*, 406.
30. Waltke and Houston, *Psalms*, 403–07; Ross, *Psalms 1–41*, 538–41.
31. Craigie, *Psalms*, 200; VanGemeren, *Psalms*, 243.
32. Compare the similarities between verses 11 (אַל־תִּרְחַק מִמֶּנִּי כִּי־צָרָה קְרוֹבָה כִּי־אֵין עֹזֵר, Ps 22:12 MT), and 19 (וְאַתָּה יְהוָה אַל־תִּרְחָק אֱיָלוּתִי לְעֶזְרָתִי חוּשָׁה׃, Ps 22:20 MT). It seems that two similar petitions (v.11 and vv. 19–21) frame the lament section (vv. 12–18).
33. Kraus, *Psalms 1–59*, 298.
34. Craigie, *Psalms*, 200; Ross, *Psalms 1–41*, 542–43; deClaissé-Walford, et al., *Psalms*, 236. LXX omits the verb.
35. Waltke and Houston, *Psalms*, 409; Ross, *Psalms 1–41*, 543–44.
36. Wilson, *Psalms*, 421; Waltke and Houston, *Psalms*, 412–14; Ross, *Psalms 1–41*, 546; deClaissé-Walford, et al., *Psalms*, 236.

our attention. First, Ps 21 (LXX) omits the phrase "you answered me" (Ps 22:22, MT). Thus, structurally, this verse does not have clear change of mood from lament to praise, possibly for the continued emphasis on the piety.[37] Second, instead of אַיֶּלֶת הַשַּׁחַר ("morning doe"; Ps 22:1 MT), Ps 21:1 (LXX) reads, "τῆς ἀντιλήμψεως τῆς ἑωθινῆς" (**the help** in the morning"). Psalm 21:2 (LXX) uses πρόσχες μοι (**Pay attention** to me") additionally in the middle of the psalmist's cry in verse 2. The two words ἀντίλημψις and πρόσχες form *inclusio* with the phrase εἰς τὴν ἀντίλημψίν μου πρόσχες in Ps 21:20 (LXX), the plea for God's salvation. The *inclusio* seems to serve as a literary signal that God answers the psalmist's prayer.[38]

Third, Ps 21 (LXX) uses semantically homogeneous word-groups that generate correspondences and analogies alien to the MT (i.e., κράζω and εἰσακούω, vv. 3, 6, 25; ῥύομαι and σώζω, vv. 5-6, 9, 21-22; ἐλπίζω and ἐλπίς, vv. 5-6, 9-10).[39] Especially, the ἐλπίζω-ἐλπίς word-group translates several Hebrew words in Ps 22 (MT) and underlines the certainty of God's salvation in Ps 21 (LXX).[40] In conclusion, Greek Ps 21 seems to stress the hope for salvation more than the MT text.[41] The Targum of Ps 22 has many minor variations from Ps 22 (MT). However, their exegetical significances are negligible. Some deviations from the MT seems to reflect the Targum's eschatological understanding of Ps 22.[42] Despite such paraphrastic translations of the Targum, the overall meaning is close to the MT. The Targum also identifies David as the author.

---

37. Fabry, "Wirkungsgeschichte," 286. See also Bons, "Septuagint-Version," 22-23. Instead, ἐν τῷ κεκραγέναι με πρὸς αὐτὸν εἰσήκουσέν μου ("when I cried out to him, he answered me," Ps 21:25) and κεκράξομαι ("I will cry out," Ps 21:3) form *inclusio*, and verse 25 connects the psalmist's personal prayer answer to the shared praise of the community.

38. Bons, "Septuagint-Version," 27.

39. Bons, "Septuagint-Version," 28-29.

40. Bons, "Septuagint-Version," 30. See also Fabry, "Wirkungsgeschichte," 282.

41. Bons, "Septuagint-Version," 32. In a similar venue, Fabry remarks, "Auch warden Elemente des direkten Gebetes an Gott genauer nuanciert: z.B. warden Elemente der beschreibenden Klage zur direkten Gebetsanrede umgeformt." Fabry, "Wirkungsgeschichte," 286.

42. Fabry, "Wirkungsgeschichte," 304.

PSALM 22 IN THE CANONICAL CONTEXT OF THE PSALTER AND OTHER OT TEXTS

The first book of the Psalter to which Ps 22 belongs consists of Pss 1–2, the gateway to the whole Psalter and Pss 3–41, the psalms of David.[43] The change of mood from a triumphant messianic psalm (Ps 2) to lament (Ps 3) appears abrupt. Starting from Ps 3, the lament psalms dominate Book I of the Psalter.[44] However, Pss 1–2 and the Davidic psalms in Book I are intimately related. In chapter 3 of this book, I already specified that Pss 1–2 introduce the theme of the Psalter as the rule of God consummated through his anointed king, the ideal royal figure, who adheres to the Deuteronomic command for the king (Deut 17:18–20).

Corresponding to this theme of the whole Psalter, Pss 3–41 demonstrate how God establishes his kingdom through his anointed king, David's constant struggle with his enemies, and victory with divine help.[45] In other words, *the lament psalms including Ps 22 in Pss 3–41 should be viewed as the part of David's ongoing struggle with his enemies to bring God's kingdom envisioned in Pss 1–2*. Also, the portrayal of David as the ideal Torah-abiding king and the motif of YHWH's rule on the mount Zion in Jerusalem run through Pss 3–41.

In a narrower scope, proposed initially by Pierre Auffret, many scholars argue that Pss 15–24 is one of the subgroups of the first book of the Psalter (Pss 1–41).[46] Some observe the chiastic structure of Pss 15–24 that has Ps 19 at the center. For example, William Brown suggests the following structure of the unit:

A Psalm 15 (Entrance Liturgy)
   B Psalm 16 (Song of Trust)
      C Psalm 17 (Prayer for Help)
         D Psalm 18 (Royal Psalm)

---

43. Psalms 9–10 and 32–33, respectively, are linked to each other. See deClaissé-Walford, "Intertextual Reading," 139n3. As the case of Ps 22, by juxtaposing the psalms of David (Pss 3–41), the editor of the Psalter seems to intend readers to view them as psalms penned by David. See Schreiner, "Stellung," 269.

44. Nancy L. deClaissé-Walford identifies twenty-seven out of forty-one psalms of Book I as lament psalms. See deClaissé-Walford, "Intertextual Reading," 139.

45. Robertson, *Flow of the Psalms*, 5.

46. Auffret, *La sagesse*, 407–38; Hossfeld and Zenger, "'Wer darf hinaufziehn," 166–82; Brown, "Here Comes," 259–77; Sumpter, "Coherence of Psalms 15–24," 186–209.

E Psalm 19 (Torah Psalm)

D' Psalms 20–21 (Royal Psalms)

C' Psalm 22 (Prayer for Help)

B' Psalm 23 (Song of Trust)

A Psalm 24 (Entrance Liturgy)[47]

This structure reflects what we have observed above: (1) Pss 15 and 24 frame the unit with the temple entry motif.[48] David, the Torah-abiding and anointed king, exemplifies the one who deserves to enter God's temple. At the same time, Ps 24 connects the Divine Warrior, YHWH, who enters the temple with David, the anointed king, who is worthy of entering the temple in Ps 15.[49] Thus, the correspondence between Pss 15 and 24 merges the messianic rule with God's rule, as envisioned by Ps 2. (2) The center of the chiastic structure (Ps 19 about Torah) is surrounded by royal psalms (Pss 18, 20–21). The unique combination of royal psalms with Torah psalms resembles the unified introduction of the Psalter in Pss 1–2.[50] It seems that the combination of Torah and royal psalms presents David as the ideal king who keeps Torah and, at the same time, as the anointed king who subjugates his enemies. (3) *The surrounding lament psalms (Pss 17 and 22) exhibit David's struggle to establish God's kingdom against his enemies.* (4) Pss 16 and 23, the psalms of trust and protection, are closely related to Pss 17–22. "Out of trust comes petition," (i.e., Pss 16–17) and "out of petition trust is vindicated" (i.e., Pss 22–23).[51]

It seems that out of all the lament psalms of David, Ps 22 illustrates most vividly how the psalmist cries out to God because of his trust and how his trust in God is vindicated, which leads to praise. Many lament psalms are followed by psalms of trust and thanksgiving (i.e., Pss 3–7 followed by Pss 8–9; Pss 25–28 followed by Pss 29–30).[52] Some lament psalms contain both lament and praise together. However, *none matches*

---

47. Brown, "Here Comes," 260.

48. Broyles, "Psalms," 248.

49. I agree with other scholars who argue that the Psalter views David as the exemplary figure for the faithful covenant people of YHWH. See Rendtorff, "Psalms of David," 63; Broyles, "Psalms," 285.

50. Robertson identifies Pss 1–2; 18–19; 118–119 as Three "Torah Psalm[s] coupled with" three messianic psalms that are pivotal in the structure of the whole Psalter. Robertson, *Flow of the Psalms*, 16. Kindle..

51. Brown, "Here Comes," 267.

52. Schreiner, "Stellung," 271; Rendtorff, "Psalms," 56.

the intensity of cry for salvation and exuberant praise for YHWH's deeds in Ps 22. As Schreiner suggests, "The editor of the Psalter might have intentionally positioned Psalm 22 right in the middle of Book I to emphasize this unique feature of Psalm 22."[53] Considering all the characteristics of Ps 22 in the canonical context of the Psalter, it is not surprising why New Testament writers, including Mark, most often either quote or allude to Ps 22.

One finds some allusive relationship between Ps 22 and other psalms in the Psalter. First, Ps 69 is another Davidic lament psalm that has similar petition and praise structure with Ps 22.[54] Especially, Ps 69:33 shows lexical and thematic parallels with Ps 22:27.[55] It seems that Ps 69:33 is the reinterpretation of Ps 22:27.[56] Second, many similarities between Ps 22 and 71 are noticeable such as (1) Pss 22:10–11 and 71:5–6 (MT),[57] (2) Pss 22:2, 20, and 71:12,[58] and (3) Pss 22:31–32 and 71:18–19.[59] Considering

---

53. Schreiner, "Stellung," 272.

54. Lyons, "Psalm 22," 651; Hoffman, "Psalm 22," 263.

55. Compare Ps 69:33 (רָאוּ עֲנָוִים יִשְׂמָחוּ דֹּרְשֵׁי אֱלֹהִים וִיחִי לְבַבְכֶם "The poor will see and rejoice. You who seek God, may your hearts revive") with Ps 22:27 (יֹאכְלוּ עֲנָוִים וְיִשְׂבָּעוּ יְהַלְלוּ יְהוָה דֹּרְשָׁיו יְחִי לְבַבְכֶם לָעַד׃ "The poor will eat and be filled. Let those who seek him will praise Yahweh. May your hearts revive forever"). Hoffman, "Psalm 22," 240–41.

56. Hoffman, "Psalm 22," 240.

57. Compare the lexical and thematic parallels between Ps 22:10–11, כִּי־אַתָּה גֹחִי מִבֶּטֶן מַבְטִיחִי עַל־שְׁדֵי אִמִּי עָלֶיךָ הָשְׁלַכְתִּי מֵרָחֶם מִבֶּטֶן אִמִּי אֵלִי אָתָּה ("Yet you are he who took me from the womb; you made me trust you at my mother's breasts. On you was I cast from my birth, and from my mother's womb you have been my God"; Ps 22:9–10 ESV) and Ps 71:5–6, כִּי־אַתָּה תִקְוָתִי אֲדֹנָי יְהוִה מִבְטַחִי מִנְּעוּרָי עָלֶיךָ נִסְמַכְתִּי מִבֶּטֶן מִמְּעֵי אִמִּי אַתָּה גוֹזִי בְּךָ תְהִלָּתִי תָמִיד ("For you, O Lord, are my hope, my trust, O LORD, from my youth. Upon you I have learned from before my birth; you are he who took me from my mother's womb. My praise is continually of you"; Ps 71:5–6 ESV). Hoffman, "Psalm 22," 78.

58. Hoffman considers that Greek version of Ps 71:11 (ὁ θεὸς μὴ μακρύνῃς ἀπ' ἐμοῦ ὁ θεός μου εἰς τὴν βοήθειάν μου πρόσχες, 70:12 LXX) depends on Ps 22:2a (ὁ θεὸς ὁ θεός μου πρόσχες μοι, Ps 21:2 LXX) and 20 (σὺ δέ κύριε μὴ μακρύνῃς τὴν βοήθειάν μου εἰς τὴν ἀντίλημψίν μου πρόσχες, Ps 21:20 LXX). Hoffman, "Psalm 22," 102.

59. Hoffman proposes the shared vocabularies and themes between Ps 22:31–32, זֶרַע יַעַבְדֶנּוּ יְסֻפַּר לַאדֹנָי לַדּוֹר יָבֹאוּ וְיַגִּידוּ צִדְקָתוֹ לְעַם נוֹלָד כִּי עָשָׂה ("Posterity shall serve him; it shall be told of the Lord to the coming generation; they shall come and proclaim his righteousness to a people yet unborn, that he has done it"; Ps 22:30–31 ESV) and Ps 71:18–19, וְגַם עַד־זִקְנָה וְשֵׂיבָה אֱלֹהִים אַל־תַּעַזְבֵנִי עַד־אַגִּיד זְרוֹעֲךָ לְדוֹר לְכָל־יָבוֹא גְּבוּרָתֶךָ׃ וְצִדְקָתְךָ אֱלֹהִים עַד־מָרוֹם אֲשֶׁר־עָשִׂיתָ גְדֹלוֹת ("So even to old age and gray hairs, O God, do not forsake me, until I proclaim your might to another generation, your power to all those to come. Your righteousness, O God, reaches the high heavens. You who have done great things, O God, who is like you?" Ps 71:18–19 ESV). Hoffman, "Psalm 22," 260.

these many correspondences, Hoffman suggests that Ps 71 is "the earliest preserved interpretation of Ps 22 available to us."[60] Therefore, the allusive relationship of Pss 69 and 71 to Ps 22 shows that *Ps 22 was an influential psalm to be appropriated by other lament psalms in the Psalter.*

In relation to other Old Testament texts, one finds few texts that clearly allude to Ps 22. However, some scholars see a couple of texts that evoke Ps 22:10–11. Both Jer 1:5 (God calling Jeremiah as a prophet even before he was born) and Isa 46:3 (God carries and upholds a remnant of Israel from their birth) share בֶּטֶן ("belly") and ("womb") with Ps 22:10–11.[61] Also, both texts evoke the motif of God's sovereign care for his covenant people (i.e., a prophet and Israel); this aligns with Ps 22:10–11.[62] If one agrees that David wrote Ps 22, it is possible that the later authors of Jeremiah and Isaiah evoked Ps 22:10–11 in the texts aforementioned.[63]

---

60. Hoffman, "Psalm 22," 263. Psalm 102 not only shares a petition-praise pattern with Ps 22 but also has an intimate relationship with Ps 22. Lyons, "Psalm 22," 651. Hoffman identifies six corresponding relationships between Pss 22 and 102. He enumerates, "1) The rather uncommon declaration that the 'nations' will praise God is matched in Ps 102:16 and Ps 22:28b. 2) Though only having minimal exact verbal parallels, Ps 102:13 is similar to Ps 22:4. 3) Ps 102:5 expresses much the same idea as 22:18a. 4) Even more closely and with greater shared vocabulary, Ps 102:19 matches the thought of Ps 22:31–32. 5) Ps 102:22 matches 22:23a. 6) There is also rabbinic evidence which linked Ps 102:1 and 22:25a.6." Hoffman, "Psalm 22," 265. In spite of such parallels between them, the general superscription of Ps 102 with no "ascription to David" makes it difficult to suggest any concrete relationship between the two psalms except that they may interpret one another mutually. Hoffman, "Psalm 22," 265.

61. Holladay, "Background," 156; Hoffman, "Psalm 22," 80.

62. If Jer 1:5 alludes to Ps 22:10–11, Isa 49:1 and 5 (YHWH's calling his servant before his birth) that are intricately connected to Jer 1:5, may be connected to Ps 22:10–11. Hoffman, "Psalm 22," 80–81.

63. Some scholars suggest there are verbal and thematic parallels between Ps 22:28 and Isa 45:22 and between Ps 22:32 and Isa 44:23. "*All the ends of the earth* [כָּל־אַפְסֵי־אֶרֶץ] shall remember and turn to the LORD, and all the families of the nations shall worship before you" (Ps 22:27 ESV); "Turn to me and be saved, *all the ends of the earth* [כָּל־אַפְסֵי־אָרֶץ]! For I am God, and there is no other" (Isa 45:22 ESV); "[T]hey shall come and proclaim his righteousness to a people yet unborn, that *he has done it* [כִּי עָשָׂה]" (Ps 22:31 ESV); "Sing, O heavens, for *the LORD has done it* [כִּי־עָשָׂה]; shout, O depths of the earth; break forth into singing, O mountains, O forest, and every tree in it! For the LORD has redeemed Jacob and will be glorified in Israel" (Isa 44:23 ESV). Lyons, "Psalm 22," 644. See also Becker, *Israel deutet seine Psalmen*, 51. Furthermore, Lyon argues that Ps 22 is edited "in light of an argument in Trito-Isaiah that extends and develops certain themes of Isaiah 40–55" (i.e., "suffering, vindication," and "proclamation of Yahweh's universal reign"). Lyons, "Psalm 22," 647–50. Lyon's argument is based on the reasoning that Ps 22:28–32 is the later addition to Ps 22:1–27 to follow the pattern of Isa 40–66. Lyons, "Psalm 22," 645. Though it is disputable whether Ps 22:28–32 is added to Ps 22:1–27, the unusual tripartite pattern of Ps 22 corresponding

PSALM 22 IN SECOND TEMPLE LITERATURE

The citations to Ps 22 are evidenced by Dead Sea Scrolls, the Pseudepigrapha and the Apocrypha. Of the Dead Sea Scrolls, 4Q88 (=4QPs^f) Frgm. 1–2 and 5/6 ḤevPs witness some quotations from Ps 22.[64] Both of them suffer from the fragmentary nature of the extant texts. However, if we consider only the compositional nature of the extant texts, we may say that the entire 4Q88 (=4QPs^f) is the extended commentary on Ps 22 as a broad lament that turns into praise.[65] Psalm 22 in 4Q88 demonstrates that the Qumran community appropriates the psalm by incorporating it as a part of their liturgy including the individual's lament, the community's praise, and the eschatological hope.[66]

Hodayot of Qumran attests a few allusions to Ps 22. In fact, Hodayot of Qumran witnesses more allusions than any other Second Temple literature to Ps 22, possibly because the book assumes the endurance of the Teacher of Righteousness who serves as a prototype of the Qumran community in "his role as a Righteous Sufferer figure . . . for his faithfulness to God."[67] Many allusions to the lament and praise sections of Ps 22 illustrate that the Teacher of Righteousness not only is aware of Ps 22 but also appropriates Ps 22 in such a way that the psalmist and his community in Ps 22 become a type for him and his community.

Concerning the Apocrypha, Wis 2–5 witnesses some possible allusions to Ps 22 lexically and thematically.[68] The adversaries of both Ps 22

---

to Isa 40–66 at least seems to be open to the possibility of his proposal.

64. Fragments 8 (i.e., Ps 22:4–9) and 9 (i.e., Ps 22:15–21) of 5/6 ḤevPs column XI are extant witnesses to Ps 22. Omerzu, "Rezeption," 53. 4Q88 (=4QPs^f) Frgm. 1–2 contain Ps 22:14–17. Omerzu, "Rezeption," 52.

65. Farby, "Wirkungsgeschichte," 298.

66. Omerzu, "Rezeption," 47.

67. Carey, *Jesus' Cry*, 120. The following texts exhibit allusions to Ps 22: (1) The unique combination of mockery (בוז) and reproof (חרפה) found in the adversaries of the psalmist in 1 QH X. 33–34 corresponds to Ps 22:7. Carey, *Jesus' Cry*, 120. (2) In 1QH XIII. 9–18, the Teacher of Righteousness depicts his enemies with the image of a lion and uses the phrase, "open their mouths against me," as in Ps 22:14. Carey, *Jesus' Cry*, 121; Omerzu, "Rezeption," 60. (3) Several allusions to the specific description on the psalmist's dead person-like status in Ps 22:15–16 are found in 1 QH XII. 33–34, 1 QH X. 28, and 1 QH XIII. 31. Carey, *Jesus' Cry*, 121–22; Omerzu, "Rezeption," 57–59. (4) Several phrases in 1 QH IX. 29–36 (i.e., "from the womb," "from the uterus," "my mother," and "breasts") seem to allude to Ps 22:10–11. Hoffman, "Psalm 22," 86–87. (5) Finally, one can attest the allusions to "the thanksgiving portion of the psalm" (i.e., Ps 22:23–25) in 1QH XX. 3, 1QH X. 33–34 and 1QH XIII. 12–19. Carey, *Jesus' Cry*, 122.

68. Thematically, both share (1) the motif of affliction and reproach of a protagonist

and Wis 2 regard their punishment on both protagonists as a test to see if God would rescue these righteous sufferers and confirm that he is their God.[69] Like the Teacher of Righteousness in QH, Wis 2–5 portrays the psalmist as a righteous sufferer.[70]

Finally, several pseudepigraphic literatures also allude to Ps 22. (1) According to Hoffman, *Apocryphal Syriac Psalm* 152:1a ("**God, God**, come to my **help**") and 152:1bc ("**assist me** and **deliver** me and rescue my soul,") allude to Ps 22:2a ("my **God**, my **God**") and 22:20–21a ("hasten to **help me. Deliver my soul** from the sword")[Emphasis mine].[71] If Hoffman's proposal about the allusion to Ps 22 in *Apocryphal Syriac Psalm* 152 is accepted, it also demonstrates how Ps 22 was appropriated for the theme of the righteous sufferer before the writing of the New Testament. (2) *Joseph and Aseneth* presents the first narration of Aseneth regarding God's rescue and her repentance from idolatry in Egypt.[72] The book suggests one possible allusion to Ps 22: her depiction of the rescue from Satan as *the deliverance from the mouth of lion* in 12:9–10 seems to allude to Ps 22:14, 22.[73] However, Aseneth's suffering is different from

---

by his adversaries, (2) "first person narration by the foes" to increase the dramatic effect of the scene, and (3) the motif of the "vindication of the protagonist" with its eschatological effects that include the gentile nations. Hoffman, "Psalm 22," 284. See also Carey, *Jesus' Cry*, 117. Lexically, Wis 2:18 (. . . ῥύσεται αὐτὸν ἐκ χειρὸς ἀνθεστηκότων . . ., ". . . he will deliver him from the hand of his adversaries . . .") seems to present a possible allusion to Ps 21:9 (ἤλπισεν ἐπὶ κύριον ῥυσάσθω αὐτόν σωσάτω αὐτόν ὅτι θέλει αὐτόν, "He hoped in the Lord: let him deliver him, let him save him, because he desires him." LXX) and 21:21(ῥῦσαι ἀπὸ ῥομφαίας τὴν ψυχήν μου καὶ ἐκ χειρὸς κυνὸς τὴν μονογενῆ μου, "Deliver my soul from the sword; my only one from the hand of the dog" LXX). Carey, *Jesus' Cry*, 117; Hoffman, "Psalm 22," 294.

69. Carey, *Jesus' Cry*, 117; Hoffman, "Psalm 22," 294. In addition, Omerzu suggests that in Wis 2:17–20, the wicked ones put the righteous ones to test if God would save them or not, which is reminiscent of Ps 21: 9 (LXX). Omerzu, "Rezeption," 72.

70. Carey, *Jesus' Cry*, 117.

71. Hoffman, "Psalm 22," 280–81. *Apocryphal Syriac Psalms* 152–153 describe the psalmist's cry to God to rescue him from a lion with 1 Sam 17:34–36 (David's fight with a lion), Dan 6 (Daniel in the den of a lion), and Ps 22 as scriptural background. Hoffman, "Psalm 22," 286.

72. Most scholars believe it was written between 100 BCE and 135 CE in Egypt. See Kraemer, *When Aseneth Met Joseph*, 5.

73. Compare *Joseph and Aseneth* 12:9–10, "For lo, the wild primaeval Lion (ὁ λέων) pursues me; And his children are the gods of the Egyptians that I have abandoned and destroyed; And their father the Devil is trying to devour me. 10. But do thou, O Lord deliver me from his hands. And *rescue me* from his mouth (ἐκ στόματος αὐτοῦ ἐξελοῦ με), lest he snatch me like a wolf and tear me," with Ps 21:14 (LXX), ἤνοιξαν ἐπ' ἐμὲ τὸ στόμα αὐτῶν ὡς λέων ὁ ἁρπάζων καὶ ὠρυόμενος ("They opened their mouth against me like a ravening and roaring lion") and 21:22 (LXX), σῶσόν με ἐκ στόματος λέοντος

Ps 22 in that her suffering relates to her past sin, which Ps 22 does not indicate.[74]

In conclusion, Ps 22 seems to be written by David during the lowest time of his life, when he was severely persecuted by his enemies. The psalm consists of both lament and praise. Despite his complaint about threat and humiliation, he experiences God's seeming absence, yet his lament is based on his covenantal trust in God. His prayer turns into praise as he is vindicated. Septuagint and Targum basically agree with MT. However, Septuagint's emphasis on hope for salvation in the lament section of Ps 22 offers the possibility that Mark uses the lament section of Ps 22 in the context of hope.[75]

The investigation of the canonical context of Ps 22 reveals that the lament psalms, including Ps 22 in Pss 3–41, need to be considered as part of David's constant struggle with his enemies to bring about God's kingdom through his messiah pictured in Pss 1–2. Out of all the Davidic lament psalms, Ps 22 demonstrates most vividly David's cry to God out of trust and his vindication that leads to praise. This uniqueness of Ps 22 explains why it is alluded to by other Psalms and OT texts (i.e., Pss 69, 71; Jer 1:5; Isa 46:3).

As for the use of Ps 22 in Second Temple period before the New Testament, first, the wide use of Ps 22 in the liturgy of Qumran community (i.e., Ps 22 in 4Q88) may imply that Second Temple Jews, including Mark, were familiar of the whole context of Ps 22, which increases the possibility that Mark may have the whole context of Ps 22 in mind.[76] Second, all Second Temple literature that either quotes or alludes to Ps 22 presents each protagonist as experiencing "persecution from his/her enemies" and seeking salvation from God.[77] Except for *Joseph and Aseneth*, all of them portray their protagonists as righteous sufferers in accordance with the psalmist in Ps 22. Also, many of them use Ps 22 in the anticipation of the eschatological vindication.[78] But none of them interpreted Ps 22 mes-

---

καὶ ἀπὸ κεράτων μονοκερώτων τὴν ταπείνωσίν μου ("*Save me* from the lion's mouth, my lowliness from the horns of the unicorns."). Carey, *Jesus' Cry*, 120; Omerzu, "Rezeption," 69–70. The translation of *Joseph and Aseneth* is from Cook, "Joseph and Aseneth," 473–503.

74. Carey, *Jesus' Cry*, 120.
75. Similarly, Stowasser, "Mein Gott, mein Gott," 180.
76. Carey, *Jesus' Cry*, 125.
77. Carey, *Jesus' Cry*, 124.
78. Marcus, *Way of the Lord*, 177–78; Watts, *Psalms*, 43; Carey, *Jesus' Cry*, 124.

sianically.⁷⁹ Mark appropriates Ps 22 to present Jesus as the Righteous Sufferer and connects his use of Ps 22 to the eschatological vindication motif in the milieu of the use of Ps 22 by his contemporaries.⁸⁰ However, unlike his contemporaries, his appropriation of Ps 22 demonstrates that Jesus is both the Messiah and the Righteous Sufferer who typologically fulfills the anticipation of the Scripture, Ps 22.

PSALM 22 IN MARK

In the previous sections of this chapter, we noticed that Ps 22 exhibits David's cry for God's deliverance, vindication, and praise most poignantly out of all the Davidic lament psalms. Also, as a part of the Davidic lament psalms, Ps 22 expresses David's intense struggle with his enemies as he brings about God's kingdom through his messiah envisioned by Pss 1–2. Among all the Davidic lament psalms, Ps 22 presents most dramatically David's cry to God out of trust and his vindication that leads to praise, which may explain several allusions to this psalm in other OT texts. And it may be the reason why Mark uses Ps 22 most profusely and at a key juncture of Markan narrative, as we will see.

Finally, most of Second Temple literature that either alludes to or quotes Ps 22 depicts a protagonist as a righteous sufferer with the anticipation of the eschatological vindication. Thus, we tentatively concluded that Mark might have followed the sociocultural milieu of his contemporaries in his appropriation of Ps 22, as he presents Jesus as the Righteous Sufferer with the anticipation of the eschatological vindication. We also suggested that Mark may have been very familiar with the whole psalm, considering that his contemporaries, the Qumran community, used the entire Ps 22 in their liturgy. But we made clear that Mark read Ps 22

---

79. Watts, "Psalms," 43.

80. Marcus cites Ruppert, who contrasts a righteous sufferer in lament psalms with a righteous sufferer in apocalyptic literature and the New Testament. The former is "a person suffering *in spite of* his righteousness and calling for God to vindicate him by destroying his enemies in *this life*." The latter "*must suffer on account of* his righteousness" but will "be *glorified at the eschaton*." Marcus, *Way of the Lord*, 177 citing Ruppert, *Jesus als der leidende Gerechte*, 42–43. As I present Jesus as the Righteous Sufferer who is the antitype of David, a righteous sufferer, I capitalize the word "righteous sufferer" when I use it for Jesus to differentiate him from other righteous sufferer figures. Jesus is perfectly sinless while others are not. Also, as we will argue, his suffering brings the eschatological salvation for all who believe in him, which is incomparable to any other righteous suffering. Thus, Jesus is the ultimate Righteous Sufferer. See also Lister, "Jesus' Righteous Suffering," 78.

messianically and used it typologically. With these things in mind, we now explore Mark's use of Ps 22 in the Markan narrative.

As aforementioned in the previous chapter of this book, Jesus reveals his identity in his climactic confrontation with the religious leaders in Mark 14:58–61, which leads to the crucifixion. Mark 15 depicts the escalation to the climax and denouement, that is, Jesus' crucifixion, death, and burial. Since Jesus' arrest, the whole narrative unfolds as Jesus predicted on the way to Jerusalem (Mark 8:31; 9:31; 10:33–34). Concerning Jesus' three predictions, Frank Matera argues that Mark 10:33–34 provides the most detailed description that aligns with the flow of Mark 14–16:

> And the Son of Man will be handed over to the chief priests and teachers of the law (cf. Mark 14:53). They will condemn him to death (cf. Mark 14:64) and hand him over to the Gentiles (cf. Mark 15:1). They will mock him, spit on him (cf. Mark 15:16–20a), flog him (cf. Mark 15:15), and kill him (cf. Mark 15:20b–39). But after three days, he will rise from the dead (cf. Mark 16:1–8).[81]

Jesus' prediction about his passion and resurrection and the scriptural citations undergird the passion narrative in Mark. Jesus indicates that his passion is according to the Scriptures (i.e., "The Son of Man goes just as it is written about him," Mark 14:21; "Day after day, I was with you in the temple teaching, but you did not arrest me, but the Scriptures must be fulfilled," Mark 14:49). Throughout all the events in Mark 15, God's sovereign purpose to inaugurate his kingdom through the death of Jesus is evident, as everything transpires according to Jesus' prediction and the Scriptures. Especially, Mark 15:20b–39, the crucifixion of Jesus, alludes to many OT passages which confirm that Jesus' death is according to the Scriptures.[82] Of these scriptural citations, the citations to Ps 22 portray that Jesus is indeed the suffering Messiah who brings about God's kingdom through his death and subsequently, his resurrection. Before we delve into Mark 15:20b–39, we will briefly examine Mark 15:1–20a to understand the narrative context for the use of Ps 22 in Mark 15:20b–39.

---

81. Matera, *Passion Narratives*, 35–36.
82. The section on Mark 15:20b–39 will treat these scriptural citations in detail.

Mark 15:1–20a

The correspondences between Mark 14:55–62 and Mark 15:1–5 show that the conflicts between the Sanhedrin and Jesus continue, even though the trial is before Pilate, such as many false charges against Jesus (Mark 15:3–4; cf. Mark 14:55–60), Jesus' silence (Mark 15:5; cf. Mark 14:61), and Jesus' affirmation of his identity (Mark 15:2; cf. Mark 14:62).[83] The scene presents Jesus as the king of the Jews, the motif that recurs in Mark 15:1–32 (Mark 15:2, 9, 12, 18, 26, 32).[84] Pilate's question to see if Jesus is the king of the Jews has a political connotation different from the kingship Jesus embodies.[85] However, ironically, the term "king of the Jews" affirms that Jesus is the Messiah in the Markan narrative.[86] This ironic portrayal of Jesus as the king who is mocked and killed by the people who are supposed to serve him dominates the entire chapter of Mark 15.

Mark 15:6–15a is pivotal in that the verdict of Jesus' crucifixion is sealed.[87] The scene reveals the guilt of the religious leaders and the crowd (i.e., Jews) for crucifying Jesus, their king (Mark 15:9–14).[88] The irony continues: the innocent king of the Jews, Jesus, dies while the murderer, Barabbas, is released.[89] Pilate's handing Jesus over for crucifixion parallels the condemnation of death by the Jewish leaders (Mark 15:15; cf. Mark 14:64).[90] *Therefore, both the trials before the Jewish religious leaders and Pilate portray Jesus as the Messiah and the Righteous Sufferer.*

The third scene (Mark 15:16–20a) describes the mockery of the Roman soldiers towards Jesus. The mockery that ensues from the Roman trial parallels the mockery after the Jewish trial (Mark 14:65).[91] Sand-

---

83. Boring, *Mark*, 418; Stein, *Mark*, 702.

84. France, *Mark*, 628. The gentile expression "king of the Jews" and the Jewish term "king of Israel" (Mark 15:32) are synonymous. Evans, *Mark*, 478; Boring, *Mark*, 418–19; Stein, *Mark*, 699.

85. Edwards, *Mark*, 458–59.

86. Strauss, *Mark*, 680.

87. The conflict transpires between Pilate, who wants to release Jesus, and the crowd, who desires to have Jesus crucified through the instigation of the religious leaders.

88. Hooker, *Mark*, 369.

89. Moloney, *Mark*, 314; Boring, *Mark*, 420. The triple repetition of παραδίδωμι in Mark 15:1, 10, 15 both highlights and completes the motif of handing over (i.e., John the Baptist, Mark 1:14; Jesus' prediction, Mark 9:31; 10:33; Judas Iscariot to the religious leaders, Mark 14:18, 21; the religious leaders to Pilate, Mark 15:1, 10; Pilate to the Roman soldiers, Mark 15:15). Matera, *Passion Narratives*, 38.

90. Moloney, *Mark*, 315.

91. Marcus, *Mark 8–16*, 1045. The series of historical present and imperfect

wiched by "two references to crucifixion" (i.e., Mark 15:15b and 20b), the scene stresses that the crucified one is the king of the Jews (i.e., the purple robe, thorny crown, and the salutation and homage; Mark 15:17–20a).[92] Their mockery ironically reveals the truth that Jesus is the king of the Jews, the suffering Messiah (cf. Isa 53:1–12).[93]

A brief examination on Mark 15:1–20a exhibits several significant aspects that set the tone of the crucifixion in Mark 15:20b–39. First, all the seemingly wrong and unjust incidents concerning Jesus ironically demonstrate that he is the Messiah who suffers innocently. Matera makes a pithy statement, "For now, his kingship is hidden in suffering and shame. He will reign from a cross."[94] Mark 15:20b–39 not only continues the ironic portrayal of Jesus' suffering messiahship but also reveals how his suffering messiahship is vindicated. Second, Jesus is handed over to gentiles and crucified as he predicted. In spite of the complete injustices concerning his crucifixion, nothing happens haphazardly.

The ensuing crucifixion and death stories highlight another aspect of God's sovereignty in that Jesus' crucifixion and death fulfill the Scripture. Unlike Mark 15:1–20a, Mark 15:20b–39 is replete with scriptural citations (i.e., Ps 22:19 in Mark 15:24; Ps 22:8–9 in Mark 15:29–30; Amos 8:9–10 in Mark 15:33; Ps 22:2 in Mark 15:34; Ps 69:22 in Mark 15:36). Of these, the citations of Ps 22 play "a central role" in Mark 15:20b–39 to which we now turn.[95]

Psalm 22 in Mark 15:20b–39[96]

Mark seems to use the consistent appropriation method and hermeneutical axiom as he uses Ps 22 in Mark 15:20b–39. Many interpreters have

---

verbs in this scene (i.e., συγκαλοῦσιν, ἐνδιδύσκουσιν, περιτιθέασιν, ἔτυπτον, ἐνέπτυον, προσεκύνουν) provides a vivid portrayal of the mockery on Jesus and intensifies the dramatic effect. Williams, *Mark*, 259. Kindle.

92. Matera, *Passion Narratives*, 38; van Iersel, *Mark*, 467–68. See also Marcus, *Mark 8–16*, 1046–48.

93. Donahue and Harrington, *Mark*, 439–40; Moloney, *Mark*, 316; Boring, *Mark*, 425.

94. Matera, *Passion Narratives*, 39.

95. Marcus, *Way of the Lord*, 174.

96. Just like Mark 15:16–20a, Mark employs several historical present and imperfect verbs to slow down the pace and present Jesus' crucifixion using a detailed description. Williams, *Mark*, 261. See the following historical present and imperfect verbs in Mark 15:20b–39: ἐξάγουσιν (Mark 15:20), ἀγγαρεύουσιν (Mark 15:21), φέρουσιν (Mar 15:22),

attempted to draw the significance of the allusion to Ps 22 in Mark 15. There are several conclusions drawn: (1) The citations to Ps 22 indicate the fulfillment of the prophecy about what would happen to Jesus.[97] (2) The citations are descriptions of the event in Old Testament language.[98] Other scholars view that the citations of Ps 22 in Mark have either (3) eschatological significance via the righteous sufferer motif,[99] (4) the role of identifying "Jesus as the Righteous Sufferer like the psalmist,"[100] or (5) the function of recounting Jesus as the Messiah.[101]

Mark's use of Ps 22, along with other scriptural citations, suggests the fulfillment of the Scriptures. Thus, it is more than mere description in OT language (option 2). Also, citations to Ps 22 are not the direct prophecy through the psalmist concerning what would happen to Jesus as option 1 suggests. Option 3 sees rightly both the righteous sufferer motif and the eschatological dimension Mark's use of Ps 22 brings. It resembles our investigation of the "social and cultural milieu" of Mark in Second Temple literature, which shows that Ps 22 was appropriated by Mark's contemporaries for the righteous sufferer motif with the eschatological vindication in mind.[102]

ἐδίδουν (Mark 15:23), σταυροῦσιν, διαμερίζονται (Mark 15:24), σταυροῦσιν (Mark 15:27), ἐβλασφήμουν (Mark 15:29), ἔλεγον (Mark 15:31), ὠνείδιζον (Mark 15:32), ἔλεγον, φωνεῖ (Mark 15:35), ἐπότιζεν, ἔρχεται (Mark 15:36). See also, Matera, *Passion Narratives*, 41. Marked by the spatial shift from the praetorium to Golgotha, the unit is divided into Mark 15:20b–27, 29–32, and 33–39. The reliable manuscripts of Mark do not contain verse 28, which is reflected in many English translations (i.e., NIV, NET, ESV, NLT, etc.).

97. Dodd, *According to the Scriptures*, 97–98.

98. Suhl, *Funktion*, 47–48.

99. Gese, "Psalm 22," 192–96; Marcus, *Way of the Lord*, 177–79.

100. Carey, *Jesus' Cry*, 169. So also, Schweizer, *Erniedrigung*, 21–33, 50; Burchard, "Markus 15.34," 5. Ahearne-Kroll, *Psalms of Lament*, 38, 108, 224. For other interpreters who view that Ps 22 portrays Jesus as a Righteous Sufferer, see Lohmeyer, *Markus*, 343; Lührmann, *Markusevangelium*, 260; Gnilka, *Markus*, 2:316–17. Lindars also concedes that Ps 22 is used for the righteous sufferer motif in the New Testament. For him, the use of Ps 22 is only "a quarry for pictorial detail in writing the story of the Passion." Lindars, *New Testament Apologetic*, 189–91.

101. Juel, *Messianic Exegesis*, 90; Collins, "Appropriation," 231. Apart from these representative interpretations, C. Focant proposes an inversed use of Ps 22 (i.e., Ps 22:19 in Mark 15:24; Ps 22:7–9 in Mark 15:29; Ps 22:2 in Mark 15:34) as the narrative technique Mark employs to intensify the tragic nature of Jesus' last word in Mark 15:34. Focant, "L'Ultime Prière," 330–37. I find his proposal implausible. It seems that Mark rather uses each citation of Ps 22 in accordance with the narrative flow.

102. Carey, *Jesus, Cry*, 94. However, none of Mark's contemporaries used Ps 22 messianically. Lange, "Relationship," 614.

Option 3 is similar to option 4, except that option 3 emphasizes the eschatological significance. For instance, Ahearne-Kroll views Jesus as a Davidic lamenter who challenges God to "answer his cries from the cross."[103] His understanding of Jesus as a Davidic lamenter leads him to conclude that the praise and thanksgiving section of the lament psalms are only means to elicit God's deliverance.[104] While not all scholars who consider Jesus as the Righteous Sufferer like David disregard the eschatological significance, they tend to focus only on Jesus as the Righteous Sufferer like the psalmist. Options 3, 4, and 5 have their own merits. However, it seems that Mark's use of Ps 22 does not side with any of these. Instead, it embraces all of them. As we have observed, Mark 15 clearly portrays Jesus as the Messiah. By appropriating the Davidic lament psalm, Mark presents Jesus as both the Messiah and the Righteous Sufferer.[105] And as we will argue, Mark's use of Ps 22 has an eschatological significance.

Thus, this section will show that Mark's appropriation of Ps 22 presents Jesus as both the Messiah and the Righteous Sufferer. It seems that Mark used Ps 22 typologically so that David's suffering as the king and the righteous sufferer becomes the type for Jesus who suffers as the Messiah and the Righteous Sufferer.[106] And his suffering and death bring the eschatological consequences (i.e., the consummation of God's eschatological kingdom via vindication of Jesus' suffering and death).[107] Both suffer innocently as they strive to establish the messianic kingdom of God. However, as the antitype, Jesus' suffering is escalated in that it (1) leads him to a death which David did not experience and (2) brings the redemption of all the nations and the eternal kingdom of God, while David's suffering is limited as the anointed king of YHWH who strives

---

103. Ahearne-Kroll, *Psalms of Lament*, 224.

104. Ahearne-Kroll, *Psalms of Lament*, 108.

105. Matera, *Passion Narratives*, 40.

106. As for the definition of typology, see Beale, *Handbook*, 13–25; Hoskins, *Scripture*, 20–36. According to Beale, "The essential characteristics of a type are (1) analogical correspondence, (2) historicity, (3) a pointing-forwardness (i.e., an aspect of foreshadowing or presignification), (4) escalation, and (5) retrospection." Beale, Handbook, 14. Jesus' appropriation of Ps 110:1 in Mark 14:62 features all these characteristics. This research has demonstrated how Mark used the Scripture typologically (i.e., Ps 2:7). It is interesting that Mark now shows how Jesus appropriated the Scripture typologically. Some scholars rightly argue that the NT writers' appropriation of the OT derives from Jesus' examples. Malcom, *Prophets*, 202–3.

107. Lagrange, "Notes sur le messianism," 53; Lange, "Relationship," 610–21; Moo, *Old Testament*, 298–99; Rowe, *God's Kingdom*, 301–02; Hoskins, *Scripture*, 37–51.

for God's kingdom.[108] Now, we will examine Mark's use of Ps 22 in the narrative context of Mark 15:20b–39 to see what role they play in the Markan narrative.

The first scene, Mark 15:20b–27 focuses on the process of the crucifixion and its significance indicated by an *inclusio*, σταυρόω (Mark 15:20b, 27) that frames the section. This passage shows Jesus' physical inability to carry his cross from the unbearable scourge he experienced.[109] Jesus' refusal to drink the wine with myrrh which may reduce pain illustrates that he willingly undergoes the full suffering of death to give his life as a ransom for many (Mark 10:45).[110]

Jesus is finally crucified in Mark 15:24. The terse statement of his crucifixion is followed by an allusion to Ps 22:18. In Mark 15:24, the soldiers cast lots and divide Jesus' garments.[111] Mark's description of Jesus' experience is similar to that of David's experience in Ps 22:18. However, Jesus' experience surpasses David's in that Jesus' suffering and shame have an eschatological and universal effect. As the suffering Messiah, Jesus will redeem many and accomplish his mission to bring about God's kingdom. By the typological use of Ps 22:18, Mark shows that Jesus' death "is being played out according to the Scriptures."[112] The terse comment on the time of crucifixion ("it was third hour") reveals that in the midst of this horrible event, what transpires is according to "'God's plan' and the fulfillment of his purpose."[113]

Mark 15:26–27 presents the crucifixion as Jesus' royal enthronement. Jesus is charged as a false messiah (i.e., the king of the Jews)

---

108. Hoskins, *Scripture*, 38.

109. Marcus, *Mark 8–16*, 1048. The place's name, Golgotha (i.e., "skull"), where Jesus was led for crucifixion, evokes impurity and death (Mark 15:22). Marcus, *Mark 8–16*, 1048–49.

110. Marcus, *Mark 8–16*, 1049. See also Hooker, *Mark*, 372–73; Matera, *Passion Narratives*, 42; Boring, *Mark*, 427; Collins, *Mark*, 743.

111. This was the typical custom for criminals approaching death, and this practice reveals the inhumane apathy shown towards the dying person. Hooker, *Mark*, 373; Boring, *Mark*, 428; Marcus, *Mark 8–16*, 1050. Also, Jesus' nakedness exposes him to the extreme shame in the shame-honor oriented Jewish context. Marcus, *Mark 8–16*, 1050.

112. Hays, *Gospels*, 83.

113. Hooker, *Mark*, 373. See also Matera, *Passion Narratives*, 42; Marcus, *Mark 8–16*, 1050. The subsequent sentence, καὶ ἐσταύρωσαν αὐτόν ("they crucified him," Mark 15:25) forms an *inclusio* with καὶ σταυροῦσιν αὐτὸν ("they crucified him") in Mark 15:25. The *inclusio* "conveys the horror and magnitude of the event without recounting it in any detail." Collins, *Mark*, 746.

unauthorized by the Roman Empire.[114] The sign was intended to show that Jesus was not the king. However, the Markan narrative reveals the ironic truth that Jesus is indeed the Messiah.[115] The co-crucifixion of two brigands on Jesus' left and right echoes James's and John's request to sit at Jesus' right and left hand in glory (cf. Mark 10:37–40).[116] Yet, instead of James and John, who should have taken up a cross and followed him, two brigands served as substitutes on Jesus' left and right.[117] The cumulative force of these ironies suggests that Mark may have pictured the crucifixion as Jesus sitting on his throne accompanied by two bandits.[118]

Mark 15:29–32 presents the litany of mockery on Jesus from passersby, the chief priests, the teachers of the law, and the two bandits. Mark alludes to Ps 22:7–8 (κινοῦντες τὰς κεφαλὰς αὐτῶν; σῶσον σεαυτὸν; Mark 15:29–30) to indicate that mocking of Jesus fulfills the Scripture typologically: in Ps 22:7–8, David, the messianic king, is mocked by the ungodly because of his trust in YHWH. The people ridicule David's faith in God because God does not appear to save David. In Mark 15:29–32, Jesus is mocked by ungodly people because of his commitment to do God's will, that is, to bring about God's kingdom through his redemptive death. Jesus' experience exceeds that of David in that Jesus experiences death and brings the ultimate kingdom of God. Jesus and his ungodly mockers are the antitypes of David and his mockers. The issue of David's mockery is that God appears not to save him in his struggle with his enemies to bring about God's kingdom. As for Jesus, people mock his profession as the Messiah with divine authority to bring about God's kingdom and a new temple order. To them, Christ's helpless situation on the cross proves that his claim as the God-ordained Messiah is wrong. Therefore, the mockery

---

114. Matera, *Passion Narratives*, 42; Boring, *Mark*, 428; France, *Mark*, 646.

115. Matera, *Passion Narratives*, 43; Collins, *Mark*, 748; Marcus, *Mark 8–16*, 1050.

116. Hooker, *Mark*, 373; Iersel, *Mark*, 470–71; France, *Mark*, 646; Collins, *Mark*, 748.

117. van Iersel, *Mark*, 470–71; Collins, *Mark*, 748. Thematically, Mark 15:26–27 parallels Isa 53:12b (ἀνθ' ὧν παρεδόθη εἰς θάνατον ἡ ψυχὴ αὐτοῦ καὶ ἐν τοῖς ἀνόμοις ἐλογίσθη, "because his soul was handed over to death and was numbered with the lawless ones" LXX). van Iersel, *Mark*, 471; Collins, *Mark*, 748. However, the lack of the linguistic correspondences between them disqualifies Mark 15:26–27 as an allusion to Isa 53:12 (LXX). Moo, *Old Testament*, 155.

118. Nickelsburg, "Genre and Function," 173; Marcus, *Mark 8–16*, 1050–51. Marcus supports the cross as the royal throne motif based on (1) the repetitious use of crucifixion in Mark 15 and (2) the fact that crucifixion was considered by some ancients as parodic royal enthronement against the one who "attempted to acquire royal power." Marcus, *Mark 8–16*, 1049–50, 1133.

in Mark 15:29–32 depicts Jesus as the Messiah and the Righteous Sufferer, the antitype of David.

The first group of mockers, the passersby, deride Jesus with contempt ("shaking their heads") and claim he is unable to destroy the temple and build a new one unless he comes down from the cross and saves himself.[119] On a narrative level, their mockery links Jesus' death on the cross to the new temple motif that runs through Mark 11–15. At the same time, their mocking challenges Jesus' action and words about the inevitability of the destruction of the temple and the creation of the new temple (i.e., Mark 11:12–15; 12:11–12; Mark 13). However, the irony is that Jesus is destroying the temple and building the new temple by *hanging on the cross and by not saving himself* (Mark 15:29–30). Therefore, Mark uses the word "blasphemy" (ἐβλασφήμουν αὐτὸν, Mark 15:29) as the "ironic double entendre."[120] These mockers may intend to insult Jesus for his immovability on the cross, but they are actually blaspheming God by "challenging Jesus to save his life" against God's will.[121] The Sanhedrin charged Jesus with blasphemy (14:64). However, as Boring perceptively states, "Those who suppose they are insulting a human blasphemer are themselves guilty of blasphemy against God."[122]

The chief priests and teachers of the law continue the mockery (ὁμοίως καὶ "in the same way, also"; Mark 15:31). They further reveal the ironic truth about Jesus' messiahship. He is ὁ χριστὸς ὁ βασιλεὺς Ἰσραὴλ ("Christ, the King of Israel"; Mark 15:32) that echoes Mark 14:61–62.[123] The logic of their mockery is that Jesus should be able to come down from the cross and save himself, if he is the Christ who is to save others.[124] Their logic closely resembles that of passersby. These "leaders" not only use a similar language ("salvation" and "come down from the cross"), but also claim that Jesus cannot be who he claims to be because of his inability to free himself from the suffering of the cross.[125] However, Jesus

---

119. Hooker, *Mark*, 373. Matera rightly points out that shaking one's head and the mocker's taunt, "Aha," that often appears in lament psalms (Pss 35:21; 40:15; 70:3), demonstrate that Mark describes Jesus as the Righteous Sufferer. Matera, *Passion Narratives*, 43–44.

120. Boring, *Mark*, 429. See also Hooker, *Mark*, 373; Evans, *Mark*, 505.

121. Matera, *Passion Narratives*, 43.

122. Boring, *Mark*, 429. See also Hooker, *Mark*, 373; Evans, *Mark*, 505; Marcus, *Mark 8–16*, 1051.

123. Evans, *Mark*, 506.

124. Evans, *Mark*, 505.

125. Gundry, *Mark*, 947.

is Christ, the king of Israel, just because he is on the cross. As Hays aptly comments, Jesus will "demonstrate his kingship not by coming down from the cross but by enduring it."[126] As the Messiah, Jesus saves others by not saving himself (Mark 8:35).[127]

The irony is augmented by their statement "so that we may see and believe," (ἵνα ἴδωμεν καὶ πιστεύσωμεν; Mark 15:32b). The crucifixion is the fulfillment of what Jesus said to the people and religious leaders (Mark 12:1–12). They see Jesus' crucifixion, that is, the coming of God's kingdom through his redemptive suffering, but they neither understand nor believe because their hearts are hardened (Mark 4:12; Isa 6:9–10).[128] They are outsiders of the kingdom of God. The third group, those who are crucified with him, also join the mockery of the other groups (Mark 15:32c). Though their verbal attacks are not written, the mocking of the criminals at Jesus' innocence completes the mockery of the ungodly towards the Righteous Sufferer. Jesus is utterly isolated.[129]

After the series of mockeries, sudden darkness covers the whole earth at noon (Mark 15:33). Scholars propose several interpretive options on the significance of the darkness such as a sign of a great man's death,[130] God's wrath on Jesus,[131] God's judgment on the mockers in Mark 15:29–32,[132] or Israel,[133] God's mourning for his beloved Son,[134] and an eschatological sign.[135] The key to interpreting this darkness in Mark 15:33 appears to be an allusion to Amos 8:9 ("καὶ ἔσται ἐν ἐκείνῃ τῇ ἡμέρᾳ λέγει κύριος ὁ θεός καὶ δύσεται ὁ ἥλιος μεσημβρίας καὶ συσκοτάσει ἐπὶ τῆς γῆς ἐν ἡμέρᾳ τὸ φῶς; Amos 8:9 LXX).[136] The verbal parallel with Mark 15:33 (σκότος ἐγένετο ἐφ᾽ ὅλην τὴν γῆν, "**the darkness was on** the **whole earth**"; Emphasis mine) points to the allusion of Amos 8:9 in Mark

---

126. Hays, *Gospels*, 56.

127. Hooker, *Mark*, 374; Boring, *Mark*, 429.

128. Marcus, *Mark 8–16*, 1053.

129. Hooker, *Mark*, 374; Boring, *Mark*, 429; Marcus, *Mark 8–16*, 1053.

130. Evans, *Mark*, 506; Boring, *Mark*, 429; Collins, *Mark*, 752; Marcus, *Mark 8–16*, 1061.

131. Collins, "Noble Death," 497.

132. Brown, *Death of the Messiah*, 2:1035.

133. Moo, *Old Testament*, 342–44; Hooker, *Mark*, 376; France, *Mark*, 651; Evans, *Mark*, 506.

134. Collins, *Mark*, 752.

135. Marcus, *Mark 8–16*, 1062.

136. "And it will be on that day, says the Lord God, that the sun will go down at noon, and the light will grow dark on the land at daytime" (Amos 8:9 LXX).

15:33.[137] Furthermore, O'Brien summarizes the structural and thematic similarities between Amos 8:9-10 and Mark 15:33 as follows: "In both, the darkness over the land comes at noon. Jesus is crucified during the Feast of Passover; in Amos 8:10, God turns their feasts into mourning, like the mourning for an only son. In LXX, יחיד (*only son*) is translated with ἀγαπητός, a word the heavenly voice uses to describe Jesus at the baptism and the transfiguration (1.11, 9.7)."[138] The verbal, conceptual, and thematic parallels between the two texts are evident.

In light of the allusion to Amos 8:9 that announces the eschatological day of the Lord, the darkness in Mark 15:33 appears to indicate God's eschatological judgment in relation to Jesus' crucifixion. As Dale Allison notes, many events in the passion narrative parallel Jesus' eschatological predictions in Mark 13 because Jesus' death commences the eschatological era.[139] Therefore, these parallels in the passion narrative seem to serve as a foretaste of the eschatological events in Mark 13.[140] In corollary, the temporary darkness in Mark 15:33 seems to function as the eschatological foretaste for the final darkness in Mark 13 that indicates the eschatological judgment at the Parousia.[141] Also, considering the thematic allusion to the mourning for the beloved son in Amos 8:10, it is possible that the darkness in Mark 15:33 may signify God's mourning for his beloved Son.[142]

At the end of this darkness ("καὶ τῇ ἐνάτῃ ὥρᾳ"), Jesus cried out with a loud voice, "ελωι ελωι λεμα σαβαχθανι" (Mark 15:34). This clear quotation from Ps 22:2 has generated many diverse interpretations. Some

---

137. O'Brien, *Use of Scripture*, 141. Emphasis mine.

138. O'Brien, *Use of Scripture*, 143.

139. For instance, handing over Jesus ("seven times in Mark 14") vs handing over disciples (Mark 13:9, 11–12), Jesus' prayer for that hour of suffering at Gethsemane (Mark 14:32–42) vs the hour for the disciples' trial (Mark 13:32–33), the Son of Man's coming (Mark 13:26; 14:62), the sun becoming dark (Mark 13:24; 15:33), the torn temple veil (Mark 15:38) vs the destruction of the temple (Mark 13:1–2), Jesus comes and finds his disciples sleeping (Mark 14:40, 47) vs a master coming and finding his servants sleeping (Mark 13:36). Allison, *End of the Ages*, 36–39.

140. Allison, *End of the Ages*, 38–39.

141. O'Brien, *Use of Scripture*, 143–44. Similarly, Smith sees the correlation between the darkness in Amos 8:9, Mark 15:33, and Mark 13:24 and states that darkness portends "the end of the old world and the beginning of the new." Smith, "Darkness at Noon," 333–34.

142. Collins, *Mark*, 752; O'Brien, *Use of Scripture*, 144.

representative ones are as follows: (1) despair,[143] (2) trust and victory,[144] (3) demon possession,[145] (4) a sense of forsakenness,[146] (5) the incipit that has the whole Ps 22 in mind (i.e., lament and praise),[147] and (6) a cry that appeals to God's rescue from the suffering.[148] In the midst of various interpretive options, one must carefully consider the significance of Jesus' cry in Mark 15:34 and its context.

First, though experiencing utter isolation from mockers and his deserted disciples, Jesus is not in despair. His suffering on the cross is voluntary, and the wording of his calling, "my God," discloses his trust and intimacy with God rather than despair. Second, Jesus' cry as trust and victory neglects the literal meaning of his cry and the narrative context. Jesus is at the brink of death with utter humiliation and suffering. Third, demon-possession is a far cry from the Markan narrative flow.

Fourth, options 4, 5, and 6 have their own merits. Many interpreters rightly point out that Jesus' cry discloses his feelings of abandonment.[149] In the midst of excruciating suffering and total desolation, Jesus is expressing his sense of forsakenness (i.e., option 4). Yet, at the same time, Jesus' cry is a prayer for God's intervention (i.e., option 6). As for option 4, many interpreters correctly call attention to the fact that all the citations of Ps 22 in Mark come from the lament section of the psalm. Therefore, some of them conclude that Mark cannot have the whole psalm in mind.[150] However, we have observed that the Markan narrative shows that Mark often appropriated psalms with their whole context in mind (i.e., Pss 2, 110, 118). Likewise, those who insist that Mark is conscious of

---

143. Robbins, "Reversed Contextualization," 1161–83; Thatcher, "(Re)mark(s) on the Cross," 360; Hooker, *Mark*, 375; Gundry, *Mark*, 966; France, *Mark*, 652–53.

144. Schwemer, "Jesu letze Worte," 5–29.

145. Danker, "Demonic Secret," 48–69.

146. Though Brown does not endorse the idea of Ps 22:1 as the incipit that has the whole Ps 22 in mind, he does not consider that Jesus' feeling forsaken equates with despair. Brown states, "Jesus is praying, and so he cannot have lost hope; calling God "My God" implies trust." Brown, *Death of the Messiah*, 2:1047–51.

147. Gese, "Psalm 22," 192–96; Pesch, *Markusevangelium*, 2: 494; Donahue and Harrington, *Mark*, 451; Carey, *Jesus' Cry*, 160–67; Hays, *Gospels*, 85–86.

148. Ahearne-Kroll, *Psalms of Lament*, 209–10; Collins, *Mark*, 755; Hoskins, *Scripture*, 50; O'Brien, *Use of Scripture*, 153; Janowski, "'Mein Gott," 399–400. As for the view that Jesus' cry in Mark 15:34 is for the Jews who are to be judged because they abandon him, see Schmidt, "Cry of Dereliction," 146, 151–52.

149. Moo, *Old Testament*, 274; Evans, *Mark*, 507; Collins, *Mark*, 755; Marcus, *Mark 8–16*, 1062; Hays, *Gospels*, 78.

150. Brown, *Death of the Messiah*, 2:1050; Gundry, *Mark*, 966.

the whole context of Ps 22 notice that the Markan narrative reflects the rest of Ps 22 (i.e., vindication).

For instance, Marcus insightfully notes that the immediate context of Mark 15:20b—16:7 follows the lament-vindication pattern of Ps 22.[151] Similarly, Carey cogently demonstrates that a "passion-resurrection narrative" runs through the whole Markan narrative and the immediate context of Mark 15:34.[152] Therefore, we may conclude that the citation of Ps 22:1 in Mark 15:34 serves as the incipit for the whole Ps 22. At the same time, it expresses Jesus' feeling of dereliction and cry for God's action.[153]

Concerning the appropriation technique, Mark uses Ps 22:1 in Mark 15:34 typologically. Like other citations of Ps 22, Mark appropriates Ps 22:1 to show that Jesus is the Righteous Sufferer and the crucified Messiah, the antitype of the righteous sufferer and king, David. Both men cry out to God in their struggle for bringing about God's kingdom. As David in Ps 22:1, Jesus expresses a sense of abandonment and desire for God's deliverance.[154] Also, like David, Jesus' cry for deliverance is answered by the torn temple veil, the centurion's confession, and resurrection in the Markan narrative (Mark 15:38—16:7). However, Jesus' final cry exceeds that of David because Jesus' cry expresses the suffering and death that usher in God's redemption and kingdom for all who believe him (Mark 8:45; 15:43).[155] All these facts affirm that Mark uses Ps 22:1 in Mark 15:34 like other allusions to Ps 22 as a typological fulfillment of the Scripture.[156]

Jesus' cry of dereliction is followed by the misunderstanding and further mockery by bystanders (Mark 15:35–37). Thinking that Jesus is calling Elijah, the bystanders attempt to prolong Jesus' life with sour wine to see if Elijah will come and save him.[157] However, ironically, Elijah has

---

151. Marcus, *Way of the Lord*, 182. The following section on Ps 22 in the Markan narrative will treat Marcus's argument. See also, Bock, "Function of Scripture," 15–16; Botner, *Jesus Christ*, 184–87.

152. Carey, *Jesus' Cry*, 45–69, 139–70.

153. Markan narrative confirms that Jesus' cry is answered by God's act such as the tearing the temple veil, the confession of the gentile centurion, and resurrection (Mark 15:38—16:7).

154. Hoskins, *Scripture*, 50.

155. Hays, *Gospels*, 83.

156. Moo, *Old Testament*, 275; Hoskins, *Scripture*, 49–51.

157. Despite the difference in wording between ελωι and Ἠλίας, the bystanders' misunderstanding may have been induced by a dying man's cry in the midst of a noisy circumstance. In addition, their traditional expectation for Elijah's coming as "the deliverer in time of need" may have increased their confusion. Moo, *Old Testament*, 268.

already come. The irony is furthered because while the people want to see, they are blind like the chief priests and teachers of the law (Cf. Mark 15:32).[158] Also, their desire to see is not genuine but a mockery to extend Jesus' agony.[159] The allusion to Ps 68:22 (LXX) supports the idea that their action is a kind of derision (γεμίσας σπόγγον ὄξους . . . ἐπότιζεν αὐτόν, "They filled a sponge with **sour wine** . . . **gave it to drink**," Mark 15:36; εἰς τὴν δίψαν μου ἐπότισάν με ὄξος, "They **gave** me **to drink sour wine** for my thirst," Ps 68:22 LXX; Emphasis mine).[160] Just as David's enemies gave him sour wine as a mockery, these bystanders gave sour wine to Jesus to mock him. By appropriating Ps 68:22 (LXX), Mark intensifies "the pathos of the mockery and humiliation" Jesus experiences at the point of his death.[161] Just like the citations of Ps 22, the typological use of Ps 68:22 (LXX) portrays Jesus as the Righteous Sufferer and the Messiah.[162]

Mark presents Jesus' death and its consequences in Mark 15:37–39. Finally, Jesus releases his spirit with a loud voice (Mark 15:37). His suffering as the Righteous Sufferer and the crucified Messiah is completed. Two events of God's vindication follow Jesus' death.[163] First, the temple veil is torn from top to bottom (Mark 15:38).[164] While Mark does not specify which veil of the temple was torn, the complete tearing of the temple veil signifies God's action ("ἐσχίσθη," the divine passive) in response to Jesus' death. It is the eschatological sign of God that the Jerusalem temple will not function as the place of worship and God's presence (cf. Mark 11:11–26; 12:1–12; 13:1–2).[165] At the same time, it signals that the death of Jesus has made the access to God available to all people (cf. Mark 12:12).[166] Therefore, the tearing of the temple veil serves to vindicate Jesus

---

158. Collins, *Mark*, 755; Marcus, *Mark 8–16*, 1065.

159. Boring, *Mark*, 431; Marcus, *Mark 8–16*, 1065.

160. Moo, *Old Testament*, 278–80; Hoskins, *Scripture*, 51; Bock, "Function of Scripture," 16; O'Brien, *Use of Scripture*, 146.

161. O'Brien, *Use of Scripture*, 146.

162. Bock, "Function of Scripture," 16.

163. Rowe, *God's Kingdom*, 304. Mark connects Jesus' death and the tearing of the temple veil with καὶ, which indicates that the two events are related.

164. Some scholars speculate whether Mark meant the inner veil to the holy of holies (i.e., Collins, *Mark*, 759–60; Marcus, *Mark 8–16*, 1067) or the outer veil to the temple. Gundry, *Mark*, 950.

165. Hooker, *Mark*, 378; Brown, *Death of the Messiah*, 2:1099–109; Donahue and Harrington, *Mark*, 452; France, *Mark*, 657–58; Boring, *Mark*, 432; Marcus, *Mark 8–16*, 1066.

166. Hooker, *Mark*, 378; Boring, *Mark*, 432; Donahue and Harrington, *Mark*, 452;

against his opponents,[167] especially, the temple authorities and those who charged and mocked him concerning the temple (Mark 14:58; 15:29–30).

Second, a gentile Roman centurion who witnesses the significance of Jesus' death ("Now when the centurion, who stood facing him, saw how he died," Mark 15:39) serves as the human counterpart to God. A gentile centurion's confession (i.e., "The man was truly the Son of God") contrasts with Jesus' Jewish opponents. Though being a gentile, he *saw* Jesus' true identity that Jesus' Jewish opponents did *not see*.[168] His confession vindicates Jesus as the Messiah, the Son of God. On a narrative level, as mentioned in chapter 3 of this book, Mark 15:38–39 forms a bookend with Mark 1:10–11, and, thus, affirms Jesus' messianic sonship and his mission to bring about God's kingdom.[169] The vindication of Jesus and extension of God's kingdom to gentiles align with the vindication and praise section of Ps 22 (Ps 22:22b–31).[170] Mark 15:37–39 is the climax of all the narrative. By his redemptive death, Jesus completes his mission to bring about God's kingdom. The tearing of the temple veil and confession of the gentile centurion vindicate Jesus by affirming the significance of his death in relation to the temple and his identity.

Psalm 22 in the Markan Narrative

Mark clearly indicates that the suffering and death of Jesus are according to the Scripture (14:21, 49). Mark employs numerous lament psalms to confirm that Jesus' suffering, death, and vindication fulfill the Scripture. We have already observed the presence of many allusions to the lament psalms in Mark 15. Likewise, Mark 14 also contains several allusions to "the Psalms of the Righteous Sufferer,"[171] such as Pss 42:5, 11; 43:5 (Mark 14:34), 140:8 (Mark 14:41), 37:32 (Mark 14:55).[172] The presence of

---

Collins, *Mark*, 760; Marcus, *Mark 8–16*, 1067; Stein, *Mark*, 717–18; Strauss, *Mark*, 72.

167. Boring, *Mark*, 432.

168. Collins, *Mark*, 760; Marcus, *Mark 8–16*, 1067.

169. Moloney, *Mark*, 330; Strauss, *Mark*, 705; Caneday, "Christ's Baptism," 76.

170. Marcus, *Way of the Lord*, 182. See especially how a gentile centurion's confession corresponds to Ps 22:27–28: "All the ends of the earth will remember and turn to the LORD, and all the families of the nations will bow down before him, for dominion belongs to the LORD and he rules over the nations" (Ps 22:27–28 NIV). Collins, *Mark*, 771.

171. Marcus, *Way of the Lord*, 174.

172. O'Brien, *Use of Scripture*, 191.

many lament psalms in the passion narrative is understandable because the basic pattern of the Markan passion narrative—suffering and vindication[173]—resembles that of many Davidic lament psalms. Of all these lament psalms, Mark appropriated Ps 22 most often to highlight Jesus as the Messiah and the Righteous Sufferer.

The citations to Ps 22 play a strategic role in the Markan narrative. I already observed that Mark 15 consistently depicts Jesus as the Messiah and the Righteous Sufferer. Starting from the trial before the Sanhedrin, one finds the threefold cycle of the revelation of Jesus' identity, followed by mockery as the form of his suffering: (1) the Messiah, the Son of God, (Mark 14:60-62) and mockery (Mark 14:65); (2) the king of the Jews (Mark 15:2) and mockery (Mark 15:16-20); (3) the Messiah, the king of the Jews, (15:26, 32) and mockery; (Mark 15:29-32, 35-36). Whenever Jesus' identity is revealed, it leads to the suffering and crucifixion, the climax of his mission to bring about God's kingdom. Therefore, the third cycle reaches the climax: Jesus is crucified. He suffers and dies as the Messiah and the Righteous Sufferer.

Interestingly, all the citations of Ps 22 are located during this last cycle. The citations of Ps 22 intensify the narrative effect of Jesus' suffering and humiliation. At the same time, they exhibit the typological fulfillment of the Scripture that Jesus is the Messiah and the Righteous Sufferer in the pattern of David, who brings about God's eternal kingdom through his redemptive suffering and death. Relatedly, Jesus' opponents who mock and attempt to kill him typologically correspond to David's enemies. Mark's intense use of Ps 22 in the narrative climax of Mark seems to be related to the fact that Ps 22 "uniquely progresses from the deepest distress and suffering" (Ps 22: 1-21b) to "the farthest-reaching praise and thanksgiving for deliverance" (Ps 22:21c-31).[174]

While all the citations to Ps 22 concern Jesus' suffering and humiliation as the Messiah and the Righteous Sufferer, the structure of the Markan narrative reveals that Mark has the whole context of Ps 22 in mind. Marcus helpfully identified how Mark 15:20b—16:7 parallels Ps 22:1-31 as follows:

---

173. Nickelsburg, "Genre and Function," 183.
174. Watts, "Psalms," 42.

	Psalm 22	*Mark*
Suffering	vv. 1–21¹	15:20b–37
Worship of Gentiles	v. 27	15:39
Kingdom of God	v. 28	15:43
Resurrection	v. 29	16:6
Proclamation to God's people	vv. 30–31	16:7[175]

Marcus's suggested correspondences between the two texts are striking. Our investigation has proved that suffering and worship by gentiles in Ps 22 are fulfilled in Jesus' suffering and the Roman centurion's confession. In addition, Marcus points out how the kingdom of God (God's rule over all nations in Ps 22:28 and Joseph of Arimathea waiting for the kingdom of God in Mark 15:43), the resurrection ("And my soul lives in him," in Ps 21:29, LXX, and "He has risen" in Mark 16:6);[176] and proclamation to God's people (proclamation to future generations in Ps 22:30–31 and "But go, tell his disciples and Peter," in Mark 16:7) motifs correspond between Ps 22:28–31 and Mark 15:43–16:7.[177] Even if one does not agree with every detail of Marcus's suggestion, the structure of Mark 15:20b–16:7 seems to show that Mark has intended to use the citations of Ps 22 with a lament and vindication pattern in mind. The anticipation of the eschatological vindication throughout Ps 22:22b–31 is finally fulfilled in Mark 15:38–16:7.

The wider context of the Markan narrative also seems to show that Mark has the whole context of Ps 22 in mind.[178] Jesus has a clear mission to bring about God's kingdom (Mark 1:14). To accomplish his mission, he must suffer, die, and be resurrected (Mark 8:31; 9:31; 10:34). Thus, the whole narrative proceeds to the passion. At the end of the passion narrative, Mark appropriates Ps 22 in such a way to present the suffering and death of Jesus in his struggle with his enemies to bring about

---

175. Marcus, *Way of the Lord*, 182.

176. Marcus seems to draw his resurrection motif from the Septuagint, καὶ ἡ ψυχή μου αὐτῷ ζῇ ("and my soul lives in him," Ps 21:30 LXX). According to Fabry, this means that the psalmist's worship will continue even after his death. Fabry, "Wirkungsgeschichte," 285. While the text does not necessarily indicate the resurrection as Marcus suggests, it seems to leave open the possibility of the resurrection.

177. Marcus, *Way of the Lord*, 182–83.

178. Similarly, focusing on "suffering, death, and resurrection" pattern throughout the Markan narrative, Carey rightly recognizes the similar pattern between the wider context of the Markan narrative and the whole context of Ps 22. Carey, *Jesus' Cry*, 45–69.

God's kingdom. Mark 15:38—16:7 parallels the vindication section of Ps 22 closely to exhibit that the anticipated vindication of Jesus has arrived.

In conclusion, it seems that, by using Ps 22 with its whole context in mind, Mark ends the narrative with the clear message: Jesus suffered as the crucified Messiah and the Righteous Sufferer. God vindicated him. As a result of Jesus' suffering, death, and resurrection, God's kingdom has come for all the nations, according to the Scriptures.

CONCLUSION

Psalm 22 is the most poignant Davidic lament psalm that expresses David's sense of God's absence, cry for salvation out of trust in the midst of unbearable suffering, humiliation, praise, and proclamation of God's rule. An examination of ancient variant texts exhibits that the LXX expresses more hope for salvation than the MT in the lament section of Ps 22. Therefore, Mark's use of Ps 21 (LXX) seems to support my argument that Mark reads the lament section in the hope for vindication. The canonical context of Ps 22 reveals that this text is a part of the Davidic lament psalms and should be viewed as part of David's ongoing struggle with his enemies as he establishes God's kingdom envisaged by Pss 1–2. Of all the Davidic lament psalms, Ps 22 stands out because it most vividly describes both an unbearable death-like suffering and humiliation of David from his enemies and the exuberant praise and proclamation of God's rule. These unique features of Ps 22 seem to be reasons for the allusions by other psalms and OT texts (i.e., Pss 69; 71; Jer 1:5; Isa 46:3).

As for the interpretation of Ps 22 in Second Temple literature, we note that (1) the use of Ps 22 clearly presents each protagonist as a righteous sufferer in the pattern of Ps 22 except *Joseph and Aseneth*, that (2) many of them anticipate the eschatological vindication, and that (3) 4Q88 attests the liturgical use of the whole Ps 22. In light of this sociocultural context of Mark's contemporaries, we conclude that Mark may have appropriated Ps 22 to portray Jesus as the Righteous Sufferer with the anticipation of the eschatological vindication in the same vein. Also, the wide use of Ps 22 in the Qumran community hints that their contemporaries, including Mark, may be very acquainted with the whole Ps 22, which increases the possibility that Mark may have the whole Ps 22 in mind.

The passion narrative in Mark demonstrates how Jesus' death and resurrection fulfill the Scriptures. The presence of numerous Davidic lament psalms in the Markan narrative reveal that Mark uses them to show that Jesus' death and suffering are patterned after David's experience as the messiah and a righteous sufferer. Of these, the unique features of Ps 22 show the suffering and vindication of David more poignantly than any other lament psalms. It may explain why Mark appropriates Ps 22 more frequently than other Davidic lament psalms. Moreover, all the citations of Ps 22 appear in Mark 15:20b–39, where Mark's consistent portrayal of Jesus as the Messiah and the Righteous Sufferer throughout Mark 15 reaches its climax. This typological use of Ps 22 suggests that David is not simply an exemplar but the type of Jesus: Jesus not only exceeds David in his experience but also fulfills the Scripture as the Messiah and the Righteous Sufferer who suffers, dies, and resurrects to bring about the ultimate eschatological kingdom of God.

Though the lament section of Ps 22 is appropriated in Mark 15, the events in the ensuing passages in Mark (i.e., Mark 15:38—16:7) closely correspond to the praise section of Ps 22 thematically. It seems reasonable to say that Mark has the whole context of Ps 22 in mind. The quotation, allusions, and echoes of Ps 22 in Mark 15:20b—16:7 cohere with the passion and vindication pattern anticipated on the level of the whole Markan narrative. All these factors point out that Mark uses Ps 22 at the key junctures of the Markan narrative. Thus, Mark uses Ps 22 in the climax of the Markan narrative (i.e., Mark 15:20b—16:7) to present Jesus as the Messiah and the Righteous Sufferer who brings about God's kingdom through his redemptive death and resurrection according to the Scriptures.

7

Conclusion

I HAVE ARGUED THAT Mark uses Pss 2, 118, 110, and 22 at the key junctures of the narrative of the Gospel of Mark to present Jesus as the Messiah, the Son of God who ushers in God's kingdom. After reviewing the history of scholarship, I pointed out the necessity to explore Mark's use of Psalms comprehensively in light of the entire Markan narrative and thus justified the validity of my study. The rest of the introduction laid out the methodology that this study utilized to explore Mark's use of Psalms, such as (1) the details of how to engage in the use of the OT in the NT and (2) the need of narrative approach to evaluate the use of Psalms in the whole literary context of Mark.

In chapter 2, I justified applying narrative criticism (i.e., setting, plot, character, andrhetoric) to identify the structure of Mark because narrative criticism faithfully reflects the literary contours of Mark. I argued for the following as the macro-level structure of the Markan narrative: Mark 1:1—8:21, Jesus' ministry in Jerusalem; [Mark 8:22–26, transition]; Mark 8:27—10:45, on the way; [Mark 10:46–52, transition]; Mark 11:1—16:8, Jesus' ministry in Jerusalem. On a micro level, I proposed the following: 1:1–15 (Prologue); 1:16–45 (the calling of the disciples and manifestation of the kingdom power in Jesus' teaching and actions); 2:1—3:6 (five conflicts between Jesus and the religious leaders); 3:7–3:35 (the second calling of the disciples, kingdom ministry, insiders and outsiders of the kingdom); 4:1–34 (revelation and concealment of the secret of God's kingdom); 4:35—6:44 (Jesus' ministry around the Sea of Galilee: the first cycle); 6:45—8:21 (Jesus' ministry around the Sea of Galilee: the second cycle); 8:27—10:45 (the prediction on Jesus' passion, death, and resurrection and teaching on discipleship); 11:1—12:44 (Jesus' entry into Jerusalem and the confrontation with theJerusalem establishment); 13:1–37 (Jesus' second teaching discourse on the temple destruction and the Parousia); 14:1—15:47 (the passion); and 16:1–8 (the resurrection).

The suggested structure of the Markan narrative reveals that Jesus' identity, his mission, and discipleship are closely interrelated. Also, the Markan narrative consistently shows that these three inseparable themes—Jesus' identity as the messianic Son of God, his ministry to usher in God's kingdom, and the participation in God's kingdom by following Jesus by faith—are according to the Scriptures. Thus, building upon the structure of the Markan narrative, we proposed the purpose of Mark as follows: (1) Mark desires to inform his readers that Jesus is the Messiah, the Son of God. (2) Mark intends to lead his readers to understand that the kingdom of God has arrived in Jesus' coming and ministry, especially in his death and resurrection. (3) Mark wants to exhort his readers to partake in God's kingdom by following Jesus with genuine faith. (4) Mark purposes to demonstrate that Jesus' identity (Christology), his mission (eschatology), and discipleship are according to the Scriptures.

Chapters 3–6 are devoted to exploring Mark's use of the four psalms and what significance they make in the Markan narrative in light of the narrative structure and the purpose of Mark. In chapter 3, after examining the textual form of Ps 2:7 in the LXX, the MT, and Mark, we identified the major theme of Ps 2 as God's rule through his messiah and his victory over the rebellious gentile rulers and nations. Psalm 2 in the context of the whole Psalter shows that Ps 2 in combination with Ps 1 functions as the gateway to the whole Psalter, as the entire Psalter points to God's rule via his messiah (i.e., the Davidic messiah). The interpretation history of Ps 2 witnessed by ancient variants (i.e., LXX and Targum) and Second Temple literature reveals the anticipation of the eschatological Davidic messiah's coming to bring God's kingdom. Interestingly, Second Temple literature appropriates several scriptural citations in tandem with Ps 2 and includes Jews into the messiah's enemies.

Mark's appropriation of Ps 2 shares some commonalities with his contemporaries: (1) Like his contemporary interpreters, Mark extends the application of the messiah's enemies in Ps 2 by replacing the rebellious rulers and the nations in Ps 2 with Satan and the disobedient Jewish rulers. Thus, Mark not only alludes to Ps 2:7 but also has the context of Ps 2:7 (God's rule through his messiah and his victory over the rebellious rulers and nations) in mind. (2) Like his contemporaries, Mark juxtaposes other scriptural citations with Ps 2:7. (3) Mark considers Jesus as the fulfilment of the eschatological Davidic messiah anticipated by his Jewish contemporaries.

However, Mark's use of Ps 2:7 exceeds the original context of Ps 2 and the interpretation of his contemporaries as he uses Ps 2:7 in tandem with other OT allusions. First, Jesus is presented as the suffering Messiah instead of the militant messiah. The suffering Messiah motif is adumbrated in Mark 1:11, where Mark uses Ps 2:7 with the allusion to Isa 42:1. The motif is more explicit when Jesus revealed his identity and mission to the disciples in the transfiguration (Mark 9:7). The echo of Ps 2:7 in the centurion's confession climaxes the suffering Messiah motif. Second, Mark interconnects the new exodus with the kingdom of God through the Messiah in the beginning and the end of Mark in such a way to present the coming of the eschatological rule of God through Jesus (i.e., Isa 64:1 and Ps 2:7 in Mark 1:10–11 and 15:38). Finally, Mark implicitly suggests the divine sonship of Jesus in the allusion to Ps 2:7 in combination of Gen 22 in Mark 1:11 and 9:7, as he does in the rest of Markan narrative (cf. Mark 2:5–11; 4:39; 6:37–44; 48–49; 7:37; 8:6–10).

As a result, Mark's allusions and echo to Ps 2:7 in Mark 1:11, 9:7, and 15:39 serve as the key framework of the entire narrative of Mark. The fact that the three occurrences of the Son of God above and the kingdom of God language in the immediate context (Mark 1:15; 9:1; 15:43) are located closely in Mark shows that Jesus' messianic sonship and the kingdom of God are correlated and function as the governing themes of Mark. Also, the allusion to Ps 2:7 in Mark 9:7 connects Jesus' messianic sonship to discipleship.

Mark's use of Ps 2:7 as the key framework of the Markan narrative and his consciousness for the whole context of Ps 2 affirm that the coming of God's kingdom through Jesus, the Son of God, is programmatic for the entire narrative of Mark. It is interesting to observe that Mark's use of Ps 2 for the narrative skeleton of Mark, with God's kingdom via his Messiah (i.e., Jesus) as the ideological view of the narrative, resembles Ps 2 as the introduction of the whole Psalter that envisages God's kingdom through his messiah, the overarching theme of the whole Psalter. It seems to imply that Mark may have been conscious of the role of Ps 2 in the whole Psalter and applied it to his own narrative structure.

In chapter 4, after probing the textual form of Ps 118:22–23, 25–26 in the LXX, the MT, and Mark, we concluded that Ps 118 is about the Davidic king who leads a procession (i.e., the nation of Israel) to the temple for thanksgiving after experiencing exodus-like salvation from his enemies. It seems that the psalm reflects the postexilic Jewish community's anticipation of the eschatological Davidic messiah, who would come and save them (i.e., the new exodus) from their oppression. Accordingly, the Targum clearly identifies the psalmist with the eschatological Davidic messiah. The witness of Second Temple literature (i.e., Dead Sea Scrolls) is not definitive due to its fragmentary nature. However, at the least, it attests the Davidic messiah motif in Ps 118.

What stands out among the interpretive history of Ps 118 before Mark is the canonical context of the Psalter and other OT texts. We observe the three major motifs, the Davidic messiah, the (new) exodus, and the temple, throughout Book V of the Psalter, especially the Egyptian Hallel (Pss 113–118) and other OT texts (i.e., Exod 15:2; 17:4; Isa 12:2, 26:4; 1 Sam 17:45; Zech 4:7). These three motifs suggest that Ps 118 portrays the coming of the Davidic messiah who will bring God's kingdom through his salvific act (i.e., the new exodus) for God's people and lead them to worship YHWH in the temple.

Mark uses Ps 118 at the critical junctures of the Markan narrative and exhibits the three motifs we identified in the previous sections. First, Mark uses Ps 118:25–26 (Mark 11:9–10) with other scriptural allusions (Gen 49:11 and Zech 9:9) in Mark 11:1–11 (the beginning of Jesus' final ministry at Jerusalem) to portray Jesus as the eschatological Davidic Messiah who will bring God's kingdom through the salvation (i.e., the new exodus). At the same time Mark closely connects the quotation of Ps 118:25–26 and Ps 118:22–23 to the temple motif: the chiastic structure, with the two citations of Ps 118:25–26 and 22–23 at the two ends and the composite citation of Isa 56:7 and Jer 7:11 (i.e., the judgment of the temple) at the center in Mark 11:1–12:12, bring out the temple motif as one of the major themes of Mark 11–16. Through the three groups of the quotations, Mark highlights that (1) Jesus' entry to Jerusalem fulfills the Davidic messiah's coming to the temple, that (2) Jesus' demonstration in the temple fulfills the judgment on the temple, and that (3) Jesus' death and resurrection fulfill the rejection and vindication of the stone as the cornerstone of the new temple.

Second, Ps 118:22–23 plays several significant roles at the key juncture of the Markan narrative: (1) It ends the parable of the wicked tenants that portrays Jesus' death and resurrection as the culmination of the salvation history. (2) It serves as the scriptural witness to Jesus' death and resurrection motif that has already run through the middle section of the Markan narrative with the three predictions (Mark 8:31-32; 9:30-31; 10:32-34). (3) It functions as the blueprint for Mark 12-16, as it forecasts Jesus' death and resurrection in tandem with the temple motif. (4) The reversal of the fortune and the salvation that evokes the wonder convey the new exodus motif (Ps 118:23). In conclusion, Mark's appropriation of Ps 118 presents Jesus as the Davidic Messiah who comes to Jerusalem to bring about God's kingdom through the judgment of the present temple and the creation of the new temple. However, unlike the anticipation of the postexilic Jewish community, he accomplishes his mission through his death and resurrection, which is the new exodus for all who put their faith in him.

In chapter 5, we investigated the textual form of Ps 110:1, which is virtually identical between the MT, the LXX, and Mark's quotation. We conclude that Ps 110 is David's prophetic psalm of twofold divine oracle concerning the enthronement of the Davidic messiah, who is also the priest-king in the manner of Melchizedek. This David's lord and his rule will ultimately fulfill the Abrahamic and Davidic covenants. In the canonical context of the whole Psalter, we observed that Ps 110 both affirms the universal rule of the Davidic messiah, the son of God, through the subjugation of his enemies envisioned in Ps 2 and culminates it with the complete subjugation of his enemies and the eternal priestly kingship.

Apart from its close relationship to Davidic and Abrahamic covenants, we do not find clear allusive relationships between Ps 110 and other OT texts and Second Temple literature. Scholars speculate that such absence may have originated either from the tension between the Hasmoneans and those who do not admit the high priesthood of the Hasmonean rulers, or from the fear of the Second Temple Jews not to infringe on their monotheistic belief by appropriating the seemingly audacious claim on the heavenly throne in Ps 110. Nevertheless, we witness some texts from the postexilic community (i.e., the LXX and the Targum) that view Ps 110 messianically (i.e., the Davidic messiah). In addition, the use of Dan 7:13 and Ps 110:1 in tandem in the *Similitudes of Enoch* seems to derive from their similarities, which may be the reason why Mark also used them together in Mark 14:62.

Mark uses Ps 110:1 twice in the Markan narrative. The first citation of Ps 110:1 appears in Mark 12:35-37 as the counterattack on the temple establishment (i.e., the scribes) after rebutting a series of hostile questions from the Jewish religious leaders concerning Jesus' authority over the temple. In the immediate context of Mark, Jesus' quotation of

Ps 110:1 serves to defeat Jesus' opponents (i.e., the scribes) by countering their teaching that the messiah is the son of David. In the wider context of Mark, Ps 110 both corrects the popular understanding of the messiahship and prepares for the full revelation of Jesus' messiahship in Mark 14:62 by building up the literary tension that is finally resolved in Mark 14:62.

The second citation of Ps 110:1 is located at the crux of the Markan narrative (Mark 14:61–62), a part of Jesus' trial by the Sanhedrin (Mark 14:55–65). Mark 14:61–62 is pivotal in the Markan narrative because it (1) recapitulates Jesus' identity as the Messiah, the Son of God (Mark 1:1), and links it to another title, the Son of Man; (2) reconnects the temple motif after Mark 13 and foreshadows another temple motif (Mark 15:29, 38); and (3) forecasts Jesus' resurrection, ascension, and second coming beyond the story narrated in Mark.

In combination with Ps 80:18 and Dan 7:13, the allusion to Ps 110:1 in Mark 14:62b plays several significant roles in the Markan narrative: (1) It affirms Jesus' heavenly enthronement and reveals the complete subjugation of his enemies. Thus, Mark's use of Ps 110 shows the consummation of God's rule through the enthronement of Jesus, the Son of God, and the subjugation of his enemies that Mark conveys by his use of Ps 2. Mark's use of these psalms corresponds to the relationship between Pss 2 and 110 in the canonical context of the Psalter. (2) With other allusions, it contributes to Jesus' prediction for his vindication through suffering, resurrection, ascension, enthronement, and the Parousia. (3) It evokes the priest-king motif. As the priestly king, Jesus will bring about the new temple order, which perfectly fits the temple motif in the immediate context (Mark 14:58–59) and in the wider context of the narrative (Mark 11–15). (4) Finally, it both accomplishes one part of the passion prediction (i.e., arrest) and becomes the basis of another part of the anticipated passion.

In chapter 6, we first established the textual form of one quotation and two allusions from Ps 22 (Ps 22:1 in Mark 15:34; Ps 22:7–8 in Mark 15:29–30; Ps 22:18 in Mark 15:24) and concluded that the textual form of Mark's citations is virtually identical with that of the LXX, except the Aramaic quotation in Mark 15:34. We argued that Ps 22 portrays (1) David's feeling of God's absence, a cry for deliverance from his intense suffering and humiliation in the lament section, and (2) praise and proclamation on the rule of God in the vindication section. The LXX uses the language of hope for salvation more than the MT in the lament section of Ps 22, which seems to support that Mark has hope for vindication in mind when he uses the lament section of Ps 22. As a part of the Davidic lament psalms in Book I of the Psalter, Ps 22 should be considered as part of David's constant struggle with his enemies as the messiah who establishes God's kingdom envisioned by Pss 1–2. Also, Ps 22 stands out from all the Davidic lament psalms because of its vivid description of the intolerable suffering and humiliation David faces from his enemies and the ebullient praise and proclamation of God's reign. These peculiarities of Ps 22 may have contributed to other OT texts alluding to the psalm (i.e., Pss 69, 71; Jer 1:5; Isa 46:3).

On the use of Ps 22 in Second Temple literature, we find that most of the texts portray their protagonists as righteous sufferers in accordance with Ps 22 and expect the eschatological vindication. Thus, Mark's use of Ps 22 may have reflected the sociocultural context of his contemporaries by depicting Jesus as the Righteous Sufferer with the anticipation of the eschatological vindication. Also, the liturgical use of the whole Ps 22 in the Qumran community attested by 4Q88 hints that Mark may have been familiar with the whole psalm, which can raise the possibility that Mark may have been conscious of the context of the entire psalm.

The passion narrative in Mark clearly shows that Jesus' passion and resurrection fulfill the Scriptures. Of the many Davidic lament psalms which exhibit that Jesus' passion is patterned after David's experience as the messiah and a righteous sufferer, Mark uses Ps 22 more often than any other Davidic lament psalm, possibly because of the unique features of the psalm we mentioned above. In his use of Ps 22, Mark portrays Jesus as the Messiah and the Righteous Sufferer who is the antitype of David, who suffers in his struggle to bring about God's kingdom. Jesus' experience exceeds that of David and fulfills the Scriptures as Jesus' suffering, death, and resurrection effect the ultimate eschatological kingdom of God.

Mark appropriates Ps 22 at the key juncture of the Markan narrative. Mark consistently presents Jesus as the Messiah and the Righteous Sufferer, especially in Mark 15. Mark locates all the citations of Ps 22 in Mark 15:20b–39 (the crucifixion scene), where the whole narrative climaxes. Also, though Mark appropriates only the lament section of Ps 22 in Mark 15, the following events in Mark 15:38—16:7 closely parallel the praise section of Ps 22 thematically. Furthermore, all the citations and echoes of Ps 22 in Mark 15:20b—16:7 follow the passion and vindication pattern on the level of the whole Markan narrative. All these features point that Mark strategically uses Ps 22 at the key juncture of the Markan narrative to present Jesus as the Messiah and the Righteous Sufferer who ushers in the kingdom of God through his passion and resurrection according to the Scriptures.

In view of our study thus far, we can highlight a few salient points in Mark's use of the given psalms. First, though Mark appropriated a part of the psalms, the Markan narrative reflects that Mark had the whole context of the psalms in mind. Our study revealed that the Markan narrative demonstrates that Mark applied the entirety of each psalm to the narrative: God's rule via his messiah and the subjugation of his enemies (Ps 2), God's exodus-like salvation through his messiah who leads God's people to worship in the temple (Ps 118), the ultimate heavenly enthronement of God's priest-king and the complete subjugation of his enemies (Ps 110), and unbearable suffering and humiliation of God's messiah and the vindication (Ps 22).

Second, Mark seems to be also conscious of each psalm's canonical context in the Psalter. (1) Mark used the allusions and echo to Ps 2 as the skeleton of Markan narrative similar to Ps 2's role as the gateway to the entire Psalter. Mark may have been aware of the significance of Ps 2 and used it as the key framework as his overarching themes of the Gospel are Jesus' identity as the messianic Son of God and God's kingdom inaugurated by him. (2) Just as Ps 110 recapitulates and expands the vision of Ps 2 in the canonical context of the Psalter, Mark's use of Ps 110 shows the consummation of God's kingdom through Jesus framed by the citations of Ps 2 and the expansion of Ps 2 with priest-king motif. (3) Likewise, the canonical context of Ps 118 (i.e., the Egyptian Hallel) shows how Ps 118 climaxes the themes of the new exodus, temple, and the Davidic messiah. Mark may have been aware of such significance of Ps 118 and used it to highlight those themes at the key juncture of Markan narrative. (4) Finally, we noted the unique features of Ps 22 in the canonical context of Mark and how Ps 22 along with other Davidic lament psalms conveys David's ongoing struggle to establish God's kingdom as his messiah. Mark's use of Ps 22 at the crucifixion of Jesus seems to indicate that Mark may have been aware of those peculiar characteristics of Ps 22.

Third, Mark shares some commonalities with his contemporaries in his use of Psalms. (1) We have observed that Mark frequently appropriated the psalms with other scriptural citations just like his contemporaries. (2) Mark's contemporaries often considered these four psalms to portray the eschatological Davidic messiah. Mark does not shy away from presenting Jesus as the eschatological Davidic Messiah in his use of these psalms, though Mark clearly shows that Jesus is more than a Davidic messiah. (3) In case of Ps 22, Mark shares the Righteous Sufferer and eschatological vindication motifs with his contemporaries.

Fourth, however, Mark's use of Psalms deviates from that of his contemporaries in that he presents Jesus and his ministry as the fulfillment of the anticipation for the coming of the eschatological Davidic messiah and God's kingdom through the new exodus. Also, unlike his contemporaries, Mark's use of psalms shows that the Messiah brings God's kingdom via suffering, death, and resurrection. He uses the psalms to show that Jesus and his ministry of God's kingdom have fulfilled the Scriptures.

As Hays perceptively states, Psalms are "particularly important intertexts for interpreting the shape of Jesus' life and death"[1] because Psalms focuses on the kingdom of God through his messiah, which perfectly coheres with the purpose of Mark (i.e., Jesus' identity as the messianic Son of God and God's kingdom he ushers in). I have demonstrated that the given psalms play a central role at the key junctures of the Markan narrative, which supports my argument that the fulfillment of the Scriptures is one element of the purpose of Mark. The paucity of discipleship motif found in Mark's use of the psalms seems to be related to the Psalter's focus on God's kingdom and his messiah.

While we explored the use of the relatively explicit and recurring psalms in Mark, the study was not able to treat Mark's use of Psalms exhaustively due to the limited scope. For the further study, it will be interesting to explore other citations of Psalms in Mark and incorporate the result into my study to see the function of Psalms in Mark more comprehensively. Also, the book addressed that the new exodus motif is found in Ps 118 and is connected to Ps 2 in Mark. Though I recognize the importance of the new exodus motif and Isaiah in Mark, I am not convinced that *Isaianic* new exodus motif is the governing theme of the Markan narrative as Watts and others suggest. However, because of sheer quantity of citations from Isaiah and Psalms in Mark and their importance in Mark, it would be a worthwhile endeavor to explore the correlations between Isaiah and Psalms in Mark. Finally, I think that the study on the use of the OT in the NT in view of the entire Gospel narrative, as I attempted in this book, will enrich our understanding on the subject matter.

---

1. Hays, *Gospels*, 83.

Bibliography

Abasciano, Brian J. "Diamonds in the Rough: A Reply to Christopher Stanley Concerning the Reader Competency of Paul's Original Audiences." *NovT* 49 (2007) 153–83.
Achtemeier, Paul. *Mark*. PC. 2nd ed. Philadelphia: Fortress, 1986.
Ådna, Jostein. *Jesu Stellung zum Tempel: Die Tempelaktion und da Tempelwort als Ausdruck seiner mesianischen Sendung*. WUNT 2/119. Tübingen: Mohr Siebeck, 2000.
Aernie, Jeffrey W. "Cruciform Discipleship: The Narrative Function of the Women in Mark 15-16." *JBL* 135 (2016) 779–97.
Ahearne-Kroll, Stephen P. *The Psalms of Lament in Mark's Passion*. Cambridge: Cambridge University Press, 2007.
Ahn, Keun Jo. "The Equivocality of Psalm 80: From Communal Lament to Royal Psalm." *KJOTS* 68 (2018) 93–117. http://doi.org/10.24333/jkots.2018.24.2.93.
Aland, K., et al., eds. *Novum Testamentum Garaece*. 28th ed. Stuttgart: Deutsche Bibelgesellschaft, 2013.
Alvarez, Francis D. "The Temple Controversy in Mark." *Landas* 28 (2014) 141–42.
Alkier, Stefan. "Intertextuality and the Semiotics of Biblical Texts." In *Reading the Bible Intertextually*, edited by Richard B. Hays, et al., 3–21. Waco, TX: Baylor University Press, 2009.
Allen, David D. "Introduction: The Study of the Use of the Old Testament in the New." *JSNT* 38 (2015) 3–16.
———. "The Use of Criteria: The State of Question." In *Methodology in the Use of the Old Testament in the New: Context and Criteria*, edited by D. David Allen and Steve Smith, 129–41. LSNT 579. New York: T&T Clark, 2019.
Allen, Leslie. C. *Psalms 101–150*. WBC. Vol. 21. Nashville: Thomas Nelson, 2002.
Allison, Dale C., Jr. *The End of the Ages Has Come: An Early Interpretation of the Passion and Resurrection of Jesus*. Philadelphia: Fortress, 1985.
Atkinson, K. *An Intertextual Study of the Psalm of Solomon Pseudepigrapha*. Lewiston, NY: Mellen, 2001.
Auffret, Pierre. *La sagesse a bâti sa maison: Études de structures littéraires dans l'Ancien Testament et spécialement dans les psaumes*. Göttingen: Vandenhoeck & Ruprecht, 1982.
———. *The Literary Structure of Psalm 2*. Sheffield: University of Sheffield Press, 1977.

Aus, R. D. *The Wicked Tenants and Gethsemane: Isaiah in the Wicked Tenants' Vineyard, and Moses and the High Priest in Gethsemane: Judaic Traditions in Mark 12:1–9 and 14:32–42*. Atlanta: Scholars, 1996.

Bail, Ulrike. "Psalm 110: Eine intertextuelle Lektüre aus alttestamentlicher Perspektive." In *Heiligkeit und Herrschaft: Intertextuelle Studien zu Heiligkeitsvorstellungen und zu Psalm 110*, edited by Dieter Sänger, 94–121. BThST 55. Neukirchen-Vluyn: Neukirchener Verlag, 2003.

Bain, Bruce Alan. "Literary Surface Structures in Mark: Identifying Christology as the Purpose of the Gospel." PhD diss., Fuller Theological Seminary, 1997.

Bakhtin, Mikhail. "Discourse in the Novel." In *The Dialogic Imagination: Four Essays*, edited by M. Holquist and translated by Caryl Emerson and M. Holquist, 259–423. Austin: University of Texas Press, 1981.

Baldwin, Joyce G. *Haggai, Zechariah, Malachi*. TOTC. Downers Grove, IL: InterVarsity, 1972.

Balhorn, Egbert. *Zum Telos des Psalters: Der Textzusammenhang des Vierten und Fünften Psalmenbuches (Ps 90–150)*. BBB 138. Berlin: Philo, 2004.

Bammel, E, ed. *The Trial of Jesus: Cambridge Studies in Honour of C. F. D. Moule*. SBT 13. London: SCM, 1970.

Barbiero, Gianni. "The Non-Violent Messiah of Psalm 110." *BZ* 58 (2014) 1–20.

Barrett, Charles K. "The House of Prayer and the Den of Thieves." In *Jesus und Paulus*, edited by E. Earle Ellis and Erich Grässer, 13–20. Göttingen: Vandenhoeck und Ruprecht, 1975.

Barthes, Roland. "The Death of the Author." In *Image, Music, Text*, 142–48. Translated by Stephen Heath. New York: Hill and Wang, 1977.

Bastard, Hans M. *A Way in the Wilderness: The Second Exodus in the Message of Second Isaiah*. JSS 12. Manchester: University of Manchester Press, 1989.

Bateman, Hebert W., IV. "Defining the Titles 'Christ' and 'Son of God' in Mark's Narrative Presentation of Jesus." *JETS* 50 (2007) 537–59.

———. "Psalm 110:1 and the New Testament." *BSac* 149 (1992) 438–53.

———. "The Recipient of Psalm 110: Who Might It Be?" *Evangelical Theological Society Papers* (1991) 1–18.

Bauckham, Richard. "Devotion to Jesus Christ in Earliest Christianity: An Appraisal and Discussion of the Work of Larry Hurtado." In *Mark, Manuscripts, and Monotheism: Essays in Honor of Larry W. Hurtado*, edited by Chris Keith and Dieter T. Roth, 176–200. LNTS 528. New York: T&T Clark, 2015.

———. *Jesus and the God of Israel*. Grand Rapids: Eerdmans, 2008.

———. "Markan Christology According to Richard Hays: Some Addenda." *JTI* 11 (2017) 21–36.

———. *Who Is God?: Key Moments of Biblical Revelation*. Grand Rapids: Baker Academic, 2020.

Baumgarten, J. M. "4Q500 and the Ancient Conception of the Lord's Vineyard." *JJS* 40 (1989) 1–6.

Beale, Gregory K. *Handbook on the New Testament Use of the Old Testament: Exegesis and Interpretation*. Grand Rapids: Baker Academic, 2012.

———. *John's Use of the Old Testament in Revelation*. Sheffield: Sheffield, 1999.

———. "Questions of Authorial Intent, Epistemology, and Presuppositions and Their Bearing on the Study of the Old Testament in the New: A Rejoinder to Steve Moyise." *IBS* 21 (1999) 1–26.

Becker, Joachim. *Israel deutet seine Psalmen: Urform und Neuinterpretation in den Psalmen*. Stuttgart: Katholisches Bibelwerk, 1966.

Berder, Michel. *"La pierre rejetée par les bâtisseurs": Psaume 118,22–23 et son emploi dans les traditions juives et dans le Nouveau Testament*. Paris: Librairie Lecoffre/J. Gabalda, 1996.

Berlin, Adele. "Critical Notes: Psalm 118:24." *JBL* 96 (1977) 567–68.

Best, Ernest. *Disciples and Discipleship*. Edinburgh: T&T Clark, 1986.

———. *Following Jesus: Discipleship in the Gospel of Mark*. Sheffield: University of Sheffield, 1981.

Bird, Michael F. *Jesus Is the Christ: The Messianic Testimony of the Gospels*. Downers Grove, IL: InterVarsity, 2013.

Black, Matthew. "The Christological Use of the Old Testament in the New Testament." *NTS* 18 (1971–72) 1–14.

Blank, Josef. "Die Sendung des Sohnes. Zur christologischen Bedeutung des Gleichnisses von den bosen Winzern Mk 12,1–12." In *Neues Testament und Kirche: Für Rudolf Schnackenburg*, edited by Joachim Gnilka, 11–41. Freiburg: Herder, 1974.

Blenkinsopp, J. "The Oracle of Judah and the Messianic Entry." *JBL* 80 (1961) 55–64.

Block, Daniel I. "My Servant David: Ancient Israel's Vision of the Messiah." In *Israel's Messiah in the Bible and the Dead Sea Scrolls*, edited by Richard S. Hess and M. Daniel Carroll R., 17–56. Grand Rapids: Backer Academic, 2003.

Bock, Darrell L. *Blasphemy and Exaltation in Judaism and the Final Examination of Jesus: A Philological-Historical Study of the Key Jewish Themes Impacting Mark 14:61–64*. WUNT 2/106. Tübingen: Mohr Siebeck, 1998.

———. *Mark*. NCBC. New York: Cambridge University Press, 2015.

———. "The Function of Scripture in Mark 15.1–29." In *Biblical Interpretation in Early Christian Gospels, Volume 1: The Gospel of Mark*, edited by Thomas R. Hatina, 8–17. New York: T&T Clark, 2006.

Boda, Mark J. "Figuring the Future: The Prophets and Messiah." In *The Messiah in the Old and New Testaments*, edited by Stanley E. Porter, 35–74. Grand Rapids: Eerdmans, 2007.

———. *The Book of Zechariah*. NICOT. Grand Rapids: Eerdmans, 2016.

Bons, Eberhard. "Die Septuaginta-Version von Psalm 110 (Ps 109 LXX): Textgestalt, Aussagen, Auswirkungen." In *Heiligkeit und Herrschaft: Intertextuelle Studien zu Heiligkeitsvorstellungen und zu Psalm 110*, edited by Dieter Sänger, 122–45. BTS 55. Neukirchen-Vluyn: Neukirchener Verlag, 2003.

———. "Die Septuagint-Version von Psalm 22." In *Psalm 22 und die Passionsgeschichten der Evangelien*, edited by Dieter Sänger, 12–32. Neukirchen: Neukirchener Verlag, 2007.

———. "Psaume 2: Bilan de recherche et essai de réinterprétation." *RevScRel* 69 (1995) 147–71.

Boring, M. Eugene. *Mark: A Commentary*. Louisville: Westminster John Knox, 2006.

———. "Markan Christology: God-Language for Jesus?" *NTS* 45 (1999) 451–71.

Botha, Phil J. "The Ideological Interface between Psalm 1 and Psalm 2." *OTE* 18 (2005) 189–203.

Botner, Max. "A Sanctuary in the Heavens and the Ascension of the Son of Man: Reassessing the Logic of Jesus' Trial in Mark 14.53–65." *JSNT* 41 (2019) 310–34.

———. *Jesus Christ as the Son of David in the Gospel of Mark*. Cambridge: Cambridge University Press, 2019.

———. "The Role of Transcriptional Probability in the Text-Critical Debate on Mark 1:1." *CBQ* 77 (2015) 467–80.

Bousset, W. *Kyrios Christos: A History of the Belief in Christ from the Beginnings of Christianity to Irenaeus*. Translated by J. E. Steely. Nashville: Abingdon, 1970.

Breu, Clarissa, ed. *Biblical Exegesis Without Authorial Intention?* Boston: Brill, 2019.

Breytenbach, Cilliers. "Das Markusevangelium, Psalm 110,1 und 118,22f . . . Folgetext und Prätext." In *The Scriptures in the Gospels*, edited by Christopher M. Tuckett, 197–222. Leuven: University Press/Peeters, 1997.

Broadhead, Edwin K. "Christology as Polemic and Apologetic: The Priestly Portrait of Jesus in the Gospel of Mark." *JSNT* 47 (1992) 21–34.

Brock, S. P. "Bibelübersetzungen I.2." *TRE* 6 (1980) 163–72.

Brooke, George J. "4Q500 1 and the Use of Scripture in the Parable of the Wicked Tenants." *DSD* 2 (1995) 268–94.

———. *Exegesis at Qumran: 4QFlorilegium in Its Jewish Context*. JSOTSS 29. Sheffield: JSOT, 1985.

———. *The Dead Sea Scrolls and the New Testament*. Minneapolis: Fortress, 2005.

———. "The Psalms in Early Jewish Literature in the Light of the Dead Sea Scrolls." In *The Psalms in the New Testament*, edited by Steve Moyise and Maarten J. J. Menken, 5–24. London: T&T Clark, 2004.

Brown, Raymond Edward. *The Death of the Messiah: From Gethsemane to the Grave; A Commentary on the Passion Narratives in the Four Gospels*. Vol. 2. ABRL. New York: Doubleday, 1994.

Brown, S. G. "Mark 11:1—12:12: A Triple Intercalation?" *CBQ* 64 (2002) 78–89.

Brown, William P. "A Royal Performance: A Critical Note on Psalm 110:3ay-b." *JBL* 117 (1998) 93–96.

———. "'Here Comes the Sun!' The Metaphorical Theology of Psalms 15–24." In *The Composition of the Book of Psalms*, edited by Erich Zenger, 259–77. BETL 238. Leuven: Peeters, 2010.

Brownlee, W. H. "Psalms 1–2 as a Coronation Liturgy." *Bib* 52 (1971) 321–36.

Broyles, Craig C. "Psalms Concerning the Liturgies of Temple Entry." In *Book of Psalms: The Composition and Reception*, edited by Peter W. Flint and Patrick D. Miller Jr., 248–87. Leiden: Brill, 2005.

Brueggemann Walter, and William H. Bellinger Jr. *Psalms*. New York: Cambridge University Press, 2014.

Brunson, Andrew C. *Psalm 118 in the Gospel of John: An Intertextual Study on the New Exodus Pattern in the Theology of John*. WUNT 2. Reihe 158. Tübingen: Mohr Siebeck, 2003.

Bucker, Ralph. "Observations on the Wirkungsgeschichte of the Septuagint Psalms in Ancient Judaism and Early Christianity." In *Septuagint Research: Issues and Challenges in the Study of the Greek Jewish Scriptures*, edited by Wolfgang Kraus and R. Glenn Wooden, 355–69. Atlanta: Society of Biblical Literature, 2006.

Bultmann, Rudolf. *The History of the Synoptic Tradition*. Translated by John Marsh. New York: Harper & Row, 1968.

Burchard, Christoph. "Markus 15.34." *ZNW* 74 (1983) 1–11.

Burkett, Delbert. "The Transfiguration of Jesus (Mark 9:2–8): Epiphany or Apotheosis?" *JBL* 138 (2019) 413–32.

Cahill, Michael. "Not a Cornerstone! Translating Ps 118,22 in the Jewish and Christian Scriptures." *RB* 106 (1999) 345–57.

Calvin, John. *Commentary on the Book of Psalms*. Vol. 1. Translated by James Anderson. Grand Rapids: Eerdmans, 1949.

———. *In Librum Psalmorum Commentarius*. CO 31. Brunswick: Schwetschke, 1887.

Campbell, Keith D. "The Appropriation of the Psalmic Lament in the Synoptic Gospels: A Study in Characterization." PhD diss., Southeastern Baptist Theological Seminary, 2011.

Caneday, Ardel B. "Christ's Baptism and Crucifixion: The Anointing and Enthronement of God's Son." *SBJT* 8 (2004) 70–85.

Carey, Holly J. *Jesus' Cry from the Cross: Towards a First-Century Understanding of the Intertextual Relationship between Psalm 22 and the Narrative of Mark's Gospel*. LNTS 398. London: T&T Clark, 2009.

Catchpole, D. R. "The Triumphal Entry." In *Jesus and the Politics of His Day*, edited by Ernst Bammel and C. F. D. Moule, 319–34. Cambridge: Cambridge University Press, 1984.

Charlesworth, J. H, ed. *The Dead Sea Scrolls: Hebrew, Aramaic, and Greek Texts with English Translations. Vol. 6B: Pesharim, Other Commentaries, and Related Documents*. Tübingen: Mohr Siebeck, 2002.

———., ed. *The Messiah: Developments in Earliest Judaism and Christianity*. Minneapolis: Fortress, 1992.

———., ed. *The Old Testament Pseudepigrapha*. 2 vols. Garden City, NY: Doubleday, 1983.

———., and Henry W. L. Rietz, eds. *The Dead Sea Scrolls: Hebrew Aramaic, and Greek Texts with English Translations. Volume 4A. Pseudepigraphic and Non-Masoretic Psalms and Prayers*. Tübingen: Mohr Siebeck, 1997.

———., H. Lichtenberger., and G. Oegema, eds. *Qumran-Messianism: Studies on the Messianic Expectations in the Dead Sea Scrolls*. Tübingen: Mohr Siebeck, 1998.

Chatman, Seymour. *Story and Discourse: Narrative Structure in Fiction and Film*. Ithaca, NY: Cornell University Press, 1978.

Chester, Andrew. "High Christology—Whence, When and Why?" *EC* 2 (2011) 22–50.

———. "Jewish Messianic Expectations and Mediatorial Figures." In *Paulus und das antike Judentum*, edited by M. Hengel and U. Heckel. Tübingen: Mohr Siebeck, 1991.

Childs, Brevard S. *Introduction to the Old Testament as Scripture*. Philadelphia: Fortress, 1979.

———. *Isaiah*. OTL. Louisville: Westminster John Knox, 2001.

———. *The Book of Exodus: A Critical, Theological Commentary*. Philadelphia: Westminster, 1974.

Chilton, Bruce D. *A Galilean Rabbi and His Bible: Jesus' Own Interpretation of Isaiah*. London: SPCK, 1984.

Chilton, Bruce D., ed. and trans. "Rabbinic Literature and the New Testament." In *The World of the New Testament: Cultural, Social, and Historical Contexts*, edited by Joel B. Green and Lee Martin McDonald, 413–23. Grand Rapids: Baker, 2013.

———. *The Isaiah Targum: Introduction, Translation, Apparatus and Notes*. The Aramaic Bible 11. Wilmington, DE: Michael Glazier, 1987.

Cho, Bernardo. *Royal Messianism and the Jerusalem Priesthood in the Gospel of Mark*. LNTS 607. London: T&T Clark, 2019.

Clendenen, E. Ray. "'Messenger of the Covenant' in Malachi 3:1 Once Again." *JETS* 62 (2019) 81–102.

Cohen, A., ed. *The Psalms: Hebrew Text, English Translation, and Commentary.* Hindhead, Surrey: Soncino, 1945.

Cole, Robert. "An Integrated Reading of Psalms 1 and 2." *SJOT* 26 (2002) 75–88.

Collins, Adela Yarbro. *Mark: A Commentary.* Minneapolis: Fortress, 2007.

———. "Mark and His Readers: The Son of God Among Greeks and Romans." *HTR* 93 (2000) 85–100.

———. "Mark and His Readers: The Son of God Among Jews." *HTR* 92 (1999) 393–408.

———. "The Appropriation of the Psalms of Individual Lament by Mark." In *The Scriptures in the Gospels,* edited by Christopher M. Tuckett, 223–41. BETL 131. Leuven: Leuven University Press/Peeters, 1997.

Collins, Adela Yarbro, and John. J. Collins. *King and Messiah as Son of God: Divine, Human, and Angelic Messianic Figures in Biblical and Related Literature.* Grand Rapids: Eerdmans, 2008.

Collins, John J. "The Interpretation of Psalm 2." In *Echoes from the Caves: Qumran and the New Testament,* edited by Florentino García Martínez, 49–66. Leiden: Brill, 2009.

———. *The Scepter and the Star: Messianism in Light of the Dead Sea Scrolls.* 2nd ed. Grand Rapids: Eerdmans, 2010.

Constant, Pierre. "*Le Psalme 118 et son employ christologique dans Luc et Actes: Une etude exegetique, litteraire et hermeneutique.*" PhD diss., Trinity International University, 2001.

Cook, David. "Joseph and Aseneth." In *The Apocryphal Old Testament,* edited by H. F. D. Sparks, 473–503. Oxford: Oxford University Press, 1984.

Corley, Jeremy. "Psalm 110 (109) and Israelite Royal Ritual." *Salm* 64 (2017) 41–71.

Cox, Claude E. "Schaper's Eschatology Meets Kraus's Theology of the Psalms." In *The Old Greek Psalter: Studies in Honour of Albert Pietersma,* edited by Robert J. V. Hiebert, et al., 289–311. JSOTSS 332. Sheffield: Sheffield, 2001.

———. "Some Things Biblical Scholars Should Know About the Septuagint." *Restor. Q.* 56 (2014) 85–98.

Craigie, P. C. *Psalms 1–50.* WBC.19. Waco, TX: Word, 1983.

Crim, Keith R. *The Royal Psalms.* Richmond: John Knox, 1962.

Crutchfield, John Charles. "Circles of Context: An Interpretation of Psalms 107–118." PhD diss., Hebrew Union College, 2000.

———. *Psalms in Their Context: An Interpretation of Psalms 107–118.* Milton Keynes: Paternoster, 2011.

Cullman, Oscar. *The Christology of the New Testament.* Translated by S. C. Guthrie and C. A. M. Hall. Philadelphia: Westminster, 1963.

Dahood, Mitchell. *Psalms III: 101–150.* AB. Garden City, NY: Doubleday, 1970.

Danker, Frederick W. "The Demonic Secret in Mark: A Reexamination of the Cry of Dereliction (15, 34)." *ZNW* 61 (1970) 48–69.

Danker, F. W., et al., ed. *Greek-English Lexicon of the New Testament and Other Early Christian Literature.* 3rd ed. Chicago: University of Chicago Press, 2000.

Daube, David. *The New Testament and Rabbinic Judaism.* Peabody, MA: Hendrickson, 1990.

Davenport, G. L. "The 'Anointed of the Lord' in the Psalm of Solomon 17." In *Ideal Figures in Ancient Judaism: Profiles and Paradigms,* edited by G. W. E. Nickelsburg and John J. Collins, 67–92. SCS12. Missoula, MT: Scholars, 1980.

Davis, Barry Craig. "A Contextual Analysis of Psalms 107–118." PhD diss., Trinity Evangelical Divinity School, 1996.

———. "Is Psalm 110 a Messianic Psalm?" *BSac* 157 (2000) 160–73.

deClaissé-Walford, Nancy L. "An Intertextual Reading of Psalms 22, 23, and 24." In *The Book of Psalms: Composition and Reception*, edited by Peter W. Flint and Patrick D. Miller Jr., 139–52. VTSup 994. Boston: Brill, 2005.

———., et al. *The Book of Psalms*. Grand Rapids: Eerdmans, 2014.

Defani, Evangelia G. "Psalm 109 (110):1–3 in the Septuagint: Its Translation-Critical, Tradition-Historical, and Theological Setting." In *Psalms and Hebrews: Studies in Reception*, edited by Dirk J. Human and Gert Jacobus Steyn, 241–59. New York: T&T Clark, 2010.

Delitzsch, Franz. *Psalms. Three Volumes in One*. Translated by Francis Bolton. Grand Rapids: Eerdmans, 1978.

Dempster, Stephen G. *Dominion and Dynasty: A Biblical Theology of the Hebrew Bible*. NSBT 15. Downers Grove, IL: InterVarsity, 2003.

Derrett, J. Duncan M. "The Stone that the Builders Rejected." In *Studies in the New Testament, Volume Two: Midrash in Action and as a Literary Device*, 60–67. Leiden: Brill, 1977.

deSilva, David A. "The Testaments of the Twelve Patriarchs as Witnesses to Pre-Christian Judaism: A Re-Assessment." *JSP* 22 (2013) 21–68.

Dewey, Joanna. *Markan Public Debate: Literary Technique, Concentric Structure, and Theology in Mark 2:1—3:6*. SBLDS 48. Chico, CA: Scholars, 1980.

Dinkler, Michal Beth. "New Testament Rhetorical Narratology: An Invitation Toward Integration." *BibInt* 24 (2016) 203–28.

Docherty, Susan E. "'Do You Understand What You Are Reading?' (Acts 8.30): Current Trends and Future Perspectives in the Study of the Use of the Old Testament in the New." *JSNT* 38 (2015) 112–25.

———. "New Testament Scriptural Interpretation in Its Early Jewish Context: Reflections on the Status Questions and Future Directions." *NovT* 57 (2015) 1–19.

Dodd, C. H. *According to the Scriptures: The Sub-Structure of New Testament Theology*. London: Nisbet, 1952.

Donahue, John R. "Temple, Trial, and Royal Christology (Mark 14:53–65)." In *The Passion in Mark: Studies on Mark 14–16*, edited by Werner H. Kelber, 61–79. Philadelphia: Fortress, 1976.

Donahue, John R., and Daniel J. Harrington. *The Gospel of Mark*. SPS. 2. Minnesota: Liturgical, 2002.

Dowd, Sharyn. *Prayer, Power, and the Problem of Suffering*. SBLDS 105. Atlanta: Scholars, 1988.

Drijvers, P. *Les Psaumes: Genres littéraires et themes doctrinaux*. Paris: Le Cerf, 1958.

Dupont, Jacques. "La Transmission des parables de Jesus sur la Lampe et la Mesure dans Marc 4,21–25 et dans la Tradition Q." In *Logia: Les Paroles de Jesus: The Sayings of Jesus: Memorial Joseph Coppens*, edited by Joël Delobel, 201–36. BETL 59. Leuven: Peeters, 1982.

Durham, John I. *Exodus*. WBC. Waco, TX: Word, 1987.

Eaton, John H. *Kingship and the Psalms*. London: SCM, 1976.

Edwards, J. R. "Markan Sandwiches: The Significance of Interpolations in Markan Narratives." *NovT* 31 (1989) 193–216.

———. "The Baptism of Jesus according to the Gospel of Mark." *JETS* 34 (1991) 43–57.

———. *The Gospel According to Mark*. PNTC. Grand Rapids: Eerdmans, 2002.
Elliger, K., and W. Rudolph, eds. *Biblia Hebraica Stuttgartensia*. Stuttgart: Deutsche Bibelgesellschaft, 1983.
Emadi, Matthew Habib. "The Royal Priest: Psalm 110 in Biblical-Theological Perspective." PhD diss., Southern Baptist Theological Seminary, 2016.
———. "You Are Priest Forever: Psalm 110 and the Melchizedekian Priesthood of Christ." *SBJT* 23 (2019) 57–84.
Ernst, Josef. *Das Evangelium nach Markus*. RNT. Regenburg: Pustet Verlag, 1981.
Estes, Daniel J. *Psalms 73–150*. NAC. Vol. 13. Nashville: B&H, 2019.
Evans, Craig A. *Jesus and His Contemporaries: Comparative Studies*. AGJU 25. Leiden: Brill, 1995.
———. *Mark 8:27—16:20*. WBC. Vol. 34B. Nashville: Thomas Nelson, 2001.
———. "On the Vineyard Parables of Isaiah 5 and Mark 12." *BZ* 28 (1984) 8–26.
———. "The Beginning of Good News and the Fulfillment of Scripture in the Gospel of Mark." In *Hearing the Old Testament in the New Testament*, edited by Stanley E. Porter, 83–100. Grand Rapids: Eerdmans, 2006.
———. "Why Did the New Testament Writers Appeal to the Old Testament?" *JSNT* 38 (2015) 36–48.
Fabry, Heinz-Josef. "Die Wirkungsgeschichte des Psalms 22." In *Beiträge zur Psalmenforschung: Psalm 2 und 22*, edited by Josef Schreiner, 279–317. Würzburg: Echter Verlag, 1988.
Fish, Stanley. *Is There a Text in This Class? The Authority of Interpretive Communities*. Boston: Harvard University Press, 1982.
Flint, Peter W. *The Dead Sea Psalms Scrolls and the Book of Psalms*. STDJ 17. Leiden: Brill, 1997.
———. "The Psalters at Qumran and the Book of Psalms." PhD diss., Notre Dame University, 1993.
Fleddermann, Harry T. "A Warning About the Scribes (Mark 12:37b–40)." *CBQ* 44 (1982) 52–67.
Fletcher-Louis, Crispin H. T. "Jesus as the High Priestly Messiah: Part 1." *JSHJ* 4 (2006) 155–75.
———. "Jesus as the High Priestly Messiah: Part 2." *JSHJ* 5 (2007) 57–79.
———. "The High Priest as Divine Mediator in the Hebrew Bible: Dan 7:13 as a Test Case." In *Society of Biblical Literature Seminar Papers, 1997*, 169–93. Soc. Biblic. Lit. Semin. 36. Chico, CA: Scholars, 1997.
Focant, Camille. "L'Ultime Prière du Pourquoi: Reflection du Ps 22 (21) dans le Récit de la Passion de Marc." In *Marc, Un Évangile Étonnant: Recueil D'Essais*, 321–37. BETL 194. Leuven: Peeters, 2006.
Fokkelman, Jan P. *Major Poems of the Hebrew Bible: At the Interface of Hermeneutics and Structural Analysis. Vol. 2. 85 Psalms and Job 4–14*. SSN 41. Assen: Van Gorcum, 2000.
Foster, Paul. "Echoes Without Resonance: Critiquing Certain Aspects of Recent Scholarly Trends in the Study of the Jewish Scriptures in the New Testament." *JSNT* 38 (2015) 96–111.
Fossum, Jarl E. *The Image of the Invisible God: Essays on the Influence of Jewish Mysticism on Early Christology*. Universitätsverlag Freiburg Schweiz and Göttingen: Vandenhoeck & Ruprecht, 1995.
Fowler, Robert M. *Loaves and Fishes: The Function of the Feeding Stories in the Gospel of Mark*. SBLDS 54. Chico, CA: Scholars, 1981.

France, R. T. *The Gospel of Mark: A Commentary on the Greek Text*. NIGTC. Grand Rapids: Eerdmans, 2002.
Fuhrmann, Justin M. "The Use of Psalm 118:22–23 in the Parable of the Wicked Tenants." *Proc.* 27 (2007) 67–81.
Funk, Robert W. *The Poetics of Biblical Narrative*. Sonoma, CA: Polebridge, 1988.
Garland, David E. *Mark*. NIVAC. Grand Rapids: Zondervan, 1996.
Gathercole, Simon. *The Preexistent Son: Recovering the Christologies of Matthew, Mark, and Luke*. Grand Rapids: Eerdmans, 2006.
Geddert, Timothy J. "The Use of the Psalms in Mark." *Dir.* 38 (2009) 179–92.
Gerstenberger, Erhard S. *Psalms: Part 1: With an Introduction to Cultic Poetry*. FOTL14. Grand Rapids: Eerdmans, 1988.
Gese, Hartmut. "Psalm 22 und das Neue Testament: Der älteste Bericht vom Tode Jesu und die Entstehung des Herrenmahles." In *Vom Sinai zum Zion*, 180–201. Munich: Chr. Kaiser Verlag, 1974.
———. *Zur biblishen Theologie: alttestamentliche Vorträge*. Tübingen: J. C. B. Mohr, 1989.
Gillingham, Susan E. *A Journey of Two Psalms: The Reception of Psalms 1 and 2 in Jewish and Christian Tradition*. Oxford: Oxford University Press, 2013.
———. "The Messiah in the Psalms." In *King and Messiah in Israel and the Ancient Near East*, edited by John Day, 209–37. JSOTSS 270. Sheffield: Sheffield Academic, 1998.
Gnilka, Joachim. *Das Evangelium nach Markus*. Vol. II/1. Zürich: Benziger Verlag, 1978.
———. *Das Evangelium nach Markus*. Vol. II/2. Zürich: Benziger Verlag, 1979.
Goldingay, John. *Daniel*. WBC. Vol. 30. Rev. ed. Grand Rapids: Zondervan Academic, 2019.
———. *Psalms. Volume 1: Psalm 1–41*. BCOTWP. Grand Rapids: Baker Academic, 2006.
———. *Psalms. Volume 2: Psalms 42–89*. BCOTWP. Grand Rapids: Baker Academic, 2007.
———. *Psalms. Volume 3: Psalms 90–150*. BCOTWP. Grand Rapids: Baker Academic, 2006.
Goulder, Michael D. *The Psalms of the Return (Book V, Psalms 107–150)*. JSOTSS 258. Sheffield: Sheffield Academic, 1998.
Gourgues, M. *A La Droite de Dieu: Résurrection de Jésus et Actualization du Psaume 110:1 dans le Nouveau Testament*. Paris: J. Gabalda, 1978.
Granerød, Gard. *Abraham and Melchizedek: Scribal Activity of Second Temple Times in Genesis 14 and Psalm 110*. BZAW 406. Berlin: De Gruyter, 2010.
Grant, Jamie A. *The King as Exemplar: The Function of Deuteronomy's Kingship Law in the Shaping of the Book of Psalms*. Atlanta: Society of Biblical Literature, 2004.
———. "The Psalms and the King." In *Interpreting the Psalms*, edited by David Firth and Philip S. Johnston, 101–18. Downers Grove, IL: InterVarsity, 2005.
Gray, T. C. *The Temple in the Gospel of Mark: A Study in Its Narrative Role*. WUNT 2:242. Tübingen: Mohr Siebeck, 2008.
Grund, Alexandra. "'Aus Gott geboren': Zu Geburt und Identität in der Bildsprache der Psalmen." In *Du hast mich aus meiner Mutter Leib gezogen*, edited by Detlef Dieckmann and Dorothea Erbele-Küster, 99–120. Neukirchen-Vluyn: Neukirchener Verlag, 2006.
Guelich, Robert A. *Mark 1—8:26*. WBC 34A. Dallas: Word, 1989.

———. "'The Beginning of the Gospel,' Mark 1.1–15." *BR* 27 (1982) 5–15.
Gundry, Robert H. *Mark, A Commentary on His Apology for the Cross*. Grand Rapids: Eerdmans, 1993.
Gunkel, Hermann. *Die Psalmen übersetzt und erklärt*. HKAT II/2. 4th ed. Göttingen: Vandenhoeck & Ruprecht, 1926.
Gunkel, Hermann, and Joachim Begrich. *Introduction to the Psalms: The Genres of the Religious Lyric of Israel*. Translated by James D. Nogalski. Macon, GA: Mercer University Press, 1998.
Haglund, Erik. *Historical Motifs in the Psalms*. Uppsala: CWK Gleerup, 1984.
Hamilton James M., Jr. *With the Clouds of Heaven: The Book of Daniel in Biblical Theology*. NSBT 32. Downers Grove, IL: Apollos, 2014.
Hartmut, Stegemann, and Eileen Schuller. *1QHodayota: With Incorporation of 1QHodayotband 4QHodayota-f*. DJD 40. Oxford: Clarendon, 2009.
Hatina, Thomas R. "Embedded Scripture Texts and the Plurality of Meaning." In *Biblical Interpretation in Early Christian Gospels, Volume 1: The Gospel of Mark*, edited by Thomas R. Hatina and Chris Keith, 81–99. New York: T&T Clark, 2006.
———. *In Search of a Context: The Function of Scripture in Mark's Narrative*. JSNTSup 232. New York: Sheffield Academic, 2002.
Hay, David. *Glory at the Right Hand: Psalm 110 in Early Christianity*. SBLMS 18. Atlanta: Society of Biblical Literature, 1989.
Hayes, Elizabeth. "The Unity of the Egyptian Hallel: Psalms 113–18." *BBR* 9 (1999) 145–56.
Hays, J. Daniel. "If He Looks Like a Prophet and Talks Like a Prophet, Then He Must Be . . . : A Response to Daniel I. Block." In *Israel's Messiah in the Bible and the Dead Sea Scrolls*, edited by Richard S. Hess and M. Daniel Carroll R., 57–69. Grand Rapids: Backer Academic, 2003.
Hays, Richard B. *Echoes of Scripture in the Gospels*. Waco, TX: Baylor University Press, 2016.
———. *Echoes of Scripture in the Letters of Paul*. New Haven: Yale University Press, 1989.
Heil, John Paul. *The Gospel of Mark as a Model for Action: A Reader-Response Commentary*. New York: Paulist, 1992.
Henderson, Suzanne Watts. *Christology and Discipleship in the Gospel of Mark*. Cambridge: Cambridge University Press, 2006.
Hellerman, Joseph H. "Challenging the Authority of Jesus: Mark 11:27–33 and Mediterranean Notions of Honor and Shame." *JETS* 43 (2000) 213–28.
Hendrick, Charles W. "What Is a Gospel? Geography, Time, and Narrative Structure." *PRSt* 10 (1983) 255–68.
Hengel, Martin. "'Sit at My Right Hand!' The Enthronement of Christ at the Right Hand of God and Psalm 110:1." In *Studies in Early Christology*, 119–225. Edinburgh: T&T Clark, 1995.
———. *Studies in the Gospel of Mark*. Translated by John Bowden. Philadelphia: Fortress, 1985.
Hibbard, J. Todd. *Intertextuality in Isiah 24–27*. FAT 2. Reihe 16. Tübingen: Mohr Siebeck, 2006.
Hilber, John W. *Cultic Prophecy in the Psalms*. BZAW 352. Berlin, New York: Walter de Gruyter, 2005.
———. "Psalm CX in the Light of Assyrian Prophecies." *VT* 53 (2003) 353–66.

Hill, Andrew E. *Daniel-Malachi*. EBC. Vol. 8. Rev. ed. Grand Rapids: Zondervan, 2008.
Hill, David. "'Son of Man' in Psalm 80 V. 17." *NovT* 15 (1973) 261–69.
Hirsch, E. D., Jr. *The Aims of Interpretation*. Chicago: University of Chicago Press, 1976.
———. *Validity in Interpretation*. New Haven: Yale University Press, 1967.
Hoffman, Mark George Vitalis. "Psalm 22 (LXX 21) and the Crucifixion of Jesus." PhD diss., Yale University, 1996.
Holladay, William L. "The Background of Jeremiah's Self-Understanding: Moses, Samuel, and Psalm 22." *JBL* 83 (1964) 153–64.
Hollander, John. *The Figure of Echo: A Mode of Allusion in Milton and After*. Berkeley, Los Angeles: University of California Press, 1981.
Hooker, M. D. *The Gospel According to Saint Mark*. BNTC. Peabody: Hendrickson, 1991.
———. "'What Doest Thou Here, Elijah?': A Look at St Mark's Account of the Transfiguration." In *The Glory of Christ in the New Testament: Studies in Christology in Memory of George Bradford Caird*, edited by L. D. Hurst and N. T. Wright, 59–70. Oxford: Clarendon, 1987.
Horbury, William. *Messianism Among Jews and Christians: Twelve Biblical and Historical Studies*. London: T&T Clark, 2003.
Horsley, Richard A. *Hearing the Whole Story: The Politics of Plot in Mark's Gospel*. Louisville: Westminster John Knox, 2001.
———. *Text and Tradition in Performance and Writing*. Eugene, OR: Cascade, 2013.
Hoskins, Paul M. *That Scripture Might Be Fulfilled: The Typology and the Death of Christ*. Longwood, FL: Xulon, 2009.
Hossfeld, Frank-Lothar, and Eric Zenger. *Die Psalmen 1–50*. Wurzburg: Echter, 1993.
Hossfeld, Frank-Lothar, and Eric Zenger. *Psalms 3: A Commentary on Psalms 101–150*. Translated by Linda M. Maloney. Minneapolis: Fortress, 2011.
Hossfeld, F-L., and E. Zenger. "'Wer darf hinaufziehn zum Berg JHWHs?' Zur Redaktionsgeschichte und Theologie der Psalmengruppe 15–24." In *Biblische Theologie und gesellschaftilicher Wandel*, edited by G. Braulik, et al., 166–82. Freiburg: Herder, 1993.
Huizenga, Leroy Andrew. "The Confession of Jesus and the Curses of Peter: A Narrative-Christological Approach to the Text-Critical Problem of Mark 14:62." *NovT* 53 (2011) 244–66.
Hurtado, Larry W. "Early Christological Interpretation of the Messianic Psalms." *Salm* 64 (2017) 73–100
———. *Lord Jesus Christ: Devotion to Jesus in Earliest Christianity*. Grand Rapids: Eerdmans, 2003.
———. "P45 and the Textual History of the Gospel of Mark." In *The Earliest Gospels: The Origins and Transmission of the Earliest Christian Gospels—The Contribution of the Chester Beatty Gospel Codex P45*, edited by Charles Horton, 132–48. JSNTSup 258. New York: T&T Clark, 2004.
———. "The Women, the Tomb, and the Climax of Mark." In *A Wandering Galilean: Essays in Honor of Seán Freyne*, edited by Zuleika Rodgers, et al., 427–50. JSJSup 132. Leiden: Brill, 2009.
Iverson, K. R. *Gentiles in the Gospel of Mark: 'Even the Dogs Under the Table Eat the Children's Crumbs.'* LNTS 339. New York: T&T Clark, 2007.
———. "Jews, Gentiles, and the Kingdom of God: The Parable of the Wicked Tenants in Narrative Perspective (Mark 12:1–12)." *BibInt* 20 (2012) 305–35.

Iverson, Kelly R., and Christopher W. Skinner, eds. *Mark as Story: Retrospect and Prospect*. Atlanta: Society of Biblical Literature, 2011.

Instone-Brewer, David. *Techniques and Assumptions in Jewish Exegesis Before 70 CE*. TSAG 30. Tübingen: Mohr Siebeck, 1992.

Iseminger, Gary, ed. *Intention and Interpretation*. Philadelphia: Temple University Press, 1992.

James, Joshua T. "'From the Narrow Straits, I Called, 'Yah': The Storied Ethics of the Thanksgiving Psalms." PhD diss., Fuller Theological Seminary, 2015.

Janse, Sam. *"You Are My Son": The Reception History of Psalm 2 in Early Judaism and the Early Church*. Leuven: Peeters, 2009.

Janowski, Bernd. "'Mein Gott, mein Gott, wozu hast du mich verlassen?': Zur Rezeption der Psalmen in der Markuspassion." *ZThK* 116 (2019) 371–401.

Jeremias, Joachim. *The Eucharistic Words of Jesus*. Translated by Norman Perrin. New York: Charles Scribner's Sons, 1966.

Johansson, Daniel L. M. "Jesus and God in the Gospel of Mark: Unity and Distinction." PhD diss., University of Edinburgh, 2011.

———. "The Identity of Jesus in the Gospel of Mark: Past and Present Proposals." *CBR* 9 (2010) 364–93.

Johnson, Bradley T. "The Form and Function of Mark 1:1–15." PhD diss., Asbury Theological Seminary, 2015.

Johnson, Elliott E. "Hermeneutical Principles and the Interpretation of Psalm 110." *BSac* 149 (1992) 428–37.

Joseph, S. J. *Jesus and the Temple: The Crucifixion in Its Jewish Context*. Cambridge: Cambridge University Press, 2015.

Juel, Donald. *A Master of Surprise: Mark Interpreted*. Minneapolis: Fortress, 1994.

———. *Messianic Exegesis: Christological Interpretation of the Old Testament in Early Christianity*. Philadelphia: Fortress, 1988.

Juncker, G. H. "Jesus and the Angel of the Lord: An Old Testament Paradigm for New Testament Christology." PhD diss., Trinity Evangelical Divinity School, 2001.

Kaiser, Walter C, Jr. "Single Meaning, Unified Referents: Accurate and Authoritative Citations of the Old Testament by the New Testament." In *Three Views on the New Testament Use of the Old Testament*, edited by Kenneth Berding and Jonathan Lunde, 45–89. Grand Rapids: Zondervan, 2009.

———. "The Messiah of Psalm 80." *BSac* 174 (2017) 387–93.

Kalt, Edmund., ed. *Herder's Commentary on the Psalms*. Translated by Bernard Fritz. Westminster, MD: Newman, 1961.

Kampling, Rainer. *Israel unter dem Anspruch des Messiahs: Studien zur Israelthematik im Markusevangelim*. SBB 25. Mainz: Verlag Katholisches Bibelwerk, 1992.

Karakolis, Christos. "Narrative Funktion und Christologische Bedeutung der Markinischen Erzählung vom Tod Johannes des Täufers (Mk 6:14–29)." *NovT* 52 (2010) 134–55.

Keck, Leander E. "The Introduction to Mark's Gospel." *NTS* 12 (1966) 352–70.

Keefer, Arthur. "The Meaning and Place of Old Testament Context in OT/NT Methodology." In *Methodology in the Use of the Old Testament in the New: Context and Criteria*, edited by D. David Allen and Steve Smith. LSNT 579. New York: T&T Clark, 2019.

Kee, Howard C. *Community of the New Age*. Philadelphia: Westminster, 1977.

———. "The Function of Scriptural Quotations and Allusions in Mark 11–16." In *Jesus and Paulus*, edited by E. E. Ellis and E. Grässer, 165–88. Göttingen: Vandenhoeck & Ruprecht, 1975.

———. "The Transfiguration in Mark: Epiphany or Apocalyptic Vision?" In *Understanding the Sacred Text: Essays in Honor of Morton S. Enslin on the Hebrew Bible and Christian Beginnings*, edited by John Reumann, 135–52. Valley Forge, PA: Judson, 1972.

Kelber, W. H. *The Kingdom in Mark: A New Place and a New Time*. Philadelphia: Fortress, 1974.

Kim, Jinkyu. "Psalm 110 in its Literary and Generic Contexts: As Eschatological Interpretation." PhD diss., Westminster Theological Seminary, 2003.

———. "The Message of Psalm 2 in the Context of the Final Shape of the Psalter." *Bible & Theology* 80 (2016) 1–35. http://dx.doi.org/10.17156/BT.80.01.

———. "The Speaker and the Addressee of Psalm 110 in the Literary Context of the Psalter." *KRT* 52 (2016) 248–82.

Kim, Sung-Soo. "The Gospels and the Contexts of the Psalms from the Perspective of Psalms 1 and 2." *BT* 59 (2011) 1–36.

Kim, Sun Wook. "Jesus' Missional Movement in Mark 4:35—8:21: Markan Spatial Presentation and its Hermeneutical Significance." PhD diss., Trinity Evangelical Divinity School, 2013.

Kingsbury, J. D. *Conflict in Mark: Jesus, Authorities, Disciples*. Minneapolis: Fortress, 1989.

———. *The Christology of Mark's Gospel*. Philadelphia: Fortress, 1983.

Kissane, Edward J. "The Interpretation of Psalm 110." *IrTheologQ* 21(1954) 103–14.

Kloppenborg, John S. *The Tenants in the Vineyard: Ideology, Economics, and Agrarian Conflict in Jewish Palestine*. WUNT 195. Tübingen: Mohr Siebeck, 2006.

Kok, Michael. "Marking a Difference: The Gospel of Mark and the 'Early High Christology' Paradigm." *JJMJS* 3 (2016) 102–24.

Kraemer, Ross Shepard. *When Aseneth Met Joseph: A Late Antique Tale of the Biblical Patriarch and His Egyptian Wife, Reconsidered*. Oxford: Oxford University Press, 1998.

Kratz, Reinhard Gregor. "Die Tora Davids: Psalm 1 und die doxologische Fünfteilung des Psalters." *ZThK* 93 (1996) 1–34.

Kraus, Hans-Joachim. *Psalms 1–59: A Continental Commentary*. Translated by Hilton C. Oswald. Minneapolis: Fortress, 1993.

———. *Psalms 60–150*. Translated by Hilton C. Oswald. Minneapolis: Fortress, 1993.

———. *The Theology of Psalms*. Translated by Keith R. Crim. Minneapolis: Augsburg, 1986.

Krause, Deborah. "The One Who Comes Unbinding the Blessing of Jacob: Mark 11.1–10 as a Midrash on Genesis 49.11, Zechariah 9.9, and Psalm 118.25–26." In *Early Christian Interpretation of the Scriptures of Israel: Investigation and Proposals*, edited by C. A. Evans and J. A. Sanders, 141–53. Sheffield: Sheffield Academic, 1997.

Kristeva, Julia. "Word, Dialogue, and Novel." In *The Kristeva Reader*, edited by Toril Moi, 34–61. New York: Columbia University Press, 1986.

Krusche, Marcel. *Göttliches und irdisches Königtum in den Psalmen*. FAT 2. Reihe 109. Tübingen: Mohr Siebeck, 2019.

Kuhn, Heinz W. "Das Reittier Jesu in der Einzusgeschichte des Markusevangelium." *ZAW* 50 (1959) 82–91.

Kutsko, John F. ed., *The SBL Handbook of Style*. 2nd ed. Atlanta: Society of Biblical Literature, 2014.

Kwon, Hyukjung. "The Reception of Psalm 118 in the New Testament: Application of a 'New Exodus Motif'?" PhD diss., University of Pretoria, 2007.

Laato, A. *A Star Is Rising: The Historical Development of the Old Testament Royal Ideology and the Rise of the Jewish Messianic Expectations*. Atlanta: Scholars, 1997.

Lafleur, Didier. *La Famille 13 dans L'évangile de Marc*. NTTSD 41. Leiden: Brill, 2013.

Lagrange, M. J. "Notes sur le messianism dans les psaumes." *RB* 2 (1905) 39–57.

Lane, William L. *The Gospel According to Mark*. NICNT. Grand Rapids: Eerdmans, 1974.

Lange, Harvey D. "The Relationship Between Psalm 22 and the Passion Narrative." *CTMV* 43 (1972) 610–21.

Larsen, Kevin W. "The Structure of Mark's Gospel: Current Proposals." *CBR* 3 (2004) 140–60.

Le Donne, A. *The Historiographical Jesus: Memory, Typology, and the Son of David*. Waco, TX: Baylor University Press, 2009.

Lee, A. *From Messiah to Preexistent Son: Jesus' Self-Consciousness and Early Christian Exegesis of Messianic Psalms*. WUNT 2/192. Tübingen: Mohr Siebeck, 2005.

Lee, Dorothy. *Transfiguration*. London: Continuum, 2004.

Lee, Peter Y. "Psalm 110 Reconsidered: Internal and External Evidence in Support of a NT Hermeneutic." *RF&P* 2 (2017) 17–47.

Leim, Joshua E. "In the Glory of His Father: Intertextuality and the Apocalyptic Son of Man in the Gospel of Mark." *JTI* 7 (2013) 213–32.

Lim, Timothy H. *Holy Scripture in the Qumran Commentaries and Pauline Letters*. Oxford: Clarendon, 1997.

———. "Qumran Scholarship and the Study of the Old Testament in the New Testament." *JSNT* 38 (2015) 68–80.

Lindars, Barnabas. *New Testament Apologetic: The Doctrinal Significance of the Old Testament Quotations*. Philadelphia: Westminster, 1961.

Lister, Rob. "What Jesus' Righteous Suffering Means for Our Perseverance." *CTR* 13 (2015) 77–91.

Loader, William R. G. "Christ at the Right Hand—PS. CX. 1 in the New Testament." *NTS* 24 (1978) 199–217.

Lochrie, Graham, Susan. "On Scripture and Authorial Intent: A Narratological Proposal." *ATR* 77 (1995) 307–20.

Lohmeyer, Ernst. *Das Evangelium des Markus*. Göttingen: Vandenhoeck & Ruprecht, 1959.

———. *Das Evangelium des Markus übersetzt und erklärt*. Göttingen: Vandenhoeck & Ruprecht, 1937.

———. "Die Verklärung Jesu nach dem Markus-Evangelium." *ZNW* 21 (1922) 185–215.

Longman, Tremper, III. "The Messiah: Explorations in the Law and Writings." In *The Messiah in the Old and New Testaments*, edited by Stanley, E. Porter, 13–34. Grand Rapids: Eerdmans, 2007.

Lövestam, Evald. "Die Davidssohnfrage," SEÅ *Svensk Exegetisk Årsbok* 27 (1962) 72–82.

Lührmann, Dieter. *Das Markusevangelium*. Tübingen: Moher Siebeck, 1987.

Lyons, Michael A. "Psalm 22 and the 'Servants' of Isaiah 54:56-66." *CBQ* 77 (2015) 640-56.

Maiberger, P. "Das Verständnis von Psalm 2 in der Septuagint aim Targum, in Qumran, im früen Judentum und im Neuen Testament." In *Beiträge zur Psalmenforschung: Psalm 2 und 22*, edited by J. Schreiner, 85-151. Würzburg: Echter Verlag, 1988.

Malbon, Elizabeth Struthers. *Mark's Jesus: Characterization as Narrative Christology*. Waco, TX: Baylor University Press, 2009.

———. "Narrative Criticism: How Does the Story Man?" In *Mark & Method: New Approaches in Biblical Studies*, edited by Janice Capel Anderson and Stephen D. Moore, 29-58. Minneapolis: Fortress, 2008.

———. "'Reflected Christology': An Aspect of Narrative 'Christology' in the Gospel of Mark." *PRSt* 26 (1999) 127-36.

———. "The Jesus of Mark and the Sea of Galilee." *JBL* 103 (1984) 363-77.

Malcom, Matthew R. *All That the Prophets Have Declared: The Appropriation of Scripture in the Emergence of Christianity*. Milton Keynes: Paternoster, 2015.

Marcus, Joel. *Mark 1-8: A New Translation with Introduction and Commentary*. AB. Vol. 27. New York: Doubleday, 2000.

———. *Mark 8-16: A New Translation with Introduction and Commentary*. AB. Vol. 27A. New Haven: Yale University Press, 2009.

———. "Polemic of the Markan Vineyard Parable." In *Tolerance and Intolerance in Early Judaism and Christianity*, edited by Graham N. Stanton and Guy G. Stroumsa, 211-27. Cambridge: Cambridge University, 1998.

———. *The Mystery of the Kingdom of God*. SBLDS 90. Atlanta: Scholars, 1986.

———. *The Way of the Lord: Christological Exegesis of the Old Testament in the Gospel of Mark*. Louisville: Westminster/John Knox, 1992.

Mark, Martin. *Meine Stärke und mein Schutz ist der Herr: Poetologisch-theologische Studie zu Psalm 118*. Würzburg: Echter Verlag, 1999.

Marshall, Christopher D. *Faith as a Theme in Mark's Narrative*. Cambridge; New York: Cambridge University Press, 1989.

Marshall, I. Howard. "An Assessment of Recent Developments." In *It Is Written: Scripture Citing Scripture: Essays in Honour of Barnabas Lindars*, edited by D. A. Carson and H. G. M. Williamson, 1-21. Cambridge: Cambridge University Press, 1988.

———. "Son of God or Servant of Yahweh?—A Reconsideration of Mark 1:11." *NTS* 14 (1969) 326-36.

Martínez, Florentino García, and Eibert J. C. Tigchelaar. "Psalms Manuscripts from Qumran Cave 11: A Preliminary Edition." *RdQ* 17 (1996) 73-107.

Marxsen, Willi. *Mark the Evangelist*. Translated by James Boyce, et al. Nashville: Abingdon, 1969.

Mason, Eric F. "Interpretation of Psalm in 4QFlorilegium and in the New Testament." In *Echoes from the Caves: Qumran and the New Testament*, edited by Florentino García Martínez, 68-82. STDJ 85. Boston: Brill, 2009.

Matera, Frank J. "Messianic Hopes in the Qumran Writings." In *The People of the Dead Sea Scrolls*, edited by F. García Martínez and J. T. Barrera, 159-89. Leiden: Brill, 1995.

———. *Passion Narratives and Gospel Theologies: Interpreting the Synoptics Through Their Passion Stories*. Mahwah, NJ: Paulist, 1986.

———. *The Kingship of Jesus: Composition and Theology of Mark 15.* SBLDS 66. Chico, CA: Scholars, 1982.

———. "The Prologue as the Interpretative Key to Mark's Gospel." *JSNT* 34 (1988) 3–20.

Mays, James Luther. "What Is a Human Being? Reflections on Psalm 8." *TToday* 50 (1994) 511–20.

McKelvey, Michael G. "The Messianic Nature of Psalm 118." *RF&P* 2 (2017) 45–55.

Meek, Russell. "Intertextuality, Inner-Biblical Exegesis, and Inner-Biblical Allusion: The Ethics of a Methodology." *Bib* 95 (2014) 280–91.

Merrill, Eugene H. "Royal Priesthood: An Old Testament Messianic Motif." *BSac* 150 (1993) 50–61.

Metzger, Bruce M. *A Textual Commentary on the Greek New Testament.* 2nd ed. Stuttgart: Deutsche Biblegesellschaft; United Bible Societies, 2000.

Milavec, Aaron. "Mark's Parable of the Wicked Husbandmen as Reaffirming God's Predilection for Israel." *JES* 26 (1989) 289–312.

Milgrom, Jacob. "Florilegium: A Midrash on 2 Samuel and Psalms in 1–2 (4Q174=4Q Flor)." In *The Dead Sea Scrolls: Hebrew, Aramaic, and Greek Texts with English Translations. Vol. 6B: Pesharim, Other Commentaries, and Related Documents,* edited by James H. Charlesworth, 248–63. Tübingen: Mohr Siebeck, 2002.

Miller, Geoffrey D. "An Intercalation Revisited: Christology, Discipleship and Dramatic Irony in Mark 6.6.b–30." *JSNT* 35 (2012) 176–95.

———. "Intertextuality in Old Testament Research." *CBR* 9 (2010) 283–309.

Mitchell, David C. *The Message of the Psalter: An Eschatological Programme in the Book of Psalms.* JSOTSup 252. Sheffield: Sheffield Academic, 1997.

Moloney, F. J. "Mark 6:6b–30: Mission, Baptist, and Failure." *CBQ* (2001) 647–63.

———. *The Gospel of Mark: A Commentary.* Peabody: Hendrickson, 2002.

Moo, Douglas J. *The Old Testament in the Gospel Passion Narratives.* Sheffield: Almond, 1983.

Moo, Douglas J., and Andrew David Naselli. "The Problem of the New Testament's Use of the Old Testament." In *The Enduring Authority of the Christian Scriptures*, edited by D. A. Carson, 702–46. Grand Rapids: Eerdmans, 2016.

Moor, J. C. de. "The Targumic Background of Mark 12:1–12: The Parable of the Wicked Tenants." *JSJ* 29 (1998) 63–80.

Moore, Stephen. *Literary Criticism and the Gospels.* New Haven: Yale University Press, 1989.

Morrison, Gregg S. *The Turning Point in the Gospel of Mark: A Study in Markan Christology.* Eugene, OR: Pickwick, 2014.

Moss, Candida R. "The Transfiguration: An Exercise in Markan Accommodation." *BibInt* 12 (2004) 69–89.

Motyer, J. Alec. *The Prophecy of Isaiah: An Introduction and Commentary.* Downers Grove, IL: InterVarsity, 1993.

Mowinckel, Sigmund. *Psalm Studies.* Vol. 2. Translated by Mark E. Biddle. Atlanta: Society of Biblical Literature, 2010.

———. *The Psalms in Israel's Worship.* Translated by D. R. Ap-Thomas. Vol. 1. New York: Abingdon, 1962.

Moyise, Steve. "Does Paul Respect the Context of His Quotations?" In *Paul and Scripture: Extending the Conversation*, edited by Christopher D. Stanley, 97–114. ECL 9. Atlanta: Society of Biblical Literature, 2012.

———. *Evoking Scripture: See the Old Testament in the New*. New York: T&T Clark, 2008.

———. "Intertextuality and the Study of the Old Testament in the New Testament." In *The Old Testament in the New Testament: Essays in Honor of J. L. North, 14–4*, edited by Steve Moyise, 14–41. Sheffield: Sheffield Academic, 2000.

Moyise, Steve, and Maarten J. J. Menken, eds. *The Psalms in the New Testament*. London: T&T Clark, 2004.

Mueller, Eike. "Cleansing the Common: A Narrative-Intertextual Study of Mark 7:1–23." PhD diss., Andrew University, 2015.

Myers, Ched. *Binding the Strong Man: A Political Reading of Mark's Story of Jesus*. Maryknoll, NY: Orbis, 1988.

Naluparayil, J. C. "Jesus of the Gospel of Mark: Present State of Research." *CBR* 8 (2000) 191–226.

———. *The Identity of Jesus in Mark: An Essay on Narrative Christology*. Jerusalem: Franciscan, 2000.

Newsom, Carol A., and Brennan W. Breed. *Daniel: A Commentary*. Louisville: Westminster John Knox, 2014.

Nickelsburg, George W. E. "The Genre and Function of the Markan Passion Narrative." *HTR* 73 (1980) 153–84.

———., and James C. Vanderkam. *1 Enoch 2: A Commentary on the Book of 1 Enoch, Chapters 37–82*. Minneapolis: Fortress, 2001.

———. *1 Enoch: The Hermeneia Translation*. Rev. ed. Minneapolis: Fortress, 2012.

Novenson, M. V. *Christ Among the Messiahs: Christ Language in Paul and Messiah Language in Ancient Judaism*. Oxford: Oxford University Press, 2012.

———. *The Grammar of Messianism*. Oxford: Oxford University Press, 2017.

Oancea, Constantin. "Psalm 2 im Alten Testament und im Frühen Judentum." *SC* 11 (2013) 159–80.

O'Brien, K. S. *The Use of Scripture in the Markan Passion Narrative*. LNTS 384. London: T&T Clark, 2010.

Öhler, Markus. "Die Verklärung (Mark 9:1–8): Die Ankunft der Herrschaft Gottes auf der Erde." *NovT* 38 (1996) 197–217.

Omerzu, Heike. "Die Rezeption von Psalm 22 im Judentum zur Zeit des Zweiten Tempels." In *Psalm 22 und die Passionsgeschicheten der Evangelien*, edited by Dieter Sänger, 33–76. Neukirchen: Neukirchener Verlag, 2007.

Paulien, Jon. "Elusive Allusions: The Problematic Use of the Old Testament in Revelation." *BR* 33 (1988) 37–53.

Peppard, M. *The Son of God in the Roman World: Divine Sonship in Its Social and Political Context*. Oxford: Oxford University Press, 2011.

Perowne, J. Stewart. *The Book of Psalms: A New Translation with Introduction and Notes, Explanatory and Critical*. Grand Rapids: Zondervan, 1976.

Perrin, N. "The Christology in Mark: A Study in Methodology." In *The Interpretation of Mark*, edited by W. R. Telford, 125–40. Edinburgh: T&T Clark, 2000.

Perrin, Norman. *The New Testament: An Introduction: Proclamation and Parenesis, Myth and History*. New York: Harcourt Brace Jovanovich, 1982.

Pesch, Rudolf. "Anfang des Evangeliums Jesu Christi: Eine Studie zum Prolog des Markusevangeliums (Mk 1, 1–15)." In *Das Markus-Evangelium*, edited by Rudolf Pesch, 311–55. WdF 411. Darmstadt: Wissenschaftliche Buchgesellschaft, 1979.

———. *Das Markusevangelium 2 Kommentar zu Kap 8,27—16,20*. HThKNT. Fridburg: Herder, 1977.
Peterson, D. N. *The Origins of Mark: The Markan Community in Current Debate*. Leiden: Brill: 2000.
Petterson, Anthony R. *Behold Your King: The Hope for the House of David in the Book of Zechariah*. New York: T&T Clark, 2009.
Phillips, George. *The Psalms in Hebrew: With a Critical, Exegetical, and Philological Commentary*. Vol. 1. London: J. W. Parker, 1846.
Pomykala, K. *The Davidic Dynasty Tradition in Early Judaism: Its History and Significance for Messianism*. Atlanta: Scholars, 1996.
Porter, Stanley E. "Further Comments on the Use of the Old Testament in the New Testament." In *The Intertextuality of the Epistles: Explorations of Theory and Practice*, edited by Thomas L. Brodie, et al., 98–110. NTMon 16. Sheffield: Sheffield Phoenix, 2006.
———. *Sacred Tradition in the New Testament: Tracing Old Testament Themes in the Gospels and Epistles*. Grand Rapids: Baker Academic, 2016.
———. "The Use of the Old Testament in the New Testament: A Brief Comment on Method and Terminology." In *Early Christian Interpretation of the Scripture of Israel: Investigations and Proposals*, edited by Craig A. Evans and James A. Sanders, 79–95. JSNTSup 148. Sheffield: Sheffield Academic, 1997.
Prinsloo, Gert T. M. "A Contextual and Intertextual Reading of Psalm 118." *OTE* 16 (2003) 401–21.
———. "Psalms 114 and 115: One or Two Poems?" *OTE* 16 (2003) 669-90.
———. "Šeʾōl → Yerûšālayim → Šāmayim: Spatial Orientation in the Egyptian Hallel (Psalms 113–118)." *OTE* 19 (2006) 739-60.
———. "Unit Delimitation in the Egyptian Hallel (Psalms 113-118): An Evaluation of Different Traditions." In *Unit Delimitation in Biblical Hebrew and Northwest Semitic Literature*, edited by Marjo C. A. Korpel and Josef M. Oesch, 232–63. Pericope 4. Assen: Koninklijke Van Gorcum, 2003.
Rahlfs, A, ed. *Septuaginta. Id est Vetus Testamentum Graece Iuxta LXX Interpres*. 2 vols. Stuttgart: Deutsche Bibelgesellschaft, 1979.
Rendtorff, Rolf. "The Psalms of David: David in the Psalms." In *The Book of Psalms: Composition and Reception*, edited by Peter W. Flint and Patrick D. Miller, 53–64. Leiden: Brill, 2004.
Rhoads, David, and Donald Michie. *Mark as Story: An Introduction to the Narrative of a Gospel*. Minneapolis: Fortress, 1982.
Robbins, Vernon K. "The Reversed Contextualization of Psalm 22 in the Markan Crucifixion: A Socio-Rhetorical Analysis." In *The Four Gospels 1992: Frestschrift Frans Neirynck*, edited by F. Van Segbroeck, 1161–83. Leuven: Leuven University Press, 1992.
Roberts, J. J. M. *First Isaiah: A Commentary*. Minneapolis: Fortress, 2015.
———. "The Enthronement of Yhwh and David: The Abiding Theological Significance of the Kingship Language of the Psalms." *CBR* 64 (2002) 679-80.
———. "The Old Testament's Contributions to Messianic Expectations." In *The Messiah: Developments in Earliest Judaism and Christianity*, edited by J. H. Charlesworth, 31–51. Minneapolis: Fortress, 1992.
———. "Whose Son Is This? Reflections on the Speaking Voice of Isaiah 9:5." In *The Bible and the Ancient Near East*, 143–56. Winona Lake, IN: Eisenbrauns, 2002.

Robertson, O. Palmer. *The Flow of the Psalms: Discovering Their Structure and Theology*. Phillipsburg, NJ: P&R, 2015.

———. *The Flow of the Psalms: Discovering Their Structure and Theology*. Philipsburg, NJ: P&R, 2015. Kindle.

Robinson, James M. "Jesus: From Easter to Valentinus (or to the Apostles Creed)." *JBL* 101 (1982) 5–37.

Rose, Christian. *Theologie als Erzählung im Markusevangelium: Eine narratologisch-rezeptionsästhetische Untersuchung zu Mk 1,1–15*. WUNT 2. Reihe 236. Tübingen: Mohr Siebeck, 2007.

Rose, Walter H. *Zemah and Zerubbabel: Messianic Expectations in the Early Postexilic Period*. Sheffield: Sheffield Academic, 2000.

Roskam, H. N. *The Purpose of Mark in Its Historical and Social Context*. NovTSup 114. Leiden: Brill, 2004.

Ross, Allen P. *A Commentary on the Psalms: Volume 1 (1–41)*. Grand Rapids: Kregel, 2011.

———. *A Commentary on the Psalms: Volume 2 (42–89)*. Grand Rapids: Kregel, 2013.

———. *A Commentary on the Psalms: Volume 3 (90–150)*. Grand Rapids: Kregel, 2016.

Routledge, Robin L. "Psalm 110, Melchizedek and David: Blessing (the Descendants of) Abraham." *BT* 1 (2009) 1–16.

Rowe, Robert D. *God's Kingdom and God's Son: The Background to Mark's Christology from Concepts of Kingship in the Psalms*. Leiden: Brill, 2002.

Ruckstuhl, Eugen. "Jesus als Gottessohn im Spiegel des markinischen Taufberichts." In *Die Mitte des Neuen Testaments: Einheit und Vielfalt neutestamentlicher Theologie: Festschrift fur Eduard Schweizer zum siebzigsten Geburtstag*, edited by Ulrich Luz and Hans Weder, 193–220. Göttingen: Vandenhoeck & Ruprecht, 1983.

Ruppert, L. *Jesus als der leidende Gerechte? Der Weg Jesus im Lichte eines alt- und zwischentestamentlichen Motivs*. Stuttgarter Biblestudien 59. Stuttgart: Katholisches Bibelwerk, 1972.

Russell, David. "The Royal and Priestly Contribution of Psalm 110 to the Book of Hebrews." PhD diss., Dallas Theological Seminary, 1998.

Sana, Nahum M. *Exodus=[Shemot]: The Traditional Hebrew Text with the New JPS Translation*. 1st ed. JPSTC. Philadelphia: Jewish Publication Society, 1991.

Sander, Paul Joseph. "Bringing Together and Setting Apart: The Theological Significance of Alternate Delimitations in the Hebrew and Greek Psalters." PhD diss., Fordham University, 2017.

Sanders, J. A. "A New Testament Hermeneutic Fabric: Psalm 118 in the Entrance Narrative." In *Early Jewish and Christian Exegesis: Studies in Memory of William Hugh Brownlee*. edited by Craig A. Evans and William F. Stinespring, 177–90. Atlanta: Scholars, 1987.

———. *The Dead Sea Psalms Scroll*. Ithaca, NY: Cornell University Press, 1967.

Sänger, Dieter, ed. *Heiligkeit und Herrschaft: Intertextuelle Studien zu Heiligkeitsvorstellungen und zu Psalm 110*. BThST 55. Neukirchen-Vluyn: Neukirchener Verlag, 2003.

Sänger, Dieter., ed. *Psalm 22 und die Passionsgeschicheten der Evangelien*. Neukirchen: Neukirchener Verlag, 2007.

Sankamo, Juho. "Jesus' Entry into Jerusalem." *AR* 4 (2014) 25–36.

Schaper, Joachim. *Eschatology in the Greek Psalter*. WUNT 2. Reihe 76. Tübingen: Mohr Siebeck, 1995.

Schiffmann, L. H. "The Concept of the Messiah in Second Temple and Rabbinic Literature." *RevExp* 84 (1987) 235–46.
Schmidt, Karl. *Der Rahmen der Geschichte Jesu: Literarkritische Untersuchungen zur ältesten Jesusüberlieferung*. Berlin: Trowitzsch, 1919.
Schmidt, Thomas E. "Cry of Dereliction or Cry of Judgment? Mark 15.34 in Context." *BBR* 4 (1994) 145–53.
Schreiber, S. *Gesalbter und König: Titel und Konzeptionen der königlichen Gesalbtenerwartung in frühjüdischen und urchristlichen Schriften*. BZAW 105. Berlin: de Gruyter, 2000.
Schreiner, Josef, ed. *Beiträge zur Psalmenforschung: Psalm 2 und 22*. Würzburg: Echter Verlag, 1988.
———. "Zur Stellung von Psalm 22 im Psalter Folgen für die Auslegung." In *Beiträge zur Psalmenforschung: Psalm 2 und 22*, edited by Josef Schreiner, 241–78 Würzburg: Echter Verlag, 1988.
Schröten, Jutta. *Entstehung, Komposition und Wirkungsgeschichte des 118. Psalms*. BBB 95. Weinheim: Beltz Athenäum Verlag, 1995.
Schweizer, Eduard. *Das Evangelium nach Markus*. Das New Testament Deutsch. 4th ed. Göttingen: Vandenhoeck & Ruprecht, 1975.
———. *Erniedringung und Erhöhung bei Jesus und seinen Nachfolgern*. Zürich: Zwingli-Verlag, 1962.
Schwemer, A. E. "Jesu letze Worte am Kreuz (Mk 5, 34; Lk 23, 46; Joh 19, 28ff)." *Theologische Beiträge* 29 (1998) 5–29.
Scott, M. Philip. "Chiastic Structure: A Key to the Interpretation of Mark's Gospel." *BTB* 15 (1985) 17–26.
Seitz, O. J. F. "The Future Coming of the Son of Man: Three Midrashic Formulations in the Gospel of Mark." In *Studia Evangelica*, vol. VI, edited by E. A. Livingstone, 478–94. Berlin: Akademie, 1973.
Seybold, Klaus. *Die Psalmen*. Tübingen: J. C. B. Mohr, 1996.
Shepherd, Tom. *Markan Sandwich Stories: Narration, Definition, and Function*. AUSDDS 18. Berrien Springs, MI: Andrews University Press, 1993.
Shively, Elizabeth E. *Apocalyptic Imagination in the Gospel of Mark: The Literary and Theological Role of Mark 3:22–30*. BZNW 189. Berlin: De Gruyter, 2012.
Skehan, P. W. "A Psalm Manuscript from Qumran (4QPsᵇ)." *CBQ* 26 (1964) 313–22.
Sloan, David B. "The Understanding of the Psalms in Luke-Acts." PhD diss., Trinity Evangelical Divinity School, 2012.
Sloan, Paul T. *Mark 13 and the Return of the Shepherd: The Narrative Logic of Zechariah in Mark*. LNTS 604. New York: T&T Clark, 2019.
Smith, Daniel Lynwood. "The Uses of 'New Exodus' in New Testament Scholarship: Preparing a Way Through the Wilderness." *CBR* 14 (2016) 207–43.
Smith, Gary V. *Isaiah 1–39*. NAC. 15A. Nashville: B&H, 2007.
Smith, Robert H. "Darkness at Noon: Mark's Passion Narrative." *CTM* 44 (1973) 325–38.
Smith, S. H. "The Literary Structure of Mark 11–12." *NovT* 31 (1989) 104–24.
Snearly, Michael K. *The Return of the King: Messianic Expectation in Book V of the Psalter*. The Library of Hebrew Bible/Old Testament Studies 624. New York: T&T Clark. 2015.
Snodgrass, K. "Recent Research on the Parable of the Wicked Tenants: An Assessment." *BBR* 8 (1998) 187–216.

———. *The Parable of the Wicked Tenants: An Inquiry into Parable Interpretation*. WUNT 27. Tübingen: Mohr Siebeck, 1983.

Snow, Robert S. *Daniel's Son of Man in Mark: A Redefinition of the Jerusalem Temple and the Formation of a New Covenant Community*. Eugene, OR: Pickwick, 2016.

Sparks, H. F. D, ed. *The Apocryphal Old Testament*. Oxford: Oxford University Press, 1984.

Stanley, Christopher D. *Arguing with Scripture: The Rhetoric of Quotations in the Letters of Paul*. New York: T&T Clark, 2004.

———. *Paul and the Language of Scripture: Citation Technique in the Pauline Epistles and Contemporary Literature*. SNTSMS 74. Cambridge: Cambridge University Press, 1992.

Stead, Michael R. *The Intertextuality of Zechariah 1–8*. New York: T & T Clark, 2009.

Stec, David M. *The Targum of Psalms: Translated with A Critical Introduction, Apparatus, and Notes*. AB 16. London: T&T Clark, 2004.

Stegner, W. Richard. "The Use of Scripture in Two Narratives of Early Jewish Christianity (Matthew 4.1–11; Mark 9.2–8)." In *Early Christian Interpretation of the Scriptures of Israel: Investigations and Proposals*, edited by Craig A. Evans and J. A. Sanders, 98–120. JSNTSup 148. Sheffield: Sheffield Academic,1997.

Steichele, H.-J. *Der leidende Sohn Gottes: Eine Untersuchung einiger alttestamentlicher Motive in der Christologie des Markusevangeliums*. BU 14. Regensburg: Pustet, 1980.

Stein, R. H. *Mark*. BECNT. Grand Rapids: Baker Academic, 2008.

———. *Jesus, the Temple, and the Coming Son of Man: A Commentary on Mark 13*. Downers Grove, IL: IVP Academic, 2014.

———. "The Ending of Mark." *BBR* 18 (2008) 79–98.

Stern, David. "Jesus' Parables from the Perspective of Rabbinic Literature: The Example of the Wicked Husbandmen." In *Parable and Story in Judaism and Christianity*, edited by Clemens Thoma and Michael Wyschogrod, 42–80. New York: Paulist, 1989.

Stowasser, Martin. "'Mein Gott, mein Gott, warum hast du mich verlassen?' (Mk 15,34). Beobachtungen zum Kontextbezug von Ps 22,2 als Sterbewort Jesu im Markusevangelium." *BZ* 58 (2014) 161–85.

Strauss, Mark L. *Mark*. ZECNT. Grand Rapids: Zondervan, 2017.

Streett, Andrew D. "From Marginal to Mainstream: The Adamic Son of Man and the Potential of Psalm 80." *CTR* 13 (2016) 77–98.

———. *The Vine and the Son of Man: Eschatological Interpretation of Psalm 80 in Early Judaism*. Minneapolis: Augsburg Fortress, 2014.

Strukenbruck, L. "Messianic Ideas in the Apocalyptic and Related Literature of Early Judaism." In *The Messiah in the Old and New Testaments*, edited by S. E. Porter, 90–113. Grand Rapids: Eerdmans, 2007.

Stuart, Douglas K. *Exodus*. NAC. Nashville: B&H, 2006.

Stuhlmueller, Carroll. "Psalm 22: The Deaf and Silent God of Mysticism and Liturgy." *BTB* 12 (1982) 86–90.

Subrahmanian, J. Samuel. *The Synoptic Gospels and the Psalms as Prophecy*. LNTS 351. New York: T&T Clark, 2007.

Suhl, Alfred. *Die Funktion der alttestamentlichen Zitate und Anspielungen im Markusevanglium*. Gütersloh: Gerd Mohn, 1965.

Sumpter, Philip. "The Coherence of Psalms 15–24." *Bib* 94 (2013) 186–209.

Tannehill, R. "The Disciples in Mark: The Function of a Narrative Role." *JR* 57 (1977) 386–405.

———. "The Gospel of Mark as Narrative Christology." *Semeia* 16 (1979) 57–95.

Tàrrech, Armand Puig i. Translated by John F. Elwolde and Roberto Martínez. "The Glory on the Mountain: The Episode of the Transfiguration of Jesus." *NTS* 58, no. 2 (2012) 151–72.

Tate, Marvin E. "An Exposition on Psalm 8." *PRSTs* 28 (2001) 343–59.

———. *Psalms 51–100*. WBC 20. Dallas: Word, 1990.

Taylor, Vincent. *The Gospel According to St. Mark: The Greek Text with Introduction, Notes, and Indexes*. London: Macmillan, 1952.

Thatcher, Tom. "(Re)mark(s) on the Cross." *BibInt* 4 (1996) 346–61.

Thompson, Alvin L. "Literary Patterns and Theological Themes in the Gospel of Mark." ThD diss., Dallas Theological Seminary, 1992.

Thompson, Michael. *Clothed with Christ: The Example and Teaching of Jesus in Romans 12.1—15.13*. JSNTSup 59. Sheffield: JSOT, 1991.

Tilly, M. "Psalm 110 zwischen hebraischer Bibel und Neuem Testament." In *Heiligkeit und Herrschaft: Intertextuelle Studien zu Heiligkeitsvorstellungen und zu Psalm 110*, edited by Dieter Sänger, 146–70. BThST 55. NeukircheN-Vluyn: Neukirchener Verlag, 2003.

Tödt, Heinz Eduard. *The Son of Man in the Synoptic Tradition*. Philadelphia: Westminster, 1965.

Tolbert, M. A. *Sowing the Gospel: Mark's World in Literary-Historical Perspective*. Minneapolis: Fortress, 1989.

Trafton, Joseph L. "What Would David Do? Messianic Expectation and Surprise in Ps. Sol. 17." In *The Psalms of Solomon: Language, History, Theology*, edited by Patrick Pouchelle and Eberhard Bons, 155–74. EJL 40. Atlanta: Society of Biblical Literature, 2015.

Treves, Marco. "Two Acrostic Psalms." *VT* 15 (1965) 81–90.

Trimaille, M. "La parabole des vignerons meurtriers (Mc 12, 1–12)." In *Les Paraboles évangéliques: Perspectives Nouvelles*, edited by J. Delorme, 247–58. Paris: Cerf, 1989.

Troyer, Kristine De. "The Septuagint and the Transmission of Jewish Scripture." In *Behind the Scenes of the New Testament: Cultural, Social, and Historical Contexts*, edited by Bruce W. Longenecker, et al., 105–12. Grand Rapids: Baker, 2024.

Trublet, Jacque. "Approche canonique des Psaumes du Hallel." In *The Composition of the Book of Psalms*, edited by Erich Zenger, 356–63. BETL 238. Leuven: Peeters, 2010.

Tucker, W. Dennis Jr. and Jamie A. Grant. *Psalms Volume 2*. NIVAC. Grand Rapids: Zondervan, 2018.

Tuckett, Christopher M., ed. *The Scriptures in the Gospels*. BETL 131. Leuven: Leuven University Press/Peeters, 1997.

Ulrich, Eugene. *Qumran Cave 4: XI*. DJD 16. Oxford: Clarendon, 2000.

Vaillancourt, Ian J. *The Multifaceted Saviour of Psalms 110 and 118: A Canonical Exegesis*. Hebrew Bible Monographs 86. Sheffield: Sheffield Phoenix, 2019.

———. "Psalm 118 and the Eschatological Son of David." *JETS* 62 (2019) 721–38.

VanGemeren, Willem A. *Psalms*. EBC. Vol. 5. Grand Rapids: Zondervan, 2008.

Vanhoozer, Kevin J. *Is There a Meaning in This Text? The Bible, the Reader, and the Morality of Literary Knowledge*. Grand Rapids: Zondervan, 2009.

van Iersel, Bas Martinus Franciscus. "Concentric Structures in Mark 1:14—3:35 (4:1): With Some Observations on Method." Translated by W. H. Bisscheroux. *BibInt* 3 (1995) 75–98.

———. *Mark: A Reader-Response Commentary*. Translated by W. H. Bisscheroux. JSNTSup 164. Sheffield: Sheffield Academic, 1998.

Vermès, G. *The Dead Sea Scrolls in English*. 4th ed. London: Penguin, 1995.

Von Rad, Gerhard. "Das Judäische Königsritual." *TLZ* 72 (1947) 211–16.

Von Nordheim, Miriam. *Geboren von der Morgenröte?: Psalm 110 in Tradition, Redaktion und Rezeption*. Neukirchen-Vluyn: Neukirchener, 2008.

Van Oyen, Geert, and Tom Shepherd, eds. *The Trial and Death of Jesus: Essays on the Passion Narrative in Mark*. Leuven: Peeters, 2006.

Waltke, Bruce K., and Charles Yu. *An Old Testament Theology: An Exegetical, Canonical, and Thematic Approach*. Grand Rapids: Zondervan, 2007.

Waltke, Bruce K., and James M. Houston. *The Psalms as Christian Worship: A Historical Commentary*. Grand Rapids: Eerdmans, 2010.

Watts, Rikki E. *Isaiah's New Exodus and Mark*. WUNT 2. Reihe 88. Tübingen: Mohr Siebeck, 1997.

———. "Mark." In *Commentary on the New Testament Use of the Old Testament*, edited by G. K. Beale and D. A. Carson, 111–250. Grand Rapids: Baker Academic, 2007.

———. "The Lord's House and David's Lord: The Psalms and Mark's Perspective on Jesus and the Temple." *BibInt* 15 (2007) 307–22.

———. "The Psalms in Mark's Gospel." In *The Psalms in the New Testament*, edited by Steve Moyise and Maarten J. J. Menken, 25–45. London: T&T Clark.

Waugh, Robin. "The Testament of Job as an Example of Profeminine Patience Literature." *JBL* 133 (2014) 777–92.

Wedderburn, Alexander J. M. *Beyond Resurrection*. London: SCM, 1999.

Wellhausen, Julius. *Das Evangelium Marci*. Berlin: E. Reimer, 1909.

Wenham, David, and D. A. Moses. "'There Are Some Standing Here . . .': Did They Become the 'Reputed Pillars' of the Jerusalem Church? Some Reflections on Mark 9:1, Galatians 2:9 and the Transfiguration." *NovT* 36 (1994) 146–63.

Westermann, Claus. *Das Buch Jesaja: Kapitel 40–66/Übers. und erklärt*. Göttingen: Vandenhoeck & Ruprecht, 1966.

Whiting, Mark J. "Psalms 1 and 2 as a Hermeneutical Lens for Reading the Psalter." *EvQ* 85 (2013) 246–62.

Whybray, R. N. *Reading the Psalms as a Book*. JSOTSup 222. Sheffield: Sheffield Academic, 1996.

Willgren, David. *The Formation of the 'Book' of Psalms*. FAT 2. Reihe 88. Tübingen: Mohr Siebeck, 2016.

Williams, Joel F. "Does Mark's Gospel Have An Outline?" *JETS* 49 (2006) 505–25.

———. "Is Mark's Gospel an Apology for the Cross?" *BBR* 12 (2002) 97–122.

———. "Literary Approaches to the End of Mark's Gospel." *JETS* 42 (1999) 21–35.

———. *Mark*. EGGNT. Nashville: B&H Academic, 2020.

———. *Other Followers of Jesus: Minor Characters as Major Figures in Mark's Gospel*. JSNTSup 102. Sheffield: Sheffield Academic, 1994.

Willis, John T. "Psalm—An Entity." *ZAW* 91 (1979) 381–401.

Wilson, Gerald H. *The Editing of the Hebrew Psalter*. SBLDS 76. Chico, CA: Scholars, 1985.

———. *Psalms, Volume 1*. NIVAC. Grand Rapids: Zondervan, 2002.

———. "Shaping the Psalter: A Consideration of Editorial Linkage in the Book of Psalms." In *The Shape and Shaping of the Psalter*, edited by J. Clinton McCann, 72–82. Sheffield: JSOT, 1993.

———. "The Structure of the Psalter." In *Interpreting the Psalms: Issues and Approaches*, edited by David Firth and Philip S. Johnston, 229–46. Downers Grove, IL: InterVarsity, 2005.

———. "Understanding the Purposeful Arrangement of the Psalms in the Psalter: Pitfalls and Promise." In *The Shape and Shaping of the Psalter*, edited by J. Clinton McCann, 42–51. Sheffield: Sheffield Academic, 1993.

———. "The Use of Royal Psalms at the 'Seams' of the Hebrew Psalter." *JSOT* 35 (1986) 85–94.

Winn, Adam. *The Purpose of Mark's Gospel: An Early Christian Response to Roman Imperial Propaganda*. WUNT 2. Reihe 245. Tübingen: Mohr Siebeck, 2008.

Wittman, Derek. "'Let Us Cast Their Ropes from Us': The Editorial Significance of the Portrayal of the Foreign Nations in Psalm 2 and 149." In *The Shape and Shaping of the Book of Psalms: The Current State of Scholarship*, edited by Nancy L. deClaissé-Walford, 53–69. Atlanta: Society of Biblical Literature, 2014.

Wright, Robert B. *The Psalms of Solomon: A Critical Edition of the Greek Text*. London: T&T Clark, 2007.

Wold, Benjamin. "Old Testament Context: Insights from the Dead Sea Scrolls." In *Methodology in the Use of the Old Testament in the New*, edited by David Allen and Steve Smith, 115–25. LNTS 579. London: T&T Clark, 2019.

Wright, N. T. *Jesus and the Victory of God*. London: SPCK, 1996.

———. *New Testament and the People of God*. Minneapolis: Fortress, 1992.

Wypadlo, Adrian. *Die Verklärung Jesu nach dem Markusevangelium: Studien zu einer christologischen Legitimationserzählung*. WUNT 308. Tübingen: Mohr Siebeck, 2013.

Yoon, David I. "The Ideological Inception of Intertextuality and Its Dissonance in Current Biblical Studies." *CBR* 12 (2012) 58–76.

Young, David M., and Michael Strickland. *The Rhetoric of Jesus in the Gospel of Mark*. Minneapolis: Fortress, 2017.

Zeitlin, Solomon. "The Hallel: A Historical Study of the Canonization of the Hebrew Liturgy." *JQR* 53 (1962) 22–29.

Zenger, Erich. "The Composition and Theology of the Fifth Book of Psalms, Psalms 107–145." *JSOT* 80 (1998) 77–102.

———. "'Dass alles Fleisch den Namen seiner Heiligung segne' (Ps 145,21): Die Komposition Ps 145–150 als Anstoss zu einer Christlich-jüdischen Psalmenhermeneutik." *BZ* 41 (1997) 1–27.

———. "'Wozu tosen die Völker . . . ?' Beobachtungen zur Entstehung und Theologie des 2. Psalms." In *Freude an der Weisung des Herrn. Beiträge zur Theologie der Psalmen*, edited by Ernst Haag and Frank-Lothar Hossfeld, 495–511. Stuttgart: Verlag Katholisches Bibelwerk, 1986.

Zimmermann, J. *Messianische Texte aus Qumran. Königliche, priesterliche und prophetische Messasvorstellungen in den Schriftfunden von Qumran*. WUNT 2/104. Tübingen: Mohr Siebeck, 1998.

Index of Authors

Note: Page numbers in *italics* indicate figures, and references following "n" refer notes.

Abasciano, Brian, 18
Achtemeier, Paul, 24n2
Ådna, Jostein, 119n123
Aernie, Jeffrey, 57n203
Ahearne-Kroll, Stephen, 8, 142n91, 177n100, 178, 184n148
Ahn, Keun Jo, 147n107
Alvarez, Francis, 112n100
Alkier, Stefan, 12n47
Allen, David, 13n50, 19n79
Allen, Leslie, 93n7, 101n52, 125n5,7, 126n12, 127n22
Allison, Dale, 55n191, 183
Auffret, Pierre, 66n6, 166
Aus, R., 116n118

Bail, Ulrike, 129n35
Bain, Bruce, 33n44
Bakhtin, Mikhail, 12
Baldwin, Joyce, 135n62
Balhorn, Egbert, 104n69
Barbiero, Gianni, 130n37
Barrett, Charles, 112n101
Barthes, Roland, 17n66
Bateman, Hebert, 162n8
Bauckham, Richard, 77n74, 79n86, 80, 84n113, 86, 87n124, 125, 88n126, 90n128, 136, 138
Beale, Gregory, 14, 16, 17n66, 19n79, 20, 21, 70n29, 178n106
Becker, Joachim, 169n63

Berder, Michel, 93n6, 100n48, 118n120
Best, Ernest, 28n21
Black, Matthew, 115n112
Blank, Josef, 79n89
Blenkinsopp, J., 108n81
Block, Daniel, 134n62, 66n6, 134n62
Bock, Darrell, 34n52, 53, 35n54, 55, 36n63, 37n73, 40n96, 41n99, 42n106, 108, 52n168, 169, 82n102, 141n86, 153n140, 185n151, 186n160, 162
Boda, Mark, 66n6, 108n82, 83, 109n85
Bons, Eberhard, 65n5, 130n39, 138n80, 165n37–41
Boring, M., 27n14, 28n20–22, 32n38, 33n40, 33n42, 36n66, 37n72, 38n80–83, 39n86, 40n92, 40n94, 41n100–1, 41n104, 42n106, 44n118, 44n120–21, 45n126, 47n134–35, 47n141, 48n145, 52n169, 53n174, 54n181–82, 55n187, 192, 78n84–85, 85n119, 116n115–16, 146n103, 152n137, 175n83–84, 89, 176n93, 179n110–11, 180n114, 181, 181n122, 182n127, 129–30, 185n151, 186n159, 186n165–67
Botha, Phil, 71n42

Botner, Max,, 29n23, 77n78–79, 78n81, 108n81, 109n84, 87, 110n93, 111n97, 118n122–23, 124n2, 142n88, 144n99, 146n102
Breytenbach, Cilliers, 5, 120n126, 124n2, 125n3, 141n85, 87, 143n96
Broadhead, Edwin, 144n99
Brock, S., 69n28
Brooke, George, 73n55, 115n122, 137n72
Brown, Raymond, 55n193, 147n104, 159n3–4, 160n6, 182n131, 184n146, 150, 186n165
Brown, William, 127n22, 166, 167n151
Brownlee, W., 72n43
Broyles, Craig, 167n48–49
Brueggemann Walter, 130n47
William H., 139n47
Brunson, Andrew, 98n41, 105n75, 106n77, 109n87–88, 111n97
Bucker, Ralph, 64n1
Bultmann, Rudolf, 81n99
Burchard, Christoph, 177n100
Burkett, Delbert, 81n99

Cahill, Michael, 96n24
Calvin, John, 65n2, 5, 162n9, 163n22
Caneday, Ardel, 30n26, 56n195, 86n122, 87n124, 187n169
Carey, Holly, 9, 23n95, 159n2, 160n5, 170n67, 177n100, 102, 184n147, 185, 189n178
Catchpole, D., 109n84
Charlesworth, J., 66n6, 105n74
Chatman, Seymour, 26n2,
Chester, Andrew, 90n128
Childs, Brevard, 72n48, 99n45, 103n67, 117n118
Chilton, Bruce, 70n29, 79, 80n91
Cho, Bernardo, 11, 77n78, 78n79–80, 108n81, 109n84, 110n91, 111n97, 112n100–1, 113n102, 114n106–7, 115n112, 118n121–22, 120n126, 153n140–41
Clendenen, E., 113n102

Cohen, A., 71n38
Cole, Robert, 71n38–40, 72n46
Collins, Adela, 4, 5n6–8, 28n18–19, 34n46, 35n61, 36n66, 38n80, 56n202, 57n203, 66n6, 77n78, 82n99, 83n109, 109n84, 115n112, 149n119, 159n3, 177n101, 179n110, 113, 180n115–17, 182n130–31, 134, 183n142, 184n148–49, 186n158, 164, 187n168, 170
Collins, John, 67n14, 68n15, 17, 69n27, 74n58–60, 75n64, 67, 70–71
Constant, Pierre, 97n37, 99n45
Cook, David, 172n73
Corley, Jeremy, 125n5, 130n36, 38, 131n41
Cox, Claude, 64n1, 69n27
Craigie, P., 67n12, 68n15, 17, 21, 162n7, 163n25, 164n31, 34
Crim, Keith, 70n34,
Crutchfield, John, 102n59, 104n69–70
Cullman, Oscar, 77n76

Dahood, Mitchell, 93n7, 97n35
Danker, Frederick, 184n145
Daube, David, 115n111
Davis, Barry, 102n59, 133n54–55, 57
deClaissé-Walford, Nancy, 71n38, 93n1–2, 94n8, 95n17, 163n18–19, 164n34, 36, 166n43–44
Defani, Evangelia, 128n22, 131n40, 42
Delitzsch, Franz, 68n21, 126n8, 162n9, 16–17
Dempster, Stephen, 132n52
Derrett, J. Duncan, 116n114
deSilva, David, 137
Dewey, Joanna, 27n11, 33
Dinkler, Michal, 25n1
Docherty, Susan, 17n62
Dodd, C., 13, 177n97
Donahue, John, 34n51, 36n66, 37n77, 38n80, 45n121, 123, 47n134, 53n178, 54n180, 55n187, 56n196, 199, 116n115,

146n102-3, 176n93, 184n147,
    186n165-66
Donald Michie, 26
Dowd, Sharyn, 45n126
Drijvers, P., 93n3
Dupont, Jacques, 34n51
Durham, John, 117n118

Eaton, John, 93n4,
Edwards, J., 27n12, 30n27, 33n40,
    34n47, 53, 35n54-55, 36n66,
    68-69, 37n74-75, 40n92,
    95, 41n100, 42n106, 43n112,
    44n117, 46n131, 47n137-38,
    48n148, 52n168-69, 54n184,
    86n121, 113n103, 175n85,
    207n59
Eibert, Tigchelaar, 105n74
Emadi, Matthew, 129, 134, 143n98-
    99, 150n121, 124
Eric Zenger, 66n6, 71n38, 95n23,
    100n48, 104n69, 126n11,
    127n17, 128n24, 130n37, 39,
    132n51, 133n52, 56, 166n46
Ernst, Josef, 36n63-64
Estes, Daniel, 95n16-17, 19, 23,
    96n26, 31-32, 104n69, 126n12,
    127n19
Evans, Craig, 29n23, 39n89, 42n107,
    43n111, 116, 45n122, 47n134,
    52n169, 53n177, 54n182-83,
    56n202, 59n205, 83n106,
    85n116, 109n84, 115n112,
    116n114-15, 141n85, 142n89-
    90, 152n137, 175n84, 181n120,
    122-24, 182n130, 133, 184n149

Fabry, Heinz-Josef, 165n37, 40-42,
    189n176
Fish, Stanley, 17n66
Flint, Peter, 105n73-74, 105n74, 76
Fleddermann, Harry, 48n147
Fletcher-Louis, Crispin, 144n99, 150
Focant, Camille, 177n101
Fokkelman, Jan, 66n6
Foster, Paul, 19, 20
Fossum, Jarl, 81n99, 83n103
Fowler, Robert, 27n14

France, R., 26n1, 28n17, 30n28,
    32n38, 33n40, 34n51, 35n54-56,
    37n74, 76, 38n80, 42n105,
    107, 109, 43n112, 116, 44n118,
    45n124, 126, 47n136, 50n157,
    51n163, 52n168, 54n182,
    55n189, 193, 56n197-98,
    202, 77n78, 78n84, 82n101,
    108n81, 109n84, 90, 115n112,
    142n89, 91, 146n103, 147n104,
    175n84, 180n114, 116, 182n133,
    184n143, 186n165
Fuhrmann, Justin, 114n106, 115,
    116b118
Funk, Robert, 30n28

Garland, David, 47n141
Gathercole, Simon, 47n141,
Geddert, Timothy, 10
Gerstenberger, Erhard, 65n5, 163n19
Gese, Hartmut, 134n58, 177n99,
    184n147
Gillingham, Susan, 71n38, 73n51-53
Gnilka, Joachim, 34n51, 50n161,
    177n100
Goldingay, John, 66n6, 67n8-9, 11,
    14, 69n23, 73n51, 93n12, 14,
    95n15, 17-18, 96n25-26, 31,
    125n4, 127n19, 21, 128n22,
    129n34, 130n36, 151n130,
    162n14, 163n24, 164n28
Goulder, Michael, 93n5
Gourgues, M., 141n87, 142n89
Granerød, Gard, 125n4
Grant, Jamie, 128n22, 132n51,
    133n56, 71n37-38, 72n46,
    73n52, 93n7, 94n9-10, 14,
    95n19-24, 96n25, 28, 30, 32,
    97n34-35, 105n53, 59
Gray, T., 44n119, 45n125, 46n131,
    47n135, 107n78, 113n103,
    116n116
Grund, Alexandra, 68n15
Guelich, Robert, 79n86, 29n24,
    30n29-30, 32n37, 33n40, 34n46,
    36n68
Gundry, Robert, 59n205, 77n73,
    78n82, 83n103, 85n115, 141n85,

(Robert Gundry continued)
  152n136, 181n125, 184n143, 150, 186n164
Gunkel, Hermann, 65, 70, 93n3

Haglund, Erik, 93n3
Hamilton James, 150n122, 124
Hatina, Thomas, 23, 24, 26, 27n10, 29n24, 30n29-30, 31n32, 32n35, 77n76, 79n88, 98n39-40, 109n87-88, 90, 111n95, 97-98, 115n113
Harrington, Daniel, 34n51, 36n66, 37n77, 38n80, 45n121, 123, 47n134, 53n178, 54n180, 55n187, 56n196, 199, 116n115, 146n102, 152n137, 176n93, 184n147, 186n165-66
Hay, David, 127n17, 131n45, 135n64, 136, 137n77, 138n81, 142n90-91, 93-94, 143n98, 149n118, 152n137,
Hayes, Elizabeth, 103n68
Hays, J., 128n25
Hays, Richard, 12, 13n49, 18-21, 23n95, 77n73, 75, 78n79, 81, 79n88, 89n127, 141n84, 142n92, 143n98, 152n135, 137, 159, 179n112, 182, 184n147, 149, 185n155, 200,
Heil, John, 26n1
Henderson, Suzanne, 26n1
Hellerman, Joseph, 113n102
Hendrick, Charles, 26n1
Hengel, Martin, 59n205, 125n5, 135-36, 135n64,
Hibbard, J., 99n45
Hilber, John, 126
Hill, Andrew, 150n128
Hill, David, 147n107
Hirsch, E., 14n52, 17n66
Hoffman, Mark, 168n54-59, 169, 170n67, 171
Holladay, William, 169n61
Hollander, John, 13n49
Hooker, M., 41n99, 55n186, 83n105, 84n111, 146n102, 152n133, 175n88, 179n110-11, 113, 180n116, 181n119-20, 122, 182n127, 129, 133, 186n165-66
Horsley, Richard, 22n91, 59n205
Hoskins, Paul, 178n106-7, 179n108, 184n148, 185n154, 156, 186n160
Hossfeld, Frank-Lothar, 66n6, 71n38, 95n23, 100n48, 104n69, 126n11, 127n17, 128n24, 130n37, 39, 132n51, 133n52, 56, 166n46
Hurtado, Larry, 27n15, 57n203, 76n72, 84n111, 90n128

Iverson, K., 36n63, 37n73, 121n99, 114n106
Instone-Brewer, David, 14n51

James, Joshua, 96n30
Jamie A., 97n34
Janse, Sam, 65n3, 69n26, 28, 70n31, 71n39-42, 73n53, 74n57, 61-62, 75n66-68, 77n76
Janowski, Bernd, 184n148
Jeremias, Joachim, 77n76, 106n77
Johansson, Daniel, 78n84-85, 82, 83n103, 109, 84n110-11, 114, 85n115, 117-19, 90n128
Johnson, Bradley, 29n24, 30-31
Johnson, Elliott, 126n9
Juel, Donald, 14n51, 87n124, 138n81, 142n90, 145n100, 146n101-3, 147n104-5, 153n139, 177n101
Juncker, G., 84n114

Kaiser, Walter, 14n52, 16, 147n107
Kalt, Edmund, 93n5
Kampling, Rainer, 78n82-83, 79n86, 89, 80n95
Karakolis, Christos, 36n68
Keck, Leander, 30n30
Keefer, Arthur, 14, 15
Kee, Howard, 59n205, 77n77, 81n99, 82n102, 83n106
Kelber, W., 35
Kim, Jinkyu, 71n37, 103n66, 132n49-50
Kim, Sung-Soo, 70n33
Kim, Sun Wook, 35, 72n50

Kingsbury, J., 26n4, 6, 43n115, 142n91
Kloppenborg, John, 114n107-8
Kok, Michael, 90n128
Kraemer, Ross, 171n72
Kratz, Reinhard, 101n52
Kraus, Hans-Joachim, 108n79
Krause, Deborah, 108n79, 81, 109n84-85
Kristeva, Julia, 12, 13n49
Krusche, Marcel, 71n37
Kuhn, Heinz, 108n81
Kutsko, John, 66n6
Kwon, Hyukjung, 106n77

Lafleur, Didier, 27n15
Lagrange, M., 178n107
Lane, William, 28n20, 30n26, 28, 33n42, 38n80-81, 39n87, 44n117, 120, 50n159, 51n163-64, 59n205, 82n102, 83n107, 108n81, 152n136
Lange, Harvey, 177n102, 178n107
Larsen, Kevin, 8n21
Lee, Dorothy, 39n88, 82n102, 84n111, 85n114
Lee, Peter, 133n57
Leim, Joshua, 152n135
Lim, Timothy, 17
Lindars, Barnabas, 13n51, 141n86, 177n100
Lister, Rob, 173n80
Loader, William, 141n86
Lochrie, Graham, 23n92
Lohmeyer, Ernst, 82n99, 142n87, 177n100
Longman, Tremper, 65n2
Lövestam, Evald, 142n90
Lührmann, Dieter, 177n100
Lyons, Michael, 168n54, 169n60, 63

Maiberger, P., 69n24, 72n44, 45
Malbon, Elizabeth, 22n90, 26n2-3, 6, 32, 35, 37n75
Malcom, Matthew, 178n106
Marcus, Joel, 4, 29n24, 33n40, 42, 35n55, 47n134, 77n73, 78, 78n80, 79n86, 82, 83n106-8, 85, 109n84, 112n100, 113n105, 114n106-7, 116n114-16, 140-41, 142n89, 144n99, 152n133-35, 137, 153n138-39, 172n78, 173n80, 175n91, 176n92, 95, 177n99, 179n109-11, 113, 180n115, 118, 181n122, 182n128-30, 135, 184n149, 185, 186n158-59, 164-65, 187n166, 168, 170-71, 188-89
Mark, Martin, 96n30, 97n33
Marshall, Christopher, 27n10, 43n115
Marshall, I., 13n51, 77n76, 78n82
Martínez, Florentino, 105n74
Marxsen, Willi, 59n205, 61n207
Mason, Eric, 73n56
Matera, Frank, 30n28, 77n78, 108n81, 152n137, 174, 175n89, 176, 177n96, 178n105, 179n110, 113, 180n114-15, 181n119, 121
Mays, James, 143n95
McKelvey, Michael, 97n34
Merrill, Eugene, 128n25, 129n30
Metzger, Bruce, 29n23
Milavec, Aaron, 115n112
Milgrom, Jacob, 73n54
Miller, Geoffrey, 17n67, 21, 36n66-67
Mitchell, David, 103
Moloney, F., 27n14, 28n21, 33n42, 36n63-64, 66, 68, 37n70, 76, 38n80, 39n84, 40n97, 42n105, 43n116, 44n117, 46n128, 130, 47n138, 48n144, 146, 49n150-52, 154, 50n156, 159, 51n166, 52n169, 53n175, 178, 55n187-89, 56n195-96, 200, 146n102, 153n142, 175n89-90, 176n93, 187n169
Moo, Douglas, 15-16, 159n1-3, 178n107, 180n117, 182n133, 184n149, 185n156-57, 186n160
Moore, Stephen, 25n1
Morrison, Gregg, 38n81, 81n97
Moss, Candida, 82n99
Motyer, J., 99n45
Mowinckel, Sigmund, 65, 67n14, 93n4

Moyise, Steve, 12, 14, 17n66
Mueller, Eike, 37n71
Myers, Ched, 86n122–23

Naselli, Andrew, 15–16
Newsom, Carol, 150n127–28
Nickelsburg, George, 75n68–69, 180n118, 188n173

Oancea, Constantin, 65n3, 70n32, 71n42
O'Brien, K., 183, 184n148, 186n160–1, 187n172
Öhler, Markus, 81n99, 83n103–4, 84n112, 85n115, 117
Omerzu, Heike, 170n64, 66–67, 171n69, 172n73

Paulien, Jon, 21
Perowne, J., 65n2, 127n18
Perrin, Norman, 26n1, 28n16, 19, 38n79, 43n114
Pesch, Rudolf, 31n32, 39n89, 43n111, 50n161, 108n81, 184n147,
Peterson, D., 100n49
Petterson, Anthony, 134n61, 135n62
Phillips, George, 65n5
Porter, Stanley, 18–22
Prinsloo, Gert, 103n68, 106n69, 71

Rendtorff, Rolf, 167n49, 52
Rhoads, David, 26
Robbins, Vernon, 184n143
Roberts, J., 66n6, 67n14, 99n45
Robertson, O., 133n57, 166n45, 167n50
Robinson, James, 81n99
Rose, Christian, 78n83, 80n95
Rose, Walter, 66n6, 135n62
Roskam, H., 59n205
Ross, Allen, 67n10–12, 14, 68n18, 20–21, 73n51, 94n9, 95n18–19, 24, 96n25–26, 30, 97n35, 126n15, 127n19–20, 128n23, 129n34, 130n37–38, 162n9–10, 13, 15–16, 163n20–21, 164n30, 34–36,
Routledge, Robin, 129n31,

Rowe, Robert, 6, 77n76, 78, 79n88, 113n104, 115n111, 141n86, 142n89, 93, 144n99, 178n107, 186n103
Ruckstuhl, Eugen, 79n86
Ruppert, L., 173n80,
Russell, David, 129n27

Sana, Nahum, 117n118
Sander, Paul, 117n119, 94n11, 104n69
Sanders, J., 93n4, 105n74, 106n77, 109n88
Sankamo, Juho, 109n86
Schaper, Joachim, 69, 131n42–43
Schmidt, Karl, 27n13
Schmidt, Thomas, 184n148
Schreiner, Josef, 166n43, 167n52, 168
Schröten, Jutta, 103n68
Schweizer, Eduard, 43n114, 177n100,
Schwemer, A., 184n144
Scott, M., 27n11
Seybold, Klaus, 133n52
Shepherd, Tom, 27n12
Shively, Elizabeth, 26n4, 34n49
Skehan, P., 105n76
Sloan, David, 74n59, 63
Sloan, Paul, 49n153, 51n164, 109n84, 110n94
Smith, Daniel, 8n21
Smith, Gary, 99n45
Smith, Robert, 183n141
Snearly, Michael, 133n57, 102–3
Snodgrass, K., 106n77, 114n107, 109, 115n110, 116n114
Snow, Robert, 144n99, 146n102, 151n129, 132, 152n133
Stanley, Christopher, 14n54, 18–19
Stead, Michael, 100n48
Stec, David, 70n30, 97n38, 131n44, 47
Stegner, W., 82n100, 102
Steichele, H.-J., 83n104, 85n155
Stein, R., 26n1, 28n22, 29n25, 33n40–42, 34n48, 52, 35n54, 36n63, 65, 67–68, 37n74, 38n78, 80, 39n89–90, 40n91, 41n99, 42n107–8, 43n111–12, 116,

44n117–20, 45n123, 47n138–40,
48n143, 145–47, 49n149, 153,
155, 50n156–57, 159, 161,
51n163–64, 52n167, 171–72,
53n175–77, 54n181–83, 56n194,
59n205, 81n98, 146n102,
152n137, 175n83–84, 187n166
Stern, David, 115n110,
Stowasser, Martin, 10, 172n75
Strauss, Mark, 30n26, 33n39–42,
34n48, 36n63, 66–68, 37n74,
76, 38n80, 39n89, 49n92, 96, 98,
41n99–100, 102–3, 42n106, 110,
43n112–13, 116, 44n117, 120,
45n121, 124, 46n127, 130, 133,
47n134–35, 138–39, 141–42,
48n144, 146, 49n149–50,
50n156–57, 159–62, 51n163–64,
52n168, 170, 172, 53n173,
175–76, 54n185, 55n190,
56n194–95, 201–2, 79n86, 89,
80n94, 86n121, 116n115–16,
146n102, 149n120, 175n86,
187n166, 169
Streett, Andrew, 72n45,
47–48, 143n95, 97, 147–50,
151n130–31
Stuart, Douglas, 117n118
Stuhlmueller, Carroll, 162n12
Subrahmanian, J., 142n90
Suhl, Alfred, 172n98
Sumpter, Philip, 166n46

Tannehill, R., 26n5
Tàrrech, Armand, 82n103
Tate, Marvin, 73n51, 143n95
Taylor, Vincent, 28n20, 59n205,
114n106
Thatcher, Tom, 184n143
Thompson, Michael, 20–21
Tilly, M., 132n42, 137
Tödt, Heinz, 152n137
Tolbert, M., 28n17, 19
Trafton, Joseph, 75n65
Treves, Marco, 65n3
Trimaille, M., 115n112
Troyer, Kristine, 64n1
Trublet, Jacque, 103n68

Tucker W., 128n22

Vaillancourt, Ian, 93n1, 94n13,
97n34–36, 98n42, 99, 101,
103n67, 104, 106n77, 111n96,
117n119, 125n6, 125n15,
127n17, 128n23–25, 129n32, 34,
130n36–38, 133n51–53, 56–57
Vanderkam, James, 75n68–69
VanGemeren, Willem, 66n6, 67n10–
11, 13, 68n18, 93n1, 95n17,
19, 128n22, 130n38, 162n7, 9,
163n18, 20, 27, 164n31
Vanhoozer, Kevin, 17n66
van Iersel, Bas Martinus, 27n11,
28n21, 32n38, 33n45, 34n50,
35n57, 44n118, 53n174, 79n86,
146n101, 176n92, 180n117
Von Rad, Gerhard, 68
Von Nordheim, Miriam, 131n48,
137, 138n80

Waltke, Bruce, 103n67, 126, 129n32,
130n36, 38, 162, 163n19, 22,
23–24, 26–27, 164n29–30,
35–36
Watts, Rikki, 4n2, 7, 8, 10–11, 26n1,
29n24, 79n86, 80n92, 85n120,
111n98, 119. 120n126, 142n89,
144n99, 149n121, 172n78,
173n79, 188n174, 200
Waugh, Robin, 136n70
Wedderburn, Alexander, 28n22
Wellhausen, Julius, 81n99
Wenham, David, 81n96
Westermann, Claus, 73n53
Whiting, Mark, 71n38–39, 41
Whybray, R., 130n37
Willgren, David, 69n25, 162n9
Williams, Joel, 26n7, 27n14, 28n17,
19, 21–22, 37n72, 43n115–16,
56n200, 59n205, 176n91, 96
Willis, John, 71n38
Wilson, Gerald, 70–71, 73n51,
101n52, 102–3, 163n27, 164n36
Winn, Adam, 59, 61n207
Wittman, Derek, 73n52
Wold, Benjamin, 14n51

Wright, N., 141n86, 142n91, 152n137
Wypadlo, Adrian, 82n100, 83n107, 84n110

Yoon, David, 12n44–45, 13n49
Yu, Charles, 103n67

Zeitlin, Solomon, 106n77
Zenger, Erich, 65n5, 66n6, 71n38, 95n23, 100n48, 102n53, 103n64, 104n69, 105n72, 126n11, 127n17, 128n24, 130n37, 39, 132n51, 133n52, 56, 166n46

Index of Scripture and Other Ancient References

OLD TESTAMENT

Genesis

5:1–11	156
14:18–24	128
15:1–6	128
22	77
49:9–11	108–9, 111, 118
49:11	119

Exodus

3:1–22	47
9:6–8, 20, 26–27, 35	99
14:8, 13, 16	99
15	117, 119
15:2, 6, 12	95, 96, 97, 99, 116, 195
15:11	99, 116
15:17	116, 117
15:18	118
15:26	84
16:16	99
17:4	195
17:11, 16	99, 116
18:1, 7, 8–9, 12, 21, 25	99
22:17	153
23:20	29
23:21	84
24:1, 9, 12–13, 15–16, 18	82
24:15–18	83
33:19	99
34:4–8, 28–30	83
34:29	82
34:35	84

Leviticus

26:14–17	84

Numbers

24:17	108

Deuteronomy

17:14–20	102
17:18–20	72, 166
18:5	82, 85
25:5–10	47

Joshua

1	72
24:13	82

1 Samuel

17:34–36	171
17:45	111

2 Samuel

7	128
7:14	74
22:5–6	104

1 Kings

8:42–43(LXX)	112

2 Chronicles

36:14–16	114

Psalms

1–2	69, 71–72, 75, 100, 102–3, 133, 166–67, 172, 190, 193, 197
1–89	103
1:1	71, 73
2	2–3, 6–7, 24, 63, 65–70, 72–76, 78, 80, 84, 86–89, 116, 128, 134, 138–39, 143, 144, 147, 154–57, 184, 194, 196, 199
2:1–2	73
2:2	75–76
2:6–8	74
2:7	2, 30, 40, 63–65, 67, 69–70, 73–74, 77–78, 80–81, 84, 86–91, 118, 121, 131, 143–44, 154, 178, 193–94
2:9	74
2:12	69, 71
3–41	166, 172
8:4–6	143
8:7	124
15	94
15–24	166–67
18:3–6	104
18:15–16	99
19	166
21:8–9(LXX)	160
21:19(LXX)	160
22	2–3, 6–7, 9–11, 24, 158–74, 176–79, 183–91, 197–99
22:1	55, 159, 184–85
22:2	9–10
22:7	5
22:7–8	55, 159, 177, 180
22:8–9	160, 176
22:18	55, 159
22:19	160, 176
24	94
35:21	181
37:32	187
40:15	181
41:9	159
42:5, 11	187
43:5	187
59:8	73
69	169, 172, 190, 197
69:9	5
69:21	159
69:22	176, 186
69:33	168
70:3	181
71	168–69, 172, 190, 197
72	71, 132
72:8	109
80	123, 147–50, 155
80:18	3, 54, 143, 147–48, 155, 157–58, 197
81:11–13	84
89	71, 74, 132, 147
94–99	71
101	132
102	169
104	105
105	105
105–6	132
107–9	133, 138
107–50	101
107–18	101–3
107:28	10
109(LXX)	124, 130–32

108–110	133	6:9	3:5
110	2, 6–7, 11, 24, 71, 123–26, 128–29, 131, 132, 134–45, 147–50, 154–58, 184, 196–97, 199	6:9–10	61, 118, 182
		8:11	73
		11	75, 99
		11:11–16	99
		12:2	99, 116, 195
110:1	3, 5, 48, 54, 123–25, 127, 135–45, 147–49, 154–57, 178, 196–97	13:10(LXX)	50, 152
		26:1–6	99
		26:4	99, 116, 195
110:4	123, 128–29, 134, 135, 138–39, 144–45, 156	29:13	37
		34:4(LXX)	50, 152
		40–55	80, 169
111–13	133, 138	40–66	169–70
113	103	40(LXX)	113
113–17	104	40:1	112
113–18	93, 101, 103, 105, 195, 121	40:3	29
		41:8–9	80
114–15	101, 104	42:1	75, 77, 80, 88–89, 194
116:1–3, 8–9, 11a, 16	104	44:23	169
117(LXX)	92, 104, 111	45:22	169
118	2, 6–7, 11, 24, 91–94, 100–1, 104–7, 109, 112, 115–23, 138, 142, 184, 194–99, 199	46:1–6	73
		46:3	169, 172, 190, 198
		46:3, 12	84
		48:12	84
		49:1	84, 169
118:1–9	121	49:3	73
118:10–12	111	50:10	100
118:14	95	51:1, 7	84
118:22	5	55:2	84
118:22–23	3, 47, 91, 112–13, 115–22	52:7	31
		53	80, 88
118:25–26	2, 45, 91–92, 96, 100, 106–9, 111, 118–21	53:1–12	176
		53:12(LXX)	180
		56(LXX)	112
118:25–29	105	56:7	45, 119, 121, 195
118:27	96	63:15–18	75
119	102	63:19	30, 75, 88
120–37	102	64:1	88, 89, 194
132	71, 132		
135	101	## Jeremiah	
138–45	102		
140:8	187	1:5	169, 172, 190, 198
144	71, 132	7:4–10	112
146–150	103	7:11	119, 121, 195
147	105	11:21	100
149	73	26:9, 16, 20	100
		30:21	128
## Isaiah		33:15	134
3:1–4	126		
5:1–7	113–14		

(Jeremiah continued)

34:14	84
51:16	100
35:15	84

Ezekiel

3:7	84
20:39	84
37:23	73

Daniel

6	171
7	123, 136, 139, 143, 148–150, 152–53
7:9–14	135
7:13	3, 50, 54, 135–37, 139–41, 143, 147, 150–52, 155, 157–58, 196–97
7:13–14	148, 151–52
7:14	151
7:17	153
7:27	151
9:27	50
11:32	73
12:10	73

Joel

2:10	50, 152
3:5	100
3:15	152

Amos

3:1–7	126
6:10	100
8:9	55, 182–83
8:9–10	176, 183
8:10	183
9:11	73

Zephaniah

3:9, 12	100

Zechariah

4	100
4:6–10	100
4:7	100, 115, 195
6:9–15	134
6:12	142, 156
6:13	134–35, 139
9	111
9:1–8	108
9:9	44, 108–9, 119, 121, 142, 195
9:9–10	108–11
13:3	100
13:7	52

Malachi

2:17–3:5	113
3:1	29, 112–13
3:1–4	113
3:2	113
4:5	29

NEW TESTAMENT

Matthew

3:17	24
21:9	109
26:64	148

Mark

1:1–8:26	144
1:1–8:21	2, 28, 62, 192
1:1–15	29, 30, 57, 60–61, 192
1:1–13	26, 30–31, 56
1:1–11	86

INDEX OF SCRIPTURE AND OTHER ANCIENT REFERENCES 237

1:1	26, 28, 30–31, 53, 58, 60, 76, 155, 198	2:24	33
1:1–3	80	3:1–6	33, 144
1:2–15	113	3:3–4	33
1:2–11	46	3:7–35	32–34, 192
1:2–8	31	3:7–12	33–34
1:2–3	24, 8, 29, 31, 78–79, 90	3:11	60, 88
1:2	76	3:13–19	33, 34
1:4–8	113	3:14–15	34
1:4–6	31	3:20–35	34
1:4–5	29	3:20–21	5, 34
1:7–8	29, 31, 76	3:22–30	34, 57
1:9–15	29, 31	3:22–27	30, 39, 87
1:9–11	76–77, 86	3:31–35	34
1:9	29, 31	3:32	57
1:10–11	30, 56, 58, 79–80, 84, 87, 89, 187, 194	4–8	27
		4:1–8:21	32
1:10	56, 77, 80, 87	4:35–8:21	32
1:11	24, 31, 60, 64, 77–82, 87–90, 114, 118, 121, 194	4	51
		4:1–34	32, 34–35, 44, 57–58, 62, 192
1:12–13	30–31	4:1–20	85
1:14–8:21	26	4:1	34, 44
1:14–15	26, 30–31	4:1–2	34–35
1:14	30, 31, 175, 189	4:3–9	34
1:15	2, 29–31, 45, 58, 87, 89, 194	4:10–12	34
		4:11–12	118
1:16–10:45	43, 60	4:12	61, 182
1:16–8:21	32, 57	4:13–20	34–35
1:16–3:35	32–33, 57	4:21–25	34–35
1:16–45	32–33, 62, 192	4:26–32	34–35
1:16–20	33, 60	4:33–34	34, 35
1:21–45	33	4:35–8:26	35
1:21–28	144	4:35–8:21	57
1:26	30	4:35–8:10	35
1:34	30	4:35–6:44	32, 35, 62, 192
1:40–45	33, 144	4:35–5:43	36
2:1–3:6	32–33, 46, 57, 62, 192	4:35	32
2:1–12	33, 144	4:35–41	27, 36
2:2–4	43	4:39	10, 90, 194
2:5–11	90, 194	5:1–20	36, 144
2:6–7	33	5:7	60, 88
2:7	194	5:21–43	36
2:13–17	33	5:24–27	43
2:16	33	6:1–6	36
2:18–22	33	6:6–30	36
2:18	33	6:6–13	36
2:23–28	33, 144	6:14–29	36
		6:30	36

6:30–44	27	8:35	29, 42, 182
6:31–44	.36	8:37	29
6:34	36	8:38–9:1	152
6:37–44	90, 194	8:38–39	85
6:39–44	36	8:38	39, 88, 152
6:45–8:26	36	9:1–8	39, 81–82, 143
6:45–8:21	62, 192	9:1	2, 39, 81–82, 85, 89, 194
6:45–8:10	32	9:2–14	39
6:45–52	27, 37	9:2–13	39
6:48–49	90, 194	9:2–8	82–86
6:53–60	36	9:5–6	40
7:1–23	37	9:7	2, 10, 40, 53, 58, 60, 64,
7:9	144		77, 79, 81–85, 87–90,
7:14–23	37		114, 118, 121, 194
7:13–14	85	9:8–13	40
7:19	85	9:8–9	40, 86
7:24–30	37	9:9–12	84
7:31–37	37	9:9	40
7:37	90, 194	9:11–13	5, 40, 61
7:45–8:10	35	9:14–29	38, 40
8:1–10	27	9:14	40
8:1–9	37	9:19	41
8:6–10	90, 194	9:20–21	41
8:10–13	37	9:22–23	41
8:11–21	32, 35	9:25–27	41
8:13–21	37–38	9:28–29	41
8:14–21	37	9:30–10:31	41
8:17–18	38	9:30–50	41
8:22–10:52	26, 38, 43	9:30–32	38
8:22–26	2, 28, 38–39, 43, 192	9:30–31	91, 119, 122, 196
8:27–10:45	2, 28, 38, 57, 62, 192	9:31	41, 51, 57, 174–75, 189
8:27–9:1	38, 81	9:33–34	38, 41
8:27–31	38	9:35–10:31	38
8:27	38	9:39–50	41
8:28–10:45	40	10	48
8:28–9:1	39, 81	10:1–31	41
8:28	84–85	10:1–12	41–42
8:29	39, 53, 58, 60	10:1–10	44
8:31–38	40, 84–86	10:1–2	42
8:31–32	91, 119, 122, 196	10:10	44
8:31	5, 38–40, 51, 57, 61, 120,	10:13–16	41–42
	122, 174, 189	10:13–14	42
8:32–9:20	40	10:14–16	42
8:32–33	38	10:14–15	42–43
8:32	40	10:17	42
8:34–9:1	38, 49	10:17–31	41–43
8:34–38	39, 85	10:17–25	42
8:35–38	150	10:26–27	42

INDEX OF SCRIPTURE AND OTHER ANCIENT REFERENCES 239

10:28–31	42	11:12–14	45
10:28	42	11:13	45
10:29	85	11:15–19	45
10:30	42	11:15–17	111–12
10:32–45	42–43	11:15	45
10:32–34	42, 91, 122, 196	11:17	45, 61
10:33–34	51, 57, 174	11:18	112
10:33	175	11:20–21	45
10:34	189	11:22–25	45
10:35–40	43, 48	11:27–12:44	45, 49, 120
10:35–37	38, 41	11:27–12:34	46
10:37–40	180	11:27–12:27	112
10:38–45	38	11:27–12:12	46
10:38	53	11:27	46–47, 112, 117, 153
10:41–45	43	11:28–12:27	140
10:41	41	11:28	112
10:42–44	43	11:29–30	112
10:45	43, 179	12–16	121, 196
10:46–52	2, 28, 38, 43, 118, 192	12	114
10:47–49	154	12:1–12	112–13, 146, 182, 186
10:47–48	44, 118, 121, 142	12:1–11	117
10:48	43	12:1–9	113, 117
10:49	43	12:1	117
11–16	58, 107, 120, 195	12:2–6	114
11:1–16:8	2, 26, 28, 44, 192	12:6	79, 88, 114
11–15	108, 156–57, 181, 195, 198	12:7–9	114
		12:7–8	46
11–13	44	12:7	114
11	58, 111	12:9	47, 117
11–12	44, 49, 58	12:10–12	111–12
11:11–2:44	44, 62, 193	12:10–11	3, 91–92, 112–13, 117, 122
11:1–12:12	119, 121, 195	12:10	114, 120
11:1–25	46	12:11–12	146, 181
11:1–11	44–45, 61, 107–8, 111, 142, 154, 195	12:11	47, 61, 114, 146
11:1–7	108–9	12:12	47, 112–13, 117–18, 186
11:1–6	52	12:13–44	47
11:2	108–9	12:13–17	47
11:8	109	12:13	118
11:9–10	2, 91–92, 107, 109, 111, 118, 121, 195	12:18–27	47
		12:28–44	48
11:9	109	12:28–34	48, 140
11:11	45, 111	12:34	46, 140
11:12–13:2	45	12:35–37	3, 5, 46, 48, 123, 140–44, 153–54, 158, 196
11:11–26	120, 186		
11:12–25	45	12:35	144
11:12–16	120	12:36–37	61, 149
11:12–15	181		

12:36	124, 143–45, 154–55, 157	14–15	44
		14:1–15:47	44, 62, 193
12:38–44	46	14:1–72	51
12:38–40	48, 145	14:1–11	51
12:41–44	48, 145	14:1	52
12:58	147	14:1–2	51–52
13	44, 49, 51, 58, 119–20, 145–46, 155, 181, 183, 198	14:39	51
		14:8	145
		14:10–11	51–52, 118
13:1–37	49, 51, 62, 193	14:11	52
13:1–4	49, 51	14:12–31	52
13:1–2	45, 146, 183, 186	14:12–16	52
13:2–4	49	14:12	52
13:3	44, 49	14:13–16	52
13:4	51	14:17–31	52
13:5–37	49–50	14:17–21	52
13:5–23	50–51	14:18–21	52
13:4	50	14:18	8, 159, 175
13:5	49, 51, 53	14:21–25	145
13:5–6	50	14:21	52, 61, 174–75, 187
13:7–20	50	14:22–26	52
13:7–8	50	14:22–25	52
13:9	51, 53, 183	14:25	52
13:7–13	50	14:27	52, 61
13:11–12	183	14:26–31	52
13:14–20	50	14:27–28	52, 145
13:14	50, 61	14:27	10
13:23	49, 23, 53	14:28	56–58, 143
13:24–27	50–51, 150, 152	14:30	52
13:24–25	50	14:32–53	53
13:24	183	14:32–42	52–53, 183
13:26–27	143	14:32	52
13:26	61, 150, 183	14:34	8, 10, 53, 61, 187
13:28–30	50–51	14:36	53, 88
13:29	51	14:37–38	53
13:30	51	14:40–41	53
13:31–37	50–51	14:40	183
13:31	85	14:41	187
13:32–33	183	14:43–52	52–53
13:32	51, 53, 88	14:43–49	53
13:33	51	147	183
13:35–37	53	14:48–49	53
13:35	51	14:49	53, 145, 174, 187
13:36	183	14:53–15:1	120
13:37	51	14:53–72	53–54, 145
14–16	44, 174	14:53	174
14	58, 135, 145, 183, 187	14:54–59	149
14:1–16:8	51, 58	14:54	53, 145

INDEX OF SCRIPTURE AND OTHER ANCIENT REFERENCES 241

14:55–65	53, 145, 154, 197	15:24	8, 61, 159–60, 176–77, 179
14:55–59	146	15:25	52, 179
14:55	61, 187	15:26–32	55
14:56–59	53	15:26–27	179–80
14:57	153	15:26	55, 87, 188
14:58–61	174	15:27	177, 179
14:58	146–47, 187	15:28	147
14:58–59	197	15:29–32	177, 180–82, 188
14:60–62	147, 188	15:29–30	61, 159, 161, 174, 180–81, 187, 197
14:60	153	15:29	8, 55, 120, 147, 155, 177, 197
14:61–62	3, 58, 123, 140, 142–43, 145, 148, 155, 158, 184, 197	15:31	55, 177, 181
14:61	60, 123	15:32	54–55, 60, 87, 175, 177, 181–82, 186, 188
14:62	3, 5, 53–54, 61, 124, 136, 139, 141, 143–45, 147–54, 155, 157, 178, 183, 196–97	15:33–41	56
		15:33–39	55, 86, 177
		15:33–34	55, 176
14:63–65	54, 153	15:33	55, 88, 182–83
14:64	174, 175, 184	15:34	8–10, 52, 61, 159–60, 177, 183–85, 197
14:65	175, 188	15:35–37	185
14:66–72	53–54, 145	15:35–36	55, 159, 177, 188
15	54, 58, 60, 159, 174, 178, 180, 187–88, 191, 198	15:36	8, 176, 186
15:14–7	54	15:37–39	55, 186–87
15:1–32	54, 175	15:38–16:7	3, 185, 189–90, 198
15:1–20	54, 174–76	15:38–39	56, 58, 87–88, 187
15:1–3	175	15:38	55, 60, 120, 147, 155, 183, 194, 198
15:1–5	54, 175	15:39	2, 56, 87–89, 187, 189, 194
15:1	52, 54, 174–75		
15:2	60, 175, 188	15:40–16:8	56
15:6–15	54, 175	15:40–47	56
15:9–14	54, 175	15:40–41	56
15:10	175	15:42–46	56
15:12	60	15:42	52
15:15	174–76	15:43–16:7	88, 189
15:16–20	55, 175, 188	15:43	2, 56, 89, 185, 188, 194
15:17–20	176	15:44–45	56
15:18	60, 87	15:46	56
15:20–16:7	158, 185, 188, 191, 198	15:47	56
15:20–39	3, 55, 158, 174, 176, 179, 191, 198	16	120
		16:1–8	44, 56, 58, 62, 174, 193
15:20–27	177, 179	16:1	52, 56
15:20–25	55	16:5	56
15:20	176, 179	16:6	56, 189
15:21	176	16:7–8	56
15:22	176, 179		
15:23	8, 177		

(Mark continued)

16:7	57–58, 60, 143, 189
16:8	57

Luke

19:38	109
22:69	148

John

12:13	109

Acts

2	141

1 Corinthians

3:16–17	146

Ephesians

2:20–22	146

Hebrews

7	144

1 Peter

2:5	146

APOCRYPHA AND PSEUDEPIGRAPHA

Apocryphal Syriac Psalm

152–53	171
152:1	171

Joseph and Aseneth

172, 190

12:9–10	.171

1 Maccabees

14:41	137

Psalms of Solomon

17	74, 76
17:1	74
17:14	74
17:21–30	74
17:21–24	74
17:22–24	74
17:22–25	75
17:22	74
17:23–24	74
17:30	74
17:32–36	74
17:32	74
17:34	74
17:36	74–75
17:37–39	74
17:42	74
17:46	74

Similitudes of Enoch (1 Enoch)

139, 157, 196

46–49	75
48:6	75
48:8–10	75–76
48:8	75
48:10	75
49:14	75
51:3	75, 136
55:4	75, 136
61:8	75, 136
62:2	75, 136
62:7	75
69:29	75

Parables of Enoch

136

Testament of Job

32:1–12	136
33:3	136

Testament of Levi

8	136–37

8:3	137
18	136–37

Testaments of the Twelve Patriarchs

137

Wisdom of Solomon

2–5	170–71

DEAD SEA SCROLLS

4Q Florilegium (=4Q174)	73, 76
I, 7–11 and I, 18–II, 2	73
4Q84 (=4QPs^b)	105
4Q87 (=4QPs^e)	105
4Q88 (=4QPs^f)	190, 198
Frgm.1–2	170
4Q173a (=4Q173 frg. 5 olim)	105
4Q246	74
5/6 ḤevPs	170

1 QH	
IX, 29–36	170
X, 33–34	170
XII, 33–34	170
XIII, 9–18	170
XIII, 12–19	170
XX, 3	170
11Q5 (=11QPs^a)	105
11Q6 (=11QPs^b)	105

OTHER JEWISH LITERATURE

Masekhet Pesachim

5.5–7	106

Masekhet Sukkah (M. Sukk)

3.9	106
4.5	106

Midrash Tehillim

106

Targum Psalms

	30, 202–3, 209–11
2:7	70
22	165
110	139
110:1, 3, 7	131
118	97
118:2	98
118:22–29	98

www.ingramcontent.com/pod-product-compliance
Lightning Source LLC
Chambersburg PA
CBHW050848230426
43667CB00012B/2192